"双高"建设规划教材

高职高专"十四五"规划教材

冶金工业出版社

TRIZ 及知识产权工程案例应用

TRIZ and Engineering Application of Intellectual Property

主　编　曹　珍　李　爽　刘　龙

副主编　赵璐璐　王　真　郝建卫　牛聚伟
　　　　吕向阳　范泠荷　张　苏

主　审　韩提文

北京

冶金工业出版社

2023

内 容 提 要

本书系统介绍了 TRIZ 及知识产权工程案例应用,书中主要内容包括基本概念、产品技术成熟度预测技术、技术进化定律、产品设计中的冲突、冲突解决理论、76个标准解、基于效应的功能设计和应用案例分析。

本书可作为普通高等学校和职业院校装备制造业、化学工程、材料工程等相关专业的教材,也可作为企业领导与管理人员、企业工程技术人员、科研院所研究人员等培训教材或技术参考书。

图书在版编目(CIP)数据

TRIZ 及知识产权工程案例应用/曹珍,李爽,刘龙主编. —北京:冶金工业出版社,2023.6

"双高"建设规划教材

ISBN 978-7-5024-9529-9

Ⅰ.①T… Ⅱ.①曹… ②李… ③刘… Ⅲ.①创造学—应用—知识产权—系统工程—教材 Ⅳ.①D913.4

中国国家版本馆 CIP 数据核字(2023)第 104901 号

TRIZ 及知识产权工程案例应用

出版发行	冶金工业出版社	**电　话**	(010)64027926
地　　址	北京市东城区嵩祝院北巷 39 号	**邮　编**	100009
网　　址	www.mip1953.com	**电子信箱**	service@ mip1953.com

责任编辑　杜婷婷　马媛馨　美术编辑　吕欣童　版式设计　郑小利
责任校对　郑　娟　责任印制　禹　蕊
三河市双峰印刷装订有限公司印刷
2023 年 6 月第 1 版,2023 年 6 月第 1 次印刷
787mm×1092mm 1/16;17.75 印张;393 千字;262 页
定价 59.00 元

投稿电话 (010)64027932 投稿信箱 tougao@cnmip.com.cn
营销中心电话 (010)64044283
冶金工业出版社天猫旗舰店 yjgycbs.tmall.com
(本书如有印装质量问题,本社营销中心负责退换)

前 言

高等职业教育在国家的大力支持下，逐渐在补齐职业教育体系的短板。在现实的实践中，高等职业教育实际已占据高等教育的半壁江山，体量如此之大的职业教育，是现代高等教育系统的一个必不可少的功能分化结果。正因如此，职教界在努力探索职业教育的大学发展模式。从 2014 年《国务院关于加快发展现代职业教育的决定》提出"探索发展本科层次职业教育"，到 2019 年《国家职业教育改革实施方案》进一步明确要求"开展本科层次职业教育试点"，国家推进本科职业教育发展，构建中国特色现代职业教育体系的决心愈加坚定，目标与路径也更为明确。中国职业教育迎来前所未有的重大发展机遇，进入高质量发展新阶段。

在国家顶层设计的指引下，多所高职院校升格为本科职业技术大学，成为试水职教本科的先行者。在此机遇与挑战背景下，职业本科大学要积极探索职业本科教育的办学模式与人才培养模式，系统提升技术技能人才培养质量，全面加强应用技术研发，对形成稳定成熟的职业本科教育办学经验与特色提出了更高要求。为落实国家大力发展职业教育精神，并推动"中国特色高水平高职学校和专业建设计划"（"双高计划"）项目建设，河北工业职业技术大学联合育米众创空间、河北日晟网络科技有限公司、石家庄及时雨科教文体设备有限公司、河北平旦科技有限公司等业内知名企业共同开发了基于"工学结合"，服务于高职和职业本科学生的产教融合创新教材。

本书编者多年从事教学研究和实践工作，重视培养学生的创新能力与专业知识的融合。本书的前半部分以被称为"点金术"的 TRIZ 理论为理论基础，包含 TRIZ 原理和工具的介绍；后半部分为运用 TRIZ 理论解决不同学科领域实际工程问题案例实操，主要包括装备制造业、化学工程、材料工程、汽车工程和建筑工程等专业。

创新方法作为一种以应用为导向的创新方法论与创新工具，与职业本科高校的人才培养定位具有高度契合性。因此，在职业本科大学中引入创新方法，将其融入应用型人才的创新创业教育，是增强大学生创新精神和创业意识、提高创新能力、丰富实践技能的必然选择。同时，聚焦应用型高校，研究并构建具有鲜明应用型特色的创新方法人才培养模式，对完善我国创新方法人才培养体系具有重要意义。本书适合企业领导与管理人员、企业工程技术人员、科研院所研究人员、机关干部和大专院校的师生作为学习、培训教材或自学参考书。

创新方法 TRIZ 理论发明与创新人类发展及科学技术进步中的每一次重大跨越和重要发现都与思维创新、方法创新、工具创新密切相关。离开了"创新"，人类社会不可能向前迈进，科学技术也不可能有实质性的进步。可以说，"创新"已经成为现代社会发展与进步的基本动力。创新理论和实践都证明，创新是人人都具有的一种潜在的能力，而且这种能力可以通过一定的学习和训练得到激发和提升。

创新方法是科学思维、科学方法和科学工具的总称，科学思维创新是科学技术取得突破性、革命性进展的先决条件，科学方法创新是实现科学技术跨越式发展的重要基础，而科学工具创新则是开展科学研究和实现发明创造的必要手段。创新方法主要以思维创新、方法创新和工具创新为主要内容，以机制创新、管理创新和体制创新为主要保障，营造良好的创新环境，建立有利于创新型人才培育的素质教育体系，形成全社会关注创新、学习创新、勇于创新的良好社会氛围，培养掌握科学思维、科学方法和科学工具的创新型人才，培育拥有自主知识产权和持续创新能力的创新型企业，研发具有自主知识产权的科学方法和科学工具，为自主创新战略、建设创新型国家提供强有力的人才、方法和工具支撑。

本书第 1 章为 TRIZ 的发展概述和基本概念；第 2 章和第 3 章，分别介绍了技术生命周期和技术进化定律；第 4 章至第 7 章分别讲述了产品设计中的冲突、冲突解决理论、76 个标准解和效应的功能设计模式；第 8 章通过七个应用案例分析讲解如何实际应用 TRIZ 理论来解决实际问题。

本书由河北工业职业技术大学曹珍、李爽、刘龙担任主编，韩提文担任主审，河北工业职业技术大学赵璐璐、王真、吕向阳、范泠荷，石家庄市市场监督管理局郝建卫、牛聚伟，河北省科学技术情报研究院张苏担任副主编，河北外国语学院何利伟，河北工业职业技术大学王子良、郭明皓、田芮畅、吉悦、曾晨、王丽佳、韩宏彦、刘明昊、马铭均、刘云青、陶萃参编。河北工院科技园有限公司刘靖华、石家庄及时雨科教文体设备有限公司宋俊峰、河北中测计量检测有限公司任贵龙参与本书部分编写工作。

由于实施创新教育与专业相融合是一项全新的课题，许多问题尚在探索之中，编者在编写过程中参考了相关论文、资料以及著作和教材，在此特向有关作者表示衷心的感谢。

本书内容涉及的有关研究得到了教育部创新方法专项（项目编号：2020IM030200）、河北省科学情报院创新方法高校人才基地建设和创新方法理论研究与人才培养基地建设项目、河北工业职业技术大学创新方法研究专项项目（编号：cx202202）的资助。

由于编者学习、研究、应用 TRIZ 时间尚短，书中内容如有不妥之处，欢迎广大读者批评指正。

编　者

2023 年 3 月

Preface

With the strong support of the state, higher vocational education is gradually making up for the shortcomings of the vocational education system. In practical practice, higher vocational education has actually accounted for half of higher education. Such a large volume of vocational education is the result of an essential functional differentiation of the modern higher education system. Because of this reason, the vocational education community is trying to explore the university development model of vocational education. From 2014 "The State Council on accelerating the development of modern vocational education" decision put forward "Explore the development of undergraduate level vocational education", to 2019 "The national vocational education reform plan" further clear requirements "The undergraduate level vocational education pilot", promote the development of undergraduate vocational education, build a modern vocational education system with Chinese characteristics more determined, goal and path is more clear. China's vocational education has ushered in unprecedented major opportunities for development and entered a new stage of high-quality development.

Under the guidance of national top-level design, many higher vocational colleges have been upgraded to undergraduate vocational and technical universities, becoming pioneers in testing the waters of vocational education undergraduate courses. In this context of opportunities and challenges, vocational undergraduate universities should actively explore the running mode and talent training mode of vocational undergraduate education, systematically improve the quality of technical and skilled personnel training, comprehensively strengthen the research and development of applied technology, and put forward higher requirements for the formation of stable and mature running experience and characteristics of vocational undergraduate education. To implement the country to develop vocational education spirit, and promote the "High level of higher vocational schools and professional construction plan" project construction, Hebei industrial vocational and technical university joint education the gen space, Hebei day sheng network technology Co., Ltd., Shijiazhuang timely rain science and education style equipment Co., Ltd., river Beijing Dan technology Co., Ltd., industry well-known enterprises jointly developed based on "engineering", service in higher vocational and vocational undergraduate students integration innovation teaching materials.

The editor of the book has been engaged in teaching research and practical work for many years, and attaches great importance to cultivating the integration of students' innovative ability and professional knowledge. The first half of this book is based on TRIZ theory called "gold", including the introduction of TRIZ principles and tools; the second half is the practice of TRIZ theory to solve practical engineering problems in different disciplines, including equipment manufacturing, chemical engineering, material engineering, automotive engineering and construction engineering.

As an application-oriented innovation methodology and innovation tool, the innovation method is highly compatible with the talent training orientation of vocational undergraduate universities. Therefore, introducing innovative methods into vocational undergraduate universities and integrating them into the innovative and entrepreneurial education of applied talents is an inevitable choice to enhance the innovative spirit and entrepreneurial consciousness, improve the innovative ability and enrich the practical skill. At the same time, it is of great significance to study and construct the innovative method talent training mode with distinct application-oriented characteristics to improve the talent training system of innovative methods in China. This book is suitable for enterprise leaders and management personnel, enterprise engineering and technical personnel, scientific research institutes and researchers, government cadres and teachers and students of colleges and universities as learning, training materials or self-study reference book.

Innovative method TRIZ theoretical invention and innovation. Every major leap and important discovery in human development and scientific and technological progress is closely related to thinking innovation, method innovation and tool innovation. Without "innovation", human society cannot move forward, and science and technology also cannot make substantial progress. It can be said that "innovation" has become the basic driving force for the development and progress of modern society. Innovation theory and practice have proved that innovation is a potential ability that everyone has, and this ability can be stimulated and improved through certain learning and training.

The innovation method is the general term of scientific thinking, scientific methods and scientific tools. The innovation of scientific thinking is a prerequisite for the breakthrough and revolutionary progress of science and technology. The innovation of scientific methods is an important foundation for the leap forward development of science and technology, and the innovation of scientific tools is a necessary means for scientific research and invention. Innovation methods mainly focus on thinking innovation, method innovation and tool innovation, and take mechanism innovation, management innovation and system innovation as the main guarantee to create a good innovation environment, establish a quality education system conducive to the cultivation of innovative talents, form a good social atmosphere for the whole society to focus on innovation, learn innovation, and be brave in innovation, and cultivate innovative talents who master scientific thinking, scientific methods and scientific tools, cultivate innovative enterprises with independent intellectual property rights and sustainable innovation capabilities, research and develop scientific methods and tools with independent intellectual property rights, and provide strong talent, methods, and tool support for independent innovation strategies and the construction of an innovative country.

Chapter 1 of this book is the development overview and basic concepts of TRIZ; Chapter 2 and Chapter 3 respectively introduce the technology life cycle and technology evolution laws; Chapter 4 to Chapter 7 respectively describe the conflict, conflict resolution theory, 76 standard solutions and effect of functional design models; Chapter 8 explains how to actually apply TRIZ theory to solve practical problems through seven application case analysis.

Book by Hebei Vocational University of Industry and Technology Cao Zhen, Li Shuang, Liu long as editor, Han Tiwen as the presiding, Hebei Vocational University of Industry and Technology Zhao Lulu, Wang Zhen, Lü Xiangyang, Fan Linghe, Shijiazhuang Market Supervision Administration Hao Jianwei, Niu Juwei, Hebei Institute of Science and Technology Information Zhang Su as deputy editor, Hebei Foreign Languages Institute He Liwei, Hebei Vocational University of Industry and Technology Wang Ziliang, Guo Minghao, Tian Ruichang, Ji Yue, Zeng Chen, Wang Lijia, Han Hongyan, Liu Minghao, Ma Mingjun, Liu Yunqing, Tao Cui participated in editing. Liu Jinghua of Hebei Industrial Technology Park Co., Ltd., Song Junfeng of Shijiazhuang Timely Science, Education and Sports Equipment Co., Ltd., and Ren Guilong of Hebei Zhongtest Measurement and Testing Co., Ltd. participated in the writing of some parts of this book.

As the integration of innovative education and professional education is a brand new topic, many problems are still being explored. The editor has referred to the relevant papers, materials, works and teaching materials in the writing process, and I would like to express my heartfelt thanks to the relational author.

The research related to the content of this book is supported by the special project of the Ministry of Education (Project No. 2020IM030200); the construction of innovative methods and universities of Hebei Scientific Information Institute; and the special project of innovative methods of Hebei Vocational University of Technology (No. cx202202).

Since the editor has short studied, studied and applied TRIZ, if there is anything wrong with the content of the book, readers are welcome to criticize and correct it.

The authors
March, 2023

目　录

Contents

0 绪 论
0 Introduction

　　TRIZ 的主要目的是研究人类进行发明创造、解决技术难题过程中所遵循的科学原理和法则，并将之归纳总结形成能指导实际新产品开发的理论方法体系。运用这一理论，可大大加快人们创造发明的进程并得到高质量的创新产品。

　　TRIZ's main purpose is to study the scientific principles and laws that human beings follow in the process of inventing and solving technical problems. And summarize it to form a theoretical method system that can guide the development of practical new products. The application of this theory can greatly speed up the process of people's creation and invention, and get high-quality innovative products.

　　TRIZ 理论也称发明问题解决理论（Theory of Inventive Problem Solving, TRIZ 是其俄文首字母缩写），是由苏联发明家阿奇舒勒（G. S. Altshuller）为首的研究团队通过对 250 万件高水平发明专利进行分析和提炼之后总结出来的指导人们进行发明创新、解决工程问题的系统化的方法学体系。

　　TRIZ theory, also known as the Theory of Inventive Problem Solving (TRIZ is its acronym in Russian), is a systematic methodological system that guides people to carry out innovation and solve engineering problems after the research team led by the former Soviet inventor G. S. Altshuler analyzed and refined 2. 5 million high-level invention patents.

　　TRIZ 理论以辩证法、系统论和认识论为哲学指导，以自然科学、系统科学和思维科学的研究成果为根基和支柱，以技术系统进化法则为理论基础，包括技术系统和技术过程、（技术系统进化过程中产生的）矛盾、（解决矛盾所用的）资源、（技术系统的进化方向）理想化等基本概念。TRIZ 理论提供了分析工程问题所需的方法，包括矛盾分析、功能分析、资源分析和物质-场分析等，同时还提供了相应的问题求解工具，包括技术矛盾创新原理、物理矛盾分离原理、科学原理知识库和发明问题标准解法等。TRIZ 理论针对复杂问题的求解提供了发明问题解决算法（ARIZ），同时 TRIZ 理论还包括了一些创新思维的方法，例如九屏幕法、智能小人法、金鱼法等。

　　TRIZ theory is philosophically guided by dialectics, system theory and epistemology, based on the research results of natural science, system science and thinking science, and based on the law of technology system evolution. It includes technology system and technology process, contradictions (generated in the process of technology system evolution), resources (used to solve contradictions), and idealization (evolution direction of technology system) and other basic concepts. TRIZ theory provides the methods needed to analyze engineering problems, including contradiction analysis, function analysis, resource analysis and matter field analysis, etc. It also provides the corresponding problem solving tools, including the innovation principle of technical contradiction, the separation principle of physical contradiction, the knowledge base of scientific principles and the standard solution of invention problems. TRIZ theory provides inventive problem-solving algorithm (ARIZ) for solving complex problems. At the same time, TRIZ theory also includes some innovative thinking methods, such as the nine screen method, intelligent villain method, goldfish method and so on.

相对于传统的创新方法，比如试错法、头脑风暴法等，TRIZ 理论具有鲜明的特点和优势。它成功地揭示了创造发明的内在规律和原理，着力于澄清和强调系统中存在的矛盾，而不是逃避矛盾；它的最终目标是完全解决矛盾，获得最终的理想解，而不是采取折中或者妥协的做法；它是基于技术的发展演化规律研究的整个设计与开发过程，而不再是随机的行为。

Compared with the traditional innovation methods, such as trial and error method and brainstorming method, TRIZ theory has distinct characteristics and advantages. It successfully reveals the inherent laws and principles of creation and invention, and focuses on clarifying and emphasizing the contradictions existing in the system, rather than evading them. Its ultimate goal is to completely solve the contradiction and obtain the final ideal solution, rather than adopt the compromise or compromise approach; it studies the whole design and development process based on the law of technological development and evolution of technology, rather than randombehavior.

具体而言，TRIZ 理论主要包含：技术系统进化法则，物质-场分析法，发明问题标准解法，发明问题解决算法 ARIZ，技术矛盾解决矩阵，40 个创新原理，39 个工程技术特性，物理学、化学、几何学等工程学原理知识库等创新设计问题解决工具。这些工具为创新理论软件化提供了基础，从而为 TRIZ 的实际应用提供了条件。

Specifically, TRIZ theory mainly includes the following innovative design problem solving tools: technology system evolution law, matter-field analysis method, standard solution of invention problem, Ariz algorithm of invention problem solving, technical contradiction solving matrix, 40 innovative principles, 39 engineering technical characteristics, knowledge base of engineering principles such as physics, chemistry, geometry, etc. These tools provide the basis for the software of innovation theory, thus providing conditions for the practical application of TRIZ.

TRIZ 理论的核心思想包括以下三个方面：第一，无论是一个简单的产品还是复杂的技术系统，其核心技术都是遵循客观规律发展演变的，即具有客观的进化规律和模式；第二，各种技术难题、冲突和矛盾的不断解决是推动这种进化过程的动力；第三，技术系统发展的理想状态是用最少的资源实现最大数目的功能。

The core idea of TRIZ theory includes the following three aspects: first, whether it is a simple product or a complex technology system, its core technology follows the objective law of development and evolution, that is, it has the objective law and mode of evolution; second, the continuous solution of various technical problems, conflicts and contradictions is the driving force to promote this process of evolution; third, the ideal state for the development of technical systems is to achieve the maximum number of functions with the minimum resources.

主要内容包括以下几个方面。

The main contents include the following aspects.

（1）创新思维方法与问题分析方法。TRIZ 理论中提供了如何系统分析问题的科学方法，如多屏幕法。而对于复杂问题的分析，它包含了科学的问题分析建模方法——物场分析法，它可以帮助快速确认核心问题，发现根本矛盾所在。

（1）Innovative thinking method and problem analysis method. TRIZ theory provides a scientific method to analyze problems systematically, such asmulti screen method. For the analysis of complex problems, it includes the scientific problem analysis modeling method——material field analysis method, which can help quickly identify the core problems and find the fundamental contradictions.

（2）技术系统进化法则。针对技术系统进化演变规律，在大量专利分析的基础上 TRIZ 理论总结提炼出 8 个基本进化法则。利用这些进化法则，可以分析确认当前产品的技术状态，并预测未来发展趋势，开发富有竞争力的新产品。

（2）Evolution law of technology system. According to the evolution law of technology system, on the basis of a large number of patent analysis, TRIZ theory summarized and refined eight basic evolution rules. Using these evolutionary rules, we can analyze and confirm the technical status of current products, predict the future development trend, and develop competitive new products.

（3）技术矛盾解决原理。不同的发明创造往往遵循共同的规律。TRIZ 理论将这些共同的规律归纳成 40 个发明原理与 11 个分离原理，针对具体的矛盾，可以基于这些创新原理寻求具体解决方案。

（3）Principle of solving technical contradiction. Different inventions often follow the same rules. TRIZ theory summarizes these common laws into 40 invention principles and 11 separation principles. In view of specific contradictions, we can find specific solutions based on these innovation principles.

（4）创新发明问题标准解法。针对具体问题物质-场模型的不同特征，分别对应有标准的模型处理方法，包括模型的修整、转换、物质与场的添加等。

（4）Standard solution of innovation and invention problem. According to the different characteristics of the matter field model of specific problems, there are corresponding standard model processing methods, including model trimming, transformation, material and field addition, etc.

（5）发明问题解决算法 ARIZ。主要针对问题情境复杂，矛盾及其相关部件不明确的技术系统。它是一个对初始问题进行一系列变形及再定义等非计算性的逻辑过程，实现对问题的逐步深入分析，问题转化，直到问题解决。

（5）Problem solving algorithm Ariz. It mainly aims at the technical system with complex problem situation, unclear contradiction and related components. It is a non-computational logical process, such as a series of deformation and redefinition of the initial problem, realizing the gradual in-depth analysis of the problem, problem transformation, until the problem is solved.

（6）基于物理、化学、几何学等工程学原理而构建的知识库。

（6）Knowledge base based on engineering principles of physics, chemistry and geometry.

体系架构包括以下几个方面：

1）8 大技术系统进化法则；

2）IFR 最终理想解；

3）40 个发明原理；

4）39 个通用参数和阿奇舒勒矛盾矩阵；

5）物理矛盾和分离原理；

6）物质-场模型分析；

7）76 个标准解法；

8）ARIZ 发明问题解决算法；

9）科学原理知识库。

The architecture includes the following aspects：

1）Evolution rules of 8 technical systems；

2）IFR final ideal solution；

3）40 invention principles；

4）39 general parameters and archishure contradiction matrix；

5）Physical contradiction and separation principle；

6）Matter field model analysis；

7）76 standard solutions；

8）Ariz invention problem solving algorithm；

9）Scientific principle knowledge base.

TRIZ 理论成功地揭示了创造发明的内在规律和原理，着力于澄清和强调系统中存在的矛盾，其目标是完全解决矛盾，获得最终的理想解。它不是采取折中或者妥协的做法，而且它是基于技术的发展演化规律研究整个设计与开发过程，而不再是随机的行为。实践证明，运用 TRIZ 理论，可大大加快人们创造发明的进程而且能得到高质量的创新产品。

TRIZ theory has successfully revealed the inherent laws and principles of invention, and focused on clarifying and emphasizing the contradictions existing in the system. Its goal is to completely solve the contradictions and obtain the final ideal solution. It is not a compromise or compromise approach, and it is based on the development and evolution of technology to study the whole design and development process, rather than a random behavior. Practice has proved that the application of TRIZ theory can greatly accelerate the process of people's creation and invention, and obtain high-quality innovative products.

1　基本概念
Chapter 1　Basic Concepts

1.1　概　　述
1.1　Summary

数学、物理、化学等科学领域，机械、化工、自动化等工程领域都以很多基本概念为基础，如几何中的点、线、面，物理中的位移、速度、加速度、力、能量、动量等。概念是对客观世界本质的概括，具有与时间无关、抽象、广泛适用、可以用各种案例说明等特点，构成了科学、技术或工程各领域的基础。TRIZ 在诞生及后续的发展过程中，形成了一些基本概念，这些概念也是 TRIZ 的基础。另外，TRIZ 也采用了其他学科领域中已存在的一些概念，学习这些概念，对理解及应用 TRIZ 十分重要。

Mathematics, physics, chemistry and other scientific fields, mechanical, chemical, automation and other engineering fields are based on many basic concepts, such as points, lines and surfaces in geometry, and displacement, velocity, acceleration, force, energy, momentum and so on in physics. The concept is a summary of the essence of the objective world, which is independent of time, abstract, widely applicable and can be illustrated by various cases. It forms the basis of science, technology or engineering. In the process of its birth and subsequent development, TRIZ has formed some basic concepts, which are also the basis of TRIZ. In addition, TRIZ has also adopted some existing concepts in other disciplines. Learning these concepts is very important for understanding and applying TRIZ.

本章主要介绍功能、理想解、创新分级、可用资源、9 窗口方法、物质-场模型等基本概念。

This chapter mainly introduces the basic concepts such as function, ideal solution, innovation classification, available resources, 9-windows method, matter field model, etc.

1.2　功　　能
1.2　Function

产品设计是包含需求分析、概念设计，技术设计及详细设计的复杂过程。概念设计阶段的根本任务是产生满足需求功能的原理解，即根据用户需求确定产品的总功能，或称为需求功能。将需求功能转变成功能结构，之后将功能结构转变成产品结构，或称为物理结构。概念设计是面向功能的设计过程。

Product design is a complex process including requirement analysis, conceptual design, technical design and detailed design. The basic task of the conceptual design stage is to produce the principle solution to meet the demand function, that is to determine the total function of the product according to the user's demand, or called the demand function. The demand function is transformed into the function structure, and then the function structure is transformed into the product structure, or the physical structure. Conceptual design is a function oriented design process.

功能是概念设计中的关键因素，这一观点在各种设计理论和方法中得到了广泛的认同。这些设计理论和方法有的给出了详细而精确的步骤以指导设计过程，如系统化设计理论依据物料流、能量流和信号流将产品的总功能分解为分功能和功能元；公理设计利用独立公理和信息公理保证功能设计的合理性；有的给出了功能的形式化表达以减少设计过程中的不确定性，如功能基使功能结构的开发具有可重复性。

Function is the key factor in conceptual design, which has been widely accepted in various design theories and methods. Some of these design theories and methods give detailed and accurate steps to guide the design process, such as systematic design theory decomposes the total function of products into sub-functions and functional elements based on material flow, energy flow and signal flow; axiomatic design uses independent axiom and information axiom to ensure the rationality of functional design; some give formal expression of functions to reduce the cost of design process, such as the function base makes the development of function structure repeatable.

1.2.1　功能的概念
1.2.1　The concept of function

产品功能分析是概念设计过程中一个重要环节，它起着承上启下、传递并生成设计信息、主导创新原理产生的重要作用。近年来，随着人们对产品概念设计的深入研究，对于功能的抽象化表达、功能分类、功能分解、功能基以及功能标准化等方面的研究越来越多。

Product function analysis is an important link in the process of conceptual design, which plays an important role in connecting the preceding and the following, transmitting and generating design information, and leading the generation of innovative principles. In recent years, with the in-depth study of product conceptual design, there are more and more researches on function abstraction, function classification, function decomposition, function base and function standardization.

20世纪40年代，美国通用电气公司工程师迈尔斯首先提出功能的概念，并把它作为价值工程研究的核心问题。迈尔斯认为顾客要购买的是产品的功能而不是产品本身，功能体现了顾客的某种需要。

In 1940s, the concept of function was first put forward by American General Electric

Engineer Miles, and it was regarded as the core problem of value engineering research. Miles thought that what customers want to buy is the function of the product rather than the product itself, and the function reflects some needs of customers.

Koller 将功能定义为输入和输出量之间的因果关系，即"什么"应当转变为"什么"。Koller 定义了 12 对基本功能：放出↔吸收，传导↔绝缘，集合↔扩散，引导↔不引导，转变↔回复，放大↔缩小，变向↔变向，调整↔振动，联结↔隔断，结合↔分离，接合↔分开，贮存↔取出。Koller 认为技术系统中一切过程都可以归诸于这 12 对功能，也就是说它们可以构成一切复杂的系统。

Koller defined function as the causal relationship between input and output, that is, "what" should be transformed into "what". Koller defines 12 pairs of basic functions: release ↔ absorption, conduction ↔ insulation, assembly ↔ diffusion, guidance ↔ no guidance, no change ↔ reply, enlarge ↔ reduce, change direction ↔ change direction, adjust ↔ vibration, connection ↔ partition, combination ↔ separation, joint ↔ separate, store ↔ take it out. Koller thought that all processes in the technological system can be attributed to these 12 pairs of functions, that is to say, they can constitute all complex systems.

Pahl 和 Beitz 将功能定义为以完成任务为目的系统的输入与输出之间的一般关系。从系统的观点出发，可将系统的功能分为总功能和分功能。每个系统都有其总功能，对系统整体的功能要求就是该系统所具有的总功能，系统输入、输出的能量、物料、信息的差别和关系反映了系统的总功能。Pahl 和 Beitz 定义了转变、变化、联结、导通和贮存五种通用功能。但同时他们指出在许多情况下，不宜用通用功能来建立功能结构，因为它们构造得太一般，以至于在后续的求解方面不能输出足够具体的相互关系设想。

Pahl and Beitz defined function as the general relationship between the input and output of the system for the purpose of completing tasks. From the perspective of system, the function of the system can be divided into total functions and sub functions. Each system has its total function. The functional requirements of the whole system are the total functions of the system. The differences and relations of the energy, materials and information input and output reflect the total functions of the system. Pahl and Beitz defined five general functions: transformation, change, connection, conduction and storage. But at the same time, they pointed out that in many cases, it is not appropriate to use the general function to establish the functional structure, because they are too general to output enough specific assumptions about the relationship in the subsequent solution.

Hubka 将功能定义为反映输入与输出间关系的技术函数。产生若干表现为一定功能的功能部件称为机体。根据功能结构，Hubka 把机械系统归为工作机体、辅助机体、驱动机体、控制调节和自动化机体、连接和支撑机体五类。

Hubka defined function as a technical function reflecting the relationship between input and output. Producing a number of functional components that perform certain functions is called the body. According to the functional structure, Hubka classified the mechanical system into five categories: working body, auxiliary body, driving body, control, regulation and automation body, connecting and supporting body.

Collins 等开发了一个主要机械功能列表用于直升机零部件的失效分析。这一列表包括了 46 个关键词和 40 个先行形容词，将它们组合后形成 105 个主要的功能。这些功能是在设计直升机时必须考虑的。

Collins et al. developed a list of major mechanical functions for failure analysis of helicopter components. This list includes 46 keywords and 40 antecedent adjectives, which are combined to form 105 main functions. These functions must be considered when designing helicopters.

功能是一个主观的概念，对于相同的行为和物理现象，不同的人或相同的人在不同的时刻，从不同的侧面，可以得到不同的表示。因此，功能不仅与物理现象行为有关，而且与设计者的意图以及观察角度有关。以往的研究中功能主要有三种表达方法：

（1）动词+名词；

（2）输入/输出变换，输入/输出可以是能量、物质或信息；

（3）行为、状态间的输入/输出变换。

Function is a subjective concept. For the same behavior and physical phenomenon, different people or the same people can get different expressions at different times and from different sides. Therefore, function is not only related to physical phenomena and behaviors, but also related to the designer's intention and observation angle. There are three ways to express function in previous studies:

（1）Verb + noun;

（2）Input/output transformation, input/output can be energy, material or information;

（3）Input/output transformation between behavior and state.

为了更好地描述语言表达功能，已提出了功能基的概念，并将其作为一种标准的设计语言。功能基包含功能和流两类术语。前者用主动动词描述，后者用名词描述。功能基可以描述所有的工作领域，而术语是独立的。其中的功能机分为八类，称为类功能或基类，每一类还可以分为第二级及第三级，后两类增加了专门化的程度。基类表示功能的空泛概念，第二级及第三级为描述功能的细节。第二级功能包含 21 个主动动词，是经常采用的功能描述。表 1-1 表示了第一级功能的所有主动动词。

In order to better describe the function of language expression, the concept of function base has been proposed and used as a standard design language. Function base includes two kinds of terms: function and flow. The former is described by active verbs and the latter by nouns. Function base can describe all work areas, while terms are independent. Among them, the functional machines are divided into eight categories, which are called class function or base class. Each category can also be divided into the second level and the third level. The latter two categories increase the degree of specialization. The base class represents the general concept of function, and the second and third levels describe the details of function. The second level function contains twenty-one active verbs, which are often used to describe functions. Table 1-1 represents the first level functions.

表 1-1　功能集及其分类

Table 1-1　Functional sets and their classification

类 Class	分开 Separate	引导 Lead	连接 Connect	控制 Control	转换 Transform	供应 Supply	发信号 Singalling	支持 Support
一级 First level	散布 Interspersal	分离 Separate 输出 Export 传递 Transmit 引导 Guide	结合 Combine 混合 Mix	启动 Firing 调节 Regulate 改变 Change 停止 Cease	转换 Transform	存储 Memory 供给 Provide	感知 Perception 显示 Display 处理 Handle	稳定 Stabilize 保证 Ensure 安置 Aftercare

功能基中的流集描述功能的输入与输出关系。与功能集相似，流集也分为三类，流的基类包括能量、物料、信号；第二级包含 20 个名词，这些名词经常被采用。表 1-2 描述了第二级流的名称。表中忽略了第三级流。

The flow set in the function base describes the relationship between the input and output of the function. Similar to function set, flow set is also divided into three categories. The basic category of flow includes energy, material and signal. The second level contains twenty nouns, which are often used. Table 1-2 describes the names of the second level flows. The third level flow is ignored in the table.

表 1-2　流集及其分类

Table 1-2　Stream sets and their classification

类 Class	物料 Materiel	信号 Signal	能量 Energy		
二级 Second level	人 People 气体 Gas 液体 Liquid 固体 Solid 等离子体 Plasma 混合物 Mixture	状态 State 控制 Control	人 People 声学 Acoustics 生物学 Biology 化学 Chemistry	电 Electric 电磁 Electromagnetism 液压 Hydraulic pressure 磁 Magnetism	机械 Mechanics 气动 Pneumatics 放射性 Radioactivity 热 Heat

1.2.2　功能模型的建立

1.2.2　**Establishment of functional model**

　　功能模型是产品或过程的一种描述，按这种描述，基本功能的组合能满足完成总功能或目的要求，功能模型的一种图形表达方式是功能结构，这种结构对设计者简明适用。对产品总的输入输出描述为总功能，总功能分解成若干分功能，一直分解到功能元，将系统的各个功能元用流有机地组合起来就得到功能结构。产品功能用动词+名词形式表示，输入/输出由用户需求确定，如图 1-1 所示。将总功能分解可得到功能结构，如图 1-2 所示。图 1-3 是咖啡壶的一个功能模型。

　　Function model is a description of product or process. According to this description, the combination of basic functions can meet the requirements of completing the total function or purpose. A graphic expression of function model is function structure, which is concise and applicable to designers. The total input and output of the product is described as the total function. The total function is decomposed into several sub functions until the function element. The function structure can be obtained by organically combining each function element of the system with flow. The product function is expressed in the form of verb + noun, and the input / output is determined by the user's requirements, as shown in Figure 1-1. The functional structure can be obtained by decomposing the total function, as shown in Figure 1-2. Figure 1-3 is a functional model of coffee pot.

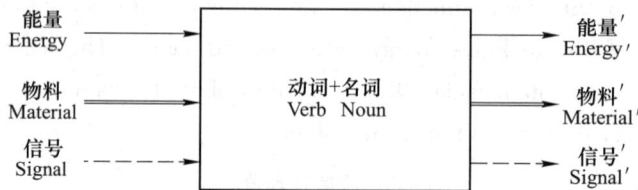

图 1-1　产品总功能

Figure 1-1　Total product function

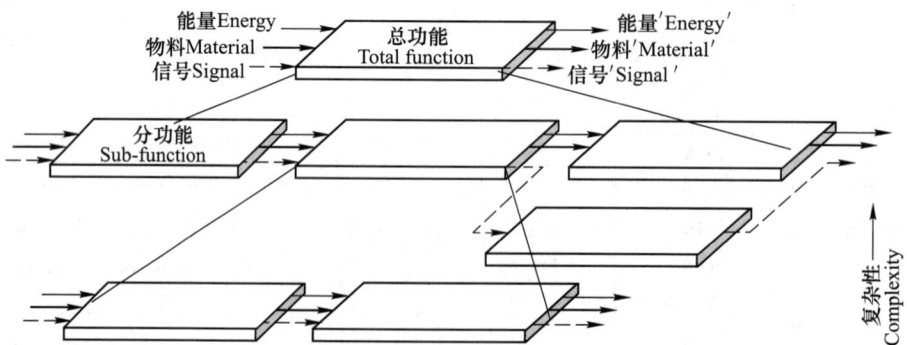

图 1-2　产品功能结构

Figure 1-2　Product functional structure

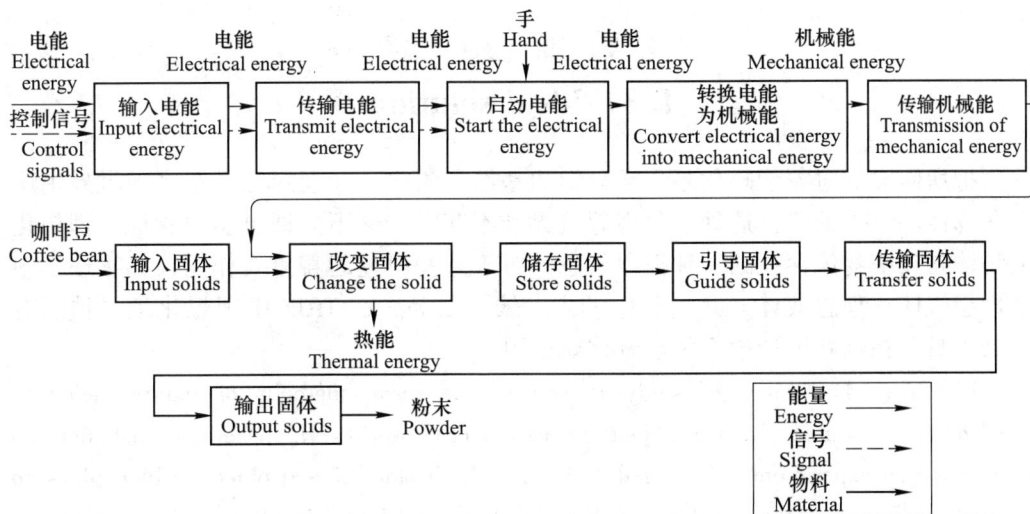

图 1-3　咖啡壶功能模型

Figure 1-3　Functional model of the coffee pot

1.2.3　功能分类

1.2.3　Function classification

一个产品或系统可能要完成多种功能，在这些功能中只有一类是主功能（PF，Primary Function）或称基本功能（BF，Basic Function），即系统存在的目的。第二类是辅助功能（AF，Auxiliary Function），该类功能是支持基本功能并使之实现的功能。辅助功能是特定设计的结果，如果改变设计，其中的一些可能要改变或取消。

A product or system may have to complete multiple functions. Only one of these functions is primary function (PF) or basic function (BF), which is the purpose of the system. The second is auxiliary function (AF), which supports and realizes basic functions. Auxiliary functions are the result of a specific design, some of which may need to be changed or cancelled if the design is changed.

每个系统提供一个或多个有用功能（UF，Useful Functions），如主功能或辅助功能，然而，系统中还存在有害功能（HF，Harmful Functions），该类功能的存在是不希望的。如一辆汽车的主要功能是载人或物，但同时也产生了噪声、振动、污染，这些都是有害功能。有用功能实现的同时，常常伴随有害功能的出现。

Each system provides one or more useful functions (UF), such as main function or auxiliary function. However, there are also harmful functions (HF) in the system, which are undesirable. For example, the main function of a car is to carry people or objects, but it also produces noise, vibration and pollution, which are harmful functions. When useful functions are realized, harmful functions often appear.

1.3 理　想　解
1.3 Ideal solution

把所研究的对象理想化是自然科学的基本方法之一。理想化是对客观世界中所存在物体的一种抽象，这种抽象客观世界既不存在，又不能通过实验验证。理想化的物体是真实物体存在的一种极限状态，对于某些研究起着重要作用，如物理学中的理想气体、理想液体，几何学中的点、线、面等。在 TRIZ 中理想化是一种强有力的工具，在创新设计过程中起着重要作用。

Idealizing the object of study is one of the basic methods of natural science. Idealization is an abstraction of objects in the objective world, which neither exists nor can be verified by experiments. Idealized object is a limit state of real object, which plays an important role in some researches, such as ideal gas and liquid in physics, point, line and surface in geometry, etc. Idealization is a powerful tool in TRIZ and plays an important role in the process of innovative design.

1.3.1 理想化
1.3.1 Idealization

在 TRIZ 中，理想化包含理想系统、理想过程、理想资源、理想方法、理想机器、理想物质等。理想化的描述如下。

（1）理想机器：没有质量，没有体积，但能完成所需的工作。

（2）理想方法：不消耗能量及时间，但通过自身调节，能够获得所需的效应。

（3）理想过程：只有过程的结果，而无过程本身，突然就获得了结果。

（4）理想物质：没有物质，功能得以实现。

In TRIZ, idealization includes ideal system, ideal process, ideal resource, ideal method, ideal machine, ideal material, etc. The idealized description is as follows.

（1）Ideal machine：no mass, no volume, but can complete the required work.

（2）Ideal method：it does not consume energy and time, but through self-regulation, it can achieve the desired effect.

（3）Ideal process：only the result of the process, but not the process itself, suddenly obtains the result.

（4）Ideal material：without material, function can be realized.

理想化分为局部理想化与全局理想化两类。局部理想化是指对于选定的原理，通过不同的实现方法使其理想化；全局理想化是指对同一功能，通过选择不同的原理使之理想化。局部理想化的过程有如下四种模式。

（1）加强：通过参数优化、采用更高级的材料、引入附加调节装置等加强有用功能的作用。

（2）降低：通过对有害功能的补偿，减少或消除损失或浪费，采用更便宜的材料、标准零部件等。

（3）通用化：采用多功能技术增加有用功能的个数。如现代化多媒体计算机具有电视机、电话、传真机、音响等的功能。

（4）专用化：突出功能的主次。如早期的汽车厂要生产零部件，最后将它们组装成汽车，今天的汽车厂主要是组装汽车，而零部件由很多专业配套厂生产。

Idealization can be divided into local idealization and global idealization. Local idealization refers to the idealization of selected principles by different implementation methods. Global idealization refers to the idealization of the same function by choosing different principles. There are four modes in the process of local idealization.

（1）Strengthen：through parameter optimization, the use of more advanced materials, the introduction of additional adjustment devices to strengthen the role of useful functions.

（2）Reduce：through the compensation for harmful functions, reduce or eliminate the loss or waste, using cheaper materials, standard parts, etc.

（3）Generalization：use multi-functional technology to increase the number of useful functions. Such as modern multimedia computer with television, telephone, fax machine, audio and other functions.

（4）Specialization：highlight the primary and secondary functions. For example, in the early days, automobile factories produced spare parts and finally assembled them into automobiles. Today's automobile factories mainly assemble automobiles, and spare parts are produced by many professional supporting factories.

1.3.2 理想化水平
1.3.2 Idealization level

技术系统是功能的实现，同一功能存在多种技术实现，任何系统在完成人们所需的功能时，都有负面作用。为了对正反两方面作用进行评价，采用如下公式：

Technology system is the realization of function. There are many technical implementations of the same function. Any system has negative effects when it completes the functions that people need. In order to evaluate the positive and negative effects, the following formula is used：

$$\text{Ideality} = \sum \text{UF} / \sum \text{HF} \tag{1-1}$$

式中　Ideality——理想化水平；

　　　$\sum$ UF ——有用功能之和；

　　　$\sum$ HF ——有害功能之和。

Where Ideality——Ideal level；

　　　$\sum$ UF ——The sum of useful functions；

　　　$\sum$ HF ——The sum of harmful functions.

该公式的意义为：技术系统的理想化水平与有用功能之和成正比，与有害功能之和成反比。当改变系统时，如果公式中的分子增加，分母减小，系统的理想化水平提高，产品的竞争能力增强。

The significance of this formula is that the idealization level of technical system is directly proportional to the sum of useful functions and inversely proportional to the sum of harmful functions. When changing the system, if the numerator in the formula increases and the denominator decreases, the idealization level of the system will increase and the competitiveness of the product will increase.

增加理想化水平有如下四种方式。

（1）$d(\sum UF)/dt > d(\sum HF)/dt$：式（1-1）中分子增加的速率高于分母增加速率。

（2）$d(\sum UF)/dt > 0$，$d(\sum HF)/dt < 0$：式（1-1）中的分子增加，分母减少。

（3）$d(\sum UF)/dt = 0$，$d(\sum HF)/dt < 0$：式（1-1）中的分子不变，分母减少，即有害功能减少。

（4）$d(\sum UF)/dt > 0$，$d(\sum HF)/dt = 0$：式（1-1）中分母不变，分子增加，即有用功能增加，有害功能不变。

There are four ways to increase the idealization level.

（1）$d(\sum UF)/dt > d(\sum HF)/dt$：the increasing rate of numerator in formula (1-1) is higher than that of denominator.

（2）$d(\sum UF)/dt > 0$，$d(\sum HF)/dt < 0$：the numerator in formula (1-1) increases and the denominator decreases.

（3）$d(\sum UF)/dt = 0$，$d(\sum HF)/dt < 0$：the numerator in formula (1-1) remains unchanged and the denominator decreases, that is, the harmful function decreases.

（4）$d(\sum UF)/dt > 0$，$d(\sum HF)/dt = 0$：in formula (1-1), the denominator remains unchanged, and the numerator increases, that is, the useful function increases, and the harmful function remains unchanged.

为使分析更加方便，将式（1-1）中的有害功能分解为代价与危害是方便的，将有用功能之和用效益之和来代替，如式（1-2）所示。

In order to make the analysis more convenient, it is convenient to decompose the harmful functions in formula (1-1) into cost and harm, and replace the sum of useful functions with the sum of benefits, as shown in formula (1-2).

$$\text{Ideality} = \sum \text{Benefits}/(\sum \text{Espenses} + \sum \text{Harms}) \tag{1-2}$$

式中　Ideality——理想化水平；

　　　Benefits——效益；

　　　Espenses——代价；

　　　Harms——副作用。

Where Ideality——Idealization level;

　　　Benefits——Benefits;

　　Espenses——Cost;

　　　　Harms——Side effects.

　　代价包括原料的成本、系统所占用的空间、所消耗的能量及所产生的噪声等。危害包括废弃物及污染等。

　　The cost includes the cost of raw materials, the space occupied by the system, the energy consumed and the noise generated. Hazards include waste and pollution.

　　该公式的意义为产品或系统的理想化水平与其效益之和成正比，与所有代价及所有危害之和成反比。不断地增加产品理想化水平是产品创新的目标。

　　The significance of the formula is that the idealized level of the product or system is directly proportional to the sum of its benefits, and inversely proportional to the sum of all costs and all hazards. The goal of product innovation is to continuously increase the level of product idealization.

1.3.3　理想解与最终理想解
1.3.3　Ideal solution and final ideal solution

　　产品处于进化之中，进化的过程就是产品由低级向高级演化的过程，如数控机床是普通机床的高级阶段，加工中心又是数控机床的高级阶段。再如彩色电视机是黑白电视机的高级阶段，高清晰度彩电是一般彩电的高级阶段。在进化的某一阶段，不同产品进化的方向是不同的，如降低成本、增加可靠性、提高可靠性、减少污染等都是产品可能的进化方向。如果将所有产品作为一个整体，低成本、高功能、高可靠性、无污染等是产品的理想状态（IFR, Ideal Final Result）。产品处于理想状态的解称为理想解。

　　The product is in the process of evolution. The process of evolution is the process of product evolution from low level to high level. For example, CNC machine tool is the advanced stage of ordinary machine tool, and machining center is the advanced stage of CNC machine tool. Another example is that color TV is the advanced stage of black and white TV, andhigh definition TV is the advanced stage of general color TV. At a certain stage of evolution, different products have different directions of evolution, such as reducing cost, increasing reliability, improving reliability, reducing pollution and so on. If all products are taken as a whole, low cost, high function, high reliability and no pollution are the ideal final results of products (IFR). The solution of product in ideal state is called ideal solution.

　　产品的理想解实现的过程是其理想化水平提高的过程，理想化水平达到无穷大状态的理想解称为最终理想解。TRIZ 中的理想物质、理想过程、理想方法、理想机器等均是某种形式的最终理想解。最终理想解很难或不可能实现，但产品进化的过程是推动理想解无限趋近最终理想解的过程。

　　The process of realizing the ideal solution of a product is the process of improving its idealization level. The ideal solution whose idealization level reaches infinity is called the final ideal solution. The ideal material, ideal process, ideal method and ideal machine in

TRIZ are all the final ideal solutions in some form. The final ideal solution is difficult or impossible to achieve, but the process of product evolution is to promote the ideal solution to reach the final ideal solution infinitely.

产品进化的过程是产品由低级向高级进化的过程，进化的极限状态是最终理想解，而进化的中间状态是理想解。为了实现低成本、高效能、高可靠性、无副作用等理想状态，产品首先实现多个理想解，通过这些理想解趋近最终理想解。

The process of product evolution is the process of product evolution from low level to high level. The limit state of evolution is the final ideal solution, while the intermediate state of evolution is the ideal solution. In order to achieve the ideal state of low cost, high efficiency, high reliability and no side effects, the product first realizes multiple ideal solutions, and then approaches the final ideal solution through these ideal solutions.

通过需求分析，可确定产品的理想解集合：

Through requirement analysis, the ideal solution set of the product can bedetermined：

$$IFR = \{ IFR_1, \ IFR_2, \ \cdots, \ IFR_k, \ \cdots, \ IFR_l \} \ (k \leq l) \tag{1-3}$$

其中 l 为理想解元素总数。

Where l is the total number of ideal solution elements.

产品从目前状态或初始状态实现每一个理想解的过程需要一系列的目标实现，而每个目标的实现都存在障碍 C_{ki}，该障碍也由一策合构成。

The process of realizing each ideal solution from the current state or initial state of a product needs a series of goals, and there are obstacles to the realization of each goal, which are also composed of a strategy.

$$C_k = \{ C_{k1}, \ C_{k2}, \ \cdots, \ C_{ki} \} \tag{1-4}$$

最终理想解与各理想解之间形成如下关系：

The relationship between the final ideal solution and each ideal solution is asfollows：

$$Ideality = [C]\{IFR\} \tag{1-5}$$

理想解可采用与技术及实现无关的语言对需要创新的原因进行描述。创新的重要进展往往对问题深入地理解所取得。确认那些使系统不能处于理想化的元件是创新成功的关键。设计过程中从一起点向理想解过渡的过程称为理想化过程。

The ideal solution can use language independent of technology and implementation to describe the reasons for innovation. Important progress in innovation is often achieved by a deep understanding of the problem. Identifying the components that keep the system from being idealized is the key to successful innovation. The process of transition from a point to an ideal solution in the design process is called idealization process.

理想解有如下的 4 个特点：

（1）消除了原系统的不足之处；

（2）保持原系统的优点；

（3）没有使系统变得更复杂（采用无成本或可用资源）；

（4）没有引入新的缺陷。

The ideal solution has the following four characteristics：

（1）The shortcomings of the original system are eliminated;

（2）Keep the advantages of the original system;

（3）It does not make the system more complex（using no cost or available resources）;

（4）No new defects were introduced.

当确定了待设计产品或系统的理想解后，可用上述 4 个特点检查，也要用式（1-1）和式（1-2）检查理想解是否正确。

When the ideal solution of the product or system to be designed is determined, the above four characteristics can be used to check, and the formula （1-1） and formula （1-2） should also be used to check whether the ideal solution is correct.

➤**例 1-1**　考虑割草机作为工具，草坪上的草作为被割的目标。割草机在割草时发出噪声、消耗燃料、产生空气污染、甩出的草片有时会伤害推割草机的工人。假如设计者的任务是改进已有的割草机，设计者可能会很快想到要减少噪声、增加安全性、降低燃料消耗。但如果确定理想解，就会勾画出未来割草机及草坪维护工业更佳的蓝图。

➤ **Example 1-1**　Consider the lawn mower as a tool and the grass on the lawn as a target to be cut. The noise, fuel consumption, air pollution and the grass flakes thrown out by the mower sometimes hurt the workers who push the mower. If the designer's task is to improve the existing mower, the designer may soon think of reducing noise, increasing safety and reducing fuel consumption. However, if we determine the ideal solution, we will draw a better blueprint for the future mower and lawn maintenance industry.

用户需要的究竟是什么？是非常漂亮且不需要维护的草坪。割草机本身不是用户需要的一部分。从割草机与草坪构成的系统看，其理想解为草坪上的草长到一定的高度就停止生长。至少国际上有两家制造割草机的公司正在实验这种理想草坪的草种，该草种被称为"漂亮草种（smart grass seed）"。

What exactly do users need? It's a very beautiful lawn that doesn't need maintenance. The mower itself is not part of the user's needs. From the system of lawn mower and lawn, the ideal solution is that the grass on the lawn stops growing when it grows to a certain height. At least two international companies that make lawn mowers are experimenting with this ideal grass seed, which is called "smart grass seed".

假定设计者的任务不是在公司或草坪维护工业水平考虑问题，而要求减少割草机的噪音，其理想解为安静的割草机。噪声低与安静是不同的概念。为了达到低噪声的目的，设计人员要为系统增加阻尼器、减震器等，这不仅增加了系统的复杂性，同时也降低了系统的可靠性。为了使割草机安静，设计人员要寻找并消除噪声源，这不仅提高了割草机效率，也达到了最初要求降低噪声的目的。

Assuming that the designer's task is not to consider the problem at the level of the company or lawn maintenance industry, but to reduce the noise of the lawn mower, the ideal solution is a quiet lawn mower. Low noise and quiet are different concepts. In order to achieve the goal of low noise, designers need to add dampers and shock absorbers to the system, which not only increases the complexity of the system, but also reduces the reliability of the system. In order to make the mower quiet, designers need to find and eliminate the noise source, which not only improves the efficiency of the mower, but also achieves the purpose of reducing the noise as originally required.

1.4 创 新 分 级
1.4 Innovation classification

TRIZ 的一个重要成果是认为创新有级别，产品创新由低级向高级的方向发展。由于这种发展，产品才一直占领老市场或又赢得新市场。Altshuller 通过研究表明，问题的解或概念分为 5 个级别，普通设计人员采用试验纠错法从产生最初的工作原理，到最终选定工作原理过程中，所产生工作原理的个数即解的个数决定解的级别。其级别与个数的关系见表 1-3。

An important achievement of TRIZ is that innovation has levels, and product innovation develops from low level to high level. As a result of this development, products have been occupying the old market or winning the new market. Altshuller's research showed that the solution or concept of the problem can be divided into five levels. Ordinary designers use the method of error detection by experiment. From the initial working principle to the final working principle selection, the number of working principles, that is, the number of solutions, determines the level of the solution. The relationship between the level and the number is shown in Table 1-3.

表 1-3 解的级别与工作原理数的关系

Table 1-3 The relationship between the level of 3 solutions and the number of working principles

级别 Level	所产生工作原理个数 Number of working principles generated
1	1-10
2	10-100
3	100-1000
4	1000-10000
5	10000-100000 或更多 10000-100000 or more

产品从低级向高级进化过程中，高级别解的产生需要更多的知识。产品的级别还与问题的难易程度、知识来源等有密切的关系。描述如下。

（1）1 级：通常的设计问题，或对已有系统的简单改进。设计人员自身的经验即可解决，不需要创新。大约有 32% 的解属于该范围。如用厚隔热层减少热量损失；用载重量更大的卡车改善运输的成本与效益比。

（2）2 级：通过解决一个技术冲突对已有系统进行少量的改进。采用行业中已有的方法即可完成。解决该类问题的传统方法是折中法。大约有 45% 的解属于该范围。如在焊接装置上增加一灭火器。

（3）3级：对已有系统有根本性的改进。要采用本行业以外已有的方法解决，设计过程中要解决冲突。大约有18%的解属于该范围。如计算机鼠标、山地自行车、圆珠笔。

（4）4级：采用全新的原理完成已有系统基本功能的新解。解的发现主要是从科学的角度而不是从工程的角度。大约有4%的解属于该类。如内燃机、集成电路、个人计算机、充气轮胎、虚拟现实。

（5）5级：罕见的科学原理导致一种新系统的发明。大约有1%属于该类。如飞机、计算机、形状记忆合金、蒸汽机。

In the process of product evolution from low level to high level, the generation of high-level solution needs more knowledge. The level of product is also closely related to the difficulty of the problem and the source of knowledge. The description is as follows.

（1）Level 1: common design problems or simple improvements to existing systems. Designers' own experience can solve the problem without innovation. About 32% of the solutions belong to this range. For example, using thick insulation layer to reduce heat loss; using trucks with larger carrying capacity to improve the cost-benefit ratio of transportation.

（2）Level 2: a small amount of improvement is made to the existing system by solving a technical conflict. It can be completed by using the existing methods in the industry. The traditional way to solve this kind of problem is compromise. About 45% of the solutions belong to this range. Such as adding a fire extinguisher on the welding device.

（3）Level 3: a fundamental improvement on the existing system. The existing methods outside the industry should be adopted, and the conflicts should be solved in the design process. About 18% of the solutions belong to this range. Such as computer mouse, mountain bike, ball point pen.

（4）Level 4: complete the new solution of the basic function of the existing system with a new principle. The discovery of solutions is mainly from the perspective of science rather than engineering. About 4% of the solutions belong to this class. Such as internal combustion engine, integrated circuit, personal computer, pneumatic tire, virtual reality.

（5）Level 5: rare scientific principles lead to the invention of a new system. About 1% of them belong to this category. Such as aircraft, computer, shape memory alloy, steam engine.

上述的描述可以看出，解的级别越高，获得该解时所需知识越多，这些知识所处的领域越宽，搜索有用知识的时间就越长，如图1-4所示。

From the above description, it can be seen that the higher the level of the solution, the more knowledge is needed to obtain the solution, the wider the domain of the knowledge, and the longer the search time for useful knowledge, as shown in Figure 1-4.

综上，产品设计中所遇到绝大多数问题或相似问题已被前人在其他地方或领域解决了。假如设计人员能按照正确路径，从低级开始，依据自身的知识与经验，向

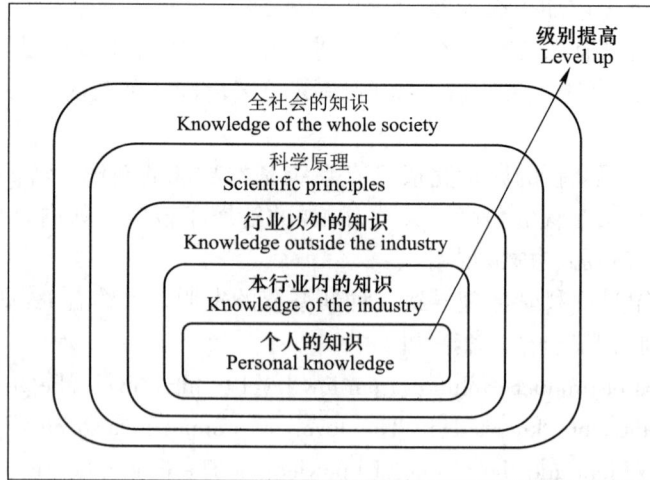

图 1-4   知识圈

Figure 1-4   Knowledge circle

高级方向努力，可从本企业、本行业及其他行业已存在的知识与经验中获得大量的解，有意识去发现这些解，将节省大量时间，降低产品开发成本。

Overall, most of the problems or similar problems encountered in product design have been solved by predecessors in other places or fields. If designers can follow the correct path, start from the low level, and work hard to the high level according to their own knowledge and experience, they can get a lot of solutions from the existing knowledge and experience of their own enterprises, their own industries and other industries. If they consciously find these solutions, they will save a lot of time and reduce the cost of product development.

1.5   可用资源
1.5   Available resources

资源一词首先涉及自然资源水、土地、木材、矿物等。在过去的多个世纪中，自然资源的丰富程度是影响一个国家或地区强弱的主要因素。后来，工业革命及资本主义的发展，产生了金融资源的概念。20世纪后半叶，由于管理革命，人力资源的概念产生了。正如自然资源在赢得战争中所起到的作用相同，金融资源及人力资源是在市场竞争中取得优势的重要因素。

The term resource first refers to natural resources such as water, land, wood, minerals, etc. In the past several centuries, the abundance of natural resources is the main factor affecting the strength of a country or region. Later, the Industrial Revolution and the development of capitalism gave birth to the concept of financial resources. In the second half of the 20th century, due to the management revolution, the concept of human resources came into being. Just as natural resources played the same role in the win war, financial resources and human resources are the important factors to gain advantages in the market competition.

　　各种社会学的研究基于自然资源、金融资源及人力资源。人类的进化伴随着可用资源的消耗，很多资源逐渐枯竭，给人类带来了巨大的恐惧及灾难。同时，人们不断地发现新的资源，如发明新的采矿方法，更好地应用各种金属、蒸汽及电，选择优良品种、采用化肥及杀虫剂增加农业产量等。很多方法用于改善自然资源的利用，如对于相同的矿石产生更多的金属、相同面积的土地产生更多的粮食等。在过去相当长的时间内，缺乏有效及可靠的方法利用自然资源。第一种以降低成本且提高效率为目标的资源分析方法是 Lawrence Miles 创造的价值工程方法（VEA，Value Engineering Analysis）。

Various sociological researches are based on natural resources, financial resources and human resources. Human evolution is accompanied by the consumption of available resources, many resources are gradually exhausted, which brings great fear and disaster to human beings. At the same time, people continue to discover new resources, such as the invention of new mining methods, better application of various metals, steam and electricity, selection of fine varieties, use of chemical fertilizers and pesticides to increase agricultural production. Many methods are used to improve the utilization of natural resources, such as producing more metals for the same ore, producing more food for the same area of land, and so on. For quite a long time in the past, there was a lack of effective and reliable methods to utilize natural resources. The first resource analysis method aiming at reducing cost and improving efficiency is value engineering analysis (VEA) created by Lawrence miles.

　　在 TRIZ 研究的历史上，1982 年 Vladimir Petrov 首先提出了技术系统超额供给的概念，认为技术系统所具有的某些能力通常都大于需求，可以利用这些多余的能力，增加系统的理想化水平，这就是系统中可用资源的概念。1985 年，Altshuller 引入了物质-场资源的概念。资源有如下分类。

In the history of TRIZ research, Vladimir Petrov first put forward the concept of excess supply of technology system in 1982. He believed that some capabilities of technology system are usually greater than the demand, and these redundant capabilities can be used to increase the idealization level of the system. This is the concept of available resources in the system. In 1985, Altshuller introduced the concept of matter field resource. Resources are classified as follows.

　　（1）基于可获得容易程度，资源可分为以下三种。

　　1）内部资源：从系统主要零部件内部获得的资源。

　　2）外部资源：包括环境中的资源，以及特别适合于本系统的资源。

　　3）超系统中的资源：由超系统得到的资源，或其他可得到的且廉价的资源（包括废料）。

　　（1）Based on the availability, resources can be divided into the following three types.

　　1）Internal resources: resources obtained from the main components of the system.

2) External resources: including the resources in the environment and the resources especially suitable for the system.

3) Resources in a supersystem: resources derived from a supersystem, or other available and inexpensive resources (including scrap).

（2）基于可否直接应用，资源可分为可直接应用的资源和导出资源（可直接应用资源的变换）。

（2）Based on direct application, resources can be divided into resources that can be applied directly and export resources (the transformation of resources can be directly applied).

总结 TRIZ 领域的研究成果，Boris zlotin 及 Alla zusman 将资源总结为发明资源和进化资源。发明资源涉及已存在的系统及其相应的环境。进化资源设计给定系统或其他系统进化的设想、概念及技术的与非技术的可能性，该类资源是直接进化理论及应用的核心。

Based on the research achievements in TRIZ, Boris zlotin and Alla zusman classified the resources into two categories: invention resources and evolutionary resources. Invention resources relate to existing systems and their corresponding environments. Evolutionary resources are the core of the theory and application of direct evolution.

利用系统或其环境中的资源可以通过产生附加有用特征，减少成本的方式增加其理想化水平，其主要包括通过利用未采用的资源、利用内部而不是外部资源、利用低成本或非常容易获取的资源。

The use of resources in the system or its environment can increase its idealization level by generating additional useful features and reducing costs, mainly including the use of unused resources, the use of internal rather than external resources, the use of low-cost or very accessible resources.

1.5.1　发明资源
1.5.1　Invention resources

发明资源定义为：系统或其环境中可利用的物质（包括废物）或由这些物质所产生的新物质，如能量储备、自由时间、未占用的空间及未采用的信息等；履行附加功能的或技术的能力，包括物质的性能及物理的、化学的、几何的效应等。

Invention resources are defined as: substances (including wastes) available in the system or its environment or new substances generated by these substances, such as energy reserve, free time, unoccupied space, unused information, etc.; the ability to perform additional functions or technologies, including material properties and physical, chemical, geometric effects, etc.

发明资源可分为内部与外部资源。内部资源是在冲突发生的时间、区域内存在的资源。外部资源是在冲突发生的时间、区域外部存在的资源。内部与外部资源又可分为直接应用、导出及差动资源三类。

Invention resources can be divided into internal and external resources. Internal resources are resources that exist in the time and region of conflict. External resources are resources that exist outside the region at the time of conflict. Internal and external resources can be divided into direct application, export and differential resources.

1.5.2　进化资源

1.5.2　**Evolutionary resources**

进化资源由知识（包括理论、事实、设想、概念、设计、过程等）、能力、技巧等构成，这些知识、能力或技巧是进化的结果，而且能够使进化向前发展一步。按进化的观点，这些资源中最重要的组成是通用进化知识、创造力及保障进化过程的技术，进化的目标是增加已存在系统的理想化水平及发明新系统。事实上，发明资源将帮助无用的甚至是有害的元素转变为有用资源。

Evolutionary resources consist of knowledge (including theory, fact, assumption, concept, design, process, etc.), ability, skill, etc. These knowledge, ability or skill are the result of evolution and can make evolution move forward. From the perspective of evolution, the most important components of these resources are universal evolutionary knowledge, creativity and technology to ensure the evolutionary process. The goal of evolution is to increase the idealization level of existing systems and invent new systems. In fact, inventing resources will help transform useless and even harmful elements into useful resources.

进化资源分为如下四类。

（1）未被采用的本领域资源：系统自诞生之日起，在系统所在领域所开发但未被采用的资源。

（2）其他领域中的技术资源：能用于本系统的其他领域技术资源，包括使能技术。

（3）社会、市场及心理学资源。

（4）关于进化的知识。

Evolutionary resources can be divided into four categories.

(1) Unused resources in the field: resources developed in the field of the system but not adopted since the birth of the system.

(2) Technical resources in other fields: technical resources in other fields that can be used in the system, including enabling technology.

(3) Social, market and psychological resources.

(4) Knowledge of evolution.

进化资源包括面向机会的进化、知识收集与利用、技术传递、技术适应性四条进化路线。

Evolutionary resources include opportunities for evolution, collection and utilization of knowledge, technology transfer and technology adaptation four evolutionary routes.

1.5.3　资源利用

1.5.3　**Resource utilization**

设计过程中所用到的资源不一定明显，需要认真挖掘才能成为有用资源。下面是一些通用的建议：

（1）将所有的资源首先集中于最重要的动作或子系统；

（2）合理有效地利用资源，避免资源损失、浪费等；

（3）将资源集中到特定的空间与时间；

（4）利用其他过程中损失的或浪费的资源；

（5）与其他子系统分享有用资源，动态地调节这些子系统；

（6）根据子系统隐含的功能，利用其他资源；

（7）对其他资源进行变换，使其成为有用资源。

不同类型资源的特殊性能帮助设计者克服资源的限制。

The resources used in the design process are not necessarily obvious, and need to be carefully excavated to become useful resources. Here are some general suggestions：

（1）All resources are first concentrated on the most important action or subsystem；

（2）Reasonable and effective use of resources to avoid loss and waste of resources；

（3）Focus resources on specific space and time；

（4）Use the resources lost or wasted in other processes；

（5）Share useful resources with other subsystems and adjust these subsystems dynamically；

（6）According to the implicit function of the subsystem, other resources are used；

（7）Transform other resources to make them useful.

The special features of different types of resources help designers overcome resource constraints.

1.5.3.1　空间

1.5.3.1　Space

（1）选择最重要的子系统，将其他子系统放在空间不十分重要的位置上。

（2）最大限度地利用闲置空间。

（3）利用相邻子系统的某些表面，或一表面的反面。

（4）利用空间中的某些点、线、面或体积。

（5）利用紧凑的几何形状，如螺旋线。

（6）利用暂时闲置的空间。

（1）Choose the most important subsystem and put other subsystems in the position where space is not very important.

（2）Maximize the use of idle space.

（3）Using some surfaces of adjacent subsystems, or the opposite side of a surface.

（4）Using some points, lines, surfaces or volumes in space.

（5）Using compact geometry, such as helix.

（6）Use temporary idle space.

1.5.3.2 时间

1.5.3.2 Time

（1）在最有价值的工作阶段，最大限度地利用时间。

（2）使过程连续，消除停顿、空行程。

（3）变换顺序动作为并行动作，以节省时间。

（1）In the most valuable stage of work, maximize the use of time.

（2）Make the process continuous and eliminate pause and empty stroke.

（3）In order to save time, the sequential action is changed into parallel action.

1.5.3.3 材料

1.5.3.3 Material

（1）利用薄膜、粉末、蒸汽，将少量物质扩大到一个较大的空间。

（2）利用与子系统混合的环境中的材料。

（3）将环境中的材料，如水、空气等，转变成有用的材料。

（1）Using film, powder and steam to expand a small amount of material to a larger space.

（2）Using materials in the environment mixed with subsystems.

（3）Materials in the environment, such as water and air, are transformed into useful materials.

1.5.3.4 能量

1.5.3.4 Energy

（1）尽可能提高核心部件的能量利用率。

（2）限制利用成本高的能量，尽可能采用低廉的能量。

（3）利用最近的能量。

（4）利用附近系统浪费的能量。

（5）利用环境提供的能量。

（1）Improve the energy efficiency of core components as much as possible.

（2）The energy with high cost should be limited and low cost should be used as far as possible.

（3）Using the nearest energy.

（4）Using the energy wasted by the nearby system.

（5）Using the energy provided by the environment.

在设计中认真考虑各种资源有助于开阔设计者的眼界，使其能跳出问题本身，这对于将全部精力都集中于特定的子系统、工作区间、特定的空间与时间的设计者解决问题特别重要。

In design, careful consideration of various resources can help designers broaden their horizons and make them jump out of the problem itself, which is particularly important for designers who focus all their energy on specific subsystems, working areas, specific space and time to solve problems.

1.6　物质-场模型
1.6　Matter field model

将复杂系统分解为简单系统是常用的分析方法。在 TRIZ 中，物质-场模型是帮助设计者进行这种分解的图形工具。一个能够工作的最小系统可以用物质-场模型表示。物质-场模型及分析提供了确定系统中核心问题的方法。

It is a common method to decompose complex system into simple system. In TRIZ, the matter field model is a graphic tool to help designers with this decomposition. A minimum system that can work can be represented by a matter field model. The matter-field model and analysis provide a method to determine the core problems in the system.

1.6.1　物质-场概念与符号
1.6.1　Concept and symbol of matter field

物质是最基本的概念。物质是具有任意复杂程度的实体，可以是简单的零部件，如螺栓、螺母、杯子、笔帽等，又可是复杂的系统，如直升飞机、宇宙飞船、港口、城市交通系统等。物质的状态不仅是通常的物理状态，如真空、等离子体、气体、液体、固体等，也可是符合状态，如悬浮物、泡沫、粉末、凝胶体、多孔物等。物质还可以具有特殊的性质，如热、电、磁、光等特性。物质本身还可以被分解，机床由床身、刀架、工作台控制等子系统等组成，每个子系统又可以分解很多零件，这些都是物质。

Matter is the most basic concept. Matter is an entity with any degree of complexity. It can be simple parts, such as bolts, nuts, cups, pen caps, etc. , but it can also be complex systems, such as helicopters, spaceships, ports, urban transportation systems, etc. The state of matter is not only the usual physical state, such as vacuum, plasma, gas, liquid, solid, etc. , but also conforms to the state, such as suspended matter, foam, powder, gel, porous material and so on. Matter can also have special properties, such as thermal, electrical, magnetic, optical and so on. The material itself can also be decomposed. The machine tool is composed of bed, turret, workbench control and other subsystems. Each subsystem can decompose many parts, which are all materials.

为了使用方便，将物质的层次结构进行如下的分解：直接可用物质，如衬衫；最小处理后的物质，如组成衬衫的纤维；大分子，如晶体、聚合物，复杂分子；分子；部分分子、原子团；原子；原子的一部分；基本粒子；微细粒子。

For the convenience of use, the hierarchical structure of materials is decomposed as follows: directly usable materials, such as shirts; the smallest processed materials, such as the fibers that make up shirts; macromolecules, such as crystals, polymers, complex molecules; molecules; partial molecules, atomic clusters; atoms; part of protons; basic particles; micro particles.

场是另一个基本概念，包括物理场、化学场等。场产生能量流、信息流、力流、相互作用、反作用等。场的出现通常伴随着物质的出现，作为物质的能源，表 1-4 给出场的名称和符号。

Field is another basic concept, including physical field, chemical field and so on. Field produces energy flow, information flow, force flow, interaction, reaction and so on. The appearance of field is usually accompanied by the appearance of matter. As the energy of matter, the name and symbol of field are given in Table 1-4.

最小技术系统由两种物质及一种场组成。两种物质分别为 S_1 与 S_2，S_1 为物质或原料，S_2 为工具，即在场的作用下操作物质，使其达到预期的结果。对于工艺过程，通常一种场作用于一种物质，该物质产生另一种场。因此，两个基本的物质-场模型如图 1-5 所示。表 1-4 是常用的作用形式。

The minimum technology system consists of two substances and one field. The two substances are S_1 and S_2 respectively. S_1 is the material or raw material, and S_2 is the tool, that is to operate the substance under the action of the field to achieve the expected results. For the process, usually one kind of field acts on one kind of material, which produces another kind of field. Therefore, the two basic matter field models are shown in Figure 1-5. Table 1-4 is a common form of action.

表 1-4 各种场

Table 1-4 Various fields

符号 Symbol	名称 Name	实例 Instance
G	重力场 Gravitational field	重力 Gravity
ME	机械场 Mechanical field	压力、惯性力、离心力 Pressure, inertial force, centrifugal force
P	流体场 Fluid field	流体静力、流体动力 Hydrostatic, fluid power
A	声场 Sound field	声、超声 Sound, ultrasonic
T	热场 Thermal field	热存储、热传导、热绝缘、热膨胀、双金属效应 Hot storage, heat conduction, thermal insulation, thermal expansion, bimetallic effect

符号 Symbol	名称 Name	实例 Instance
C	化学 Chemistry	燃烧、氧化、腐蚀 Burn，oxidation，corrode
E	电场 Electric field	静电、电感应、电容 Electrostatics，inductance，capacitance
M	磁场 Magnetic field	静磁、铁磁 Magnetostatic，ferromagnetic
O	光场 Light field	光、反射、折射 Light，reflection，refraction
R	辐射 Madiation	X 射线、不可见电磁波 X-ray，no electromagnetic waves are visible
B	生物场 Biological field	发酵、腐烂 Fement，rot
N	核能场 Nuclear energy field	α、β、γ 射线束、中子、电子 α，β，γ ray beam，reutron，electron

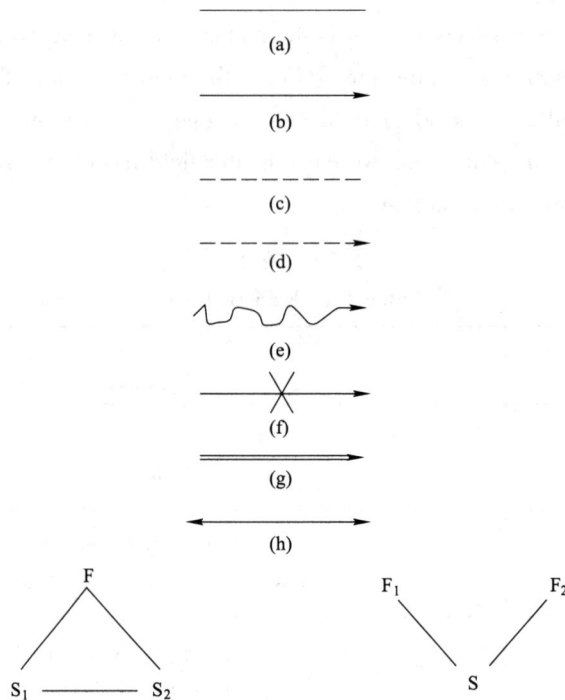

图 1-5　物质-场模型中的各种作用关系

Figure 1-5　Various interaction relationships in matter field model

（a）连接；（b）有指向的作用；（c）无作用；（d）不足作用；（e）有害作用；

（f）断开连接；（g）变换；（h）相互作用

（a）Connect；（b）Having directional effects；（c）No effect；（d）Insufficient effect；

（e）Harmful effects；（f）Disconnect；（g）Transform；（h）Interaction

不完善的物质-场模型如图 1-6 所示。

The imperfect matter field model is shown in Figure 1-6.

$$S_1 \qquad F_1 \qquad S_1 \text{———} S_2 \qquad S_1 \text{———} F$$

图 1-6 不完善物质-场

Figure 1-6 Imperfect matter field

1.6.2 物质-场特性

1.6.2 Matter field characteristics

物质-场是系统中的一部分，通常是设计者关注的重要部分。最重要的五个物质-场特性如下。

（1）假如所研究的子系统或部分是不完整的物质-场，可以将其变为完整的物质-场。如图 1-7 所示，将研究的部分仅有 S_1，将其变化成完整的物质-场。

（2）对物质-场元件的不同作用，导致对相关元件作用的变化。因此，可以对物质-场中的某个元件施加控制，以获得所希望的变化。

（3）假如一个物质-场元件具有特定的空间-时间结构，另一个物质-场元件也具有这样的相似结构。

（4）作用于物质元件之间的场的数量没有限制，这种数量由相互作用的物理性质等确定。

（5）一个物质-场中的元件可以同时是另一个物质-场中的元件，如图 1-8 所示。

Matter field is a part of the system, which is usually an important part of designers. The five most important matter field properties are as follows.

（1）If the subsystem or part studied is an incomplete matter field, it can be transformed into a complete matter field. As shown in Figure 1-7, only S_1 will be studied and transformed into a complete matter field.

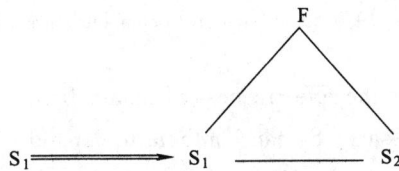

图 1-7 物资-场模型变换

Figure 1-7 Matter field model transformation

（2）The different effects on the matter field elements lead to the changes of the effects on the related elements. Therefore, control can be applied to a certain element in the matter field to obtain the desired change.

（3）If one matter field element has a specific space-time structure, another matter field element also has such a similar structure.

（4）There is no limit to the number of fields acting between material elements, which is determined by the physical properties of the interaction.

（5）An element in a matter field can be an element in another matter field at the same time, as shown in Figure 1-8.

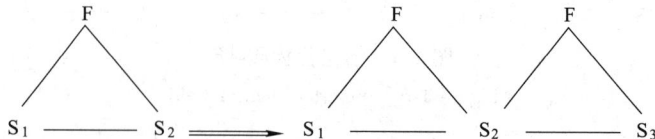

图 1-8　同一元件在不同物质—场模型

Figure 1-8　The same element in different matter field models

物质-场模型可以在宏观或微观层面上变化，以帮助设计者解决问题。变化的规则如下。

（1）在解决问题的过程中，如果物质-场不完整，要将其变换成完整的物质-场模型，如图 1-9 所示。

（2）为了增加物质-场的有效性，可以将其中的工具扩展为另一个物质-场。如果有必要，S_3 可以继续扩展，如图 1-10 所示。

（3）在一些检测与测量问题中，有时需要按图 1-11 所示扩展物质-场模型。

Matter field model can be changed at macro or micro level to help designers solve problems. The rules of change are as follows.

（1）In the process of solving the problem, if the matter field is not complete, it should be transformed into a complete matter field model. As shown in Figure 1-9.

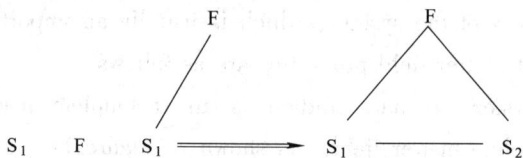

图 1-9　变换成完整物质-场

Figure 1-9　Transformation to complete matter field

（2）In order to increase the effectiveness of matter field, the tool can be extended to another matter field. If necessary, S_3 can continue to expand. As shown in Figure 1-10.

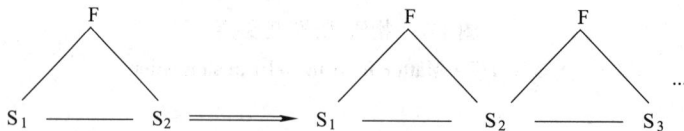

图 1-10　变换成完整物质-场

Figure 1-10　Transformation to complete matter field

（3）In some detection and measurement problems, it is sometimes necessary to expand the matter field model as shown in Figure 1-11.

➤例 1-2　应用榔头在木板上钉钉子。在人手产生力的条件下，力作用于榔头，榔头作用于钉子，钉子进入木板。图 1-12 是该过程的物质-场模型。

➤ **Example 1-2** Nail the board with hammer. Under the condition of manual force, the force acts on the hammer, the hammer acts on the nail, and the nail enters the board. Figure 1-12 shows the matter field model of the process.

➤**例 1-3** 热作用于固体，固体将产生力及变形。其物质-场模型如图 1-13 所示。

➤ **Example 1-3** Heat is applied to solid, which will produce force and deformation. The matter field model is shown in Figure 1-13.

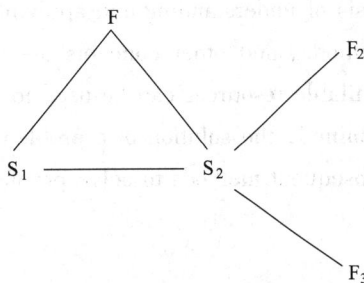

图 1-11　物质-场的检测

Figure 1-11　Detection of matter field

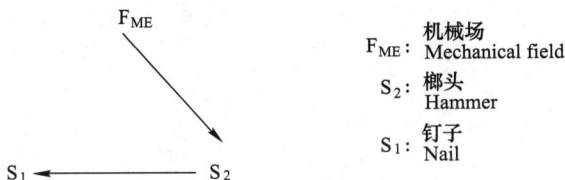

图 1-12　钉钉子模型

Figure 1-12　Nail model

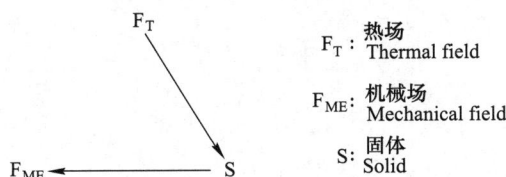

F_{ME}: 机械场 Mechanical field

S_2: 榔头 Hammer

S_1: 钉子 Nail

图 1-13　热作用于固体产生力模型

Figure 1-13　Force model of heat acting on solid

F_T: 热场 Thermal field

F_{ME}: 机械场 Mechanical field

S: 固体 Solid

1.7　本章小结

1.7　Summary of this chapter

功能、理想解、创新分级、可用资源、9 窗口、物质-场模型都是 TRIZ 中的基本且非常重要的概念。掌握这些概念，是理解及应用 TRIZ 的基础。功能是其他设计方法中经常采用的概念，其他几个概念是 TRIZ 中专用的。有的基本概念，如可用资源可单独用于解决问题，如果能获得某些可用资源，则可能直接得到某个问题的解。另一些概念与后续的方法一起用于解决问题。

Function, ideal solution, innovation level, available resources, 9 windows and matter-field model are basic and very important concepts in TRIZ. Mastering these concepts is the basis of understanding and applying TRIZ. Function is a concept often used in other design methods, and other concepts are specially used in TRIZ. Some basic concepts, such as available resources can be used to solve problems alone. If some available resources can be obtained, the solution of a problem may be obtained directly. Other concepts are used with subsequent methods to solve problems.

2 产品技术成熟度预测技术
Chapter 2 Product Technology Maturity Prediction Technology

2.1 概　　述
2.1 Overview

世界处于变化之中，能够预测未来技术的发展，快速开发新一代技术和产品，对企业的生存发展十分重要。作为能够实行技术预测的公司在以下方面占有优势：

(1) 打败竞争对手，及早占领市场；

(2) 合理规划和配置资源；

(3) 增加市场监控的有效性，获得市场需求；

(4) 最大限度地增加利润，将成本降到最低限；

(5) 改善产品决策量。

The world is changing. It is very important for the survival and development of enterprises to be able to predict the future development of technology and quickly develop new generation technology and products. As a company that can implement technology forecasting, it has advantages in the following aspects：

(1) Defeat the competitors and occupy the market as soon as possible；

(2) Rational planning and allocation of resources；

(3) Increase the effectiveness of market monitoring to obtain market demand；

(4) Maximize profits and minimize costs；

(5) Improve the quality of product decisions.

随着全球性竞争越来越激烈，拥有一种能够对即将出现的技术精确而细致的预测能力，对于企业的长远发展越来越重要。假如技术进化本身是随机的，任何预测都非常困难。大量的研究表明，任何领域的产品改进、技术的变革、创新和生物系统一样，都存在产生、生长、成熟、衰老、灭亡的过程，是有规律可循的，是可预测的。

With the increasingly fierce global competition, it is more and more important for the long-term development of enterprises to have a kind of ability to predict the coming technology accurately and carefully. If technology evolution itself is random, any prediction is very difficult. A large number of studies have shown that any field of product improvement, technological change, innovation and biological systems, there is a process of production, growth, maturity, aging, extinction, which is regular and predictable.

企业在制订研发计划时，知道自己的产品技术处于技术发展所处的阶段，即技术成熟度是正确决策的关键。但很多企业的决策并不科学。Ellen Domb 认为："人们往往基于他们的情绪与状态来对其产品技术成熟程度做出预测，假如人们处于兴奋状态，则常把他们的产品置于'成熟期前期'，如果他们受了挫折，则可能认为其产品已处于退出期。"因此，需要一种系统化的产品技术成熟度预测方法。

When making R & D plan, enterprises know that their product technology is in the stage of technology development, that is, technology maturity is the key to correct decision-making. But the decision-making of many enterprises is not scientific. Ellen Domb believed："People often make predictions about the technological maturity of their products based on their emotions and states. If people are excited, they often put their products in the 'early stage of maturity'. If they are frustrated, they may think that their products are in the exit stage. "Therefore, a systematic prediction method of product technology maturity is needed.

本章介绍技术成熟度的概念、预测方法及工程实例。

This chapter introduces the concept of technology maturity, prediction methods and engineering examples.

2.1.1　技术生命周期
2.1.1　Technology life cycle

技术发展是从一项新发明开始的，其后的发展轨迹称为技术生命周期，如图 2-1 所示。图中横坐标为时间，即依据一项核心技术所推出的一系列产品的时间；纵坐标为技术的性能参数值，该参数值不能超过自然限制。从横坐标上将产品分为新发明、技术改进及技术成熟三个阶段。

Technology development begins with a new invention, and the subsequent development path is called technology life cycle, as shown in Figure 2-1. The abscissa in the figure is the time, that is, the time of a series of products launched according to a core technology. The ordinate is the performance parameter value of the technology, which cannot exceed the natural limit. From the abscissa, the product is divided into new invention, technology improvement and technology maturity three stages.

在新发明阶段，一项新的物理的、化学的、生物的发现，被设计人员转变成产品。不同的设计人员对同一原理的实现是不同的，已设计出的产品还要不断改善。因此，随时间的推移，产品的性能指标不断提高。

In the new invention stage, a new physical, chemical or biological discovery is transformed into a product by designers. The realization of the same principle is different for different designers, and the designed products need to be improved continuously. Therefore, with the passage of time, the performance index of the product continues to improve.

在上一阶段结束时，很多企业已认识到，基于该发现的产品有很好的市场潜力，应大力开发。因此，将投入很多的人力、物力与财力用于新产品开发，新产品的性

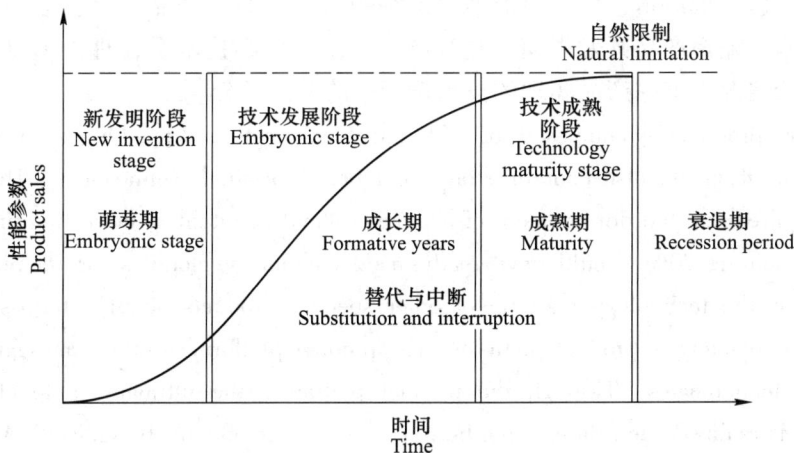

图 2-1 技术生命周期

Figure 2-1 Technology life cycle

能参数快速增长。这就是技术改进阶段。

At the end of the last stage, many enterprises have realized that the products based on this discovery have good market potential and should be vigorously developed. Therefore, a lot of human, material and financial resources will be invested in the development of new products, and the performance parameters of new products will grow rapidly. This is the stage of technical improvement.

随着产品进入技术成熟阶段，所推出的新产品性能参数只有少量增长。继续投入进一步完善已有技术的效益减少，企业应研究新的核心技术以在适当的时间替代已有产品的核心技术。

As the products enter the mature stage of technology, the performance parameters of the new products only increase a little. Enterprises should study new core technology to replace the core technology of existing products at an appropriate time.

最后一个阶段是技术退出期。此阶段，新的替代技术已出现，已有技术将中断，退出市场。

The last stage is the technology exit period. At this stage, new alternative technologies have emerged, and existing technologies will be discontinued and withdrawn from the market.

2.1.2 技术与产品生命周期

2.1.2 Technology and product life cycle

一个新产品是由不同的技术组成，除一部分新技术外，还应该包含大量原有技术，业界通常要求一个产品的开发最多包含30%的创新，而剩下的70%都应该有现成的技术模块可借鉴。核心技术是企业的其他具体产品的技术平台，是公司产品平台的基础，产品平台往往是众多核心技术的集合体，通过产品平台实现了核心技术的最终价值，有效实现产品间的共享，同时还有效实现了技术的保密，产品平台是终端产品快速、低成本、低风险地推向市场的基础，通过产品平台可以有效降低产品开发成本、缩短产品开发周期、提升产品质量。核心技术是在理论基础上，在确定技术路线情况下支撑产品实现的技术选择中的关键部分。

A new product is composed of different technologies. In addition to some new technologies, it should also contain a large number of original technologies. The industry usually requires that the development of a product should contain at most 30% innovation, and the remaining 70% should have ready-made technology modules for reference. Core technology is the technology platform of other specific products of an enterprise and the basis of the company's product platform. The product platform is often the aggregation of many core technologies. Through the product platform, the ultimate value of the core technology is realized, and the sharing between products is effectively realized. At the same time, the confidentiality of technology is also effectively realized. The product platform is the rapid, low-cost and low-risk marketing of terminal products. The product platform can effectively reduce the product development cost, shorten the product development cycle and improve the product quality. Core technology is the key part of technology selection to support product realization on the basis of theory and technology route.

核心技术诞生后往往带来后续的一系列新产品。技术先于产品的产生，两者的生命周期具有相似性，但产品的生命周期滞后于技术的生命周期，如图 2-2 所示。

After the birth of core technology, it often brings a series of new products. Technology comes before products, and their life cycles are similar, but product life cycle lags behind technology life cycle, as shown in Figure 2-2.

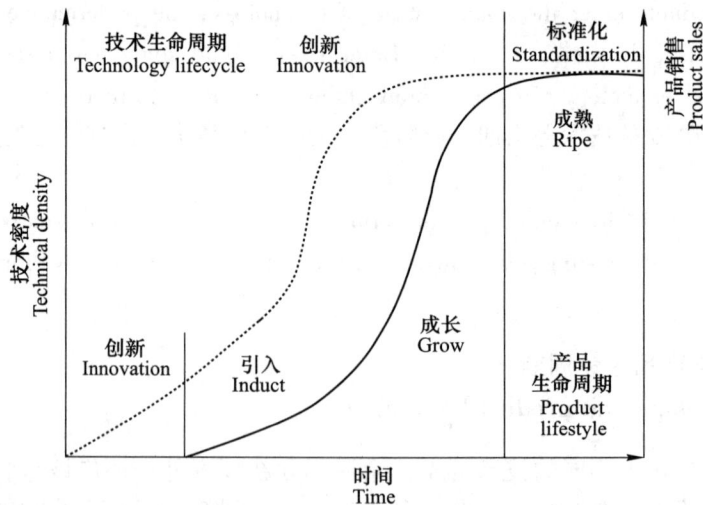

图 2-2　技术与产品的生命周期

Figure 2-2　Life cycle of technology and product

2.2 TRIZ 中的 S-曲线及技术成熟度预测
2.2 S-curve and technology maturity prediction in TRIZ

2.2.1 分段 S-曲线
2.2.1 Piecewise S-curve

通过对大量专利的分析，Altshuller 发现产品的进化规律满足 S-曲线。但进化过程是靠设计者推动的，当前的产品如没有设计者引入新的技术，它将停留在当前的水平上，新技术的引入使其不断沿某些方向进化。Altshuller 用如图 2-3 所示分段线性 S-曲线表示性能随时间的变化规律，从而更加明确地把产品进化分为了婴儿期、成长期、成熟期和退出期四个阶段。

Through the analysis of a large number of patents, Altshuller found that the evolution law of products meets the S-curve. But the evolution process is driven by the designer. If the current product does not have the designer to introduce new technology, it will stay at the current level. The introduction of new technology makes it continue to evolve in some directions. Altshuller used piecewise linear S-curve as shown in Figure 2-3 to express the change rule of performance with time, so as to more clearly divide the product evolution into infancy, growth, maturity and exit four stages.

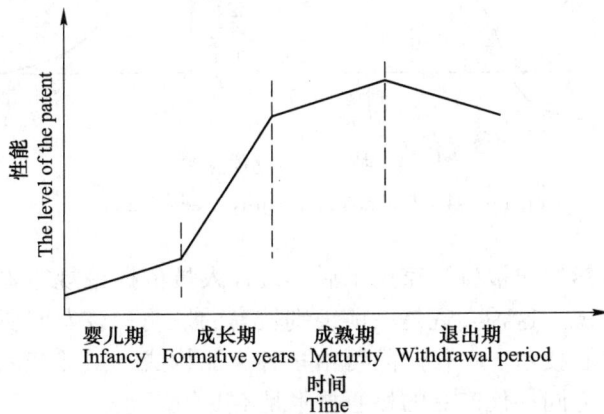

图 2-3 分段线性 S-曲线
Figure 2-3 Piecewise linear S-curve

2.2.2 技术成熟度预测
2.2.2 Technology maturity prediction

确定组成产品的技术在 S-曲线上的位置是产品进化理论的重要研究内容，并称为技术成熟度预测。

It is an important research content of product evolution theory to determine the position of technology in S-curve, which is also called technology maturity prediction.

　　Altshuller 分析了专利数量、专利等级和产品的获利能力、性能四个指标随着产品进化而变化的规律，与 S-曲线一起组成产品技术成熟度预测算子，用于产品技术成熟度预测。四个指标随技术进化而变化的曲线的形状如图 2-4 所示。收集当前产品的四方面数据所建立曲线的形状与图 2-4 四条曲线的形状比较，即可确定当前产品的技术成熟度。

　　Altshuller analyzed the law that the number of patents, patent grade, profitability and performance of products change with the evolution of products. Together with S-curve, altshuller forms a product technology maturity prediction operator, which is used to predict product technology maturity. The shape of the curve of the four indicators changing with the evolution of technology is shown in Figure 2-4. The technology maturity of the current product can be determined by comparing the shape of the established curve with that of the four curves in Figure 2-4.

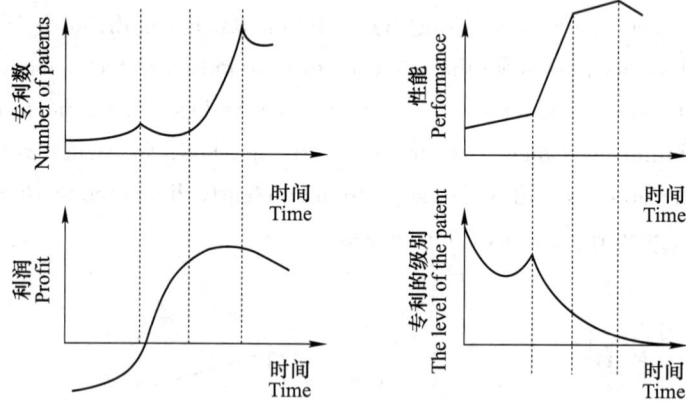

图 2-4　技术成熟度预测曲线

Figure 2-4　Technology maturity prediction curve

　　当一条新的自然规律被科学家揭示后，设计人员依据该规律提出产品实现的工作原理，并使之实现。这种实现是一项级别较高的发明，该发明所依据的工作原理是这一代产品的核心技术。一代产品可由多种产品构成，虽然产品要不断完善，不断推陈出新，但作为同一代产品的核心技术是不变的。

　　When a new natural law is revealed by scientists, the designer puts forward the working principle of product realization according to the law and makes it come true. This kind of realization is a higher level invention. The working principle of this invention is the core technology of this generation of products. A generation of products can be made up of many kinds of products. Although the products need to be constantly improved and innovated, the core technology of the same generation of products remains unchanged.

　　一代产品的第一个专利是一个高级别的专利，如图 2-4 中时间-专利的级别曲线所示，后续的专利级别逐步降低。但当产品由婴儿期向成熟期过渡时，伴随着限制产品性能的关键问题的解决会出现一些高级别的专利，正是这些专利的出现，推动产品从婴儿期过渡到成长期。

The first patent of a generation of products is a high-level patent, as shown in the time-patent level curve in Figure 2-4. The subsequent patent level was gradually reduced. However, when the product is transiting from infancy to maturity, some advanced patents will appear along with the solution of the key problems that limit the product performance. It is the emergence of these patents that promote the transition of the product from infancy to growth.

图 2-4 中的时间-专利数曲线表示专利数随时间的变化。在婴儿期和成长期前期由于参与开发的企业和人员较少，因此专利数较少，在成熟期由于激烈的竞争，企业新专利不断涌现，专利数最多。之后产品到了退出期，企业进一步增加投入已没有什么回报。因此，专利数降低。

图 2-4 中的时间-获利能力曲线表明：开始阶段，企业仅仅是投入并没有赢利。到成长期产品虽然还有待于进一步完善，但产品已出现利润。之后利润逐年增加，到成熟期的某一时间达到最大，之后开始降低。

图 2-4 中的时间-性能曲线表明，随时间的延续，产品性能不断增加，但到了退出期，其性能很难再有提高。

The time patent number curve in Figure 2-4 shows the change of patent number over time. In infancy and early growth period, due to fewer enterprises and personnel involved in the development, the number of patents is less. In mature period, due to fierce competition, new patents of enterprises continue to emerge, with the largest number of patents. After the product to the exit period, enterprises to further increase investment has no return. As a result, the number of patents decreased.

The time profitability curve in Figure 2-4 shows that in the initial stage, the enterprise only invests and does not make profits. In the growth period, although the product still needs to be further improved, the profit of the product has appeared. After that, the profit increased year by year, reached the maximum at a certain time of maturity, and then began to decrease.

The time performance curve in Figure 2-4 shows that the performance of the product increases with time, but it is difficult to improve again when it comes to the exit period.

如果能收集到产品的有关数据，绘出上述 4 条曲线，通过曲线的形状，可以判断出产品在 S-曲线上所处的位置，从而可对其技术成熟度进行预测。

If we can collect the relevant data of the product and draw the above four curves, we can judge the position of the product on the S-curve by the shape of the curve. Thus, the technology maturity can be predicted.

图 2-5 表示了产品技术成熟度预测后的两种结果。如果产品处于婴儿期或成长期，则需要对产品进行持续创新与优化，以改善已有的 S-曲线；反之，则需要产品突破性创新以产生新的核心技术，替代已有的核心技术，即使产品移入新的 S-曲线。

Figure 2-5 shows two results of product technology maturity prediction. If the product is in infancy or growth period, it needs continuous innovation and optimization to improve the existing S-curve; on the contrary, it needs breakthrough innovation to generate new core technology to replace the existing core technology, even if the product moves into the new S-curve.

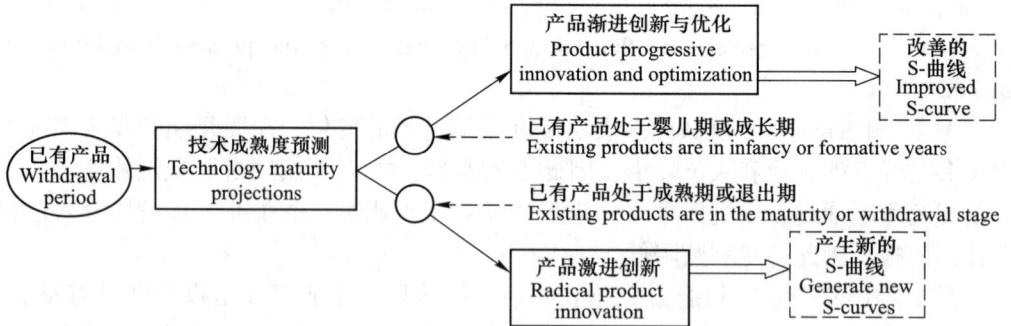

图 2-5　产品技术成熟度预测及决策

Figure 2-5　Product technology maturity prediction and decision making

　　为了改善 S-曲线，需对产品进行优化设计。已有产品的优化是指产品的核心技术即工作原理不变，而对其实现技术进行优化，包括材料选择、结构加工工艺、结构的装拆、性能、造型等的优化。

In order to improve the S-curve, it is necessary to optimize the product design. The optimization of existing products means that the core technology of the product, namely the working principle, remains unchanged, while the realization technology is optimized, including the optimization of material selection, structure processing technology, structure assembly and disassembly, performance, modeling, etc.

2.2.3　基于专利分析的技术成熟度预测
2.2.3　Technology maturity prediction based on patent analysis

　　专利制度是随着人类社会向商品经济和工业化发展的过程中产生和发展起来的，到现在世界上绝大多数国家都实行了专利制度以保护发明人或设计人的合法权益，目的是鼓励发明创造、促进工业发展和推动科学技术进步。

Patent system is produced and developed with the development of human society to commodity economy and industrialization. Up to now, most countries in the world have implemented patent system to protect the legitimate rights and interests of inventors or designers. The purpose is to encourage invention and creation, promote industrial development and promote scientific and technological progress.

　　世界知识产权组织统计表明，全世界每年发明成果的 90%～95% 首先是在专利文献上发表的，而在其他科技文献中只反映出 5%～10%，目前全世界专利文献已超过 4000 万件，并且每年以 100 万件的速度递增，占全世界各种图书、期刊每年总出版量的四分之一。这些专利文献凝聚了全世界科技创造的精华，形成了庞大的科技信息宝库，是非常重要的科技信息源。

According to the statistics of the World Intellectual Property Organization (WIPO),

90% to 95% of the world's annual invention achievements are first published in patent literature, while only 5% to 10% are reflected in other scientific and technological literature. At present, there are more than 40 million patent literatures in the world, increasing at the rate of 1 million every year, accounting for one fourth of the total annual publications of various books and journals in the world. These patent documents have condensed the essence of technological creation all over the world, and formed a huge treasure house of scientific and technological information, which is a very important source of scientific and technological information.

专利保护的发明创造是人类脑力劳动的成果。人类的大脑可以创造出多种方法和各种装置以利用周围的自然，使发明创造层出不穷。现在用于制造产品的工业设备和方法是几千年来发展的结果，是在原有的发明创造基础上不断出现新的发明创造的结果。有些发明现在看来很普通，以至于我们可能意识不到在当时的确是一项新颖的发明。

The invention creation of patent protection is the result of human brain work. The human brain can create a variety of methods and devices to make use of the surrounding nature, so that inventions emerge in endlessly. The industrial equipment and methods now used to manufacture products are the result of thousands of years of development, and are the result of the continuous emergence of new inventions and creations on the basis of the original inventions and creations. Some inventions now seem so common that we may not realize that they were really novel at that time.

可授予专利权的发明创造必须是工业领域的新产品、新方法和新应用。这里指的工业是广义的，包括农业、畜牧业等在内。不能导致工业技术变化的发明创造一般不能得到专利权。

A patentable invention creation must be a new product, a new method and a new application in the industrial field. The industry referred to here is in a broad sense, including agriculture, animal husbandry, etc. The invention creation that can't lead to the change of industrial technology can't get patent right.

一项发明是基于通过采用某些措施而达到某种特定的效果。发明人没有必要对此作出科学解释，只要确保所采取的这些措施能够产生所述的特定效果就够了。一般说来，一项发明创造可以看作是一个解决技术问题的实施方案。在寻找一种途径或方法以解决某一现存问题而且最终找到了解决方案的情形下，这一点就更为明显。有些发明创造是针对早已存在的但却不为人知的问题的解决方案。也就是说，所解决的问题是在发明出现之后才被认识的。

An invention is based on the adoption of certain measures to achieve a certain effect. There is no need for inventors to give a scientific explanation for this, as long as they ensure that the measures taken can produce the specific effects described. Generally speaking, an invention can be regarded as a solution to technical problems. This is more obvious when a way or method is found to solve an existing problem and a solution is finally found. Some inventions are solutions to long-standing but unknown problems. That is to say, the problem solved was only recognized after the invention appeared.

专利权只授予新的发明创造，这在世界范围内是一致的。中国专利法第 22 条规定：授予专利权的发明和实用新型，应当具备新颖性、创造性和实用性。

（1）新颖性。指在申请日以前没有同样的发明或者实用新型在国内外出版物上公开发表过、在国内公开使用过或者以其他方式为公众所知，也没有同样的发明或者实用新型由他人向专利局提出过申请，并且记载在申请日以后公布的专利申请文件中。

（2）创造性。指同申请日以前已有的技术相比，该发明具有突出的实质性特点和显著的进步，该实用新型有实质性特点和进步。

（3）实用性。指该发明或者实用新型能够制造或者使用，并且能够产生积极的效果。

It is consistent worldwide that patents are granted only to new inventions. Article 22 of the Chinese patent law stipulates that an invention or utility model for which a patent right is granted shall possess novelty, creativity and practicality.

（1）Novelty. It means that before the application date, no identical invention or utility model has been publicly published in publications at home and abroad, publicly used in China or known to the public in other ways, and no other person has applied to the Patent Office for the same invention or utility model, which is recorded in the patent application documents published after the application date.

（2）Creativity. It means that the invention has prominent substantive features and significant progress compared with the technology existing before the application date, and the utility model has substantive features and progress.

（3）Practicality. It means that the invention or utility model can be manufactured or used, and can produce positive effects.

专利之所以能够作为研究对象来预测技术的成熟度，是因为专利具有以下特点：

（1）专利申请活动是反映新技术、新产品开发活动的一个极为重要的方面，任何一件专利都必须具备新颖性、创造性和工业实用性；

（2）专利文献是专利活动的完整记录，它能够反映各个技术领域中技术活动的现状，又能够用来研究某个特定技术领域技术活动的发展历史；

（3）专利信息内容新颖、广泛，分类系统、详尽，实用性强，出版迅速，时效性强，格式统一、规范，便于查阅，优于一般意义上的科技信息，尤其是网络技术的发展，使得专利信息查询更加快捷便利。

The reason why patents can be used as research objects to predict the maturity of technology is that patents have the following characteristics:

（1）Patent application is a very important aspect reflecting the development of new technology and new products, any patent must have novelty, creativity and industrial practicability;

（2）Patent literature is a complete record of patent activities, it can reflect the status quo of technical activities in various technical fields, and can be used to study the development history of technical activities in a specific technical field；

（3）The content of patent information is novel and extensive, the classification system, detailed, practical, published quickly, timeliness, the format is unified and standardized, which is easy to consult and superior to the general sense of scientific and technological information, especially with the development of network technology, patent information query is more convenient.

正是因为专利具有以上特点，所以关于某项技术的专利所支持的技术性能代表了该技术的发展过程，关于某项技术参数的专利所支持的技术性能代表了该技术参数的发展过程。研究关于某项技术或某个技术参数的专利所支持的技术性能，其增长都应该符合 S-曲线规律。正是通过研究专利，Altshuller 发现了技术进化规律，创立了发明问题解决理论（TRIZ）。很多技术预测的专家也都把目光投向了专利分析统计，得出了很多有实践意义的成果。专利的特点和前人的实践都说明专利比较适合作为产品技术成熟度预测的研究对象。

Because the patent has the above characteristics, the technical performance supported by the patent on a certain technology represents the development process of the technology, and the technical performance supported by the patent on a certain technical parameter represents the development process of the technical parameter. To study the technical performance supported by a patent about a certain technology or a certain technical parameter, its growth should conform to the S-curve law. It is through the study of patents that Altshuller discovered the law of technological evolution and founded the theory of inventive problem solving（TRIZ）. Many experts of technology prediction also pay attention to patent analysis and statistics, and get a lot of practical results. The characteristics of patents and previous practices show that patents are more suitable as the research object of product technology maturity prediction.

2.2.4 TMMS 的预测模型
2.2.4 TMMS prediction model

产品技术成熟度预测系统（TMMS, Technology Maturity Mapping System）是基于专利分析的产品成熟度预测软件。以往的技术成熟度预测方法都存在一些问题：应用 Altshuller 专利考察模式进行技术成熟度预测时，由于某些技术的性能指标和获利能力指标难以精确表示，数据获取相对较难，难以实施；应用 Darrell Mann 专利考察模式进行技术成熟度预测时，只能预测技术是否已经过了成熟期，而国内专利文件的形式限制了依赖于专利引用次数的 Aurigin 专利考察模式的应用。基于性能的模型，一方面性能指标不易正确确定，另一方面现有的数学模型对预测技术成熟度都有一定缺陷。

Technology maturity mapping system（TMMS）is a product maturity prediction software based on patent analysis. There are some problems in the past technology maturity prediction methods：when using Altshuller patent investigation model to predict technology maturity, it is difficult to accurately express the performance index and profitability index of some technologies, and it is relatively difficult to obtain data, so it is difficult to implement; when Darrell Mann patent inspection model is applied to predict technology maturity, it can only predict whether the technology has passed the maturity period. However, the form of domestic patent documents limits the application of aurigin patent investigation mode which depends on the number of patent citations. On the one hand, the performance index of performance-based model is not easy to determine correctly; on the other hand, the existing mathematical models have some defects in predicting technology maturity.

　　另外，根据曲线形状来判断技术成熟度的方法，需要得出所研究技术系统的所有历史数据，一方面进行历史数据分析所耗用的时间较长，另一方面对于国内专利数据不完全的现状不适用。为了使技术成熟度预测方法具有一定的普适性，TMMS应用了一种新的基于专利分析的技术成熟度预测模型。

On the one hand, it takes a long time to analyze the historical data, on the other hand, it is not applicable to the current situation of incomplete domestic patent data. In order to make the technology maturity prediction method universal, TMMS applies a new technology maturity prediction model based on patent analysis.

2.2.4.1　基于专利分析的技术成熟度预测的模型指标
2.2.4.1　Model index of technology maturity prediction based on patent analysis

　　Darrell Mann 的研究成果是为了加速预测过程而得出的，因此可以在应用 Altshuller 研究结果时，抛开较难获得的性能指标和获利能力指标，而引入弥补缺陷的专利数量（Number of SCP）这一指标。因为在研究专利过程中，相对于专利分级来说，对专利按照是否弥补缺陷进行分类是一个很简单的过程，仅仅根据专利摘要就能确定，不会增加太多工作量，所以 TMMS 通过利用专利数量、专利等级和弥补缺陷的专利数量三项指标进行技术成熟度预测，其指标模型分别来自 Altshuller 的专利考察成果和 Darrell Mann 的专利考察成果，如图2-6所示。专利数量反映技术研究活跃程度；专利等级反映研究成果的水平，Altshuller 在研究发明过程中根据获得发明所需要反复尝试的次数把发明分为五个等级，其分级原则用于分析专利，就是专利等级；弥补缺陷的专利是指通过引入补充技术、结构或方法来弥补专利所指向的技术中所存在的缺陷，以在不致对技术系统做出太多改变的前提下提高技术性能，其数量反映研究重点的转移。由于三条曲线表现的都是关于某技术的专利指标的特点，所以在 TMMS 中称为技术的专利特性曲线。

Darrell Mann's research results are obtained in order to speed up the prediction process. Therefore, when applying the Altshuller research results, we can put aside the difficult performance indicators and profitability indicators and introduce the number of patents to make up for defects (SCP). In the process of patent research, compared with patent classification, it is a very simple process to classify Patents according to whether they can make up for defects. It can be determined only according to patent abstracts and will not increase too much workload. Therefore, TMMS predicts the technology maturity by using three indicators: the number of patents, patent grade and the number of patents that can make up for defects. The index models are derived from the patent investigation results of altshuller and Darrell Mann respectively as shown in Figure 2-6. The number of patents reflects the activity of technology research. The patent grade reflects the level of research results. Altshuller divides the invention into five grades according to the number of repeated attempts needed to obtain the invention in the process of research and invention. The grading principle is used to analyze the patent, which is the patent grade. The patent to make up for defects refers to the introduction of complementary technology, structure or method to make up for the defects in the technology pointed by the patent, so as to improve the technical performance without making too much changes to the technical system. The number of patents reflects the shift of research focus. Because the three curves are all about the characteristics of the patent index of a technology, it is called the patent characteristic curve of technology in TMMS.

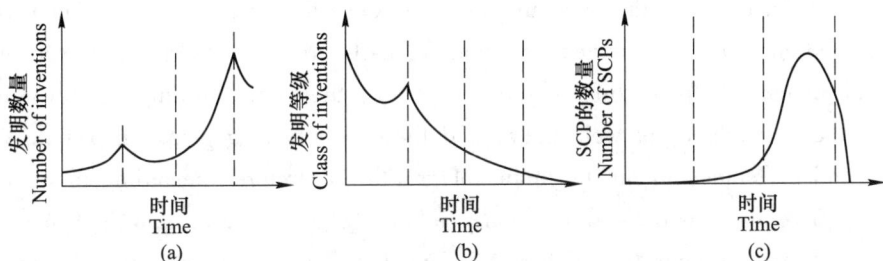

图 2-6　基于专利分析的技术成熟度预测模型指标

Figure 2-6　Indicators of technology maturity prediction model based on patent analysis

（a）发明数量与时间关系图；（b）发明等级与时间关系图；（c）SCP 的数量与时间关系图

（a）Diagram of the number of inventions versus time；（b）Diagram of invention rank and time；（c）Diagram of the number of SCP and time

　　不难发现，所采用的三项指标来自于一个数据源，实质上是考察一个问题的多个方面，因此可比性更强。为了提高预测的精度，可以选择某一性能指标和获利能力指标进行对照，根据预测结果对照出现的偏差，并分析出现偏差的原因。

　　It is not difficult to find that the three indicators used come from one data source, which is essentially to examine multiple aspects of a problem, so they are more comparable. In order to improve the prediction accuracy, we can select a performance index and profitability index for comparison, according to the prediction results, compare the deviation, and analyze the reasons for the deviation.

2.2.4.2　技术成熟度预测的算法分析

2.2.4.2　Algorithm analysis of technology maturity prediction

　　如图 2-7 所示，图中箭头所指的是各条曲线上的转折点（极值点）。从图 2-7 （a）可以发现，在技术的婴儿期结束到成长期开始有一个转折点（极大值），在成熟期前期中期有一个转折点（极小值），在成熟期结束到退出期开始有一个转折点

（极大值）。如果按照图 2-7（a）中的转折点划分可以把曲线划分为婴儿期、成长期前期、成长期后期+成熟期、退出期。从图 2-7（b）可以发现，在技术的婴儿期中期有一个转折点（极小值），在婴儿期结束到成长期开始有一个转折点（极大值）。因此，根据图 2-7（b）可以把曲线划分为婴儿期前期、婴儿期后期、成长期+成熟期+退出期。从图 2-7（c）可以发现，曲线只有一个转折点，该转折点将成熟期分为两部分即成熟期前期和成熟期后期。因此，综合各曲线上的转折点对曲线的划分，以及 Altshller 对技术生命周期的划分可以把技术生命周期分为婴儿期前期、婴儿期后期、成长期前期、成长期后期、成熟期前期，成熟期后期和退出期七部分，如图 2-8 所示。

As shown in Figure 2-7, the arrow in the figure refers to the turning point（extreme point）on each curve. From Figure 2-7（a）, we can find that there is a turning point（maximum）from the end of infancy to the beginning of growth. There is a turning point（minimum）in the early and middle stage of maturity, and a turning point（maximum）from the end of maturity to the beginning of exit. According to the turning point in Figure 2-7（a）, the curve can be divided into infancy, early growth, late growth + maturity and withdrawal. It can be found from Figure 2-7（b）, there is a turning point（minimum value）in the mid infancy of technology, and there is a turning point（maximum value）from the end of infancy to the beginning of growth. Therefore, according to Figure 2-7（b）, the curve can be divided into early infancy, late infancy, growth + maturity + withdrawal. It can be found from Figure 2-7（c）that there is only one turning point in the curve, which divides the mature stage into two parts: early mature stage and late mature stage. Therefore, the technology life cycle can be divided into seven parts: early infancy, late infancy, early growth, late growth, early maturity, late maturity and exit as shown in Figure 2-8.

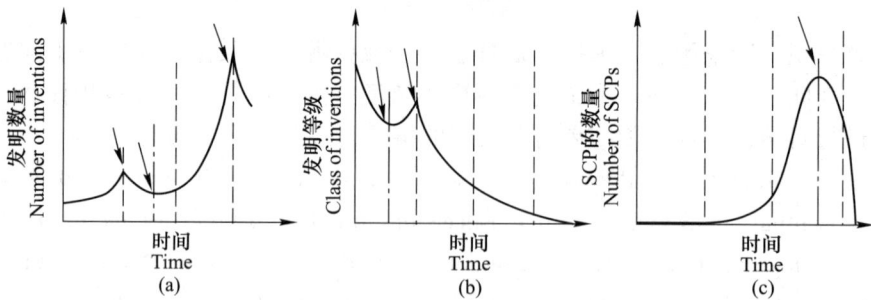

图 2-7　各曲线上的极值点和基于极值点的技术生命周期的重新划分

Figure 2-7　Extreme points on each curve and re division of technology life cycle based on extreme points

（1）婴儿期前期和后期。任何一项技术都是源自某个重要发现或某个等级很高的发明或想法，然后围绕这项发现或发明开展一系列应用探索，导致一系列低等级的发明或想法，这就是婴儿期前期。随着经验的积累和限制技术应用的一系列主要问题的解决，导致一系列较高等级的发明或想法，这就是技术的婴儿期后期。随着原有技术退出市场，新技术就进入成长期。成长期又分为成长期前期和成长期后期。制约新技术应用的关键技术问题的解决，推动技术进入成长期前期。但是技术真正进入成长期前期是由于拥有关键技术的公司放弃原有技术，而转向新技术产品的开发。企业的先发优势和技术的垄断（专利权），以及多数企业对新技术还持怀疑的态度，一定时期内发明相对减少，这段时间就是成长期前期。随着技术垄断的打破和技术的扩散以及行业内对新技术的信心加强，越来越多的企业加入到对该技术的进一步研发，专利数量迅速增加，迅速推动技术进入成熟期，这段时间就是成长期后期。

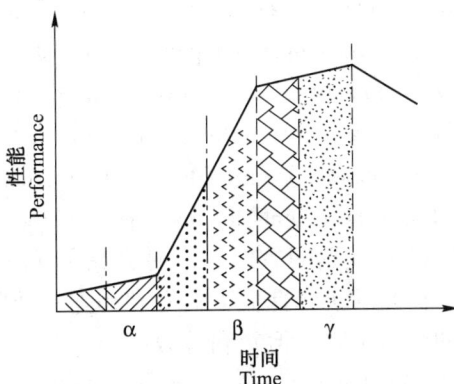

图 2-8 技术生命周期的重新划分

Figure 2-8 Redivision of technology life cycle

(1) Early and late infancy. Any technology is derived from an important discovery or a high-level inventions or ideas, and then a series of application explorations are carried out around this discovery or invention, leading to a series of low-level inventions or ideas, which is called early infancy. With the accumulation of experience and the solution of a series of major problems limiting the application of technology, a series of higher level inventions or ideas have been made, which is the late infancy of technology. With the original technology out of the market, new technology will enter the growth period. Growth period is divided into early growth period and late growth period. To solve the key technical problems that restrict the application of new technology, and promote the technology into the early stage of growth. But technology really enters the early stage of growth period because companies with key technology give up the original technology and turn to the development of new technology products. Because of the first mover advantage of enterprises, the monopoly of technology (patent right) and the skepticism of most enterprises towards new technology, inventions are relatively reduced in a certain period of time, which is the early growth period. With the break of technology monopoly, the spread of technology and the strengthening of confidence in new technology in the industry, more and more enterprises have joined in the further research and development of the technology, the number of patents has increased rapidly, and the technology has rapidly entered the mature period, which is the late growth period.

(2) 成熟期前期。进入成熟期后，产品的性能接近极限，决定产品竞争力的因素不再是产品的性能，而变成产品的成本。激烈的市场竞争使得各个企业加大研发力度，一方面使产品尽善尽美，另一方面降低产品成本，在所申请的专利中，Darrell Mann 所论及的两种专利（降低成本的专利和弥补缺陷的专利）占了绝大多数。

(2) In the early stage of maturity. After entering the mature period, the performance

of the product is close to the limit. The factor determining the competitiveness of the product is no longer the performance of the product, but the cost of the product. Fierce market competition makes every enterprise to increase R & D efforts. On the one hand, it makes the products perfect, on the other hand, it reduces the cost of products. Among the patents applied, Darrell Mann's two kinds of patents (the patents for reducing the cost of wood and the patents for making up defects) account for the vast majority.

（3）成熟期后期。这时产品的成本和性能接近极限，虽然专利申请依然很积极，但是对于降低成本的专利和弥补缺陷的专利因为专利空间越来越小，这两种专利的数量下降，但专利总数还会上升。

（3）Later stage of maturity. At this time, the cost and performance of the product are close to the limit. Although the patent application is still very active, the number of patents that reduce the cost and those that make up for defects is declining, this is because the patent space is getting smaller and smaller. But the total number of patents will rise.

（4）退出期。技术的性能已经达到极限，成本也达到极限值，这时决定产品竞争力的是各种销售手段的应用和良好的售后服务及企业的信誉。

（4）Exit period. The performance of technology has reached the limit and the cost has reached the limit. At this time, the application of various sales means, good after-sales service and the reputation of the enterprise determine the competitiveness of the product.

根据专利特性曲线上的极值点把技术分为上述的 7 个阶段，每个阶段的专利特性都有自己的基本特征。最基本的特征是特性曲线的升降的趋势，即各阶段上特性曲线的斜率。另外，通过图 2-7（a）与（c）比较可以大致观察同期专利中弥补缺陷的专利在同期专利中的比例变化。从图 2-7 得出特性曲线的斜率和弥补表面缺陷的专利在同期专利中的大致比例。

According to the extremum of the patent characteristic curve, the technology is divided into the above seven stages, and each stage has its own basic characteristics. The most basic characteristic is the rising and falling trend of the characteristic curve, that is, the slope of the characteristic curve at each stage. In addition, by comparing (a) and (c) in Figure 2-7, we can roughly observe the change of the proportion of the patents that make up for defects in the patents of the same period in the patents of the same period. Figure 2-7 shows the slope of the characteristic curve and the approximate proportion of the patents to make up the surface defects in the patents of the same period.

2.3 本 章 小 结
2.3 Summary of this chapter

产品是不断发展的，每个产品都有核心技术，其技术的发展存在一个生命周期，在进行产品开发时对产品的技术生命周期进行预测，可以帮助设计者进行正确的决策。本章介绍了产品技术预测的方法、产品生命周期、S-曲线以及 TRIZ 的阶段性 S-曲线、TRIZ 基于专利的技术成熟度预测，并通过实例说明技术成熟度预测对产品开发战略制定的指导意义。

Products are constantly developing. Every product has its core technology. There is a life cycle in the development of its technology. Predicting the technology life cycle of products during product development can help designers make correct decisions. This chapter introduces the method of product technology prediction, product life cycle, S-curve, TRIZ S-curve and TRIZ patent based technology maturity prediction, and illustrates the guiding significance of technology maturity prediction to product development strategy formulation through examples.

3 技术进化定律
Chapter 3 Law of Technological Evolution

3.1 概 述
3.1 Overview

市场竞争的日益加剧、买方市场的形成和产品更新速度的加快是当今制造业的显著特点。由于市场的复杂多变和不可预期，要求企业具有快速响应市场的能力，迅速开发出满足市场需求的产品。

Today's manufacturing industry is characterized by increasingly fierce market competition, the formation of buyer's market and the acceleration of product renewal. Due to the complexity and unpredictability of the market, enterprises are required to have the ability to quickly respond to the market and quickly develop products to meet the market demand.

企业在新产品研发决策过程中，要预测当前产品的技术水平及新一代产品可能的进化方向，这种预测的过程称为技术预测（Technology Forecasting）。技术预测的研究起始于半个世纪以前。在长期的研究过程中，理论界提出了技术预测的多种方法，这些方法被分为规范化方法（Normative）与探索性方法（Exploratory）两类。上述方法是西方世界提出的方法。MIT 的 Frauens 在 2000 年指出西方传统的技术预测存在如下 3 条缺点：

（1）预测所需要的准则太弱；

（2）支持提出及实现可能特征的工具集是有限的；

（3）确定目前产品功能的潜力主要取决于专家。

In the process of new product R & D decision-making, enterprises need to predict the technology level of current products and the possible evolution direction of new generation products, which is called technology forecasting. The research of technology prediction started half a century ago. In the long-term research process, many methods of technology prediction have been put forward in the theoretical circle. These methods are divided into two categories: normative method and exploratory method. The above method is proposed by the western world. In 2000, Frauens of MIT pointed out that there are three shortcomings in the western traditional technology prediction:

（1）The criteria needed for forecasting are too weak；

（2）There is a limited set of tools for proposing and implementing possible features；

（3）It is up to the experts to determine the potential of current product functions.

Altshuller 通过对世界专利库的分析，发现并确认了技术在结构上进化的趋势，即技术进化定律与进化路线，而且还发现，在一个工程领域中总结出的进化定律与进化路线可在另一工程领域实现，即技术进化定律与进化路线具有可传递性，从而形成了 TRIZ 中的技术预测系统。Frauens 指出：苏联 TRIZ 中的技术系统进化 (Technology System Evolution) 理论已提供了强有力的技术预测工具，这些工具包括产品进化定律及进化路线等。

Through the analysis of the world patent database, Altshuller found and confirmed the trend of technology evolution in structure, that is, the law and route of technology evolution, and also found that the evolution law and route summarized in one engineering field can be realized in another engineering field, that is, the law and route of technology evolution are transitive, thus forming the technology prediction in TRIZ System. Frauens pointed out: the theory of technology system evolution in TRIZ of the Soviet Union has provided powerful technology prediction tools, including product evolution law and evolution route.

本章系统介绍 TRIZ 中的产品进化理论成果及应用实例。

This chapter systematically introduces the product evolution theory achievements and application examples in TRIZ.

3.2 技术进化阶段
3.2 Technology evolution stage

3.2.1 技术系统的诞生及进化
3.2.1 Birth and evolution of technology system

技术系统是人造物，如投影仪、激光笔、手机、桌椅等，设计及制造这些人造物均能满足特定的功能。技术系统按功能或结构均可以划分为层次结构，如图 3-1 所示。

Technology system is a kind of artifact, such as projector, laser pen, mobile phone, desk and chair. The design and manufacture of these artifact can meet the specific function. The technical system can be divided into hierarchical structure according to function or structure, as shown in Figure 3-1.

如果图 3-1 是某个待设计系统的功能树，则第三层为系统的功能元，将功能元用能量流、物料流及信息流连接起来形成功能结构。由每个功能元确定其实现的过程首先在工业界已开发的技术中选择，如果某些零部件或系统能用，则直接选用。如果找不到能用的已有技术，则需要创新。

If Figure 3-1 is the function tree of a system to be designed, the third layer is the function elements of the system. which are connected by energy flow, material flow and information flow to form a functional structure. Each functional element determines its implementation process. First, it is selected from the developed technologies in the

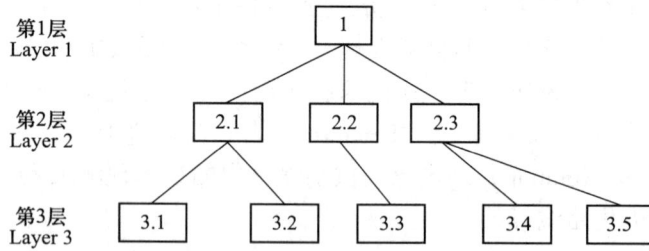

图 3-1　典型的层次结构

Figure 3-1　Typical hierarchy

industry. If some parts or systems can be used, it is directly selected. If we can't find the available technology, we need to innovate.

3.2.2　产品进化的四个阶段

3.2.2　Four stages of product evolution

从历史的观点看，产品进化分为如下 4 个阶段：

（1）为系统选择零部件；

（2）改善零部件；

（3）系统动态化；

（4）系统的自控制。

From a historical point of view, product evolution can be divided into the following four stages:

（1）Select components for the system;

（2）Improve parts and components;

（3）The system is dynamic;

（4）Self control of the system.

为系统选择零部件。飞机的发明是从 100 多年前开始的。当时的发明人所考虑的问题是：飞行的部件是什么？发动机是否在机翼内？机翼是固定的还是活动的？如果是活动的，是否与鸟的翅膀相同？发动机的类型是什么？蒸汽发动机还是电动发动机？经过多次实验，选用了固定式机翼及内燃机。

Choosing components for the system. The invention of the airplane began more than 100 years ago. The question that the inventors considered at that time was: what are the flying parts? Is the engine in the wing? Is the wing fixed or movable? If it is active, is it the same as a bird's wing? What is the type of engine? Steam engine or electric engine? After many experiments, fixed wing and internal combustion engine were selected.

改善零部件。发明人改进组成技术系统的不同零部件，对其形状、各种关系进行优化，采用更合适的材料、尺寸等。对于飞机的改进，该阶段的问题是：一架飞机采用几个机翼，一个、两个还是三个；控制系统放在什么位置，前部还是后部；发动机的具体位置；螺旋桨应如何设计，是推动型还是拉动型；一架飞机应采用多少个齿轮等。经过该阶段的进化所设计的飞机与今天的飞机已很相似了。

Improving parts. The inventor improves different parts of the technical system, optimizes their shapes and various relationships, and adopts more appropriate materials and sizes. For the improvement of the aircraft, the problems in this stage are: how many wings should an aircraft adopt, one, two or three; where should the control system be placed, front or rear; the specific position of the engine; how to design the propeller, push or pull; how many gears should an aircraft adopt, and so on. After this stage of evolution, the aircraft designed is very similar to today's aircraft.

系统动态化。在该阶段，很多采用刚性连接的零部件改为柔性连接，如发明了飞机的可伸缩起落架，能改变形状的机翼，机身的前部可上下移动，发明了使飞机垂直升降的发动机等。由于系统动态化进化，系统性能空前提高。

System dynamics. At this stage, many parts that use rigid connection are changed to flexible connection, such as the invention of the aircraft's retractable landing gear, wings that can change shape, the front of the fuselage can move up and down, and the invention of the engine that can make the aircraft lift vertically. Due to the dynamic evolution of the system, the performance of the system has been improved unprecedentedly.

系统的自控制。这一进化步骤还没有广泛实现，但可从火箭、航天器的设计中看出该进化步骤已初露端倪，如运行中的航天器可对其自身的某些行为进行自组织。这只是该进化步骤的开始，未来的系统将能够自动地适应环境。

Self control of the system. This evolutionary step has not been widely realized, but it can be seen from the design of rockets and spacecraft that this evolutionary step has begun to emerge, such as the spacecraft in operation can self organize some of its own behaviors. This is just the beginning of the evolutionary process, and the future system will automatically adapt to the environment.

3.3 技术进化系统
3.3 Technology evolution system

3.3.1 技术进化系统组成
3.3.1 Composition of technology evolution system

技术及其产品要通过不断变化满足用户新的需求，以提高市场竞争力。技术系统的进化分为不同的阶段，目前的阶段与过去及未来的阶段是不同的。从某一阶段开始，经过大量的研发与知识积累之后技术系统进化到下一阶段。

Technology and its products to meet the new needs of users through continuous changes, in order to improve market competitiveness. The evolution of technology system is divided into different stages. The present stage is different from the past and future stages. From a certain stage, after a lot of R & D and knowledge accumulation, the technology system evolves to the next stage.

由于市场的压力，技术系统要不断改变，如性能更好、重量更轻、所需制造资源更少，完成的功能更多，即技术系统要向最终理想解进化。技术系统每进化一步都是发明人努力的结果。成千上万的人，包括有资格的工程师及普通人，每年在进行高级别与低级别的创新活动，仅有少量的创新结果被实施，对技术系统的进化做出贡献。发明人作为一个整体是不可控的，他们的工作受市场及兴趣的驱动，通常也不知道其他人正在从事同样的发明创造。这些人的工作似乎处于一种随机状态。但从历史的观点研究，一项发明最终被接受的原因是遵循了技术进化的逻辑。

Due to the pressure of the market, the technology system needs to change constantly, such as better performance, lighter weight, less manufacturing resources and more functions, that is, the technology system needs to evolve to the final ideal solution. Every step of technological system evolution is the result of the efforts of inventors. Thousands of people, including qualified engineers and ordinary people, are engaged in high-level and low-level innovation activities every year, and only a small number of innovation results are implemented to contribute to the evolution of technology system. The inventor as a whole is uncontrollable, their work is driven by the market and interests, and usually does not know that other people are engaged in the same invention. The work of these people seems to be in a random state. But from a historical point of view, the reason why an invention is finally accepted is that it follows the logic of technological evolution.

TRIZ 创始人 G. S. Altshuller 及研究人员经过分析大量专利，发现不同领域中技术进化过程的规律是相同。如果掌握了这些规律，就能主动预测未来技术的发展趋势，今天设计明天的产品。TRIZ 中的技术进化定律及技术进化路线正是这些客观规律的一种总结。其基本原理如下：

（1）技术进化定律及路线应是技术进化的真实描述，能被不同历史时期的大量专利及技术所证实；

（2）技术进化定律及路线应能协助研发人员预测技术未来的发展；

（3）技术进化定律及路线应是开放系统，随技术发展所产生的新模式及路线应能加入到已有的系统中。

After analyzing a large number of patents, TRIZ founder G. S. Altshuller and researchers found that the law of technology evolution in different fields is the same. If we master these laws, we can actively predict the development trend of future technology and design tomorrow's products today. The law and route of technology evolution in TRIZ is a summary of these objective laws. The basic principle is as follows：

（1）The law and route of technological evolution should be the true description of technological evolution, which can be confirmed by a large number of patents and technologies in different historical periods；

（2）The law and route of technology evolution should help researchers predict the future development of technology；

（3）The law and route of technology evolution should be an open system, and the new pattern and route generated with the development of technology should be able to be added to the existing system.

TRIZ 中的技术进化理论反映了技术系统、组成元件、系统与环境之间在进化过程中重要的、稳定的和重复性的相互作用。Fry 及 Rivin 在以往 TRIZ 研究成果的基础上，将技术进化定律归纳为九条。

定律 1：提高理想化水平。技术系统向提高理想化水平的方向进化。

定律 2：子系统的非均衡发展。组成系统子系统发展不均衡，系统越复杂不均衡的程度越高。

定律 3：动态化增长。组成技术系统的结构更加柔性化，以适应性能要求、环境条件的变化及功能的多样性要求。

定律 4：向超系统进化。技术系统由单系统向双系统及多系统进化。

定律 5：向微观系统进化。技术系统更多地采用微结构及其组合。

定律 6：完整性。一个完整系统包含执行、传动、能源动力和操作控制四个部分。

定律 7：缩短能量流路径长度。技术系统向着缩短能量流经系统的路径长度的方向进化。

定律 8：增加可控性。进一步增强物质-场之间的相互作用，使系统可控性程度提高。

定律 9：增加和谐性。周期性作用与完成这些作用的各部分之间的和谐性增加。

The theory of technology evolution in TRIZ reflects the important, stable and repetitive interaction among technology system, component, system and environment in the process of evolution. Based on the previous TRIZ research results, Fry and Rivin summed up nine laws of technological evolution.

Law 1: improve the level of idealization. Technology system to improve the level of idealization in the direction of evolution.

Law 2: unbalanced development of subsystems. The more complex the system, the higher the degree of imbalance.

Law 3: dynamic growth. The structure of the technical system is more flexible to meet the requirements of performance, environmental conditions and functional diversity.

Law 4: evolution to super systems. Technology system evolves from single system to double system and multi system.

Law 5: evolution to microsystems. Microstructures and their combinations are more used in technological systems.

Law 6: integrity. A complete system consists of four parts: execution, transmission, energy and power, and operation control.

Law 7: shorten energy flow path length. Technology system evolves in the direction of shortening the path length of energy flow through the system.

Law 8: increase controllability. Further enhance the interaction between matter and field to improve the controllability of the system.

Law 9: increased harmony. Increased harmony between periodic actions and the parts that fulfill them.

技术进化定律给出了技术系统进化的一般方向，但没有给出每个方向进化的细节。每条定律之下有多条技术进化路线，每条技术进化路线由技术所处的不同状态构成，表明了技术进化由低级向高级进化的过程，可以作为技术预测的依据。

The law of technology evolution gives the general direction of technology system evolution, but does not give the details of each direction of evolution. There are several technological evolution routes under each law, and each technological evolution route is composed of different states of technology, which indicates the process of technological evolution from low level to high level, and can be used as the basis of technological prediction.

基于 TRIZ 的技术进化系统组成如图 3-2 所示。技术进化模式之下是技术进化路线，每条路线由不同的状态组成，并由工程实例库支持。其中的实例库来自大量专利分析的结果。图 3-2 中的产品或某项技术是技术进化系统的输入，首先选择可能应用的技术进化定律，之后在其下选择技术进化路线及与这些路线对应的工程实例，类比产生新技术概念。

The composition of technology evolution system based on TRIZ is shown in Figure 3-2. In technology evolution mode, there are technology evolution routes. Each route is

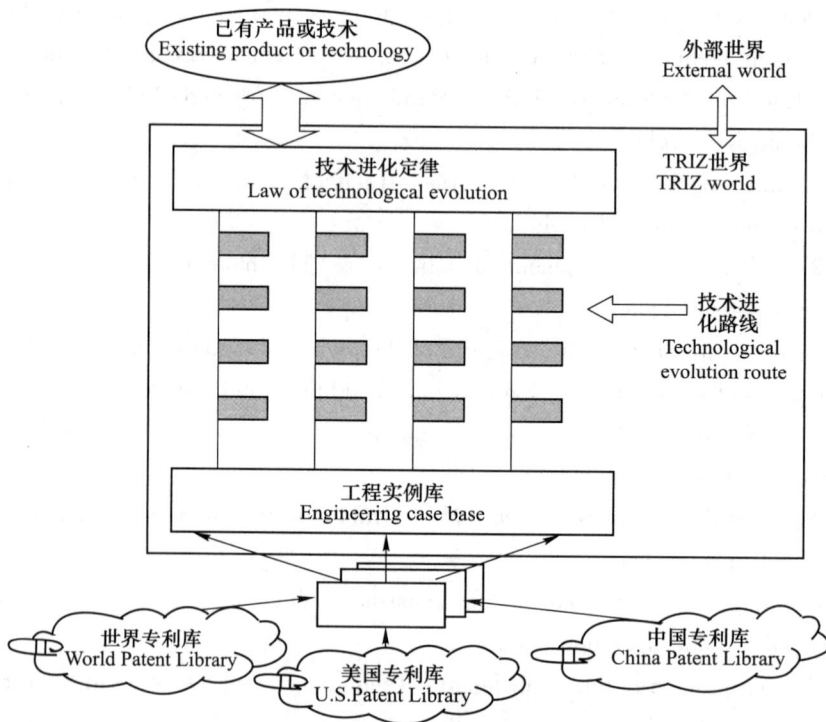

图 3-2　技术进化系统组成

Figure 3-2　Composition of technology evolution system

composed of different states and supported by engineering case base. The case base comes from a large number of patent analysis results. The product or a technology in Figure 3-2 is the input of the technology evolution system. First, we select the law of technology evolution that may be applied, then select the technology evolution route and the engineering examples corresponding to these routes, and generate new technology concepts by analogy.

3.3.2 技术进化定律与进化路线定律
3.3.2 Law of technology evolution and law of evolution route

3.3.2.1 定律1：提高理想化水平
3.3.2.1 Law 1：raise the level of idealization

提高理想化水平定律是指技术系统向提高理想化水平的方向进化。按式（3-1）计算，增加技术系统的效益，如实现更多的功能、更好的实现功能，减少成本或副作用，均可增加技术系统的理想化水平。该定律是技术进化的根本性定律，描述了技术系统进化总的方向，也是判断一个技术创新是否有效的重要判据。

$$理想化水平=收益/（成本+副作用）\qquad(3-1)$$

Law of raising the level of idealization refers to the evolution of technology system to improve the level of idealization. According to the formula（3-1）, increasing the benefits of the technical system, such as realizing more functions and better functions, reducing costs or side effects, can increase the idealization level of the technical system. This law is the fundamental law of technological evolution, describes the general direction of technological system evolution, and is also an important criterion to judge whether a technological innovation is effective or not.

$$Idealization\ level = benefit/（cost + side\ effect）\qquad(3-1)$$

➤路线1-1 空洞程度增加

图 3-3 是该路线所包含的几个状态。为了增加理想化水平，最初采用实体的系统增加一个空洞及几个空洞，之后采用毛细孔实体及多孔实体，最后采用多微空洞实体。空心砖、空心楼板、保温杯等均是按该路线进化的实例。

➤ Route 1-1 Increased void

Figure 3-3 shows the status of the route. In order to increase the level of idealization, a void and several voids were added to the solid system at first, then microporous solid and porous solid were used, and finally multi micro void solid was used. Hollow brick, hollow floor and insulation cup are all examples of evolution according to this route.

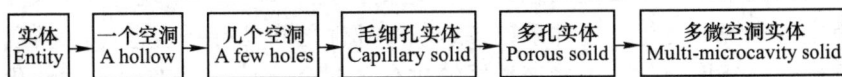

| 实体
Entity | → | 一个空洞
A hollow | → | 几个空洞
A few holes | → | 毛细孔实体
Capillary solid | → | 多孔实体
Porous soild | → | 多微空洞实体
Multi-microcavity solid |

图 3-3 空洞程度增加路线

Figure 3-3 Route of increasing void degree

3.3.2.2 定律 2：子系统的非均衡发展

3.3.2.2 Law 2: unbalanced development of subsystems

组成系统的子系统发展非均衡，系统越复杂非均衡的程度越高。非均衡的出现是由于系统中的某些子系统满足了新的需求，从而其发展快于其他子系统。非均衡将导致系统内部子系统间或子系统与系统间出现冲突，不断消除该类冲突使系统得到进化。消除冲突的手段是新发明的应用。

应用该定律的建议步骤如下：

（1）确定系统中的不同子系统及其功能；

（2）选择感兴趣的子系统及其主要功能；

（3）确定由该子系统对其他子系统所产生的副作用或危害，明确冲突；

（4）解决冲突；

（5）重复（1）~（4）。

发明问题解决理论中有 40 条发明原理并可以用于解决冲突。

The more complex the system is, the higher the degree of disequilibrium is. The emergence of disequilibrium is due to the fact that some subsystems of the system meet the new requirements, so its development is faster than other subsystems. Non equilibrium will lead to conflicts between subsystems or between subsystems in the system, and the system will evolve by constantly eliminating such conflicts. The means to eliminate conflicts is the application of new inventions.

The suggested steps to apply the law are as follows：

(1) Determine the different subsystems and their functions in the system;

(2) Select the interested subsystem and its main functions;

(3) Determine the side effects or hazards caused by the subsystem to other subsystems, and define the conflicts;

(4) Conflict resolution;

(5) Repeat (1) - (4).

There are 40 inventive principles in the theory of inventive problem solving, which can be used to solve conflicts.

3.3.2.3 定律 3：动态化增长

3.3.2.3 Law 3: dynamic growth

动态化增长定律是指组成技术系统的结构更加柔性化，以适应性能需求、环境条件的变化及功能的多样性需求。

研发新的技术系统主要是解决一个特定的问题，即至少实现一个特定的功能，并在一特定的环境下运行。这种系统各组成零部件之间具有刚性连接的特征，因此，不能很好地适应环境变化。很多该类系统进化的过程表明，动态化或柔性化是一种进化趋势。在进化的过程中，系统的结构逐步适应变化的环境，而且具有多种功能。

Dynamic growth law means that the structure of the technology system is more flexible to meet the requirements of performance, environmental conditions and functional diversity.

The main purpose of developing new technology system is to solve a specific problem, that is, to realize at least one specific function and run in a specific environment. The components of this system have the characteristics of rigid connection, so it can not adapt to the changes of environment. Many evolutionary processes of this kind of system show that dynamic or flexible is an evolutionary trend. In the process of evolution, the structure of the system gradually adapts to the changing environment and has multiple functions.

➢路线 3-1 向连续状态变化系统进化（见图 3-4）

➢ Route 3-1 Evolution to continuous state change system (as shown in Figure 3-4)

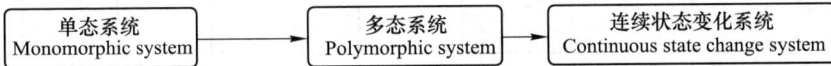

单态系统 Monomorphic system	→	多态系统 Polymorphic system	→	连续状态变化系统 Continuous state change system

图 3-4 向连续变化系统进化路线

Figure 3-4 Evolution route to continuous change system

➢路线 3-2 向自适应系统进化（见图 3-5）

图 3-5 中表明系统进化有被动适应、人工控制（人工适应）及主动适应三种状态。被动适应系统是在没有设置动力驱动或伺服控制机构的条件下，系统能够适应环境的变化。分级控制系统是指操作人员或通过传感器感知的信号下达指令改变系统的构型，从而改变系统的运行状态，但这种系统改变是分级的，而不是连续的。主动适应系统是装有传感器的系统，传感器自动检测环境的变化，并将这种变化传递给控制机构，从而实施控制，改变系统的运行状态。

➢ Route 3-2 Evolution to adaptive systems (as shown in Figure 3-5)

Figure 3-5 shows that there are three states of system evolution: passive adaptation, artificial control (artificial adaptation) and active adaptation. Passive adaptive system is that the system can adapt to the change of environment without setting power drive or servo control mechanism. Hierarchical control system means that the operator or the signal sensed by the sensor gives the command to change the configuration of the system, so as to change the operation state of the system. But this kind of system change is hierarchical, not continuous. Active adaptive system is a system with sensors. Sensors automatically detect the changes of the environment, and transmit the changes to the control mechanism, so as to implement control and change the operation state of the system.

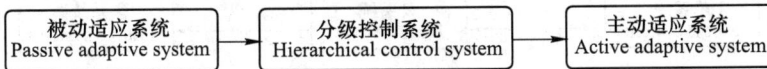

被动适应系统 Passive adaptive system	→	分级控制系统 Hierarchical control system	→	主动适应系统 Active adaptive system

图 3-5 向主动系统传递路线

Figure 3-5 Route to active system

➢路线 3-3 向流体或场进化

增加柔性化的过程通常包含固定或刚性部件被活动或柔性部件代替的过程。因此，存在该路线，如图 3-6 所示。

➤ Route 3-3　Evolution to fluid or field

The process of increasing flexibility usually involves the replacement of fixed or rigid parts by moving or flexible parts. Therefore, there is a route, as shown in Figure 3-6.

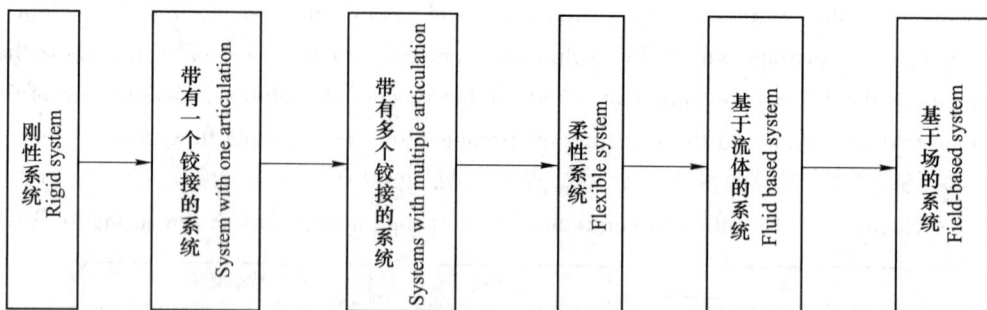

图 3-6　向流体或场传递路线

Figure 3-6　Transfer route to fluid or field

3.3.2.4　定律 4：向超系统进化
3.3.2.4　Law 4: evolution to supersystems

技术系统由单系统向双系统及多系统进化。单系统具有一个功能，双系统含有两个单系统，这两个单系统可以相同，也可以不同。多系统含有三个或多个相同或不同的单系统。将单系统集成为双系统或多系统是系统升级的一种形式。形成复杂系统的方法是将已有的两个或多个相互独立的单系统集成。集成后的系统实现性能提高，新的有用功能显现。因此，由单系统向双系统及多系统进化是一种技术系统进化的趋势，如图 3-7 所示。

Technology system has evolved from single system to double system and multi system. Single system has one function, dual system contains two single systems, which can be the same or different. A multiple system consists of three or more identical or different single systems. It is a form of system upgrading to integrate a single system into two or more systems. The method of forming complex system is to integrate two or more independent single systems. The performance of the integrated system is improved, and new useful functions appear. Therefore, the evolution from single system to dual system and multi system is a trend of technology system evolution, as shown in Figure 3-7.

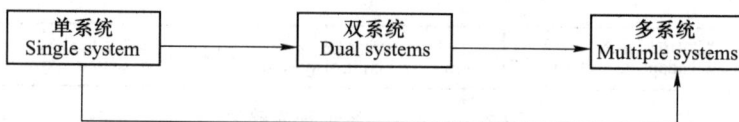

图 3-7　单系统向多系统进化

Figure 3-7　Evolution from single system to multiple systems

双系统及多系统的组成部件多样性会产生新的效果。如双金属片由热膨胀系数不同的两金属条组成，对于少量的温度变化，它将产生较大的变形。任何单金属片没有这种效果。在同质双系统或多系统的基础上，使其组成部件的性能变化，可以得到少量变化的多样性，如眼镜的镜片往往具有不同的度数，以适应每只眼睛不同近视程度的需求。

The diversity of components of dual system and multi system will produce new effects. If the bimetallic sheet is composed of two metal strips with different thermal expansion coefficient, it will produce larger deformation for a small amount of temperature change. No single sheet metal has this effect. On the basis of homogeneous dual system or multi system, the performance of its components can be changed to obtain a small amount of variety. For example, the lenses of glasses often have different degrees to meet the needs of different myopia degrees of each eye.

3.3.2.5 定律 5：向微观系统进化
3.3.2.5 Law 5：evolution to microsystems

技术系统是由物质组成的，物质分为不同层次的微观物理结构，常用的结构为晶体结构、分子团、分子、原子、离子、基本粒子。宏观的物质结构是由微观的物质结构所组成。技术系统由宏观向微观系统传递是一种进化趋势。即由宏观的物质所完成的功能，如轴、杠杆、齿轮等的功能，由微观物质完成。由宏观系统向微观系统进化的过程可以解决宏观系统中出现的冲突。

Technology system is composed of matter, which is divided into different levels of micro physical structure. The commonly used structures are crystal structure, molecular group, molecule, atom, ion and basic particle. Macro material structure is composed of micro material structure. It is an evolutionary trend for technology system to transfer from macro system to micro system. That is to say, the functions completed by macro materials, such as shaft, lever, gear and so on, are completed by micro materials. The process of evolution from macro system to micro system can solve the conflicts in macro system.

➢路线 5-1 向微观系统进化

该路线如图 3-8 所示，系统由晶体或分子团状态向分子态、原子与离子态、基本粒子态进化。

➢ Route 5-1 Evolution to microsystems

This route is shown in Figure 3-8, the system evolves from crystal or molecular group state to molecular state, atomic and ionic state, and elementary particle state.

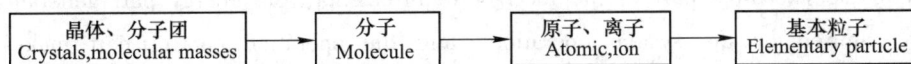

| 晶体、分子团
Crystals,molecular masses | → | 分子
Molecule | → | 原子、离子
Atomic,ion | → | 基本粒子
Elementary particle |

图 3-8 向微观系统传递路线

Figure 3-8 Transfer route to microsystem

该定律的应用遵循以下两条规则。

（1）微观系统或结构的采用应实现宏观结构或系统所完成的功能，如电化学加工是采用分子之间的相互作用完成加工，即用分子加工代替在力的作用下传统刀具直接加工工件。

（2）微观结构控制宏观结构的特性及行为。如对不同光照变色的眼镜采用了该规则，由于这种眼镜的镜片在强光下变黑，所以戴该黑眼镜的人不再需要太阳镜或遮阳罩。制造过程中在镜片中添加银氯化物，使眼镜镜片具有这种透光性的变化。其原理为：光线与氯化物的离子相互作用产生氯化物原子与电子，该类电子与银的离子作用，产生银的原子。银原子积聚阻碍的穿透，使镜片变黑。其变黑的程度与光线密度成正比。

The application of this law follows the following two rules.

（1）The application of micro system or structure should realize the function of macro structure or system. For example, electrochemical machining is to use the interaction between molecules to complete the machining, that is, to use molecular machining instead of traditional cutting tools to directly process the workpiece under the action of force.

（2）Microstructure controls the characteristics and behavior of macro structure. If the rule is applied to glasses with different light discoloration, because the lenses of the glasses turn black under strong light, the person wearing the black glasses no longer needs sunglasses or sunshades. In the manufacturing process, silver chloride is added to the lens to make the lens have this change of light transmittance. The principle is：the interaction of light and chloride ions produces chloride atoms and electrons, which interact with silver ions to produce silver atoms. The accumulation of silver atoms blocks the penetration of the lens, making it black. The degree of darkening is proportional to the density of light.

3.3.2.6　定律6：完整性
3.3.2.6　Law 6：integrity

完整性定律是指自治系统包含执行、传动、能源和操作控制四个部分。其中执行部分是直接完成系统主要功能的部分，传动部分将能源以要求的形式传递到执行部分，能源部分产生系统运行所需要的能量，控制部分使各部分的参数与行为按需要改变。

Integrity law means that the autonomous system consists of four parts：execution, transmission, energy and operation control. Among them, the executive part is the part that directly completes the main functions of the system, the transmission part transfers the energy to the executive part in the form of requirements, the energy part generates the energy required by the system operation, and the operation control part makes the parameters and behaviors of each part change as needed.

➤例3-1　液压传动系统的组成

液压泵是系统的能源装置，它将电能转变为液压能。液压油起传动的作用，将能量传递到所需要的位置。液压缸是执行部分，它将液压能转变为机械能，并作为系统的输出，完成所规定的操作。各种控制阀，如压力控制阀、方向控制阀、流量控制阀等控制系统协调有序的工作。

➢ **Example 3-1　Composition of hydraulic transmission system**

Hydraulic pump is the energy device of the system, which converts electric energy into hydraulic energy. Hydraulic oil plays the role of transmission, transferring energy to the required position. The hydraulic cylinder is the executive part, which transforms the hydraulic energy into mechanical energy, and as the output of the system, completes the specified operation. Various control valves, such as pressure control valve, direction control valve, flow control valve and other control systems work in a coordinated and orderly manner.

➢路线6-1　完整性路线（减少人的介入路线）

最初的技术系统常常是人工过程的一种替代，这种技术系统通常只有工具部分。随着技术进化的过程，传动部分被引入，之后是能源及控制部分的引入，从而最后取代了人工的参与。完整性路线如图3-9所示。

➢ Route 6-1　Integrity route（reducing human intervention route）

The original technology system is often an alternative to the artificial process, which usually has only the tool part. With the process of technological evolution, the transmission part is introduced, followed by the introduction of energy and control part, thus finally replacing the participation of human. The integrity route is shown in Figure 3-9.

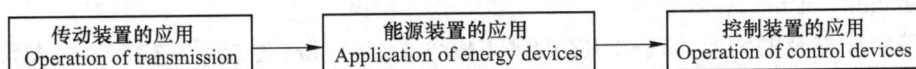

图 3-9　完整性路线

Figure 3-9　Integrity route

3.3.2.7　定律7：缩短能量流路径长度

3.3.2.7　Law 7：shorten energy flow path length

技术系统向着缩短能量流经系统路径长度的方向发展。技术系统运行的基本条件是能量能够从能源装置传递到执行装置，该路径的长度向缩短的方向进化。该定律含有两种技术进化趋势。

The technology system is developing in the direction of shortening the path length of energy flowing through the system. The basic condition of technical system operation is that the energy can be transferred from the energy device to the executive device, and the length of the path will be shortened. The law contains two trends of technological evolution.

（1）减少能量传递的级数。减少能量形式的转换次数，如能量的路径由电能转换为机械能，再由机械能转换为热能构成，将中间环节机械能去掉；减少参数的转换次数，如电动机输出的转速经过3级减速传递给丝杠，丝杠驱动执行机构，将3级减速减为2级减速。

（2）增加能量的可控性。即将可控性较差的能量形式变为可控性较好的形式。能量控制的难易顺序为：万有引力形成的势能、机械能、热能、电磁能。因此，将势能转变为机械能，将机械能转变为热能，将热能转变为电磁能是技术进化的趋势。

（1）Reduce the number of energy transfer. Reduce the number of energy form conversion, such as the energy path from electrical energy to mechanical energy, and then from mechanical energy to thermal energy, remove the mechanical energy in the middle link. Reduce the number of parameter conversion, such as the motor output speed is transmitted to the lead screw through three-stage deceleration, and the lead screw drives the actuator to reduce the three-stage deceleration to two-stage deceleration.

（2）Increase the controllability of energy. That is to say, the energy form with poor controllability will be changed into one with better controllability. The difficulty order of energy control is: potential energy, mechanical energy, thermal energy and electromagnetic energy formed by gravitation. Therefore, it is the trend of technological evolution to transform potential energy into mechanical energy, mechanical energy into thermal energy, and thermal energy into electromagnetic energy.

3.3.2.8 定律 8：增加可控性
3.3.2.8 Law 8: increase controllability

进一步增强物质与场之间的相互作用，可以增加系统的可控性。

Further enhancing the interaction between matter and field can increase the controllability of the system.

该定律涉及的物质-场是 TRIZ 的基本概念。Altshuller 通过对功能的研究发现：

（1）所有的功能都可分解为三个基本元件；

（2）一个存在的功能必定由三个基本元件构成；

（3）相互作用的三个基本元件有机组合将产生一个功能。

The matter field involved in the law is the basic concept of TRIZ. Altshuller found that:

（1）All functions can be divided into three basic components;

（2）An existing function must consist of three basic elements;

（3）The organic combination of the three basic elements of interaction will produce a function.

组成功能的三个基本元件分别为两种物质和一种场。物质可是任何东西，如太阳、地球、轮船、飞机、计算机、水、X-射线、齿轮、分子等。场是能量的总称，可以是核能、电能、磁能、机械能、热能等。

The three basic elements of the function are two substances and a field. Matter can be anything, such as the sun, the earth, ships, airplanes, computers, water, X-rays, gears, molecules, etc. Field is the general term of energy, which can be nuclear energy, electric energy, magnetic energy, mechanical energy, thermal energy, etc.

在 TRIZ 中，功能的基本描述如图 3-10 所示。图中 F 为场，S_1 及 S_2 分别为物质。其意义为 S_1 与 S_2 之间通过场 F 的相互作用，改变 S_1。

In TRIZ, the basic description of functions is shown in Figure 3-10. F is the field, S_1 and S_2 are the matter. Its significance is S_1 and S_2 change S_1 through the interaction of field F.

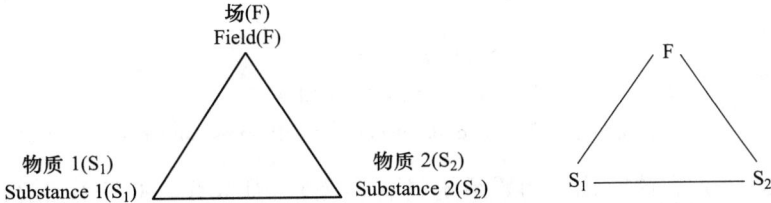

图 3-10 简化的物质-场符号

Figure 3-10 Simplified matter field notation

组成功能的每个元件都有其特殊的角色。S_1 为被动元件，起被作用、被操作、被改变的角色。S_2 为主动元件，起工具的作用，它操作、改变或作用于被动元件 S_1，S_2 又常被称为工具。F 为使能元件，它使 S_1 与 S_2 相互作用。

Each component of a function has its own special role. S_1 is a passive component, which plays the role of being acted, operated and changed. S_2 is an active component and acts as a tool. It operates, changes or acts on the passive component S_1. S_2 is also often called a tool. F is the enabling element, which makes S_1 interact with S_2.

物质-场中的物质通过场相互作用，如图 3-11 所示。图中，（a）表示物质产生场，（b）表示场作用于物质，（c）表示物质 S 将场 F_1 转变为 F_2。F_1 与 F_2 可以是相同或不同的场。

Matter matter in the field interacts through the field, as shown in Figure 3-11. In the figure, (a) indicates that matter produces a field, (b) indicates that the field acts on matter, and (c) indicates that matter s transforms field F_1 into F_2. F_1 and F_2 can be the same or different fields.

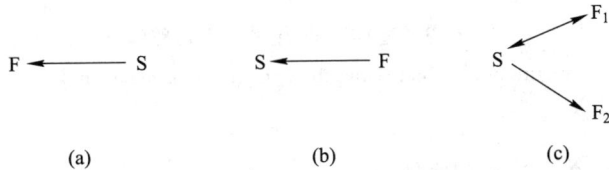

图 3-11 物质与场间可能的相互作用

Figure 3-11 Possible interaction between matter and field

图 3-12 为物质-场表示的功能。可解释为：人手产生的机械能（F）驱动牙刷（S_2）刷牙（S_1）；电能（F）驱动车床（S_2）车削工件（S_1）；机械能（F）驱动主轴（S_2）带动三爪卡盘上的工件（S_1）旋转。

Figure 3-12 shows the function of matter field representation. It can be interpreted as: the mechanical energy (F) generated by human hand drives toothbrush (S_2) to brush teeth (S_1); the electric energy (F) drives lathe (S_2) to turn workpiece (S_1); the mechanical energy (F) drives spindle (S_2) to drive workpiece (S_1) on three jaw chuck to rotate.

➤路线 8-1 增加物质-场的复杂性

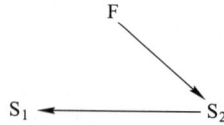

图 3-12　物质-场表示的功能

Figure 3-12　Function of matter field representation

图 3-13（a）为该路线。初始系统具有不完整物质-场，如图 3-13（b）所示中缺少场；首先将其进化为完整的物质-场，如图 3-13（c）所示；之后是将其进化为复杂的物质-场，如图 3-13（d）~（f）所示；图 3-13（d）、（e）中增加了场 F_2，经常起控制作用，使不可控的物质-场变得可控；图 3-13（f）表示物质-场的串联。

➢ Route 8-1　Increasing the complexity of matter field

（a）in Figure 3-13 shows the route. The initial system has an incomplete matter field, as shown in Figure 3-13（b）, which lacks a field; first, it is evolved into a complete matter field, as shown in Figure 3-13（c）; then it is evolved into a complex matter field, as shown in Figures 3-13（d）to（f）; in Figures 3-13（d）and（e）, field F_2 is added, which often plays a controlling role, making the uncontrollable matter field controllable; and Figure 3-13（f）shows the series connection of matter field.

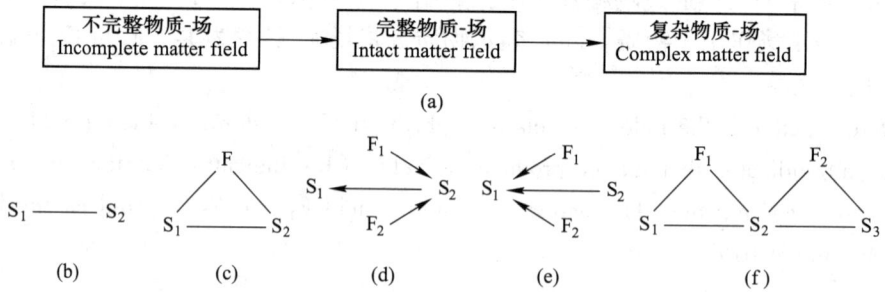

图 3-13　增加物质-场的复杂性路线

Figure 3-13　Increasing the complexity of matter field

3.3.2.9　定律 9：增加和谐性

3.3.2.9　Law 9: increase harmony

增加和谐性定律指交变作用本身与完成这些作用的零部件之间要和谐，且不断增加其和谐性。实际运行中的系统的主要部件或子系统都要互相配合、和谐工作，这是系统产生规定运动或动作基本保证。如果组成系统的主要部件或子系统不和谐，将出现部件或子系统间的干涉，系统的性能将会受到影响，甚至不能正常工作。

Increase harmony law means that there should be harmony between the alternating action itself and the parts that complete these actions, and the harmony should be continuously increased. In actual operation, the main components or subsystems of the system should cooperate with each other and work harmoniously, which is the basic guarantee for the system to produce specified movement or action. If the main components or subsystems of the system are not harmonious, there will be interference between components or subsystems, and the performance of the system will be affected, or even can not work normally.

该条定律的应用可以有多种方法：

（1）保持子系统、部件或零件间交变运动或参数的和谐性；

（2）应用谐振；

（3）避免采用不必要的交变运动。

部件或子系统间的和谐性有时与自然频率或动态特性无关，而与各部件或子系统间的运动或动作顺序有很大的关系。合理地安排该类顺序，系统的和谐性将得到改善。

There are many ways to apply this law:

（1）Keep the harmony of alternating motion or parameters among subsystems, components or parts;

（2）Applicationof resonance;

（3）Avoid unnecessary alternating motion.

Sometimes the harmony between components or subsystems has nothing to do with the natural frequency or dynamic characteristics, but has a great relationship with the motion or action sequence of each component or subsystem. Reasonable arrangement of this kind of sequence will improve the harmony of the system.

➢例 3-2　油漆喷枪的改进

传统的油漆喷枪有两个阀门分别控制进入喷嘴的油漆及空气，其动作顺序为：喷枪被激发后，空气控制阀门首先开启，之后油漆控制阀门开启，系统进入工作状态。为了停止工作，油漆控制阀门首先关闭，之后空气控制阀门关闭。该喷枪所喷油漆表面存在质量问题，即当喷枪开始工作及停止后，均有油漆液滴从喷口流到被喷漆表面。

改变交变运动的和谐性可以解决该问题。美国专利 No. 4759502 提出的解决方案为：油漆控制阀门首先开启与关闭，在很短的时间差内空气阀门要开启或关闭，两者的时间差要能够调节。该解决方案改善了被喷油漆表面的质量。

➢ Example 3-2　Improvement of paint spray gun

The traditional paint spray gun has two valves to control the paint and air entering the nozzle respectively. The action sequence is: after the spray gun is activated, the air control valve is opened first, then the paint control valve is opened, and the system enters the working state. In order to stop the work, the paint control valve is closed first and then the air control valve is closed. There is a quality problem on the surface of the paint sprayed by the spray gun, that is, when the spray gun starts to work and stops, the paint droplets flow from the nozzle to the painted surface.

This problem can be solved by changing the harmony of alternating movement. The solution proposed by US patent No. 4759502 is: the paint control valve shall be opened and closed first, and the air valve shall be opened or closed within a short time difference, and the time difference between the two shall be adjustable. The solution improves the quality of the sprayed surface.

➤路线 9-1　功能-时间动力学

该路线如图 3-14 所示。完成每项功能都需要时间，如图 3-14 中的功能 1、2、3 所示，可以同时完成几项功能，如路径（a）同时完成功能 1 及 2，节省了总的时间；路径（b）表明减少完成某项功能（如功能 1）的时间；路径（c）表明要顺序地完成多项功能，但每一项功能都要节省时间。

➤ Route 9-1　Function time dynamics

The route is shown in Figure 3-14. It takes time to complete each function. As shown in functions 1, 2 and 3 in Figure 3-14, several functions can be completed at the same time. For example, path (a) completes functions 1 and 2 at the same time, saving the total time; path (b) indicates reducing the time to complete a certain function (such as function 1); path (c) indicates that multiple functions should be completed in sequence, but each function should save time.

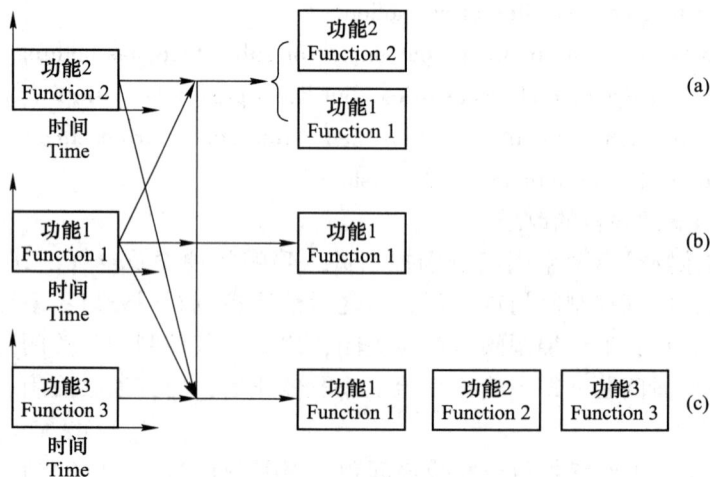

图 3-14　功能-时间动力学路线

Figure 3-14　Function time dynamics route

3.4　本　章　小　结
3.4　Summary of this chapter

产品的发展过程是性能由低到高逐渐提高的过程，在产品发展的过程中具有一定的规律，这个规律就是技术进化定律，每个产品的发展都符合一条或更多的技术进化定律，在每个技术定律下包含若干条进化路线，进化路线描述了具体的产品技术发展所经历的各个阶段。本章介绍了产品进化的基本概念、进化模式和路线及其应用与实现方法，用实例说明进化理论的应用。企业的决策层如能掌握这些理论，将使企业的研发决策更加科学合理，增加企业的创新能力及市场竞争力。

The process of product development is the process of performance improving gradually from low to high. There is a certain law in the process of product development, which is the law of technology evolution. The development of each product conforms to one or more laws of technology evolution. Under each law of technology, there are several evolution routes. The evolution route describes each stage of specific product technology development Paragraph. This chapter introduces the basic concept of product evolution, evolution mode and route, and its application and implementation method, and illustrates the application of evolution theory with examples. If the decision-makers of enterprises can master these theories, they will make the R & D decisions more scientific and reasonable, and increase the innovation ability and market competitiveness of enterprises.

4 产品设计中的冲突
Chapter 4　Conflict in Product Design

4.1　概　述
4.1　Overview

产品设计具有相同的规律，即产品处于进化之中并受客观定律支配，最普遍的支配定律是对立统一、从量变到质变、否定之否定三大定律，这构成了发明问题解决理论（TRIZ）的内容基础。TRIZ 认为产品创新的核心是解决设计中的冲突或矛盾，如能发现需求与已有产品或产品内部的冲突，开发新产品或改进已有的产品，解决这些已发现的冲突，不仅满足社会日益增长的需求，同时为新产品生产企业带来效益。

Product design has the same law, that is, the product is in the process of evolution and dominated by objective laws. The most common dominant laws are unity of opposites, from quantitative change to qualitative change, and negation of negation, which constitute the content basis of TRIZ. TRIZ believes that the core of product innovation is to solve the conflict or contradiction in design. If we can find the conflict between demand and existing products or within products, develop new products or improve existing products, and solve these conflicts, we can not only meet the growing needs of society, but also bring benefits to new product manufacturers.

在 TRIZ 意义下，解决发明问题的核心是克服冲突，未克服冲突的设计不是创新设计。产品进化过程就是不断解决产品所存在冲突的过程，一个冲突解决后，产品进化过程处于停顿状态；之后解决另一个冲突，使产品移到一个新的状态。设计人员在设计过程中不断的发现并解决冲突，是推动其向理想化方向进化的动力。

In the sense of TRIZ, the core of solving the problem of invention is to overcome the conflict, and the design without overcoming the conflict is not innovative design. The process of product evolution is the process of constantly solving the conflicts existing in the product. After one conflict is solved, the process of product evolution is at a standstill; after another conflict is solved, the product moves to a new state. Designers constantly find and solve conflicts in the design process, which is the driving force to promote its evolution in the direction of idealization.

产品是功能的实现。任何产品都包含一个或多个功能，为了实现这些功能，产品要由具有相互关系的多个零部件组成。为了提高产品的市场竞争力，需要不断对产品进行改进设计。当改变某个零件、部件的设计，即提高产品某些方面的性能时，可能会影响到与这些被改进设计零部件相关联的零部件，结果可能使产品或系统另一些方面的性能受到影响。如果这些影响是负面影响，则设计出现了冲突。TRIZ 所强调的冲突是针对功能与预期目标之间存在的差距，通过对产品的功能分析去发现并解决冲突。

Product is the realization of function. Any product contains one or more functions, in order to achieve these functions, the product should be composed of multiple components with mutual relationship. In order to improve the market competitiveness of products, we need to constantly improve the design of products. When the design of a part or component is changed, that is to say, the performance of some aspects of the product is improved, the parts associated with these improved design parts may be affected. As a result, the performance of other aspects of the product or system may be affected. If these effects are negative, the design conflicts. The conflict emphasized by TRIZ is to find and solve the conflict through the functional analysis of the product in view of the gap between the function and the expected goal.

本章介绍冲突及其类型、技术冲突、物理冲突的基本概念，标准工程参数，以及发现冲突的基本方法。

This chapter introduces conflict and its types, basic concepts of technical conflict and physical conflict, standard engineering parameters, and basic methods of finding conflict.

4.2 冲突及其分类
4.2 Conflict and classification

无论是新设计还是已有产品的改进设计，设计人员在设计过程中首先要保证或提高产品的某些内部性能，但这种提高往往导致产品其他内部性能的降低。即设计中往往存在冲突，冲突普遍存在于各种产品的设计之中。产品设计中的冲突是设计出现问题的根本原因，因此在产品设计和改进的过程中，必须发现并解决冲突，而不是采用折中的方法来平衡问题的双方，这是 TRIZ 理论之所以能从根本上解决问题的关键。

Whether it is a new design or an improved design of an existing product, designers should first ensure or improve some internal performance of the product in the design process, but this improvement often leads to the reduction of other internal performance of the product. That is to say, there are often conflicts in the design, which generally exist in the design of various products. The conflict in product design is the root cause of design problems, so in the process of product design and improvement, we must find and solve the conflict, rather than using a compromise method to balance the two sides of the problem, which is the key to TRIZ theory to fundamentally solve the problem.

G. S. Altshuller 将冲突分为三类，即管理冲突、物理冲突和技术冲突。

G. S. Altshuller divides conflicts into three categories: administrative conflicts, physical conflicts and technical conflicts.

管理冲突是指为了避免某些现象或希望取得某些结果，需要做一些事情，但不知如何去做。如希望提高产品质量、降低原材料的成本，但不知方法。管理冲突本身具有暂时性，而无启发价值。因此，不能表现出问题的解的可能方向，不属于传统 TRIZ 的研究内容。

Management conflict means that in order to avoid some phenomena or hope to achieve some results, we need to do something, but we don't know how to do it. If you want to improve the quality of products, reduce the cost of raw materials, but do not know the way. Management conflict itself is temporary, but not enlightening. Therefore, it can not show the possible direction of the solution of the problem, which does not belong to the research content of traditional TRIZ.

物理冲突是指为了实现某种功能，一个子系统或元件应具有一种特性，但同时出现了与此特性相反的特性。物理冲突出现的几种情况如下：

（1）一个子系统中有用功能加强的同时导致该子系统中有害功能的加强；

（2）一个子系统中有害功能降低的同时导致该子系统中有用功能的降低。

Physical conflict means that in order to achieve a certain function, a subsystem or component should have a characteristic, but at the same time, the opposite characteristic appears. There are several situations of physical conflict:

（1）The enhancement of useful functions in a subsystem leads to the enhancement of harmful functions in the subsystem;

（2）The decrease of harmful functions in a subsystem leads to the decrease of useful functions in the subsystem.

技术冲突是指一个作用同时导致有用及有害两种结果，也可指有用作用的引入或有害效应的消除导致一个或几个子系统或系统变坏。技术冲突常表现为一个系统中两个子系统之间的冲突。技术冲突出现的几种情况如下：

（1）在一个子系统中引入一种有用功能，导致另一个子系统产生一种有害功能，或加强了已存在的一种有害功能；

（2）消除一种有害功能导致另一个子系统有用功能变坏；

（3）有用功能的加强或有害功能的减少使另一个子系统或系统变得太复杂。

Technology conflict means that one action leads to both useful and harmful results. It can also mean that the introduction of useful effect or the elimination of harmful effect leads to one or more subsystems or systems deterioration. Technology conflict is often manifested as the conflict between two subsystems in a system. There are several situations of technology conflict:

(1) The introduction of a useful function into one subsystem leads to a harmful function in another subsystem, or strengthens an existing harmful function;

(2) The elimination of one harmful function leads to the deterioration of another subsystem's useful function;

(3) The enhancement of useful functions or the reduction of harmful functions make another subsystem or system too complex.

4.3 技术冲突的通用化
4.3 Generalization of technical conflicts

产品设计中的冲突是普遍存在的，应该有一种通用化、标准化的方法描述设计冲突，设计人员使用这些标准化的方法共同研究与交流将促进产品创新。

Conflicts in product design are common. There should be a general and standardized method to describe design conflicts. Designers using these standardized methods to study and communicate together will promote product innovation.

通过对 250 万件专利的详细研究，TRIZ 理论提出用 39 个通用过程参数描述冲突。实际应用中，首先要把一组或多组冲突均用该 39 个工程参数来表示。利用该方法把实际工程设计中的冲突转化为一般的或标准的技术冲突。

Based on the detailed study of 2.5 million patents, TRIZ theory proposes 39 general process parameters to describe conflicts. In practical application, one or more groups of conflicts should be represented by the 39 engineering parameters. Using this method, the conflicts in practical engineering design are transformed into general or standard technical conflicts.

39 个工程参数中常用到运动物体与静止物体两个术语，分别介绍如下：

（1）运动物体是指自身或借助于外力可在一定的空间内运动的物体；

（2）静止物体是指自身或借助于外力都不能使其在空间内运动的物体。

Among the 39 engineering parameters, two terms, moving objects and stationary objects, are commonly used:

(1) A moving object is an object that can move in a certain space by itself or by means of external force;

(2) A static object is one that cannot move in space by itself or by means of external force.

表 4-1 是 39 个通用工程参数名称的汇总。

Table 4-1 is a summary of 39 common engineering parameter names.

表 4-1　通用工程参数名称

Table 4-1　Name of general engineering parameters

序号 Serial	名称 Name	序号 Serial	名称 Name
No. 1	运动物体的重量 Weight of moving objects	No. 21	功率 Power
No. 2	静止物体的重量 Weight of stationary objects	No. 22	能量损失 Energy loss
No. 3	运动物体的长度 Length of moving objects	No. 23	物质损失 Material loss
No. 4	静止物体的长度 Length of stationary objects	No. 24	信息损失 Information loss
No. 5	运动物体的面积 Area of moving objects	No. 25	时间损失 Time loss
No. 6	静止物体的面积 Area of stationary objects	No. 26	物质或事物的数量 Quantity of matter or thing
No. 7	运动物体的体积 Volume of moving objects	No. 27	可靠性 Reliability
No. 8	静止物体的体积 Volume of stationary objects	No. 28	测试精度 Testing accuracy
No. 9	速度 Speed	No. 29	制造精度 Manufacturing accuracy
No. 10	力 Force	No. 30	物体外部有害因素作用的敏感性 Sensitivity of external harmful factors
No. 11	应力或压力 Stress or pressure	No. 31	物体产生的有害因素 Harmful factors resulting from an object
No. 12	形状 Shape	No. 32	可制造性 Manufactureability
No. 13	结构的稳定性 Stability of structures	No. 33	可操作性 Operationalization
No. 14	强度 Srengtht	No. 34	可维修性 Maintainability
No. 15	运动物体作用时间 Time of action of a moving objects	No. 35	适应性及多用性 Adaptability and versatilitys
No. 16	静止物体作用时间 Time of action of a stationary objects	No. 36	装置的复杂性 Complexity of installations
No. 17	温度 Temperature	No. 37	监控与测试的困难程度 Difficulties in monitoring and testing
No. 18	光照强度 Light intensity	No. 38	自动化程度 Automation
No. 19	运动物体的能量 Energy of moving objects	No. 39	生产率 Productivity
No. 20	静止物体的能量 Energy of stationary objects		

4. 4　物理冲突
4. 4　Physical conflict

物理冲突的核心是指对一个物体或系统中的一个子系统有相反的、矛盾的需求。物理冲突的例子很多。

The core of physical conflict is to have opposite and contradictory requirements for an object or a subsystem of a system. There are many examples of physical conflict.

工程中的实例如下：

（1）侦察机应飞行得很快，以便尽快离开被侦察的地区；但在被侦查的地区上空又应飞行得很慢，以便多收集数据。

（2）飞机的机翼应有大的面积以便起飞与降落，但又要较小以便高速飞行。

相对于技术冲突，物理冲突是尖锐的冲突，但设计中如果能确定，较容易解决。物理冲突的确定可通过对问题的详细分析及深刻理解的基础上确定，也可通过对已有技术冲突的进一步分析来确定。

Examples in the project are as follows：

（1）The reconnaissance plane should fly very fast so as to leave the reconnaissance area as soon as possible；However, in order to collect more data, we should fly very slowly over the investigated area.

（2）The wing of an aircraft should have a large area for take-off and landing, but a small area for high-speed flight.

Compared with the technical conflict, the physical conflict is sharp, but if it can be determined in the design, it is easier to solve. The determination of physical conflict can be based on the detailed analysis and deep understanding of the problem, and can also be determined through the further analysis of the existing technical conflict.

4. 5　技术冲突与物理冲突
4. 5　Technical conflict and physical conflict

技术冲突总是涉及两个基参数 A 与 B，当 A 得到改善时，B 变得更差。物理冲突仅涉及系统中的一个子系统或部件，而对该子系统或部件提出了相反的要求。往往技术冲突的存在隐含物理冲突的存在，有时物理冲突的解比技术冲突更容易。

Technical conflict always involves two basic parameters A and B. When A is improved, B becomes worse. The physical conflict only involves one subsystem or component in the system, and puts forward the opposite requirements for the subsystem or component. Often the existence of technical conflict implies the existence of physical conflict, and sometimes the solution of physical conflict is easier than technical conflict.

从技术冲突出发确定物理冲突的核心是确定另一参数或物体，该参数或物体控制着技术冲突的两个参数 A 与 B。

Starting from the technical conflict, the core of determining the physical conflict is to determine another parameter or object, which controls the two parameters A and B of the technical conflict.

➢例 4-1 用化学的方法为金属表面镀层的过程如下：金属制品放置于充满金属盐溶液的池子中，溶液中含有镍、钴等金属元素，在化学反应过程中，溶液中的金属元素凝结到金属制品表面形成镀层。温度越高，镀层形成的速度越快，但温度高有用元素沉淀到池子底部与池壁的速度也越快，温度低又大大降低生产率。

➢ **Example 4-1** The process of coating metal surface by chemical method is as follows: the metal products are placed in a pool filled with metal salt solution, which contains nickel, cobalt and other metal elements. In the process of chemical reaction, the metal elements in the solution condense to the surface of the metal products to form a coating. The higher the temperature is, the faster the coating is formed. However, the higher the temperature is, the faster the useful elements precipitate to the bottom and wall of the pool. The lower the temperature is, the lower the productivity is.

该问题的技术冲突为：两个标准参数为生产率（A）与材料浪费（B），加热溶液使生产率（A）提高，同时材料浪费（B）增加。

The technical conflict of this problem is: the two standard parameters are productivity (A) and material waste (B), heating solution makes productivity (A) increase and material waste (B) increase.

为了将该问题转变成为物理冲突，将温度作为另一参数（C）。物理冲突可描述为：溶液温度（C）增加，生产率（A）提高，材料浪费（B）增加；反之，生产率（A）降低，材料（B）浪费减少；溶液温度既应该高，以提高生产率，又应该低，以减少材料消耗。

In order to turn the problem into a physical conflict, temperature is chosen as another parameter (C). The physical conflict can be described as follows: with the increase of solution temperature (C), the productivity (A) increases and the material waste (B) increases; on the contrary, with the decrease of productivity (A), the material waste (B) decreases; the solution temperature should be high to improve the productivity and low to reduce the material consumption.

➢例 4-2 波音公司改进 737 设计过程中出现的一个技术冲突：既希望发动机吸入更多的空气以提高燃料的利用率（A），但又不希望发动机罩与地面的距离减少以保证飞机的安全性（B）。现将该技术冲突转变为物理冲突：发动机罩的直径（C）应该加大，以吸入更多的空气，但机罩直径（C）又不能加大，以不使路面与机罩之间的距离减少。

➢ **Example 4-2** A technical conflict occurred in the process of Boeing's 737 design improvement: it not only hopes that the engine will inhale more air to improve fuel utilization (A), but also does not want to reduce the distance between the hood and the ground to ensure the safety of the aircraft (B). Now the technical conflict is transformed into physical conflict: the diameter (C) of the hood should be increased to absorb more air, but the diameter (C) of the hood should not be increased to avoid reducing the distance between the road and the hood.

4.6 本 章 小 结
4.6 Summary of this chapter

冲突广泛存在于产品设计之中，发现冲突并彻底地解决冲突是创新设计的核心，通过不断地解决产品中的冲突使产品的性能不断提高。本章介绍了冲突的分类，并详细介绍了技术冲突与物理冲突，重点介绍了技术冲突和物理冲突出现的情况，并用不同领域中的实例说明两种冲突的特征、区别和联系。TRIZ 的核心是解决冲突，本章还介绍了 TRIZ 与其他理论结合的冲突分析方法，指导设计人员如能发现待设计产品或已有产品中的冲突。本章介绍的确定产品设计中冲突的四种方法，即基于物质-场分析的冲突分析方法、基于 QFD 的冲突分析方法、基于 AD 的冲突分析方法和基于 TOC 的冲突分析方法。第一种方法特别适用于已有产品冲突的确定，第二、三、四种方法既适用于全新产品开发，也适用于已有产品的改进设计。本章的方法与后面几章的内容结合，将形成从冲突确定，到冲突求解的系统化方法，并用于指导创新设计。

Conflict exists widely in product design. The core of innovative design is to find and solve the conflict thoroughly. By constantly solving the conflict in the product, the performance of the product is improved. This chapter introduces the classification of conflict, and introduces the technical conflict and physical conflict in detail, focusing on the situation of technical conflict and physical conflict, and illustrates the characteristics, differences and relations of the two conflicts with examples in different fields. As the core of TRIZ is to solve conflicts, this chapter also introduces the conflict analysis method of TRIZ combined with other theories to guide designers to find conflicts in products to be designed or existing products. This chapter introduces four methods to determine conflicts in product design: conflict analysis method based on matter field analysis, conflict analysis method based on QFD, conflict analysis method based on AD and conflict analysis method based on TOC. The first method is especially suitable for the determination of existing product conflicts. The second, third and fourth methods are suitable for both new product development and improved design of existing products. The method of this chapter combined with the content of the following chapters will form a systematic method from conflict determination to conflict resolution, and will be used to guide innovative design.

5 冲突解决理论
Chapter 5 Conflict Resolution Theory

5.1 概 述
5.1 Overview

在技术创新的历史中，人类已完成了很多产品的设计，一些设计人员或发明家已积累了很多发明创造的经验。进入 20 世纪，技术创新已逐渐成为企业市场竞争的焦点。为了指导技术创新，一些研究人员开始总结前人发明创造的经验。这种经验的总结可分为适应于本领域的经验与适应于不同领域的通用经验两类。

In the history of technological innovation, human beings have completed a lot of product design, and some designers or inventors have accumulated a lot of experience in invention and creation. In the 20th century, technological innovation has gradually become the focus of market competition. In order to guide technological innovation, some researchers began to summarize the experience of previous inventions. This kind of experience can be divided into two categories: the experience adapted to this field and the general experience adapted to different fields.

第一类经验主要由本领域的专家、研究人员本身总结，或与这些人员讨论并整理总结。这些经验对指导本领域的产品创新有一定的参考意义，但对其他领域的创新意义不大。第二类经验由专门研究人员对不同领域的已有创新成果进行分析、总结，得到具有普遍意义的规律，这些规律对指导不同领域的产品创新都有重要参考价值。

The first type of experience is mainly summarized by experts and researchers in this field, or discussed with them. These experiences have certain reference significance for guiding product innovation in this field, but have little significance for innovation in other fields. The second type of experience is analyzed and summarized by special researchers on the existing innovation achievements in different fields, and the general rules are obtained, which have important reference value for guiding product innovation in different fields.

TRIZ 中的冲突解决原理属于第二类经验，这些原理是在分析全世界大量专利的基础上提出的。通过对专利的分析，TRIZ 研究人员发现，在以往不同领域的发明中所用到的规则并不多，不同时代的发明，不同领域的发明，这些规则反复被采用。每条规则并不限定于仅能用于某一领域，融合了物理的、化学的以及各工程领域的原理，适用于不同领域的发明创造。

The conflict resolution principles in TRIZ belong to the second kind of experience, which are based on the analysis of a large number of patents in the world. Through the analysis of patents, TRIZ researchers found that in the past, there were not many rules used in inventions in different fields. For inventions in different times and in different fields, these rules were repeatedly adopted. Each rule is not limited to a certain field, it integrates the principles of physical, chemical and engineering fields, and is suitable for invention and creation in different fields.

本章将介绍解决技术冲突的发明原理和解决物理冲突的分离原理以及相关工程案例。

This chapter will introduce the invention principle of solving technical conflict and the separation principle of solving physical conflict, as well as related engineering cases.

5.2 技术冲突解决理论
5.2 Technology conflict resolution theory

5.2.1 发明原理
5.2.1 Principle of invention

在对全世界专利进行分析研究的基础上，Altshuller 等提出了 40 条发明原理。实践证明，这些原理对于指导设计人员的发明创造具有重要的作用。表 5-1 是 40 条发明原理的名称。

On the basis of analyzing and studying the patents all over the world, Altshuller and others put forward 40 principles of invention. Practice has proved that these principles play an important role in guiding designers' invention and creation. Table 5-1 shows the names of 40 principles of the invention.

表 5-1 40 条发明原理
Table 5-1 40 principles of invention

序号 Serial	名称 Name	序号 Serial	名称 Name
No. 1	分割 Division	No. 7	套装 Package
No. 2	分离 Separation	No. 8	重量补偿 Weight compensation
No. 3	局部质量 Local mass	No. 9	预加反作用 Pre-action
No. 4	不对称 Asymmetric	No. 10	预操作 Pre-operation
No. 5	合并 Consolidation	No. 11	预补偿 Pre-compensation
No. 6	多用性 Multipurpose	No. 12	等势性 Isopotential

序号 Serial	名称 Name	序号 Serial	名称 Name
No. 13	反向 Reverse	No. 28	机械系统的替代 Replacement of mechanical systems
No. 14	曲面化 Surfaces	No. 29	气动与液压结构 Pneumatic and hydraulic structures
No. 15	动态化 Dynamic		
No. 16	未达到或超过的作用 Effects not achieved or exceeded	No. 30	柔性壳体或薄膜 Flexible shell or film
NO. 17	维数变化 Change in dimension	No. 31	多孔材料 Porous materials
No. 18	振动 Vibration		
No. 19	周期性作用 Periodicity	No. 32	改变颜色 Change colors
No. 20	有效作用的连续性 Continuity of effective action	No. 33	同质性 Homogeneity
No. 21	紧急行动 Urgent action	No. 34	抛弃与修复 Abandonment and rehabilitation
No. 22	变有害为有益 Turn harmful into beneficial		
No. 23	反馈 Feedback	No. 35	参数变化 Changes in parameters
No. 24	中介物 Intermediates	No. 36	状态变化 State change
No. 25	自服务 Self-discipline	No. 37	热膨胀 Thermal expansion
No. 26	复制 Copy	No. 38	加速强氧化 Accelerating strong oxidation
No. 27	低成本、不耐用的物体 代替昂贵、耐用的物体 Low-cost, non-durable objects instead of expensive, durable objects	No. 39	惰性环境 Inert environment
		No. 40	复合材料 Composite materials

下面将对各发明原理的含义及应用实例进行详细介绍。

The meaning and application examples of each invention principle will be introduced in detail below.

5.2.1.1　发明原理 1：分割

5.2.1.1　Principle of invention 1：division

将一个物体分成相互独立的部分，例：

（1）用多台个人计算机代替一台大型计算机完成相同的功能；

（2）用一辆卡车加拖车代替一辆载重量大的卡车；

（3）将大的工程项目分解为子项目；

（4）强势、弱势、机会、危险（SWOT）分析；

（5）多房间、多层住宅群；

（6）将企业的办公区与制造车间分开。

To divide an object into separate parts, for example：

（1）Using multiple personal computers instead of a large computer to complete the same function；

（2）Replace a heavy truck with a truck and trailer；

（3）Decompose a large project into subprojects；

（4）SWOT analysis of strength, weakness, opportunity and danger；

（5）Multi room and multi-storey residential complex；

（6）Separate the office area from the manufacturing workshop.

5.2.1.2 发明原理2：分离

5.2.1.2 Principle of invention 2：separation

（1）将一个物体中的"干扰"部分分离出去，例：

1）在飞机场环境中，采用播放刺激鸟类的声音使鸟与机场分离；

2）将空调中产生噪声的空气压缩机放于室外；

3）别墅中的车库。

（2）将物体中的关键部分挑选或分离出来，例：

1）飞机场候机大厅中的专用吸烟室；

2）加工车间中的休息室；

3）办公区中的透明（如玻璃）隔离室。

（1）Separate the "interfering" part of an object, for example：

1）In the airport environment, the sound of stimulating birds is played to separate the birds from the airport；

2）Put the air compressor that produces noise in the air conditioner outdoors；

3）Garage in Villa.

（2）To select or separate key parts of an object, for example：

1）Special smoking room in airport waiting hall；

2）Rest room in processing workshop；

3）A transparent（e. g. glass）isolation room in an office area.

5.2.1.3 发明原理3：局部质量

5.2.1.3 Principle of invention 3：local mass

（1）将物体或环境的均匀结构变成不均匀结构，例：

1）用变化中的压力、温度、或密度代替正常的压力、温度或密度；

2）不采用刚性工资结构，而采用计件工资；

3）弹性工作时间；

4）无噪声工作区；

5）材料表面的热处理、涂层、自清洁处理等；

6）增加建筑物下部墙的厚度使其能承受更大的负载；

7）混凝土中的非均匀分布钢筋产生所需要的强度特性；

8）石工术中的拱形。

（2）使组成物体的不同部分完成不同的功能，例：

1）午餐盒被分成放热食、冷食及液体的空间，每个空间功能不同；

2）使每个雇员的工作位置适应其生理、心理需要，以最大限度地发挥作用；

3）定制式软件；

4）根据不同功能需求将房间设计成不同形状。

（3）使组成物体的每一部分都最大限度地发挥作用，例：

1）带有橡皮的铅笔，带有起钉器的榔头等；

2）按功能划分机构，而不是按产品划分；

3）具有一流研究条件中的一流研究人员；

4）雇用本地雇员以适应本地文化特色；

5）有线电视提供电话、互联网、远程医疗诊断等服务；

6）屋顶上的通风瓷砖；

7）阻燃油漆。

（1）To change the uniform structure of an object or environment into an inhomogeneous structure, for example:

1）Replacing steady pressure, temperature or density with changing pressure, temperature or density;

2）Instead of adopting rigid wage structure, we should adopt piecework wage;

3）Flexible working hours;

4）Noiseless working area;

5）Material surface heat treatment, coating, self-cleaning treatment, etc;

6）Increase the thickness of the lower wall of the building so that it can bear more load;

7）The non-uniform distribution of reinforcement in concrete produces the required strength characteristics;

8）Arch in stonework.

（2）To make different parts of an object perform different functions, for example:

1）Lunch boxes are divided into spaces for hot food, cold food and liquid, each space has different functions;

2）So that each employee's work position to adapt to their physical and psychological needs, in order to maximize the role;

3）Customized software;

4）According to different functional requirements, the room is designed into different shapes.

（3）Make every part of an object work to the maximum，for example：

1）Pencil with rubber，hammer with stapler，etc；

2）Organization by function，not by product；

3）First class researchers with first class research conditions；

4）Employ local employees to adapt to local culture；

5）Cable TV provides telephone，Internet，telemedicine diagnosis and other services；

6）Ventilation tiles on the roof；

7）Flame retardant paint.

5.2.1.4　发明原理4：不对称

5.2.1.4　Principle of invention 4：asymmetric

（1）将物体的形状由对称变为不对称，例：

1）不对称搅拌容器，或对称搅拌容器中的不对称叶片；

2）将O形圈的截面形状改为其他形状，以改善其密封性能；

3）非正态分布；

4）对不同的顾客群采用不同的营销策略；

5）非圆截面的烟囱改变气流的分布；

6）倾斜的屋顶。

（2）如果物体是不对称的，增加其不对称的程度，例：

1）轮胎的一侧强度大于另一侧，以增加其抗冲击的能力；

2）管理者与雇员之间的双向对话；

3）复合的多斜面屋顶；

4）钢索加固的悬臂式屋顶。

（1）Change the shape of an object from symmetry to asymmetry，for example：

1）Asymmetric stirring vessel，or asymmetric blade in symmetric stirring vessel；

2）In order to improve the sealing performance，the cross-section shape of O-ring is changed to other shapes；

3）Non normal distribution；

4）Adopt different marketing strategies for different customer groups；

5）The chimney with non-circular cross section changes the distribution of air flow；

6）A sloping roof.

（2）If the object is asymmetric，increase the degree of asymmetry，for example：

1）The strength of one side of a tire is greater than that of the other side to increase its impact resistance；

2）Two way dialogue between managers and employees；

3）Composite multi slope roof；

4）Cable reinforced cantilever roof.

5.2.1.5　发明原理5：合并

5.2.1.5　Principle of invention 5：consolidation

（1）在空间上将相似的物体连接在一起，使其完成并行的操作，例：

1）网络中的个人计算机；

2）安装在电路板两面的集成电路；

3）单元制造技术；

4）具有相关产品的公司合并；

5）双板散热器；

6）多功能厅。

（2）在时间上合并相似或相连的操作，例：

1）同时分析多个血液参数的医疗诊断仪；

2）具有保护根部功能的草坪割草机；

3）设计过程中倾听用户的意见；

4）多媒体演示；

5）气、光缆、电等的协同定位服务，最大限度地减少地下管网的施工工作量；

6）混水阀；

7）预先制造的配件。

（1）Connect similar objects together in space to complete parallel operation, for example：

1）Personal computer in network；

2）Integrated circuits installed on both sides of a circuit board；

3）Cell manufacturing technology；

4）Merger of companies with related products；

5）Double plate radiator；

6）Multifunction Room.

（2）Merging similar or connected operations in time, for example：

1）A medical diagnostic instrument for simultaneously analyzing multiple blood parameters；

2）Lawn mower with root protection function；

3）Listen to users' opinions in the design process；

4）Multimedia presentation；

5）The collaborative positioning service of gas, optical cable and electricity can minimize the construction workload of underground pipe network；

6）Mixing valve；

7）Pre manufactured accessories.

5.2.1.6　发明原理6：多用性

5.2.1.6　Principle of invention 6：multipurpose

（1）使一个物体能完成多项功能，可以减少原设计中完成这些功能多个物体的数量，例：

1）装有牙膏的牙刷柄；

2）能用作婴儿车的儿童安全座椅；

3）一站购物：超市提供保险、银行服务，销售燃料、报纸及各种日用品；

4）快速反应部队；

5）房间中自带壁橱；

6）同时具备透明、隔热、透气功能的窗户；

7）屋顶的水箱既能隔热又提供水头。

（2）利用标准的特性，例：

1）采用国际或国家标准，如安全标准；

2）采用具有标准尺寸的空心砖；

3）采用标准件，如螺钉、螺母等；

4）采用 STEP 标准。

（1）Making an object complete multiple functions can reduce the number of multiple objects to complete these functions in the original design, for example：

1）Toothbrush handle with toothpaste；

2）It can be used as a child safety seat for baby carriage；

3）One stop shopping：supermarkets provide insurance, banking services, selling fuel, newspapers and various daily necessities；

4）Rapid response force；

5）The room has its own closet；

6）Windows with transparent, heat insulation and ventilation functions；

7）The water tanks on the roof provide both heat insulation and water head.

（2）Using the characteristics of the standard, for example：

1）Adopt international or national standards, such as safety standards；

2）Use hollow brick with standard size；

3）Use standard parts, such as screws, nuts, etc；

4）Adopt step standard.

5.2.1.7 发明原理7：套装

5.2.1.7 Principle of invention 7：package

（1）将一个物体放在第二个物体中，将第二个物体放在第三个物体中，可进行下去，例：

1）儿童玩具不倒翁；

2）套装式油罐，内罐装黏度较高的油，外罐装黏度较低的油；

3）仓库中的仓库；

4）雇员的层次结构，如基本的、环境相关、简单知识结构的、复合型的、卓越的；

5）超市中的监视系统；

6）在墙内或地板内设置保险箱；

7）在三维结构中设置空腔；

8）地板内部沟槽式加热方式；

9）布在墙内的电缆。

（2）使一个物体穿过另一物体的空腔，例：

1）收音机伸缩式天线；

2）伸缩液压缸；

3）伸缩式钓鱼竿；

4）汽车安全带卷收器；

5）音乐厅观众席内的可回收式座椅；

6）带有空气加热系统的商场出/入口循环空间；

7）可回收楼梯；

8）推拉门。

（1）Put one object in the second object, put the second object in the third object, can go on, for example：

1）Children's toy tumbler；

2）The inner tank is filled with oil with higher viscosity and the outer tank is filled with oil with lower viscosity；

3）Warehouse in warehouse；

4）Employee's hierarchy, such as basic, environment related, simple knowledge structure, compound and excellent；

5）Monitoring system in supermarket；

6）Set a safe in the wall or floor；

7）Setting cavities in 3D structures；

8）Grooved heating method in floor；

9）Cables in walls.

（2）To pass one object through a cavity in another, for example：

1）Radio telescopic antenna；

2）Telescopic hydraulic cylinder；

3）Telescopic fishing rod；

4）Automobile safety belt retractor；

5）Recyclable seats in auditorium of Concert Hall；

6）Circulation space of entrance / exit of shopping mall with air heating system；

7）Recyclable stairs；

8）Sliding door.

5.2.1.8 发明原理8：重量补偿

5.2.1.8 Principle of invention 8: weight compensation

（1）用另一个能产生提升力的物体补偿第一个物体的重量，例：

1）在圆木中注入发泡剂，使其更好地漂浮；

2）用气球携带广告条幅；

3）合并的两公司中，一个以其自身的资金、核心技术、市场等优势提升另一个；

4）公司中借助于一种旺销产品促进另一种产品的销售；

5）浮动门；

6）起重机配重；

7）大型阀门控制系统配重。

（2）通过与环境相互作用产生空气动力或液体动力的方法补偿第一个物体的重量，例：

1）飞机机翼的形状使其上部空气压力减少，下部压力增加，以产生升力；

2）升力涡轮改善飞机机翼所产生的升力；

3）船在航行过程中船身浮出水面，以减少阻力；

4）小公司借助于环境中的某种资源（如邮局快递业务）提升自己；

5）采用产品加服务的营销策略；

6）游艇；

7）被动式太阳能加热器采用自然方式使水循环。

（1）Compensate the weight of the first object with another object that produces lifting force, for example：

1）Inject foaming agent into the log to make it float better；

2）Carrying advertising banners with balloons；

3）Among the two companies merged, one promotes the other with its own capital, core technology, market and other advantages；

4）The company promotes the sale of another product with the help of one popular product；

5）Floating door；

6）Crane counterweight；

7）Counterweight of large valve control system.

（2）Compensates the weight of the first object by interacting with the environment to generate aerodynamic or hydrodynamic forces, for example：

1）The shape of an aircraft wing reduces the upper air pressure and increases the lower pressure to produce lift；

2）A lift turbine improves the lift of an aircraft wing；

3）In the course of sailing, the hull surfaced to reduce resistance；

4）Small companies improve themselves with the help of certain resources in the environment（such aspost office express service）；

5）Adopt the marketing strategy of product plus service；

6）Yacht；

7）Passive solar heater uses natural way to make water circulation.

5.2.1.9　发明原理9：预加反作用

5.2.1.9　Principle of invention 9：pre-action

（1）预先施加反作用，例：

1）缓冲器能吸收能量、减少冲击带来的负面影响；

2）当向公众公布消息时，要包括消息的全部内容，而不仅仅是负面的消息；

3）在项目开始前，采用形式化风险评估方法确定风险并消除风险；

4）新产品的用户实验、分期分批投放市场；

5）使用可循环的材料；

6）使用可再生的能量。

（2）如果某一物体处于或将处于受拉伸状态，预先增加压力，例：

1）浇混凝土之前的预压缩钢筋；

2）在从事产品开发活动之前，Epson 的工程师要从事销售及售后服务工作；

3）失业潮发生前，要准备提供所涉及雇员的补偿、新职介绍；

4）预压缩螺栓；

5）允许水蒸气穿透的油漆能预防木材的腐烂；

6）分开相异的金属可防止电解腐蚀。

（1）Pre reaction, for example：

1）The buffer can absorb energy and reduce the negative impact of impact；

2）When publishing news to the public, it should include all the contents of the news, not just the negative news；

3）Before the start of the project, the formal risk assessment method is used to identify and eliminate the risks；

4）User experiment of new products and putting them on the market by stages and batches；

5）Use recyclable materials；

6）Use renewable energy.

（2）If an object is or will be stretched, increase the pressure in advance, for example：

1）Pre compressed steel bar before concrete pouring；

2）Epson's engineers are engaged in sales and after-sales services before engaging in product development activities；

3）Before the occurrence of unemployment, we should be prepared to provide compensation and new job introduction for the employees involved；

4）Precompression bolt；

5）Paint that allows water vapor to penetrate prevents wood from rotting；

6）Separating dissimilar metals prevents electrolytic corrosion.

5.2.1.10 发明原理 10：预操作

5.2.1.10 Principle of invention 10：pre-operation

（1）在操作开始前，使物体局部或全部产生所需的变化，例：

1）预先涂上胶的壁纸；

2）在手术前为所有器械杀菌；

3）项目的预先计划；

4）尽早完成非关键路径的任务；

5）在改变管理与经营中的重大活动前与雇员们对话；

6）供应链管理；

7）预制窗户单元、洗澡间或其他结构；

8）已搅拌好的水泥；

9）预先充有焊料的铜管连接件。

（2）预先对物体进行特殊安排，使其在时间上有准备，或已处于易操作的位置，例：

1）柔性生产单元；

2）灌装生产线中使所有瓶口朝一个方向，以增加灌装效率；

3）开会前要有确定的议程；

4）磨刀不误砍柴工；

5）汽车零部件供应商的预先装配，如 CD 机、车轮、空调等；

6）中央真空清扫系统；

7）点火系统；

8）停车场内的预付款机。

（1）Before the start of operation, make the required changes to the whole or part of the object, for example：

1）Wallpaper pre coated with glue；

2）Sterilize all instruments before operation；

3）Advance planning of the project；

4）Complete non critical path tasks as early as possible；

5）Dialogue with employees before major activities in management and operation change；

6）Supply chain management；

7）Prefabricated window units, bathrooms or other structures；

8）Mixed cement；

9）Copper pipe connectors pre filled with solder.

（2）Make special arrangements for objects in advance, so that they are ready in time or in easy to operate position, for example：

1）Flexible production unit；

2）In the filling production line, all the bottle mouths are in one direction to increase the filling efficiency；

　　3）There should be a definite agenda before the meeting；

　　4）Sharpening the knife does not make mistakes in cutting firewood；

　　5）Pre assembly of auto parts suppliers，such as CD player，wheel，air conditioner，etc；

　　6）Central vacuum cleaning system；

　　7）Ignition system；

　　8）Prepaid machines in car parks.

5.2.1.11　发明原理 11：预补偿

5.2.1.11　Principle of invention 11：pre-compensation

采用预先准备好的应急措施补偿物体相对较低的可靠性，例：

（1）飞机上的降落伞；

（2）汽车安全气囊；

（3）应急电路照明；

（4）双通道控制系统；

（5）防火通道；

（6）避雷针；

（7）安全阀；

（8）抗 SARS 预案；

（9）谈判前考虑最坏情况及最不利的位置；

（10）备份计算机数据；

（11）运行反病毒软件。

The relatively low reliability of the object is compensated by pre prepared emergency measures for example：

　　（1）Parachute on an airplane；

　　（2）Automobile airbag；

　　（3）Emergency circuit lighting；

　　（4）Dual channel control system；

　　（5）Fire escape；

　　（6）Lightning arrester；

　　（7）Safety valve；

　　（8）Anti SARS plan；

　　（9）Consider the worst case and the most unfavorable position before negotiation；

　　（10）Backup computer data；

　　（11）Run anti virus software.

5.2.1.12　发明原理 12：等势性

5.2.1.12　Principle of invention 12：isopotential

改变工作条件，使物体不需要被升高或降低，例：

（1）与冲床工作台高度相同的工件输送带，将冲好的零件输送到另一工位；

（2）通过压力补偿所形成的等压面；

（3）汽车修理平台汽车高度不变，修理工改变位置；

（4）在同级别的不同单位工作以扩大知识面；

（5）每个雇员都倾向于提高工作水平，以达到公司内部公认的标准。

Change working conditions so that objects do not need to be raised or lowered, for example：

（1）The workpiece conveyor belt with the same height as the punch table conveys the punched parts to another station；

（2）Isobaric surface formed by pressure compensation；

（3）The height of the car remains the same, and the repairman changes his position；

（4）Work in different units at the same level to expand knowledge；

（5）Every employee tends to improve their work to meet the recognized standards within the company.

5.2.1.13　发明原理13：反向

5.2.1.13　Principle of invention 13：reverse

（1）将一个问题说明中所规定的操作改为相反的操作，例：

1）为了拆卸处于紧配合的两个零件，采用冷却内部零件的方法，而不采用加热外部零件的方法；

2）在工商业衰退期进行企业扩张而不是收缩；

3）制定最坏状态的标准，而不制定最理想状态的标准；

4）发现过程中的失误，而不责怪过程中的人；

5）自服务柜台；

6）开放式监狱；

7）翻转型窗户，使在屋内擦外面的玻璃成为可能。

（2）使物体中的运动部分静止，静止部分运动，例：

1）使工件旋转，使刀具固定；

2）扶梯运动，乘客相对扶梯静止；

3）风洞中的飞机静止；

4）送货上门；

5）用信用卡，不用现金；

6）拥挤城市中的停车与上路计划；

7）假如你遵循了所有的规则，你会失去所有乐趣。

（3）使一个物体的位置颠倒，例：

1）将一个部件或机器总成翻转，以安装紧固件；

2）楼上为起居室（美景），楼下为卧室（凉爽）；

3）步行街；

4）劳埃德建筑将管路等置于外部，而不是内部；

5）苏联政府为专利申请者付费，西方国家的专利申请者要为专利申请付费。

（1）Change the operation specified in a problem description to the opposite, for example：

1）In order to remove two parts in a tight fit, the method of cooling the internal parts is adopted instead of heating the external parts;

2）Expansion rather than contraction in a recession;

3）Set standards for the worst, not the best;

4）Discover the mistakes in the process without blaming the people in the process;

5）Self service counter;

6）Open prison;

7）Flipped windows make it possible to clean the outside glass inside the house.

（2）To make the moving part of an object stand still and the stationary part move, for example：

1）Make the workpiece rotate and fix the tool;

2）The escalator is moving and the passengers are stationary relative to the escalator;

3）Aircraft standstill in wind tunnel;

4）Provide home delivery service;

5）Credit card, no cash;

6）Parking and road planning in crowded cities;

7）If you follow all the rules, you will lose all the fun.

（3）To reverse the position of an object, for example：

1）Turn over a component or machine assembly to install a fastener;

2）Upstairs for the living room (beautiful scenery), downstairs for the bedroom (cool);

3）Pedestrian Street;

4）Lloyd's architecture places piping, etc. outside, not inside;

5）The Soviet Union government pays for patent applicants, while western countries pay for patent applications.

5.2.1.14　*发明原理14：曲面化*

5.2.1.14　Principle of invention 14：surfaces

（1）将直线或平面部分用曲线或曲面代替，立方形用球形代替，例：
1）为了增加建筑结构的强度，采用弧形或拱形;
2）绕过一些官僚机构，以最短的路径到达用户;
3）在结构的某些位置引入应力释放孔;
4）环形截面建筑物;
5）利用最少的材料覆盖最大的空间。
（2）采用辊、球、螺旋，例：
1）螺旋齿轮提供均匀的承载能力;

2）采用球或滚珠为笔尖的钢笔增加了墨水的均匀程度；

3）车轮上的晚餐—上门送餐服务；

4）图书馆上门送书服务；

5）阿基米德螺线水泥泵；

6）螺旋形楼梯；

7）鼠标采用球形结构产生计算器屏幕内光标的运动。

（3）用旋转运动代替直线运动，采用离心力，例：

1）洗衣机采用旋转产生离心力的方法，去除湿衣服中的部分水分；

2）宾馆的旋转门保持室内的温度；

3）高层建筑上的旋转餐厅；

4）带有螺纹的螺杆；

5）离心铸造；

6）轮流坐庄；

7）环行工作单元。

（1）The straight line or plane part is replaced by curve or surface, and the cubic part is replaced by sphere, for example:

1）In order to increase the strength of the building structure, arc or arch is used;

2）Bypass some bureaucracies and get to users in the shortest way;

3）Stress relief holes are introduced in some positions of the structure;

4）Circular section building;

5）Cover the largest space with the least material.

（2）Using roller, ball and screw, for example:

1）Helical gears provide uniform load carrying capacity;

2）A pen with a ball or ball tip increases the uniformity of the ink;

3）Dinner on wheels door to door service;

4）Library door to door book delivery service;

5）Archimedes spiral cement pump;

6）Spiral staircase;

7）The mouse uses the spherical structure to produce the movement of the cursor in the calculator screen.

（3）The linear motion is replaced by the rotary motion and the centrifugal force is used, for example:

1）The washing machine uses the method of centrifugal force generated by rotation to remove part of the moisture in wet clothes;

2）The revolving door of the hotel keeps the temperature in the room;

3）Revolving restaurant on high rise building;

4）Screw with thread;

5）Centrifugal casting;

6）Take turns in business;

7）Circular work unit.

5.2.1.15　发明原理15：动态化

5.2.1.15　Principle of invention 15：dynamic

（1）使一个物体或其环境在操作的每一个阶段自动调整，以达到优化的性能，例：

1）可调整驱动轮、可调整座椅、可调整反光镜；

2）用户快速响应小组；

3）过程的连续改进；

4）形状记忆合金；

5）柔性写字间布置。

（2）划分一个物体成具有相互关系的元件，元件之间可以改变相对位置，例：

1）计算机蝶形键盘；

2）链条；

3）竹片凉席。

（3）如果一个物体是刚性的，使之变为可活动的或可改变的，例：

1）检测发动机用柔性光学内孔检测仪；

2）可回收房顶结构；

3）浮动房顶；

4）电梯代替楼梯；

5）冗余结构；

6）无级变速器。

（1）Make an object or its environment automatically adjust at every stage of operation to achieve optimal performance, for example：

1）Adjustable driving wheel, adjustable seat and adjustable reflector；

2）User quick response team；

3）Continuous process improvement；

4）Shape memory alloy；

5）Flexible office layout.

（2）Divide an object into components with mutual relationship, and the relative positions of components can be changed, for example：

1）Computer butterfly keyboard；

2）Chain；

3）Bamboo mat.

（3）If an object is rigid, make it movable or changeable, for example：

1）Flexible optical bore detector for testing engine；

2）Recyclable roof structure；

3）Floating roof；

4）Elevators instead of stairs；

5) Redundant structure;

6) Continuously variable transmission.

5.2.1.16 发明原理 16：未达到或超过的作用

5.2.1.16 Principle of invention 16：effects not achieved or exceeded

如果 100% 达到所希望的效果是困难的，稍微未达到或超过预期的效果将大大简化问题，例：

（1）缸筒外壁刷漆可将缸筒浸泡在盛漆的容器中完成，但取出缸筒后外壁粘漆太多；

（2）可通过快速旋转可以甩掉多余的漆；

（3）用灰泥填墙上的小洞时首先多填一些，之后再将多余的部分去掉；

（4）对于某些设计，如供热系统、停车场，满足 95% 的需求通常是一种实际的设计；

（5）由一定技术水平的工人或技术人员完成预制件的安装。

If it is difficult to achieve the desired effect by 100%, it will greatly simplify the problem if the expected effect is not achieved or exceeded slight, for example：

（1）The painting of the outer wall of the cylinder can be completed by immersing the cylinder in the paint container, but there is too much paint on the outer wall after taking out the cylinder；

（2）The excess paint can be removed by rapid rotation；

（3）When filling small holes in the wall with plaster, first fill in more and then remove the excess；

（4）For some designs, such as heating system and parking lot, meeting 95% of the demand is usually a practical design；

（5）The installation of prefabricated parts shall be completed by workers or technicians with certain technical level.

5.2.1.17 发明原理 17：维数变化

5.2.1.17 Principle of invention 17：change in dimension

（1）将一维空间中运动或静止的物体变成在二维空间中运动或静止的物体，在二维空间中的物体变成三维空间中的物体，例：

1) 为了扫描物体，红外线计算机鼠标在三维空间运动，而不是在平面内运动；

2) 五轴机床的刀具可被定位到任意所需的位置上；

3) 全面评估；

4) 多维组织层次图，如 3 维或 4 维（包括时间）；

5) 质量部门提出质量要求并检查，每个员工负责自己工序的质量；

6) 用三角形改进框架结构的强度及稳定性；

7) 金字塔结构（非垂直墙结构）；

8) 间接光线；

9）槽型固定装置；

10）螺旋形楼道节省空间；

11）波浪形的屋顶材料刚度高且重量轻。

（2）将物体用多层排列代替单层排列，例：

1）能装 6 个 CD 盘的音响不仅增加了连续放音乐的时间，也增加了选择性；

2）立体车库；

3）立体仓库；

4）多用途建筑，如购物中心；

5）站在巨人的肩膀上。

（3）使物体倾斜或改变其方向，例：

1）自卸车；

2）思维模式从纵向转向横向，或从横向转向纵向；

3）管理模式由线管理转向项目管理。

（4）使用给定表面的反面，例：

1）叠层集成电路；

2）内嵌式门铰链；

3）由外部直接诊断一个机构，或通过咨询公司诊断该机构。

（1）In this paper, we change a moving or stationary object in one-dimensional space into a moving or stationary object in two-dimensional space, and an object in two-dimensional space into an object in three-dimensional space, for example：

1）In order to scan objects, the infrared computer mouse moves in three dimensions, not in a plane；

2）The cutting tool of five axis machine tool can be positioned at any desired position；

3）Comprehensive assessment；

4）Multi dimensional organization hierarchy, such as 3D or 4D（including time）；

5）The quality department puts forward quality requirements and checks, and each employee is responsible for the quality of his own process；

6）Improving the strength and stability of frame structure with triangle；

7）Pyramid structure（non vertical wall structure）；

8）Indirect light；

9）Slot type fixture；

10）Spiral corridor saves space；

11）The wavy roof material has high rigidity and light weight.

（2）Replace single layer arrangement with multi layer arrangement, for example：

1）The sound system with six CDs not only increases the time of playing music continuously, but also increases the selectivity；

2）Stereo garage；

3）Stereoscopic warehouse；

4）Multi purpose buildings such as shopping malls；

5) Standing on the shoulders of giants.

(3) Tilt or change the direction of an object, for example:

1) Dump truck;

2) Mode of thinking from vertical to horizontal, or from horizontal to vertical;

3) From line management to project management.

(4) Use the opposite side of a given surface, for example:

1) Stacked integrated circuit;

2) Embedded dumpling chain;

3) Diagnose an institution directly from outside or through a consulting firm.

5.2.1.18 发明原理 18：振动
5.2.1.18 Principle of invention 18: vibration

(1) 使物体处于振动状态，例：

1) 电动雕刻刀具有振动刀片；

2) 振动棒的有效工作可避免水泥中的空穴；

3) 一个机构中所害怕的波动、骚动、不平衡正是创新的源泉。

(2) 如果振动存在，增加其频率，甚至可以增加到超声，例：

1) 通过振动分选粉末；

2) 采用时事通信、互联网、会议等多种形式频繁交流；

3) 我们所处的信息时代强烈地影响着世界；

4) 用白噪声伪装谈话；

5) 超声清洗；

6) 超声探伤。

(3) 使用共振频率，例：

1) 利用超声共振消除胆结石或肾结石；

2) 制订战略计划使机构处于谐振状态，在该谐振频率处，机构最容易实现突破策略；

3) "Kansei"—日文术语，表示产品与用户之间处于谐振状态；

4) 利用 H 型共鸣器吸收声音。

(4) 使压电振动代替机械振动，例：

1) 石英晶体振动驱动高精度的表；

2) 喷嘴处的石英振荡器改善流体雾化效果；

3) 将新鲜血液吸收到队伍中来；

4) 聘请顾问。

(5) 使超声振动与电磁场耦合，例：

1) 如在高频炉中混合合金；

2) 超声探伤；

3) 地球物理技术能协助确定地下的结构。

(1) Make the object vibrate, for example:

1) The electric carving knife has a vibrating blade;

2) The effective operation of the vibrator can avoid voids in the cement;

3) The volatility, turmoil and imbalance that anorganization fears is the source of innovation.

(2) If vibration exists, increasing its frequency can even increaseto ultrasonic, for example:

1) Powder separation by vibration;

2) Frequent communication in the form of newsletters, Internet, conferences, etc;

3) The information age we live in strongly influences the world;

4) Camouflage conversation with white noise;

5) Ultrasonic cleaning;

6) Ultrasonic inspection.

(3) Use resonance frequency, for example:

1) The use of ultrasound resonance to eliminate gallstones or kidney stones;

2) Make a strategic plan to keep the organization in resonance, at this resonance frequency, the organization is most likely to achieve breakthrough strategy;

3) "Kansei" is a Japanese term for resonance between products and users;

4) Using H-type resonator to absorb sound.

(4) Piezoelectric vibration instead of mechanical vibration, for example:

1) Quartz crystal vibration driven high precision watch;

2) Quartz oscillator at the nozzle improves the atomization effect;

3) Absorb fresh blood into the team;

4) Engagement of consultants.

(5) Coupling ultrasonic vibration with electromagnetic field, for example:

1) Mixing alloy in high frequency furnace;

2) Ultrasonic inspection;

3) Geophysical techniques can help determine the structure of the ground.

5.2.1.19 发明原理 19：周期性作用

5.2.1.19 Principle of invention 19：periodicity

(1) 用周期性运动或脉动代替连续运动，例：

1) 使报警器声音脉动变化，代替连续的报警声音；

2) 设计供热及光线管理系统时要充分考虑白天与夜间的温度及光；

3) 线效应不同；

4) 脉冲淋雨要比连续喷水淋雨省水；

5) 点焊；

6) 打桩；

7) 批量制造（外贸出口）；

8) 轮流坐庄（如 EU 轮值主席）；

9) 周期性休息可以更新人的某些观点；

10) 采用月报或周报代替年报。

(2) 对周期性的运动改变其运动频率，例：

1) 通过调频传递信息；

2) 用变幅值与变频率的报警器代替脉动报警器。

(3) 在作用之间增加新的作用，例：

1) 医用呼吸器系统中，每压迫胸部 5 次，呼吸 1 次；

2) 当过滤器暂停使用时，通过倒流将其冲洗干净；

3) 采用电池、飞轮等方法储存能量。

(1) Using periodic motion or pulsation instead of continuous motion, for example：

1) Make the alarm sound pulsating change, instead of continuous alarm sound；

2) When designing the heating and light management system, the temperature and light of day and night should be fully considered；

3) The line effect is different；

4) Pulse rain is more water saving than continuous spray rain；

5) Spot welding；

6) Piling；

7) Batch manufacturing (export)；

8) Take turns (e. g. EU chairman in office)；

9) Periodic rest can update some people's views；

10) Using monthly or weekly reports instead of annual reports.

(2) Change the frequency of periodic motion, for example：

1) Ttransmitting information through FM；

2) The pulse alarm is replaced by the alarm with variable amplitude and frequency.

(3) Add new effects between the effects, for example：

1) In the medical respirator system, every time the chest is compressed 5 times, one breath is taken；

2) When the filter is out of service, flush it through the inflow；

3) Battery and flywheel are used to store energy.

5.2.1.20 发明原理 20：有效作用的连续性

5.2.1.20 Principle of invention 20：continuity of effective action

(1) 不停顿地工作，物体的所有部件都应满负荷地工作，例：

1) 多岗位雇员；

2) 经常消除企业中的瓶颈问题，使企业处于最优的状态；

3) Otis 电梯的连续在线监测——全面售后服务职责；

4) 汽车保险中的 24h 服务——第一天无论在何处抛锚，第二天早饭前被拖回；

5) 瀑布的能量是无数水滴的能量之合。

(2) 消除运动过程中的中间间歇，例：

1）针式打印机的双向打印；

2）瓶颈处的多功能设备或操作者改变工作流程；

3）终身学习；

4）生产调整期的员工培训；

5）自清洁过滤器消除生产过程中的停顿；

6）快速干燥油漆。

（3）用旋转运动代替往复运动。

（1）Keep working, all parts of the object should work at full load, for example：

1）Multi position employees；

2）Often eliminate the bottleneck problem in the enterprise, make the enterprise in the optimal state；

3）Continuous online monitoring of Otis Elevator；

4）24-hour service in auto insurance-no matter where the anchor breaks down on the first day, it will be towed back before breakfast the next day；

5）The energy of a waterfall is the energy of countless drops of water.

（2）Eliminate the intermittence in the process of exercise, for example：

1）Bidirectional printing of needle printer；

2）The multi-functional equipment or operator at the bottleneck changes the workflow；

3）Lifelong learning；

4）Staff training in production adjustment period；

5）Self cleaning filter eliminates the pause in the production process；

6）Quick drying paint.

（3）Rotary motion instead of reciprocating motion.

5.2.1.21　发明原理21：紧急行动

5.2.1.21　Principle of invention 21：urgent action

以最快的速度完成有害的操作，例：

（1）修理牙齿的钻头高速旋转，以防止牙组织升温；

（2）在热量还没有传递前就突然切断了可塑制品，使其无变形；

（3）连续浇注水泥；

（4）渐进主义是创新的敌人；

（5）快速原型；

（6）快速经历痛苦的过程。

Complete harmful operations as quickly as possible, for example：

（1）The drill for repairing teeth rotates at high speed to prevent tooth tissue from heating up；

（2）Before the heat is transferred, the plastic product is suddenly cut off to make it no deformation；

（3）Continuous casting of cement；

（4）Gradualism is the enemy of innovation;

（5）Rapid prototyping;

（6）Go through the painful process quickly.

5.2.1.22 发明原理22：变有害为有益

5.2.1.22 Principle of invention 22: turn harmful into beneficial

（1）利用有害因素，特别是对环境有害的因素，获得有益的结果，例：

1）利用余热发电，利用秸秆作板材原料；

2）收集信息，找出有害因素，采取行动克服这些因素；

3）"激怒"是一种鼓励产生新想法的方法；

4）堆制肥料型厕所；

5）城市垃圾焚烧发电装置。

（2）通过与另一种有害因素结合消除一种有害因素，例：

1）用有毒的化学物质保护木材不受昆虫的袭击，且不腐蚀；

2）通过引入竞争力消除员工对变化的恐惧；

3）亏本销售策略能增加销售量；

4）通过增加市内停车费用，减少市外停车费用的策略，可以减轻市内交通拥挤状况。

（3）加大一种有害因素的程度使其不再有害，例：

1）善意的专政；

2）减少做某项工作的资源，以至于不得不发现新方法来解决问题；

3）限制某种产品的生产，使市场上该产品的供应不足。

（1）Using harmful factors, especially those harmful to the environment, to obtain beneficial results, for example:

1）Using waste heat to generate electricity, using straw as raw material for board;

2）Collect information, identify harmful factors and take action to overcome them;

3）Anger is a way to encourage new ideas;

4）Composting toilet;

5）Municipal solid waste incineration power plant.

（2）Eliminate one harmful factor by combining with another harmful factor, for example:

1）Use toxic chemicals to protect wood from insects and corrosion;

2）Eliminate employees' fear of change by introducing competitiveness;

3）Loss selling strategy can increase sales;

4）By increasing the parking cost in the city and reducing the parking cost outside the city, the traffic congestion in the city can be reduced.

（3）Increase the degree of a harmful factor to make it no longer harmful, for example:

1）Good will dictatorship;

2）Reduce the resources to do a job, so that we have to find new ways to solve the problem;

3）To restrict the production of a product so that it is in short supply on the market.

5.2.1.23　发明原理 23：反馈

5.2.1.23　Principle of invention 23：feedback

（1）引入反馈以改善过程或动作，例：

1）音频电路中的自动音量控制；

2）加工中心自动检测装置；

3）运动敏感光线控制系统（厕所光线敏感冲水系统）；

4）用于探测火与烟的热/烟传感器；

5）供应价格链管理；

6）统计过程控制（SPC）——用于确定修改过程的时间；

7）预算；

8）设计过程引入顾客参加。

（2）如果反馈已经存在，改变反馈控制信号的大小或灵敏度，例：

1）飞机接近机场时，改变自动驾驶系统的灵敏度；

2）在预算允许的范围内改变管理措施，以满足客户需求；

3）使设计人员及销售人员与客户紧密接触；

4）多标准决策分析；

5）在设计的早期阶段包含制造的信息；

6）含有模糊控制器的温度调节装置。

（1）Introduce feedback to improve process or action, for example：

1）Automatic volume control in audio circuit;

2）Automatic detection device of machining center;

3）Motion sensitive light control system（toilet light sensitive flushing system）;

4）Heat / smoke sensors for detecting fire and smoke;

5）Supply price chain management;

6）Statistical process control（SPC）-used to determine the timing of the modification process;

7）Budget;

8）Customer participation in design process.

（2）If the feedback already exists, change the size or sensitivity of the feedback control signal, for example：

1）When the aircraft approaches the airport, it changes the sensitivity of the autopilot system;

2）Change management measures within budget to meet customer needs;

3）Close contact between designers and salesmen and customers;

4）Multi criteria decision analysis;

5) Include manufacturing information in the early stages of design;

6) Temperature adjusting device with fuzzy controller.

5.2.1.24 发明原理 24：中介物

5.2.1.24 Principle of invention 24：Intermediates

（1） 使用中介物传递某一物体或某一种中间过程，例：

1) 机械传动中的惰轮；

2) 管路绝缘材料；

3) 催化剂；

4) 中介机构对项目的评估；

5) 产品生产企业与用户之间的总经销商；

6) 旅行社。

（2） 将一容易移动的物体与另一物体暂时结合，例：

1) 机械手抓取重物并移动该重物到另一处；

2) 请故障诊断专家帮助诊断设备；

3) 磨粒能改善水射流切割的效果 。

（1） The use of intermediaries to convey an object or an intermediate process，for example：

1) Idler in mechanical transmission；

2) Pipeline insulation material；

3) Catalyzer；

4) Evaluation of projects by intermediaries；

5) General distributor between product manufacturer and user；

6) Travel agency.

（2） To temporarily engage an easily moving object with another，for example：

1) A manipulator grabs a heavy object and moves it to another place；

2) Ask the fault diagnosis expert to help diagnose the equipment；

3) Abrasive particles can improve the effect of water jet cutting.

5.2.1.25 发明原理 25：自服务

5.2.1.25 Principle of invention 25：self-discipline

（1） 使某一物体通过附加功能产生自己服务于自己的功能，例：

1) 自清洁水槽——不会由于树叶或其他杂物堵塞；

2) 自排泄涂层；

3) 自测量匀泥尺；

4) 品牌效应环——哈佛管理学院培养了一些著名人士，这些人士增加了学院的知名度，很多学生申请入学，学院仅招收最优秀的学生，培养的学生也是最优秀的，形成了良性循环。

（2） 利用废弃的材料、能量与物质，例：

1）钢铁厂余热发电装置；

2）重新雇用有经验的退休员工，让他们发挥作用；

3）包装材料的再利用；

4）工业生态系统；

5）太阳能利用；

6）地热利用。

（1）Make an object produce its own service function through additional function，for example：

1）Self cleaning sink will not be blocked by leaves or other debris；

2）Self draining coating；

3）Self measuring mud leveling ruler；

4）Brand effect ring——Harvard School of management has trained some famous people，who have increased the popularity of the school. Many students apply for admission. The school only recruits the best students，and the students trained are the best，forming a virtuous circle.

（2）Utilization of waste materials，energy and materials，for example：

1）Waste heat power generation device in iron and steel plant；

2）Re hire experienced retirees and make them work；

3）Reuse of packaging materials；

4）Industrial ecosystem；

5）Utilization of solar energy；

6）Geothermal utilization.

5.2.1.26　发明原理26：复制

5.2.1.26　Principle of invention 26：copy

（1）用简单的、低廉的复制品代替复杂的、昂贵的、易碎的或不易操作的物体，例：

1）通过虚拟现实技术可以对未来的复杂系统进行研究；

2）通过对模型的实验来代替对真实系统的实验；

3）旅游景点的多媒体导游；

4）雕像。

（2）用光学拷贝或图像代替物体本身，可以放大或缩小图像，例：

1）通过看一名教授的讲座录像可代替亲身自参加他的讲座；

2）为了勘测，采用卫星或飞机上拍摄的照片代替陆地；

3）测量某一物体的照片代替测量该物体；

4）风景壁画。

（3）如果已使用了可见光拷贝，用红外线或紫外线代替，例：

1）利用红外线成像探测热源；

2）红外线成像可检测热源，如农作物的病虫害、安全保卫系统范围内的入侵者；

3）用紫外线作为无损探伤的一种方法；

4）用 X-射线检测结构缺陷。

（1）Replace complex, expensive, fragile, or difficult objects with simple, inexpensive copies, for example：

1）Through virtual reality technology, we can study the complex system in the future；

2）The experiment of real system is replaced by the experiment of model；

3）Multimedia guide of tourist attractions；

4）Statue.

（2）Using optical copy or image instead of the object itself can enlarge or reduce the image, for example：

1）Instead of attending a lecture in person, you can watch a video of a professor's lecture；

2）In order to survey, the land is replaced by pictures taken by satellites or airplanes；

3）A photograph of an object instead of measuring it；

4）Landscape fresco.

（3）If a visible copy has been used, use infrared or ultraviolet instead, for example：

1）Using infrared imaging to detect heat source；

2）Infrared imaging can detect heat sources, such as crop diseases and insect pests, intruders within the scope of security system；

3）Using ultraviolet as a method of nondestructive testing；

4）X-ray detection of structural defects.

5.2.1.27　发明原理27：低成本、不耐用的物体代替昂贵、耐用的物体

5.2.1.27　Principle of invention 27：low-cost, non-durable objects instead of expensive, durable objects

用一些低成本物体代替昂贵物体，用一些不耐用物体代替耐用物体，有关特性折中处理，例：

（1）一次性纸杯子；

（2）门前的擦鞋垫；

（3）有规律地涂漆，以免表面损坏；

（4）塑料整体一次成型椅子；

（5）汽车操纵动力学系统、飞机飞行、原子弹爆炸的计算机仿真；

（6）数字天气预报；

（7）飞行驾驶模拟器。

Some low-cost objects are used to replace expensive objects, and some non durable objects are used to replace durable objects, and compromise the relevant characteristics, for example：

（1）Disposable paper cup；

（2）Doormat；

（3）Paint regularly to avoid surface damage；

（4）One step plastic chair；

（5）Computer simulation of vehicle control dynamics system，aircraft flight and atomic bomb explosion；

（6）Digital weather forecast；

（7）Flight simulator.

5.2.1.28　发明原理28：机械系统的替代

5.2.1.28　Principle of invention 28：replacement of mechanical systems

（1）用视觉、听觉、嗅觉系统代替部分机械系统，例：

1）在天然气中混入难闻的气体代替机械或电子传感器来警告人们天然气的泄漏；

2）运动感知开关代替机械开关；

3）计算机之间的无线信息传输；

4）不透明镀层处理过的玻璃可以不用窗帘。

（2）用电场、磁场及电磁场完成与物体的相互作用，例：

1）为了混合两种粉末，使其中一种带正电荷，另一种带负电荷；

2）火警系统报警时，该系统所控制的电磁装置打开；

3）GPS系统能确定有关卡车或出租车的位置；

4）电子标签。

（3）将固定场变为移动场，将静态场变为动态场，将随机场确定场，例：

1）记忆中所形成的地图；

2）定点加热系统；

3）居住者能调节的房间彩色光线系统。

（4）将铁磁粒子用于场的作用之中，例：用变磁场加热含有铁磁材料的物质，当温度达到居里点时，铁磁材料变成顺磁体，不再吸收热量。

（1）Replace part of the mechanical system with visual，auditory and olfactory systems，for example：

1）In the natural gas mixed with bad gas instead of mechanical or electronic sensors to warn people of natural gas leakage；

2）Motion sensing switch instead of mechanical switch；

3）Wireless information transmission between computers；

4）Opaque coated glass can be used without curtains.

（2）Using electric field，magnetic field and electromagnetic field to complete the interaction with objects，for example：

1）In order to mix two powders，one is positively charged and the other is negatively charged；

2）When the fire alarm system alarms，the electromagnetic device controlled by the system is turned on;

3）GPS system can determine the location of the truck or taxi;

4）Electronic label.

（3）The fixed field is changed into a moving field, the static field is changed into a dynamic field, and the random field is determined, for example：

1）A map formed in memory;

2）Fixed point heating system;

3）Room color light system adjustable by occupants.

（4）Ferromagnetic particles are used in the field, for example：when a ferromagnetic material is heated by a variable magnetic field, when the temperature reaches Curie point, the ferromagnetic material becomes paramagnetic and no longer absorbs heat.

5.2.1.29 发明原理29：气动与液压结构
5.2.1.29 Principle of invention 29：pneumatic and hydraulic structures

物体的固体零部件可用气动或液压零部件代替，例：
（1）车辆减速时由液压系统储存能量，车辆运行时放出能量；
（2）充气床垫；
（3）液压电梯替代机械电梯；
（4）利用水平面保证地基是水平的；
（5）热空气加热系统；
（6）清算资产。

The solid parts of the object can be replaced by pneumatic or hydraulic parts, for example：

（1）When the vehicle decelerates, the energy is stored by the hydraulic system and released when the vehicle is running;

（2）Inflatable mattress;

（3）Hydraulic elevator replaces mechanical elevator;

（4）Use horizontal plane to ensure that the foundation is horizontal;

（5）Hot air heating system;

（6）Liquidation of assets.

5.2.1.30 发明原理30：柔性壳体或薄膜
5.2.1.30 Principle of invention 30：flexible shell or film

（1）用柔性壳体或薄膜代替传统结构，例：
1）用薄膜制造的充气结构作为网球场的冬季覆盖物；
2）刷卡代替现金——公司的工资已不是现金，而被打到银行账号，具有特定ID号的卡即可使用；
3）充气服装模特；
4）I、C、U形截面梁代替实心梁；

5）网状结构；

6）膨胀形油漆保护钢结构免受大火的袭击。

（2）使用柔性壳体或薄膜将物体与环境隔离，例：

1）在水库表面漂浮一种由双极性材料制造的薄膜，一面具有亲水性能，另一面具有疏水性能，以减少水的蒸发；

2）餐厅内部的屏风；

3）舞台上的幕布将舞台与观众隔开；

4）充气外衣；

5）鸡蛋专用箱。

（1）Flexible shell or membrane instead of traditional structure, for example：

1）Inflatable structure made of film is used as winter cover of tennis court；

2）Credit card instead of cash——the company's salary is no longer cash, but is called to the bank account, with a specific ID card can be used；

3）Inflatable dress model；

4）I, C, U-section beam instead of solid beam；

5）Reticular structure；

6）Intumescent paint protects rigid structures from fire.

（2）Use a flexible shell or membrane to isolate objects from the environment, for example：

1）Floating on the surface of a reservoir is a film made of bipolar materials, which has hydrophilic properties on one side and hydrophobic properties on the other, so as to reduce the evaporation of water；

2）The screen inside the restaurant；

3）The curtain on the stage separates the stage from the audience；

4）Inflatable coat；

5）Egg box.

5.2.1.31　发明原理31：多孔材料

5.2.1.31　Principle of invention 31：porous materials

（1）使物体多孔或通过插入、涂层等增加多孔元素，例：

1）在某一结构上钻孔，以减少重量；

2）充气砖；

3）泡沫材料；

4）采用类似海绵的材料吸水；

5）氧气呼吸膜。

（2）如果物体已是多孔的，用这些孔引入有用的物质或功能，例：

1）利用一种多孔材料吸收接头上的焊料；

2）利用多孔绝储藏液态氢。

（1）To make an object porous or to add porous elements by insertion, coating, etc., for example：

1）Drill a hole in a structure to reduce weight；

2）Inflatable brick；

3）Foam material；

4）Use sponge like material to absorb water；

5）Oxygen breathing membrane.

（2）If the object is already porous，use these holes to introduce useful substances or functions，for example：

1）Using a porous material to absorb solder on the joint；

2）Storage of liquid hydrogen by porous insulator.

5.2.1.32 发明原理 32：改变颜色
5.2.1.32 Principle of invention 32：change colors

（1）改变物体或环境的颜色，例：

1）在洗像的暗房中要采用安全的光线；

2）反照率（天体）；

3）用不同的颜色（如红、黄、蓝、绿等）表示不同警报；

4）彩色喷墨打印机。

（2）改变一个物体的透明度，或改变某一过程的可视性，例：

1）采用透明绷带缠绕伤口，可以从绷带外部观察伤口变化的情况；

2）增加管理的透明度；

3）问题的清晰、简明的描述是重要的；

4）光线敏感玻璃。

（3）采用有颜色的添加物，使不易被观察到的物体或过程被观察到，例：

1）为了实验透明管路内的流动状态，使带颜色的某种流体从入口流入；

2）使用相反的光线增加可视性，如屠夫采用绿色包装使瘦肉显得更红；

3）红色警示牌。

（4）如果已增加了颜色添加物，则采用发光的轨迹。

（1）Change the color of an object or environment，for example：

1）Safe light should be used in the darkroom of image washing；

2）Albedo（celestial body）；

3）Use different colors（such as red，yellow，blue，green，etc.）to indicate different alarms；

4）Colour inkjet printer.

（2）Change the transparency of an object or the visibility of a process，for example：

1）Using transparent bandage around the wound，you can observe the changes of the wound from the outside of the bandage；

2）Increase the transparency of management；

3）A clear and concise description of the problem is important；

4）Light sensitive glass.

（3）The use of colored additives to make objects or processes difficult to observe visible，for example：

1）In order to test the flow state in a transparent pipe，some colored fluid flows in from the inlet；

2）Use the opposite light to increase visibility，such as the butcher using green packaging to make the lean meat appear more red；

3）Red warning sign.

（4）If the color additive has been added，the luminous track is used.

5.2.1.33　发明原理33：同质性
5.2.1.33　Principle of invention 33：homogeneity

采用相同或相似的物质制造与某物体相互作用的物体，例：
（1）为了减少化学反应，盛放某物体的容器应与该物体用相同的材料制造；
（2）为了防止变形，邻接的材料应有相似的膨胀系数；
（3）为了防止点腐蚀，邻接的金属应有相似的特性；
（4）内部用户；
（5）产品族；
（6）不同机构之间的通用数据传递协议。

Making objects that interact with the same or similar substances，for example：

（1）In order to reduce chemical reaction，the container containing an object should be made of the same material as the object；

（2）In order to prevent deformation，adjacent materials should have similar coefficient of expansion；

（3）In order to prevent pitting corrosion，adjacent metals should have similar characteristics；

（4）Internal users；

（5）Product family；

（6）Common data transfer protocol between different organizations.

5.2.1.34　发明原理34：抛弃与修复
5.2.1.34　Principle of invention 34：abandonment and rehabilitation

（1）当一个物体完成了其功能或变得无用时，抛弃或修改该物体中的一个元件，例：
1）用可溶解的胶囊作为药面的包装；
2）可降解餐具；
3）子弹壳；
4）协议租用某专用设备；
5）合同制雇员。

（2）立即修复一个物体中所损耗的部分，例：

1）割草机的自刃磨刀具；

2）水循环系统；

3）终生学习，不断获得新知识。

（1）When an object completes its function or becomes useless, discard or modify one of its components, for example:

1）Use a soluble capsule as a package for the medicine;

2）Biodegradable Cutlery;

3）Bullet shells;

4）Agreement to rent a special equipment;

5）Contract employee.

（2）Repair the damaged part of an object immediately, for example:

1）Self sharpening cutter of lawn mower;

2）Water circulation system;

3）Lifelong learning, continuous access to new knowledge.

5.2.1.35 发明原理35：参数变化

5.2.1.35 Principle of invention 35: changes in parameters

（1）改变物体的物理状态，即使物体在气态、液态、固态之间变化，例：

1）使氧气处于液态，便于运输；

2）黏接代替机械交接方法；

3）快速模具技术中可用液态速凝塑料；

4）虚拟原型。

（2）改变物体的浓度或黏度，例：

1）从使用的角度看，液态香皂的黏度高于固态香皂，且使用更方便；

2）改变合成水泥的成分可改变其性能；

3）采用不同黏度的润滑油。

（3）改变物体的柔性，例：

1）用三级可调减振器代替轿车中不可调减振器；

2）在建筑物内的可调减振器可提供主动减振功能；

3）安到橡胶支撑上的窗户改善了振动性能；

4）提供智能在线目录；

5）对新手提供专家服务的软件。

（4）改变温度，例：

1）使金属的温度升高到居里点以上，金属由铁磁体变为顺磁体；

2）为了保护动物标本，需将其降温；

3）借助产品的兴趣质量使用户兴奋（热）；

4）通过参与公司长远规划的制定，使员工处于兴奋状态。

（5）改变压力，例：

1）采用真空吸入的方法改变水泥的流动性；

2）利用大气压力差改变高层建筑的空气流动性能；

3）用形状记忆合金制成的窗户合叶能自动调节。

（1）Change the physical state of an object, even if the object changes between the gaseous state, liquid state and solid state, for example：

1）Make oxygen in liquid state, easy to transport；

2）Bonding instead of mechanical comparison；

3）Liquid quick setting plastics can be used in rapid tooling technology；

4）Virtual prototype.

（2）Change the concentration or viscosity of an object, for example：

1）From the perspective of use, the viscosity of liquid soap is higher than that of solid soap, and it is more convenient to use；

2）The properties of synthetic cement can be changed by changing its composition；

3）Lubricating oil with different viscosity.

（3）Changing the flexibility of objects, for example：

1）Three stage adjustable shock absorber instead ofnon adjustable shock absorber in car；

2）Adjustable dampers in buildings provide active damping；

3）Windows attached to rubber supports improve vibration performance；

4）Provide intelligent online directory；

5）Software that provides expert services to novices.

（4）Change the temperature, for example：

1）The temperature of the metal is raised above the Curie point, and the metal changes from ferromagnetic to paramagnetic；

2）In order to protect animal specimens, it is necessary to cool them down；

3）Excite users with interest quality of products；

4）By participating in the formulation of the company's long-term plan, employees are excited.

（5）Change the pressure, for example：

1）Change the fluidity of cement by vacuum inhalation；

2）Using atmospheric pressure difference to change air flow performance of high rise buildings；

3）Window hinges made of shape memory alloy can be adjusted automatically.

5.2.1.36　发明原理36：状态变化

5.2.1.36　Principle of invention 36：state change

在物质状态变化过程中实现某种效应，例：

（1）合理利用水在结冰时体积膨胀的原理；

（2）热泵利用吸热散热原理工作；

（3）热管；

（4）利用状态变化储存能量；

（5）制冷工厂；

（6）轴与轴套的加热装配；

（7）股市由牛市转向熊市；

（8）优秀教学评估过后的放松状态。

Realizing some effect in the process of material state change, for example:

（1）The principle of rational use of water volume expansion when it freezes;

（2）Heat pump works on the principle of heat absorption and heat dissipation;

（3）Heat pipe;

（4）Use state change to store energy;

（5）Refrigeration plant;

（6）Heating assembly of shaft and sleeve;

（7）Stock market turns from bull market to bear market;

（8）Relaxed state after excellent teaching evaluation.

5.2.1.37 发明原理37：热膨胀

5.2.1.37 Principle of invention 37: thermal expansion

（1）利用材料的热膨胀或热收缩性质，例：

1）装配紧配合的两个零件时，将内部零件冷却，外部零件加热，之后装配在一起，并置于常温中；

2）膨胀接头；

3）假如员工处于兴奋状态（热膨胀），在规定的时间及空间内做的更多。

（2）使用具有不同热膨胀系数的材料，例：

1）双金属片传感器；

2）市场的扩张或收缩取决于产品销售量与效益；

3）工作团队中的个性匹配；

4）双金属片合叶能根据室内温度自动调节窗户的开口量。

（1）Utilizing the thermal expansion or shrinkage properties of materials, for example:

1）When assembling two tight fitting parts, cool the internal parts and heat the external parts, then assemble them together and place them in normal temperature;

2）Expansion joint;

3）If the employee is in a state of excitement (thermal expansion), do more in the specified time and space.

（2）Materials with different coefficient of thermal expansion are used, for example:

1）Bimetal Sensor;

2）The expansion or contraction of the market depends on the sales volume and benefit of the products;

3）Personality matching in work teams;

4) The bimetallic hinge can automatically adjust the opening of the window according to the indoor temperature.

5.2.1.38　发明原理38：加速强氧化

5.2.1.38　Principle of invention 38：accelerating strong oxidation

使氧化从一个级别转变到另一个级别，如从环境气体到充满氧气，从充满氧气到纯氧气，从纯氧到离子态氧，例：

（1）为了获得更多的热量，焊枪里通入氧气，而不是用空气；

（2）氧吧；

（3）讨论会中的特约嘉宾；

（4）用仿真训练代替讲课。

Make oxidation change from one level to another, such as from ambient gas to full oxygen, from full oxygen to pure oxygen, from pure oxygen to ionic oxygen, for example：

（1）In order to get more heat, put oxygen into the welding gun instead of air；

（2）Oxygen bar；

（3）Special guests in the seminar；

（4）Replacing lectures with simulation training.

5.2.1.39　发明原理39：惰性环境

5.2.1.39　Principle of invention 39：inert environment

（1）用惰性环境代替通常环境，例：

1）为了防止炽热灯丝的失效，让其置于氩气中；

2）消除评估、评奖等过程中的混乱局面，由一自然的工作系统代替谈判过程中的休会期；

3）硅片加工所需要的净化车间；

（2）在某一物体中添加自然部件或惰性成分，例：

1）难燃材料添加到泡沫状材料构成的墙体中；

2）悬挂系统中的阻尼器；

3）吸声面板；

4）在困难的谈判过程中，引入公正的第三者做评判；

5）在办公区内引入一个安静区。

（1）Use inert environment instead of normal environment, for example：

1）In order to prevent the failure of the hot filament, put it in argon；

2）To eliminate the confusion in the process of evaluation and award, a natural working system should replace the recess in the negotiation process；

3）Purification workshop for silicon wafer processing.

（2）Add natural parts or inert ingredients to an object, for example：

1）Fire resistant materials are added to walls made of foamy materials；

2）Damper in suspension system；

3）Sound absorbing panel；

4）In the difficult negotiation process，the introduction of a fair third party to judge；

5）Introduce a quiet area in the office area.

5.2.1.40 发明原理40：复合材料
5.2.1.40 Principle of invention 40：composite materials

将材质单一的材料改为复合材料，例：

（1）玻璃纤维与木材相比较轻并且在形成不同形状时更容易控制；

（2）钢筋混凝土结构；

（3）玻璃纤维加强结构；

（4）混合纤维地毯；

（5）机电一体化；

（6）多学科项目小组；

（7）高/低风险投资策略。

Change single material to composite material，for example：

（1）Glass fiber is lighter than wood and easier to control when forming different shapes；

（2）Reinforced concrete structure；

（3）Glass fiber reinforced structure；

（4）Mixed fiber carpet；

（5）Mechatronics；

（6）Multidisciplinary project team；

（7）High / low risk investment strategy.

上述这些原理都是通用发明原理，未针对具体领域，其表达方法是描述可能解的概念。如几个原理建议采用柔性方法，问题的解要涉及到在某种程度上改变已有系统的柔性或适应性，设计者根据该建议提出已有系统的改进方案，这将有助于问题的迅速解决。还有一些原理范围很宽，应用面广，即可应用于工程，又可用于管理、广告、市场等领域。

The above principles are general invention principles, which are not specific to specific fields. The expression method is to describe the concept of possible solutions. If several principles suggest adopting flexible method, the solution of the problem involves changing the flexibility or adaptability of the existing system to some extent. The designer puts forward the improvement scheme of the existing system according to the suggestion, which will help to solve the problem quickly. There are also some principles with a wide range of applications, which can be applied to engineering, management, advertising, marketing and other fields.

5. 2. 2　冲突矩阵
5. 2. 2　Conflict matrix

在设计过程中如何选用发明原理作为产生新概念的指导是一个具有现实意义的问题。通过多年的研究、分析、比较，Altshuller 提出了冲突矩阵，该矩阵将描述技术冲突的 39 个工程参数与 40 条发明原理建立了对应关系，很好地解决了设计过程中选择发明原理的难题。

In the design process, how to choose the principle of invention as a guide to generate new concepts is a practical problem. Through years of research, analysis and comparison, Altshuller proposed a conflict matrix, which established the corresponding relationship between 39 engineering parameters describing technical conflicts and 40 invention principles, and solved the problem of selecting invention principles in the design process.

冲突解决矩阵为 40 行 40 列的一个矩阵，其中第 1 行或第 1 列为按顺序排列的 39 个描述冲突的工程参数序号。除第 1 行与第 1 列以外，其余 39 行与 39 列形成一个矩阵，矩阵元素中或空、或有几个数字，这些数字表示 40 条发明原理中的推荐采用原理序号。表 5-2 为矩阵简图。矩阵中的行所描述的工程参数为冲突中改善的一方，列所代表的工程参数是恶化的一方。

The conflict resolution matrix is a matrix of 40 rows and 40 columns, in which the first row or column is the sequence number of 39 engineering parameters describing the conflict. In addition to the first row and the first column, the remaining 39 rows and 39 columns form a matrix. The matrix elements are either empty or have several numbers. These numbers represent the number of recommended principles in the 40 principles of the invention. Table 5-2 is the matrix diagram. The engineering parameters described by the row in the matrix are the improving party in the conflict, and the engineering parameters represented by the column are the deteriorating party.

表 5-2　冲突解决矩阵
Table 5-2　Conflict resolution matrix

序号 Number	No. 1	No. 2	No. 3	No. 4	No. 5	...	No. 39
No. 1			15,8,29,34		29,17,38,34		35,3,24,37
No. 2				10,1,29,35			1,28,15,35
No. 3	8,15,29,34				15,17,4		14,4,28,29
No. 4		35,28,40,29					30,14,7,26
No. 5	2,17,29,4		(14,15,1) 6,4				10,26,3 4,2
⋮							
No. 39	35,6,24,37	28,27,15,3	18,4,28,38	30,7,14,26	10,26,34,31		

应用该矩阵的过程为：首先在 39 个标准工程参数中，确定使产品某一方面质量提高及降低（恶化）的工程参数 A 及 B 的序号，之后将参数 A 及 B 的序号从第 1

列及第 1 行中选取对应的序号，最后在两序号对应行与列的交叉处确定某一特定矩阵元素，该元素所给出的数字为推荐采用的发明原理序号。如希望质量提高与降低的工程参数序号分别为 No. 5 及 No. 3，在矩阵中，第 5 行与第 3 列交叉处所对应的矩阵元素见表 5-2 中的椭圆所示，该元素中的数字 14、15、16 及 4 为推荐的发明原理序号。

The process of applying the matrix is as follows: firstly, among 39 standard engineering parameters, the serial numbers of engineering parameters A and B which can improve or reduce the quality of a certain aspect of the product are determined, and then the parameters A and B are determined and select the corresponding serial number from the first column and the first row, and finally determine a specific matrix element at the intersection of the corresponding rows and columns of the two serial numbers. The number given by the element is the recommended serial number of the invention principle. In the matrix, the matrix elements corresponding to the intersection of the fifth row and the third column are shown in the ellipse in Table 5-2, and the numbers 14, 15, 16 and 4 in the elements are the recommended invention principle numbers.

5.2.3 技术冲突问题解决过程
5.2.3 Technical conflict resolution process

Altshuller 的冲突理论似乎是产品创新的灵丹妙药，实际在应用该理论之前的前处理与应用之后的后处理仍然是关键的问题。图 5-1 表明了问题求解的全过程。

Altshuller's conflict theory seems to be a panacea for product innovation. In fact, the pre-processing and post-processing after the application of the theory are still the key problems. Figure 5-1 shows the whole process of problem solving.

当针对具体问题确认了一个技术冲突后，要用该问题所处技术领域中的特定术语描述该冲突。之后，要将冲突的描述翻译成一般术语，由这些一般术语选择标准工程参数。由标准工程参数在冲突解决矩阵中选择可用解决原理。一旦某一或某几个原理被选定后，必须根据特定的问题应用该原理以产生一个特定的解。对于复杂的问题一条原理是不够的，原理的作用是使原系统向着改进的方向发展。在改进的过程中，对问题的深入思考、创造性、经验都是需要的。

When a technical conflict is identified for a specific problem, the specific terms in the technical field of the problem should be used to describe the conflict. After that, the conflict description is translated into general terms, and the standard engineering parameters are selected by these general terms. The available resolution principles are selected from the conflict resolution matrix by standard engineering parameters. Once one or several principles are selected, they must be applied to a specific problem to produce a specific solution. For complex problems, one principle is not enough. The function of principle is to improve the original system. In the process of improvement, deep thinking, creativity and experience are needed.

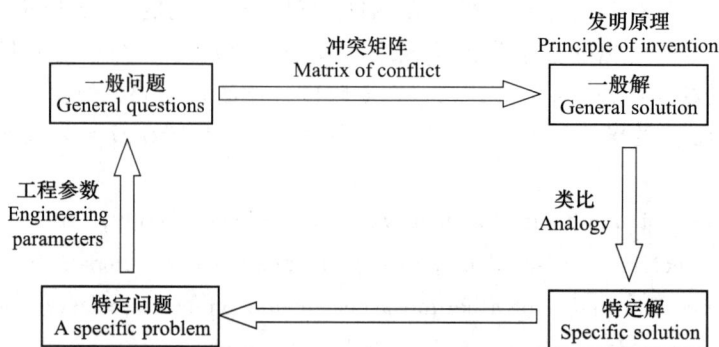

图 5-1   技术冲突解决原理

Figure 5-1   Technology conflict resolution principle

可把上述技术冲突解决原理具体化为 12 步：

（1）定义待设计系统的名称；

（2）确定待设计系统的主要功能；

（3）列出待设计系统的关键子系统、各种辅助功能；

（4）对待设计系统的操作进行描述；

（5）确定待设计系统应改善的特性、应该消除的特性；

（6）将涉及的参数要按标准的 39 个工程参数重新描述；

（7）对技术冲突进行描述：如果某一工程参数要得到改善，将导致哪些参数恶化；

（8）对技术冲突进行另一种描述：假如降低参数恶化的程度，要改善参数将被削弱，或另一恶化参数被加强；

（9）在冲突矩阵中由冲突双方确定相应的矩阵元素；

（10）由上述元素确定可用发明原理；

（11）将所确定的原理应用于设计者的问题；

（12）找到、评价并完善概念设计及后续的设计。

The above technical conflict resolution principle can be embodied into 12 steps：

（1）Define the name of the system to be designed；

（2）Determine the main functions of the system to be designed；

（3）The key subsystems and auxiliary functions of the system to be designed are listed；

（4）Describe the operation of the system to be designed；

（5）The characteristics to be improved and eliminated of the system to be designed are determined；

（6）The parameters involved should be re described according to the standard 39 engineering parameters；

（7）Describe the technical conflict：if a certain engineering parameter is to be improved，which parameters will deteriorate；

（8）Another description of technology conflict is： if the deterioration degree of parameters is reduced， the parameters to be improved will be weakened， or another deterioration parameter will be strengthened；

（9）In the conflict matrix， the corresponding matrix elements are determined by both sides of the conflict；

（10）The available principles of the invention are determined from the above elements；

（11）The principle is applied to the designer's problem；

（12）Find，evaluate and improve the concept design and subsequent design.

通常所选定的发明原理多于一个，这说明前人已用这几个原理解决了一些特定的技术冲突。这些原理仅仅表明解的可能方向，即应用这些原理过滤掉了很多不太可能的解的方向。尽可能将所选定的每条原理都用到待设计过程中去，不要拒绝采用推荐的任何原理。假如所有可能的解都不满足要求，对冲突重新定义并求解。

Generally， more than one invention principle is selected， which indicates that the predecessors have used these principles to solve some specific technical conflicts. These principles only indicate the possible direction of the solution， that is， the application of these principles filters out many unlikely directions of the solution. Try to use each principle selected in the design process，and do not refuse to use any recommended principle. If all possible solutions do not meet the requirements，the conflict is redefined and solved.

5.3 物理冲突解决理论
5.3 Physical conflict resolution theory

5.3.1 分离原理
5.3.1 Separation principle

物理冲突是 TRIZ 要研究解决的关键问题之一。当对一子系统具有相反的要求时就出现了物理冲突。例如，为了容易起飞机，飞机的机翼应有较大的面积，但为了高速飞行，机翼又应有较小的面积，这种要求机翼具有大的面积与小的面积同时存在的情况，对于机翼的设计就是物理冲突，解决该冲突是机翼设计的关键。与技术冲突相比，物理冲突是一种更尖锐的冲突，设计中必须解决。

Physical conflict is one of the key problems in TRIZ. Physical conflict occurs when there are opposite requirements for a subsystem. For example， in order to get off the plane easily， the wing should have a larger area， but in order to fly at a high speed， the wing should have a smaller area. This situation requires that the wing has both a large area and a small area. The design of the wing is a physical conflict， and solving the conflict is the key to the wing design. Compared with technical conflict， physical conflict is a more acute conflict， which must be solved in design.

现代 TRIZ 在总结物理冲突解决的各种研究方法的基础上，提出了采用如下的分离原理解决物理冲突的方法：

（1）空间分离；

（2）时间分离；

（3）基于条件的分离；

（4）整体与部分的分离。

On the basis of summarizing various research methods of physical conflict resolution, modern TRIZ puts forward the following separation principle to solve physical conflict：

（1）Spatial separation；

（2）Time separation；

（3）Condition based separation；

（4）The separation of the whole from the part.

通过采用内部资源，物理冲突已用于解决不同工程领域中的很多技术问题。所谓的内部资源是在特定的条件下，系统内部能发现及可利用的资源，如材料及能量。假如关键子系统是物质，则几何或化学原理的应用是有效的，如关键子系统是场，则物理原理的应用是有效的。有时从物质到场，或从场到物质的传递是解决问题的有效方案。

By using internal resources, physical conflicts have been used to solve many technical problems in different engineering fields. The so-called internal resources are the resources that can be found and utilized in the system under specific conditions, such as materials and energy. If the key subsystem is matter, the application of geometric or chemical principles is effective. If the key subsystem is field, the application of physical principles is effective. Sometimes from the material to the field, or from the field to the material transfer is an effective solution to the problem.

5.3.1.1 空间分离原理

5.3.1.1 Principle of space separation

所谓空间分离原理是将冲突双方在不同的空间分离，以降低解决问题的难度。当关键子系统冲突双方在某一空间只出现一方时，空间分离是可能的。应用该原理时，首先应回答如下问题：

（1）是否冲突一方在整个空间中"正向"或"负向"变化；

（2）在空间中的某一处冲突的一方是否可不按一个方向变化，如果冲突的一方可不按一个方向变化，利用空间分离原理是可能的。

The so-called spatial separation principle is to separate the two sides of the conflict in different spaces, so as to reduce the difficulty of solving the problem. When there is only one side of the key subsystem conflict in a certain space, space separation is possible. When applying this principle, we should first answer the following questions：

（1）Does one side of the conflict change "positively" or "negatively" in the whole space；

（2）Is it possible for the conflicting party to change in a certain direction in space, if one side of the conflict can not change in one direction, it is possible to use the principle of spatial separation.

5.3.1.2 时间分离原理
5.3.1.2 Time separation principle

所谓时间分离原理是将冲突双方在不同的时间段分离，以降低解决问题的难度。当关键子系统冲突双方在某一时间段只出现一方时，时间分离是可能的。应用该原理时，首先应回答如下问题：

（1）是否冲突一方在整个时间段中"正向"或"负向"变化；

（2）在时间段中冲突的一方是否可不按一个方向变化，如果冲突的一方可不按一个方向变化，利用时间分离原理是可能的。

The so-called time separation principle is to separate the two sides of the conflict in different time periods, so as to reduce the difficulty of solving the problem. Time separation is possible when there is only one conflict party in a certain period of time. In order to understand the principle, we should first answer the following questions:

（1）Does one side of the conflict change "positively" or "negatively" over the entire period of time;

（2）Can the conflicting party not change in one direction during the period of time, if one side of the conflict can not change in one direction, it is possible to use the principle of time separation.

5.3.1.3 基于条件的分离
5.3.1.3 Condition based separation

所谓基于条件的分离原理是将冲突双方在不同的条件下分离，以降低于解决问题的难度。当关键子系统冲突双方在某一条件下只出现一方时，基于条件分离是可能的。应用该原理时，首先应回答如下问题：

（1）是否冲突一方在所有条件下都要求"正向"或"负向"变化；

（2）在某些条件下，冲突的一方是否可不按一个方向变化，如果冲突的一方可不按一个方向变化，利用基于条件的分离原理是可能的。

The so-calledcondition based separation principle is to separate the two sides of the conflict under different conditions, so as to reduce the difficulty of solving the problem. It is possible to separate key subsystems based on conditions when only one of the two conflicting parties appears under certain conditions. When applying this principle, we should first answer the following questions:

（1）Does one side of the conflict require a "positive" or "negative" change under all conditions;

（2）Under certain conditions, can the party to the conflict not change in one direction, if one side of the conflict can not change in one direction, it is possible to use conditional separation principle.

5.3.1.4　总体与部分的分离

5.3.1.4　Separation of the whole from the part

所谓总体与部分的分离原理是将冲突双方在不同的层次分离，以降低解决问题的难度。当冲突双方在关键子系统层次只出现一方，而该方在子系统、系统或超系统层次内不出现时，总体与部分的分离是可能的。

The so-called separation principle of the whole and the part is to separate the two sides of the conflict at different levels, so as to reduce the difficulty of solving the problem. It is possible to separate the whole from the part when only one party appears at the key subsystem level and the other party does not appear at the subsystem, system or super system level.

5.3.2　分离原理与发明原理的关系

5.3.2　Relationship between separation principle and invention principle

Mann 通过研究提出，解决物理冲突的分离原理与解决技术冲突的发明原理之间存在关系，对于一条分离原理，可以有多条发明原理与之对应。表 5-3 是其研究结果。

Mann proposed through research that there is a relationship between the separation principle to solve the physical conflict and the invention principle to solve the technical conflict. For a separation principle, there can be multiple invention principles corresponding to it. The results are shown in Table 5-3.

表 5-3　分离原理和发明原理对应的关系

Table 5-3　Corresponding relationship between separation principle and invention principle

分离原理 Separation principle	发明原理 Principle of invention
空间分离 Spatial separation	1、2、3、4、7、13、17、24、26、30
时间分离 Time separation	9、10、11、15、16、18、19、20、21、29、34、37
整体与部分分离 Separation of whole and part	12、28、31、32、35、36、38、39、40
条件分离 Conditional separation	1、7、25、27、5、22、23、33、6、8、14、25、35、13

只要能确定物理冲突及分离原理的类型，40 条发明原理及发明原理的工程实例可帮助设计者尽快确定新的设计概念。

As long as the types of physical conflicts and separation principles can be determined, 40 invention principles and engineering examples of invention principles can help designers to determine new design concepts as soon as possible.

5.4 本章小结
5.4 Summary of this chapter

  本章详细介绍了设计过程中技术冲突和物理冲突解决方法：应用40条发明原理解决技术冲突，应用4条分离原理解决物理冲突。经过不断努力，设计人员会逐渐了解这些原理的含义和应用流程，并能够熟练地应用于解决实际问题。经验表明，不断地应用这些原理，将大大提高设计人员的创新能力。

  This chapter introduces the solution of technical conflict and physical conflict in the design process in detail: 40 invention principles are applied to solve the technical conflict, and 4 separation principles are applied to solve the physical conflict. After continuous efforts, designers will gradually understand the meaning and application process of these principles, and can skillfully apply them to solve practical problems. Experience shows that continuous application of these principles will greatly improve the innovation ability of designers.

6 76 个标准解
Chapter 6　76 Standard Solutions

6.1　概　　述
6.1　Overview

物质-场分析法应用多年，特别是应用于不同领域的专利分析，Altshuller 利用它揭示了问题解决的标准条件及解决问题的标准方法。在 TRIZ 中"标准"这一术语表示解决不同领域问题的通用解决"诀窍"。标准条件及基本相同的解称为标准解。

Matter field analysis has been used for many years, especially in patent analysis in different fields. Altshuller used it to reveal the standard conditions and methods of problem solving. In TRIZ, the term "standard" denotes a common "knack" for solving problems in different fields. Standard conditions and basically the same solutions are called standard solutions.

标准解是 G. S. Altshuller 等，在 1975—1985 年之间完成的，共有 76 个并被分为 5 类，其分类如下。

The standard solution was obtained by G. S. altshuller et al. from 1975 to 1985. There are 76 of them and they are divided into five categories.

第1类：不改变或仅少量改变以改进系统　　　　　　　　　　13个标准解
Class1：No changes or only minor changes to improve the system　　13 standard solutions

第2类：改变系统　　　　　　　　　　　　　　　　　　　　23个标准解
Class2：Change the system　　　　　　　　　　　　　　　　23 standard solutions

第3类：系统传递　　　　　　　　　　　　　　　　　　　　6个标准解
Class3：Transfer of system　　　　　　　　　　　　　　　　6 standard solutions

第4类：检测与测量　　　　　　　　　　　　　　　　　　　17个标准解
Class4：Detection and measurement　　　　　　　　　　　　17 standard solution

第5类：简化与改进策略　　　　　　　　　　　　　　　　　17个标准解
Class5：Simplify and improve the strategy　　　　　　　　　17 standard solutions

76 个标准解对获得高级别的原理解是有效的。通常 76 个标准解可作为一步用于 ARIZ 之中，这在进行物质-场分析，并确定了约束之后进行。在 TRIZ 中，常认为建立物质-场模型的区域是创新设计感兴趣的区域。

76 standard solutions are effective for obtaining high-level original understanding. Generally, 76 standard solutions can be used in ARIZ as a step after the matter field analysis and the determination of constraints. In TRIZ, it is often considered that the area of matter field model is the area of interest in innovative design.

6.2 物质-场模型的建立
6.2 Establishment of matter field model

6.2.1 符号系统
6.2.1 Symbol system

物质-场分析的基础是用图形表示待设计系统。图 6-1 所示为 Altshuller 的功能图形表示，Zinovy、Teminko 等又对其进行了发展，本节介绍发展了的符号系统。

The basis of matter field analysis is to use graphics to represent the system to be designed. Figure 6-1 shows the functional graphical representation of altshuller, which has been developed by zinovy and teminko. This section introduces the developed symbol system.

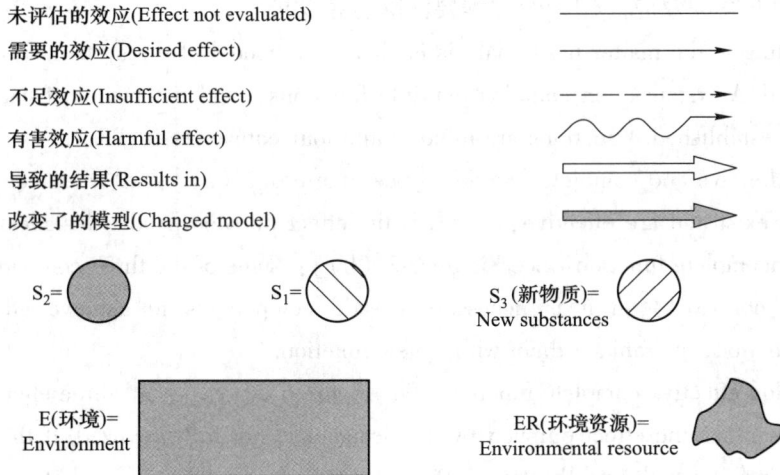

未评估的效应(Effect not evaluated)

需要的效应(Desired effect)

不足效应(Insufficient effect)

有害效应(Harmful effect)

导致的结果(Results in)

改变了的模型(Changed model)

$S_2=$　　　$S_1=$　　　S_3(新物质)= New substances

E(环境)= Environment　　　ER(环境资源)= Environmental resource

图 6-1 物质-场分析符号系统

Figure 6-1 Symbolic system of matter field analysis

常用字母及意义。

（1）Ftype：场的类型。常用类型有 Me-机械、Th-热、Ch-化学、E-电、M-磁、G-重力。

（2）U：有用效应。

（3）H：有害效应。

Common letters and meanings.

（1）Ftype：the type of field. The common types are as follows：Me-mechanical，Th-thermal，Ch-chemical，E-Electrical，M-magnetic，G-gravity.

（2）U：Useful effect.

（3）H：Harmful effects.

6. 2. 2　功能分类及其模型
6. 2. 2　Function classification and its model

按物质-场分析方法，首先建立待设计系统的模型。一个系统往往包含多个功能，需要建立每个功能的模型。TRIZ 中将功能分为四类。

（1）有效完整功能［见图 6-2（a）］：该功能的三个元件都存在，且都有效，是设计者追求的效应。

（2）不完整功能［见图 6-2（b）］：组成功能的三元件中部分元件不存在，需要增加元件来实现有效完整功能，或用一些功能代替。

（3）非有效完整功能［见图 6-2（c）］：功能中的三元件都存在，但设计者所追求的效应未能完全实现。如产生的力不足够大、温度不足 够高等，需要改进以达到要求。

（4）有害功能［见图 6-2（d）］：功能中的三元件都存在，但产生与设计者所追求效应相冲突的效应。创新的过程要消除有害功能。

According to the matter field analysis method, the model of the system to be designed is established. A system often contains multiple functions, and the model of each function needs to be established. Functions are divided into four categories in TRIZ.

（1）Effective and complete function ［See Figure 6-2（a）］: all three components of the function exist and are effective, which is the effect pursued by the designer.

（2）Incomplete function ［See Figure 6-2（b）］: some of the three components of the function do not exist, so it is necessary to add components to achieve effective and complete function, or replace them with a new function.

（3）Non effective complete function ［See Figure 6-2（c）］: all three elements in the function exist, but the effect pursued by the designer is not fully realized. If the generated force is not large enough and the temperature is not high enough, it needs to be improved to meet the requirements.

（4）Harmful function ［See Figure 6-2（d）］: all three elements in the function exist, but produce effects that conflict with the effects pursued by the designer. The process of innovation should eliminate harmful functions.

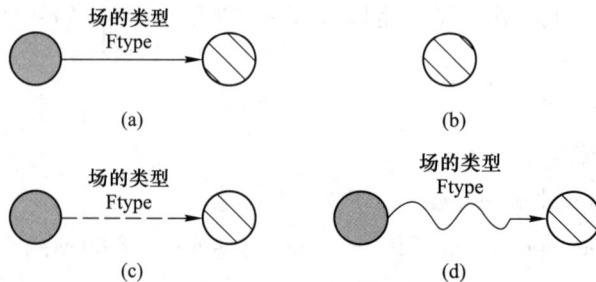

图 6-2　各种功能模型

Figure 6-2　Various functional models

6.3 76 个标准解
6.3 76 standard solutions

6.3.1 第 1 类标准解
6.3.1 Class 1 Standard Solution

改进一个系统使其具有所需要的输出或消除不理想的输出。对系统只有少量的改变或不改变。

Improve a system to have desired output or eliminate undesirable output. Little or no change to the system.

该类解包含完善一个不完整系统或非有效完整系统所有需要的解。在物质-场模型中，不完整系统是指一个系统中不包含 S_1 或 S_2 或 F，非 A 效完整功能可指 F 不足够大。

These solutions contain all the necessary solutions to perfect an incomplete system or an inefficient holonomic system. In matter field model, incomplete system means that a system does not contain S_1 or S_2 or F, and non-A-effect complete function means that F is not large enough.

6.3.1.1 改进具有非完整功能的系统（1.1）
6.3.1.1 Improving systems with incomplete functions （1.1）

（1）No.1（1.1.1）完善具有不完整功能的系统：假如只有 S_1，增加 S_2 及场 F。

（2）No.2（1.1.2）假如系统不能改变，但可接受永久的或临时的添加物，可以在 S_1 或 S_2 内部添加来实现。

（3）No.3（1.1.3）假如系统不能改变，但永久的或临时的外部添加剂改变 S_1 或 S_2 是可接受的。

（4）No.4（1.1.4）假定系统不能改变，但可用环境资源作为内部或外部添加剂。

（5）No.5（1.1.5）假定系统不能改变，但可以改变系统所处的环境。

（6）No.6（1.1.6）微小量的精确控制是困难的，但可以通过增加一个附加物并在之后除去来控制微小量。

（7）No.7（1.1.7）一个系统中场强度不够，增加场强又会损坏系统，强度足够大的一个场施加到另一个元件上，该元件连接到原系统上。同理，一种物质不能很好的发挥作用，但连接到另一种可用物质上则能发挥作用。

（8）No.8（1.1.8）同时需要大的/强的及小的/弱的效应时，小效应的位置可由物质 S_3 保护。

（1）No.1（1.1.1）improve the system with incomplete function: if there is only S_1, add S_2 and field F.

（2）No.2（1.1.2）if the system cannot be changed, but permanent or temporary additives can be accepted, they can be added in S_1 or S_2.

（3）No.3（1.1.3）if the system cannot be changed, permanent or temporary external additive changes S_1 or S_2 are acceptable.

（4）No.4（1.1.4）assumes that the system cannot be changed, but environmental resources can be used as internal or external additives.

（5）No.5（1.1.5）assumes that the system cannot be changed, but it can change the environment of the system.

（6）It is difficult to control the tiny amount of No.6（1.1.6）, but it can be controlled by adding an additive and removing it later.

（7）No.7（1.1.7）if the field strength of a system is not enough, increasing the field strength will damage the system. A field with enough strength is applied to another component, which is connected to the original system. In the same way, one substance can't work well, but connecting to another substance can work.

（8）When No.8（1.1.8）needs both large / strong and small / weak effects, the location of small effect can be protected by S_3.

6.3.1.2　消除或抵消有害效应（1.2）

6.3.1.2　Eliminate or offset harmful effects（1.2）

（1）No.9（1.2.1）在一个系统中有用及有害效应同时存在。S_1 及 S_2 不必直接接触，引入 S_3 消除有害效应。

（2）No.10（1.2.2）与 No.9 类似，但不允许增加新物质，通过改变 S_1 或 S_2 消除有害效应。该类解包括增加"虚无物质"，如空位、真空、空气、汽泡、泡沫等，或加一种场，场的作用相当于增加一种物质。

（3）No.11（1.2.3）有害效应是由一种场引起的，引入物质 S_3 吸收有害效应。

（4）No.12（1.2.4）在一个系统中有用及有害效应同时存在，但 S_1 及 S_2 必须处于接触状态。增加场 F_2，使之抵消 F_1 的影响，或得到一附加的有用效应。

（5）No.13（1.2.5）在一个系统中，由于一个元件存在磁性而产生有害效应，将该元件加热到居里点以上磁性将不存在，或引入一相反的磁场消除原磁场。

（1）No.9（1.2.1）has both useful and harmful effects in a system. S_1 and S_2 do not need to be contacted directly, and S_3 is introduced to eliminate harmful effects.

（2）No.10（1.2.2）is similar to No.9, but new substances are not allowed to be added, and harmful effects can be eliminated by changing S_1 or S_2. Such solutions include increasing the "void substance" such as vacancy, vacuum, air, bubble, foam, etc., or adding a field. The action of the field is equivalent to adding one substance.

（3）No.11（1.2.3）the harmful effect is caused by a kind of field, which is absorbed by S_3.

（4）No.12（1.2.4）has both useful and harmful effects in a system, but S_1 and S_2 must be in contact. The field F_2 is added to counteract the effect of F_1, or an additional useful effect is obtained.

(5) No. 13 (1.2.5) in a system, a harmful effect is produced due to the existence of magnetism in an element. If the element is heated above the Curie point, the magnetism will not exist, or an opposite magnetic field will be introduced to eliminate the original magnetic field.

6.3.2 第2类标准解
6.3.2 Class 2 standard solution

该类标准解的特点是通过对描述系统物质-场模型的较大改变来改善系统。

The characteristic of this kind of standard solution is to improve the system by changing the matter field model.

6.3.2.1 传递到复杂物质-场模型 (2.1)
6.3.2.1 Transfer to complex matter field model (2.1)

(1) No. 14 (2.1.1) 串联物质-场模型：将第一个模型的 S_2 及 F_1 施加到 S_3，S_3 及 F_2 施加到 S_1。串联的两个模型是独立可控的。

(2) No. 15 (2.1.2) 并联物质-场模型：一可控性很差的系统需要改进，但已存在的部分不能改变，并联第二个场，并作用到 S_2 上。

(1) No. 14 (2.1.1) tandem matter field model：S_2 and F_1 of the first model are applied to S_3, and S_3 and F_2 are applied to S_1. The two models in series are independent and controllable.

(2) No. 15 (2.1.2) parallel matter field model：a system with poor controllability needs to be improved, but the existing part can not be changed. The second field is paralleled and acts on S_2.

6.3.2.2 加强物质-场 (2.2)
6.3.2.2 Enhanced matter field (2.2)

(1) No. 16 (2.2.1) 对于可控性差的场，用一易控场代替，或增加一易控场。如由重力场变为机械场，由机械变为电或电磁场。其核心是由物体的物理接触到场的作用。

(2) No. 17 (2.2.2) 将 S_2 由宏观变为微观。

(3) No. 18 (2.2.3) 改变 S_2 成为允许气体或液体通过的多孔的或具有毛细孔的材料。

(4) No. 19 (2.2.4) 使系统更具有柔性或适应性。通常的方式由刚性变为一个铰接，到连续柔性系统。

(5) No. 20 (2.2.5) 使一个不能控制的场具有永久或临时确定的模式。

(6) No. 21 (2.2.6) 将单一物质或不可控物质变成确定空间结构的非单一物质，这种变化可以是永久的或临时的。

(1) No. 16 (2.2.1) for the field with poor controllability, an easy field is used to

replace or add an easy field. For example, from gravity field to mechanical field, from machinery to electricity or electromagnetic field. Its core is the action of the field by the physical contact of the object.

（2）No. 17 （2.2.2） changed S_2 from macro to micro.

（3）No. 18 （2.2.3） changes S_2 into a porous or porous material that allows gas or liquid to pass through.

（4）No. 19 （2.2.4） makes the system more flexible or adaptable. The usual way is changed from rigid to hinged to continuous flexible system.

（5）No. 20 （2.2.5） gives a field that cannot be controlled a permanent or temporary mode.

（6）No. 21 （2.2.6） changes a single substance or uncontrollable substance into a non single substance that determines the spatial structure, which can be permanent or temporary.

6.3.2.3　控制频率使其与一个或两个元件的自然频率匹配或不匹配，以改善性能 （2.3）

6.3.2.3　Control the frequency to match or not match the natural frequency of one or two components to improve performance （2.3）

（1）No. 22 （2.3.1） 使 F 与 S_1 或 S_2 的自然频率匹配或不匹配。

（2）No. 23 （2.3.2） 与 F_1 或 F_2 的固有频率匹配。

（3）No. 24 （2.3.3） 两个不相容或独立的动作可以一个接一个地完成。

（1）No. 22 （2.3.1） makes F match or not match the natural frequency of S_1 or S_2.

（2）No. 23 （2.3.2） matches the natural frequency of F_1 or F_2.

（3）No. 24 （2.3.3） two incompatible or independent actions can be completed one by one.

6.3.2.4　铁磁材料与磁场结合 （2.4）

6.3.2.4　Combination of ferromagnetic materials and magnetic fields （2.4）

（1）No. 25 （2.4.1） 在一个系统中增加铁磁材料和或磁场。

（2）No. 26 （2.4.2） 将 No. 16 与 No. 25 结合，利用铁磁材料与磁场增加场的可控性。

（3）No. 27 （2.4.3） 磁流体的应用。磁流体是 No. 26 的一个特例。

（4）No. 28 （2.4.4） 利用含有磁粒子或液体的毛细结构。

（5）No. 29 （2.4.5） 利用附加物，如涂层，使非磁性物体永久或临时具有磁性。

➢**例 6-1**　在理疗过程中，在药物粒子中增加一磁性粒子，体内的磁性粒子将被吸引到外部磁性线周围，达到磁力线精确定位的目的。

（6）No. 30 （2.4.6） 假如一个物体不能具有磁性，将铁磁物质引入到环境之中。

（7）No. 31 （2.4.7） 利用自然现象，如物体按场排列，或在居里点以上物体将失去磁性。

（8） No. 32 （2.4.8） 利用动态、可变、或自调整的磁场。

（9） No. 33 （2.4.9） 加入铁磁粒子改变材料的结构，施加磁场移动粒子。通过这种途径，使非结构化系统变为结构化系统，或反之。

（10） No. 34 （2.4.10） 与 F 场的自然频率相匹配。对于宏观系统，采用机械振动增强铁磁粒子的运动。在分子及原子水平上，材料的复合成分可通过改变磁场频率的方法用电子谐振频谱确定。

（11） No. 35 （2.4.11） 用电流产生磁场并可以代替磁粒子。

（12） No. 36 （2.4.12） 电流变流体具有被电磁场控制的黏度。它们可以与其他方法一起使用。

（1） No. 25 （2.4.1） adding ferromagnetic materials and or magnetic fields to a system.

（2） No. 26 （2.4.2） combines No. 16 with No. 25. Ferromagnetic materials and magnetic field are used to increase the field controllability.

（3） Application of No. 27 （2.4.3） magnetic fluid. MHD is a special case of No. 26.

（4） No. 28 （2.4.4） uses capillary structure containing magnetic particles or liquid.

（5） No. 29 （2.4.5） permanent or temporary magnetism of non-magnetic objects by means of additives, such as coating.

➤**Example 6-1** In the process of physical therapy, a magnetic particle is added to the drug particles, and the magnetic particles in the body will be attracted around the external magnetic line, so as to achieve the purpose of accurate positioning of the magnetic line of force.

（6） No. 30 （2.4.6） if an object cannot be magnetic, ferromagnetic material is introduced into the environment.

（7） No. 31 （2.4.7） makes use of natural phenomena, such as objects arranged in fields or above Curie point will lose magnetism.

（8） No. 32 （2.4.8） uses dynamic, variable, or self-adjusting magnetic fields.

（9） No. 33 （2.4.9） ferromagnetic particles were added to change the structure of the material, and magnetic field was applied to move the particles. In this way, unstructured system can be changed into structured system, or vice versa.

（10） No. 34 （2.4.10） matches the natural frequency of F field. For the macro system, mechanical vibration is used to enhance the motion of ferromagnetic particles. At the molecular and atomic level, the composition of the material can be determined by changing the frequency of the magnetic field.

（11） No. 35 （2.4.11） can generate magnetic field by electric current and replace magnetic particles.

（12） No. 36 （2.4.12） ER fluid has viscosity controlled by electromagnetic field. They can be used with other methods.

6.3.3　第3类标准解

6.3.3　Class 3 standard solution

该类标准的特点是系统传递到双系统、多系统或微观水平。

The characteristic of this kind of standard is that the system transfers to the level of dual system, multi system or micro level.

6.3.3.1　传递到双系统或多系统（3.1）

6.3.3.1　Transfer to dual system or multi system（3.1）

（1）No. 37（3.1.1）系统传递（a）：产生双系统或多系统。

（2）No. 38（3.1.2）改进双系统或多系统中的连接。

（3）No. 39（3.1.3）系统传递（b）：在元件之间增加其不同性质。

（4）No. 40（3.1.4）双系统及多系统的简化。

（5）No. 41（3.1.5）系统传递（c）：整体与部分之间的相反特性。

（1）No. 37（3.1.1）system transfer（a）：generating two or more systems.

（2）No. 38（3.1.2）improves connectivity in dual or multiple systems.

（3）No. 39（3.1.3）system transfer（b）：adding different properties between components.

（4）No. 40（3.1.4）simplification of dual system and multi system.

（5）No. 41（3.1.5）system transfer（c）：the opposite characteristic between whole and part.

6.3.3.2　传递到微观水平（3.2）

6.3.3.2　Transfer to micro level（3.2）

No. 42（3.2.1）系统传递（d）：传递到微观水平。

No. 42（3.2.1）system transfer（d）：transfer to micro level.

6.3.4　第4类标准解

6.3.4　Class 4 Standard solution

该类标准解是检测与测量。检测与测量是典型的控制环节。检测是指检查某种状态发生或不发生。测量具有定量化及一定精度的特点。一些创新解是采用物理的、化学的、几何的效应完成自动控制，而不采用检测与测量。

The standard solution is detection and measurement. Detection and measurement are typical control links. Detection is to check whether a certain state occurs or does not occur. The measurement has the characteristics of quantification and certain precision. Some innovative solutions use physical, chemical and geometric effects to complete automatic control, instead of detection and measurement.

6.3.4.1　*间接法*（4.1）

6.3.4.1　Indirect method（4.1）

（1）No. 43（4.1.1）替代系统中的检测与测量，使之不再需要。

（2）No. 44（4.1.2）假如 No. 43 不可能，测量一复制品或肖像。

（3）No. 45（4.1.3）假如 No. 43 及 No. 44 不可能，利用两个检测量代替连续测量。

（1）No. 43（4.1.1）replaces the detection and measurement in the system and makes it unnecessary.

（2）No. 44（4.1.2）if No. 43 is not possible, measure a copy or portrait.

（3）No. 45（4.1.3）if No. 43 and No. 44 are not possible, two measurements are used instead of continuous measurement.

6.3.4.2　*将零件或场引入到已存在的系统中*（4.2）

6.3.4.2　Introducing a part or field into an existing system（4.2）

（1）No. 46（4.2.1）假如一个不完整物质-场系统不能被检测或测量，增加单一或双物质-场，且一个场作为输出。假如已存在的场是非有效的，在不影响原系统的条件下，改变或加强该场。加强了的场应具有容易检测的参数，这些参数与设计者所关心的参数有关。

（2）No. 47（4.2.2）测量一引入的附加物。引入的附加物在原系统中变化，测量附加物的这种变化。

（3）No. 48（4.2.3）假如系统中不能增加其他附加物，在环境中增加附加物使其对系统产生场，检测或测量场对系统的影响。

（4）No. 49（4.2.4）假如附加物不能被引入到环境中去（No. 48），分解或改变环境中已存在的物质，使其产生某种效应，测量这种效应。

（1）No. 46（4.2.1）if an incomplete matter field system cannot be detected or measured, add a single or dual matter field, and a field as the output. If the existing field is not effective, it can be changed or strengthened without affecting the original system. The enhanced field should have parameters that are easy to detect, which are related to the parameters concerned by the designer.

（2）No. 47（4.2.2）was used to measure an introduced additive. The changes of the introduced additives in the original system are measured.

（3）No. 48（4.2.3）if other additives cannot be added to the system, add the additives in the environment to produce a field to the system, and detect or measure the influence of the field on the system.

（4）No. 49（4.2.4）if the additive cannot be introduced into the environment（No. 48）, decompose or change the existing substances in the environment to produce some effect, and measure this effect.

6.3.4.3　加强测量系统（4.3）

6.3.4.3　Enhanced measurement system（4.3）

（1）No.50（4.3.1）利用自然现象。如利用系统中出现的已知科学效应，通过观察效应的变化，决定系统的状态。

（2）No.51（4.3.2）假如系统不能直接或通过场测量，测量系统或元件被激发的固有频率来确定系统的变化。

（3）No.52（4.3.3）假如No.51不可能。测量与已知特性相联系的物体的固有频率。

（1）No.50（4.3.1）uses natural phenomena. For example, the state of the system can be determined by observing the changes of the known scientific effects in the system.

（2）No.51（4.3.2）if the system cannot be measured directly or through field measurement, the change of the system can be determined by measuring the excited natural frequency of the system or component.

（3）No.52（4.3.3）if No.51 is not possible. Measure the natural frequency of an object associated with a known characteristic.

6.3.4.4　测量铁磁场（Fe-场）（4.4）

6.3.4.4　Measurement of ferromagnetic field（Fe field）（4.4）

在遥感、微装置、光纤、微处理器应用之前，为测量引入铁磁材料是流行的方法。

（1）No.53（4.4.1）增加或利用磁物质或系统中的磁场以便测量。

（2）No.54（4.4.2）增加磁性粒子或改变一种物质成为铁磁粒子以便测量，测量所导致的磁场即可。

（3）No.55（4.4.3）假如No.54不可能，建立一复合系统，添加铁磁粒子附加物到系统中去。

（4）No.56（4.4.4）假如系统不允许增加铁磁物质，将其加到环境之中。

（5）No.57（4.4.5）测量与磁性有关的现象。

Before the application of remote sensing, micro devices, optical fibers and microprocessors, the introduction of ferromagnetic materials for measurement is a popular method.

（1）No.53（4.4.1）increases or utilizes the magnetic field in a magnetic substance or system for measurement.

（2）No.54（4.4.2）add magnetic particles or change a substance into ferromagnetic particles for measurement, and then measure the magnetic field.

（3）No.55（4.4.3）if No.54 is not possible, a composite system should be established and ferromagnetic particle additives should be added to the system.

（4）No.56（4.4.4）if the system does not allow the addition of ferromagnetic material, add it to the environment.

（5）No. 57（4.4.5）measures the phenomena related to magnetism.

6.3.4.5 测量系统的进化方向（4.5）
6.3.4.5 Evolution direction of measurement system（4.5）

（1）No. 58（4.5.1）传递到双或多系统。假如单一测量系统不能给出足够的精度，可应用双系统或多系统。

（2）No. 59（4.5.2）代替直接测量，可测量时间或空间的一阶或二阶导数。

（1）No. 58（4.5.1）to dual or multiple systems. If a single measurement system can not give enough accuracy, two or more systems can be used.

（2）No. 59（4.5.2）can measure the first or second derivative of time or space instead of direct measurement.

6.3.5 第5类标准解
6.3.5 Class 5 standard solution

该类标准解是简化或改进上述的标准解，以得到简化的方案。

This kind of standard solution is to simplify or improve the above standard solution to get a simplified scheme.

6.3.5.1 引入物质（5.1）
6.3.5.1 Introduced substances（5.1）

（1）No. 60（5.1.1）间接方法主要有以下几种。

1）（5.1.1.1）使用无成本资源，如空气、真空、气泡、泡沫、空洞、缝隙等。

2）（5.1.1.2）利用场代替物质。

3）（5.1.1.3）用外部附加物代替内部附加物。

4）（5.1.1.4）利用少量但非常活化的附加物。

5）（5.1.1.5）将附加物集中到一特定的位置上。

6）（5.1.1.6）暂时引入附加物。

7）（5.1.1.7）假如原系统中不允许附加物，可在其复制品中增加附加物。这包括仿真器的使用。

8）（5.1.1.8）引入化合物，当它们起反应时产生所需要的化合物，而直接引入这些化合物是有害的。

9）（5.1.1.9）通过对环境或物体本身的分解获得所需的附加物。

（2）No. 61（5.1.2）将元件分为更小的单元。

（3）No. 62（5.1.3）附加物被使用完后自动消除。

（4）No. 63（5.1.4）假如环境不允许大量使用某种材料，使用对环境无影响的东西。

（1）No. 60（5.1.1）indirect method.

1）（5.1.1.1）the use ofcost free resources, such as air, vacuum, bubbles, bubbles, holes, gaps, etc.

2）（5.1.1.2）using field instead of matter.

3）（5.1.1.3）replace internal additions with external ones.

4）（5.1.1.4）use of small but very active additives.

5）（5.1.1.5）concentrate the addition on a specific location.

6）（5.1.1.6）temporary introduction of additives.

7）（5.1.1.7）if the addition is not allowed in the original system, the addition can be added to the copy. This includes the use of simulators.

8）（5.1.1.8）introduction compounds, when they react, produce the desired compounds, and direct introduction of these compounds is harmful.

9）（5.1.1.9）obtain the necessary additives by decomposing the environment or the object itself.

（2）No. 61（5.1.2）divides the components into smaller units.

（3）No. 62（5.1.3）is automatically eliminated after use.

（4）No. 63（5.1.4）if the environment does not allow the use of a large number of certain materials, use things that have no impact on the environment.

6.3.5.2　使用场（5.2）

6.3.5.2　Field of use（5.2）

（1）No. 64（5.2.1）使用一种场来产生另一种场。

（2）No. 65（5.2.2）利用环境中已存在的场。

（3）No. 66（5.2.3）使用属于场资源的物质。

（1）No. 64（5.2.1）uses one field to generate another.

（2）No. 65（5.2.2）uses the existing field in the environment.

（3）No. 66（5.2.3）uses materials belonging to field resources.

6.3.5.3　状态传递（5.3）

6.3.5.3　State transfer（5.3）

（1）No. 67（5.3.1）状态传递1：替代状态。

（2）No. 68（5.3.2）状态传递2：双态。

（3）No. 69（5.3.3）状态传递3：利用状态转换过程中的伴随现象。

（4）No. 70（5.3.4）状态传递4：传递到双态。

（5）No. 71（5.3.5）部件或物质之间的相互作用。引入系统中元件或物质之间的相互作用使系统更有效。

（1）No. 67（5.3.1）state transfer 1：alternative state.

（2）No. 68（5.3.2）state transition 2：two states.

（3）No. 69（5.3.3）state transfer 3：using the accompanying phenomenon in the process of state transition.

（4）No. 70（5.3.4）state transfer 4：transfer to two states.

(5) No. 71 (5.3.5) interaction between components or substances. The interaction between components or substances in the system is introduced to make the system more effective.

6.3.5.4 应用自然现象 (5.4)
6.3.5.4 Applicationof natural phenomena (5.4)

(1) No. 72 (5.4.1) 自控制传递。假如一物体必须具有不同的状态，应使其自身从一个状态传递到另一个状态。

(2) No. 73 (5.4.2) 当输入场较弱时，加强输出场。通常在接近状态转换点处实现。

(1) No. 72 (5.4.1) self control transfer. If an object must have different states, it should transfer itself from one state to another.

(2) No. 73 (5.4.2) when the input field is weak, the output field is strengthened. It is usually implemented near the state transition point.

6.3.5.5 产生高等或低等结构水平的物质 (5.5)
6.3.5.5 Substances with high or low structure level (5.5)

(1) No. 74 (5.5.1) 通过分解获得物质粒子。

(2) No. 75 (5.5.2) 通过结合获得物质。

(3) No. 76 (5.5.3) 应用 No. 74 及 No. 75 时，假如高等结构物质需要分解，但又不能分解，由次高一级的物质状态代替。反之，如果物质是通过低结构物质组合而成，而该物质不能应用，则采用高一级的物质代替。

(1) No. 74 (5.5.1) is obtained by decomposition.

(2) No. 75 (5.5.2) was obtained by binding.

(3) No. 76 (5.5.3) when No. 74 and No. 75 are applied, if higher structural substances need to be decomposed, but can not be decomposed, they will be replaced by the next higher material state. On the contrary, if the material is composed of low structure material, and the material can not be applied, thehigher level material is used instead.

6.4 标准解应用过程
6.4 Application process of standard solution

产品设计中的问题要用简练的语言说明，并且包括问题的约束或限制性条件的说明。当问题符合以上条件时，76 个标准解可以作为解决问题的模板。

Problems in product design should be explained in concise language, including the description of constraints or restrictive conditions. When the problem meets the above conditions, 76 standard solutions can be used as templates to solve the problem.

76 个标准解最有代表性的应用是在建立了物质-场模型，并确定了解的所有约束条件之后，作为 TRIZ 中 ARIZ 算法的一个步骤。模型和约束条件用于确定解的类别直至特定的解。76 个标准解在 ARIZ 之外也有广泛应用，特别是在系统的基本模型能够建立的情况下。建立的模型可以是物质-场模型的形式，也可以是功能结构。功能结构在没有明显的技术或物理约束的时候也很有用。

The most representative application of the 76 standard solutions is to establish the matter field model and determine all the constraints of the solution as a step of ARIZ algorithm in TRIZ. Models and constraints are used to determine the class of solutions up to a specific solution. 76 standard solutions are also widely used outside ARIZ, especially when the basic model of the system can be established. The model can be in the form of matter field model or functional structure. Functional structures are also useful when there are no obvious technical or physical constraints.

第 1 类到第 4 类标准解常常使系统更复杂，这是由于这些解都需要引入新的物质或场。第 5 类标准解是简化系统的方法，使系统更理想化。当从解决性能问题的第 1 类到第 3 类标准解或解决检测/测量问题的第 4 类标准解决定了一个解之后，第 5 类可用来简化这个解。流程图 6-3 详细表达了 76 个标准解的每个类别在问题求解和技术预测两个方面应用。

Class 1 to class 4 standard solutions often make the system more complex, because these solutions need to introduce new matter or field. The fifth standard solution is a method to simplify the system and make the system more ideal. When a solution is determined from the first class to the third class standard solution for performance problems or the fourth class standard solution for detection / measurement problems, the fifth class can be used to simplify the solution. Flow Figure 6-3 shows in detail the application of each category of 76 standard solutions in problem solving and technical prediction.

6.5　本章小结
6.5　Summary of this chapter

本章系统介绍了 TRIZ 中的 76 个标准解，选择标准解的过程，并以实例说明标准解的应用。标准解适合于求解高级别的问题，如果问题可用标准解描述与解决，不必再确定冲突及解决冲突。

This chapter systematically introduces 76 standard solutions in TRIZ, the process of selecting standard solutions, and illustrates the application of standard solutions with examples. Standard solution is suitable for solving high-level problems. If the problems can be described and solved by standard solution, it is no longer necessary to determine and solve conflicts.

图例说明：
- 分析 Analyse
- 76个标准 76 standards
- 决策 Decision
- 图例 Legend

选择需要改进的系统
Select the system that needs improvement

关注问题范围
——确定系统的特征要素
Focus on problem scope——identify the characteristic elements of the system

问题的简洁描述
Aconcise description of the problem

预测改变的潜力
Predict the potential for change

需要？
Need？

检测/测量
Test/measure

第4类标准解
Class 4 standard solution

系统改进
Improvement of system

建立系统的物质-场模型
Establish the matter-field model of the system

1.1类标准解
Class 1.1 standard solution

缺乏
Lack

相互作用？
Interaction？

有害
Harmful

1.2类标准解
Class 1.2 standar solution

改变的规模
The scale of change

最小改变？
Minimal change？

不充分
Not enough

第1类或第2类标准解
Class 1 or Class 2 standard solution

超系统或子系统的改变？
A change in a supersystem or subsystem

第2类标准解
Class 2 standard solution

第3类标准解
Class 3 standard solution

否
No

充分？
Sufficient？

第3类标准解
Class 3 standard solution

是
Yes

解充分吗？
Is the solution sufficient？

否
No

提炼问题描述
Refining the problem description

是
Yes

第5类标准解
Class 5 standard solution

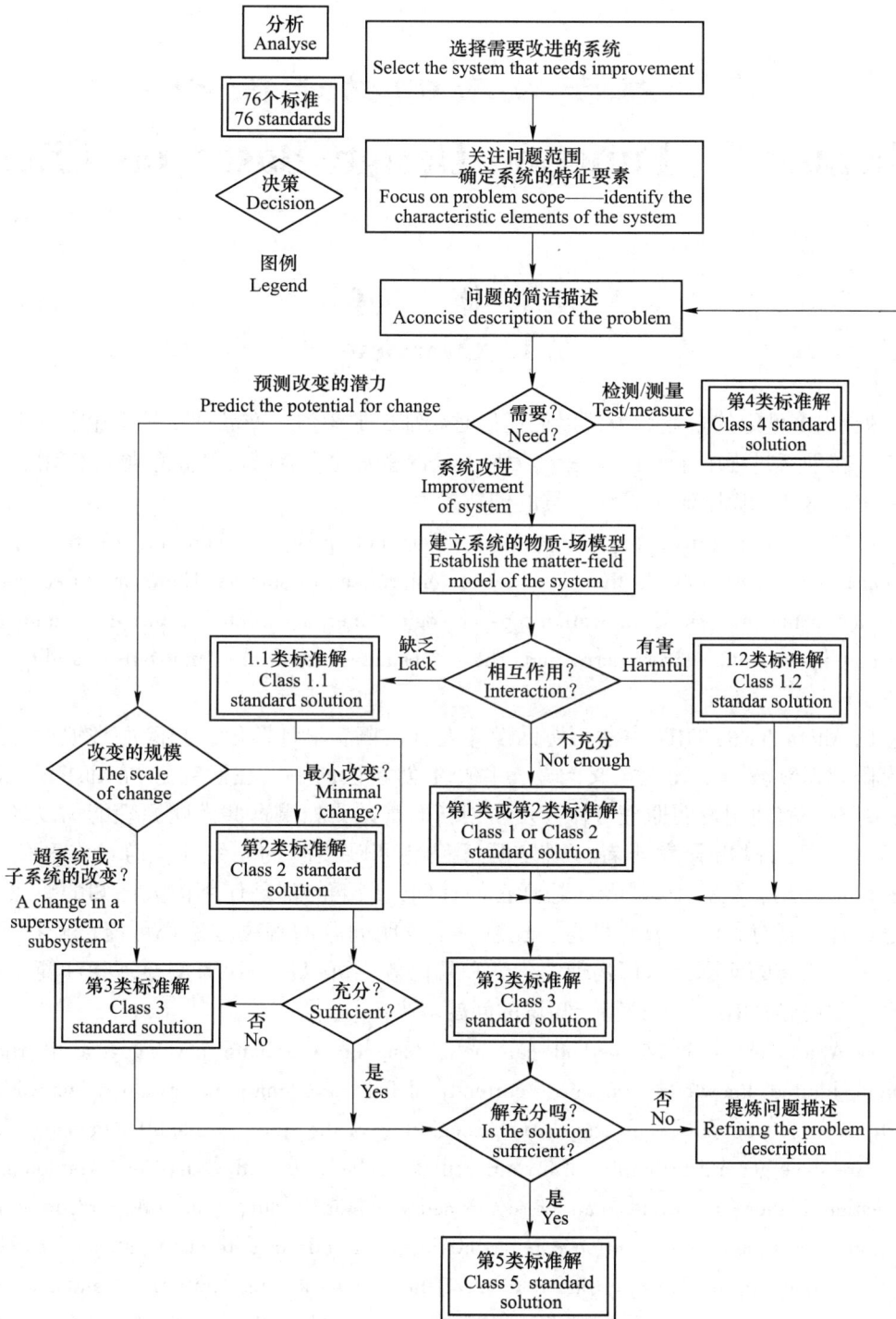

图 6-3　76 个标准解应用流程

Figure 6-3　Application process of 76 standard solutions

7 基于效应的功能设计
Chapter 7 Function Design Based on Effect

7.1 概　　述
7.1 Overview

处于 21 世纪的企业竞争比以往任何时候都更加激烈，产品创新是企业唯一生存之道。在创新过程中主要存在三个障碍，即心理惯性、有限的知识领域和使用实验纠错法。这些障碍限制了设计人员的创新能力。

In the 21st century, the competition among enterprises is more intense than ever before. Product innovation is the only way for enterprises to survive. There are three main obstacles in the process of innovation: psychological inertia, limited knowledge, and the use of experimental error correction. These obstacles limit the innovative ability of designers.

G. Altetmller 的 TRIZ 方法可协助设计人员在概念设计阶段，扫除心理惯性，扩展有限知识领域，正确地定义问题，并产生创新性的解。在研究之初 Altshuller 认为：存在一些通用发明原理可作为发明创新的基础，如果这些发明原理能加以确认与整理，并用以指导发明者，则发明过程是可以预测的。另外，通过专利研究 Altshuller 指出，只有 1% 的专利是真正的首创，剩下的都是使用前人已知的想法或概念，加上新奇方法。因此可得，任意一个发明问题的解决方法都可能已经存在。对于一个给定的问题，运用物理、化学和几何效应可以使解决方案更理想和简单地实现。效应是 TRIZ 中一种基于知识的问题解决工具。

G. Altetmller's TRIZ method can help designers eliminate psychological inertia, expand limited knowledge domain, correctly define problems and produce innovative solutions in conceptual design stage. At the beginning of the study, Altshuller believed that there are some general principles of invention that can be used as the basis for invention and innovation. If these principles can be confirmed and sorted out, and used to guide the inventor, the process of invention can be predicted. In addition, through patent research, Altshuller pointed out that only one percent of the patents are real initiative, and the rest are using previously known ideas or concepts, plus novel methods. Therefore, it can be concluded that the solution to any invention problem may already exist. For a given problem, the application of physical, chemical and geometric effects can make the solution more ideal and simple. Effect is a knowledge-based problem-solving tool in TRIZ.

本章将介绍效应的概念，应用效应进行功能设计一般过程以及相关工程案例。

This chapter will introduce the concept of effect, the general process of applying effect to functional design and related engineering cases.

7.2 效应及效应链
7.2 Effect and effect chain

效应与产品之间存在关联性，可用于产品设计中原理解的确定。TRIZ 将专利作为效应知识库中效应的主要信息源。通过专利分析，效应确定了专利中产品的功能与实现该功能的科学原理之间的相关性，将物理、化学等科学原理与其工程应用有机结合在一起，从本质上解释了功能实现的科学依据，有利于高级别创新解的产生。

There is correlation between effect and product, which can be used to determine the original understanding in product design. TRIZ regards patent as the main information source of effect in effect knowledge base. Through the patent analysis, the correlation between the function of the product in the patent and the scientific principle to realize the function is determined. The scientific principle of physics and chemistry and its engineering application are organically combined to explain the scientific basis of function realization in essence, which is conducive to the generation of high-level innovative solutions.

7.2.1 效应
7.2.1 Effect

效应是对系统输入/输出间转换过程的描述，该过程由科学原理和系统属性支配，并伴有现象发生。基于专利分析，效应将科学原理、系统属性和现象与其工程应用有机地联系在一起，确定了在科学原理和系统属性支配下输入/输出流之间的因果关系。

Effect is a description of the process of input/output conversion, which is dominated by scientific principles and system attributes, accompanied by phenomena. Based on patent analysis, the effect connects scientific principles, system attributes and phenomena with their engineering applications, and determines the causal relationship between input/output flows under the control of scientific principles and system attributes.

每一个效应都有输入和输出，因此效应模型有输入和输出两个接口（两极），如图 7-1（a）所示。效应还可以通过辅助量来控制或调整其输出，可控制的效应模型扩展为三个接口（三极），如图 7-1（b）所示。

Each effect has input and output, so the effect model has two interfaces (two poles), as shown in Figure 7-1 (a). The effect can also be controlled or adjusted by auxiliary quantity. The controllable effect model is extended to three interfaces (three poles), as shown in Figure 7-1 (b).

一个效应可以有多个输入流、输出流或控制流，例如库仑效应中带电体所带电量（Q_1、Q_2）为两个输入流，库仑力（F）为输出流，相对介电常数私（ε_r）和带电体间距离（r）为控制流，如图 7-2 所示。效应应该用具有多个输入流、输出流

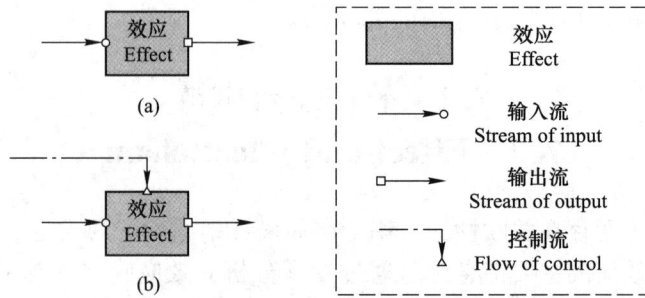

图 7-1   效应模型
（a）两极效应模式；（b）三级效应模式

Figure 7-1   Effect model
（a）Bipolar effect model；（b）Three pole effect model

或控制流的多极效应模型表示，如图 7-3 所示。

An effect can have multiple input streams, output streams or control streams. For example, in the Coulomb effect, the charged quantity （Q_1, Q_2）of the charged body is two input streams, the Coulomb force （F）is the output stream, and the relative permittivity （ε_r）and the distance between the charged bodies （r）are the control streams, as shown in Figure 7-2. The effect should be represented by a multipole effect model with multiple input, output or control flows, as shown in Figure 7-3.

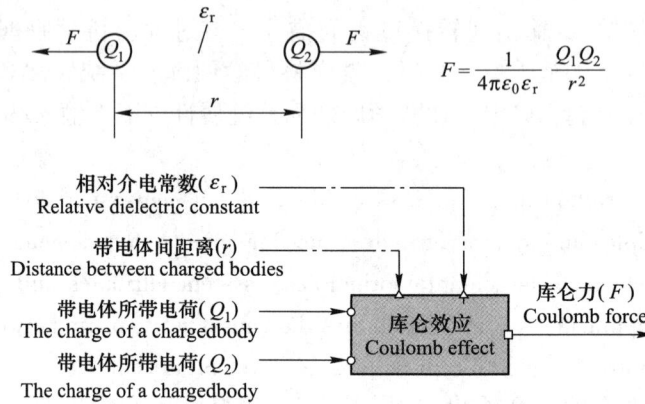

$$F = \frac{1}{4\pi\varepsilon_0\varepsilon_r} \frac{Q_1 Q_2}{r^2}$$

图 7-2   库仑效应模型

Figure 7-2   Coulomb effect model

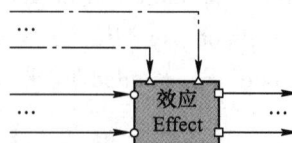

图 7-3   具有多流的多效应模型

Figure 7-3   Multi effect model with multi flow

7.2.2 效应模式
7.2.2 **Effect mode**

依据效应规定的输入/输出流之间的因果关系可以实现预期的输入/输出转换。预期的输入/输出转换可以由一个效应实现。如果没有可以直接实现预期转换的效应，可以按照邻接效应输入/输出流之间的相容关系，将多个效应组合成效应链。基于多流多极效应模型构建效应链的基本组成方式称为效应模式，效应模式有以下几种。

The expected input/output conversion can be achieved according to the causal relationship between the input/output flows specified by the effect. The expected input/output conversion can be achieved by an effect. If there is no effect that can directly achieve the desired conversion, multiple effects can be combined into an effect chain according to the compatible relationship between adjacent effect input/output streams. Based on the multi current and multi pole effect model, the basic composition of the effect chain is called the effect mode.

（1）串联效应模式：预期的输入/输出转换由按顺序相继发生多个效应共同实现，如图 7-4 所示。

（1）Series effect mode：the expected input/output conversion is realized by multiple effects occurring in sequence, as shown in Figure 7-4.

图 7-4　串联效应模型

Figure 7-4　Series effect model

（2）并联效应模式：预期的输入/输出转换由同时发生的多个效应共同实现，如图 7-5 所示。

（2）Parallel effect mode：the expected input/output conversion is realized by multiple simultaneous effects, as shown in Figure 7-5.

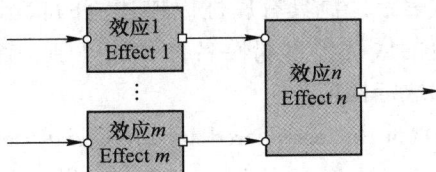

图 7-5　并联效应

Figure 7-5　Parallel effect

（3）环形效应模式：预期的输入/输出转换由多个效应共同实现，后一效应的输出流通过一定的方式返回到前一效应的输入端，如图 7-6 所示。

（3）Ring effect mode：the expected input/output conversion is realized by multiple effects, and the otput flow of the latter effect returns to the input of the former effect in a certain way, as shown in Figure 7-6.

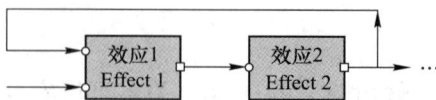

图 7-6　环形效应模式

Figure 7-6　Annular effect pattern

（4）控制效应模式：预期的输入/输出转换由多个效应共同实现，其中一个或多个效应的输出流由其他效应的输出流控制，如图 7-7 所示。

（4）Control effect mode：the expected input/output conversion is realized by multiple effects，and the output flow of one or more effects is controlled by the output flow of other effects，as shown in Figure 7-7.

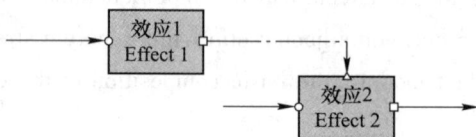

图 7-7　控制效应模型

Figure 7-7　Control effect model

7.2.3　效应链推理方法
7.2.3　Effect chain reasoning method

效应模式是实现输入/输出转换的几种基本方式。在实际应用过程中，通常需要将多种效应模式组合成复合效应链来实现预期的输入/输出转换。

Effect mode is the basic way to realize input/output conversion. In practical application，it is usually necessary to combine multiple effect modes into a composite effect chain to achieve the desired input/output conversion.

流是任何设计问题中都要考虑的基本对象，它包含了产品模型中关键的物理信息。流通常分为物质流、能量流和信号流，并可以进一步细化。物质最好用物料表示，信息更具体地用参数表示。流具有属性以描述流的状态，流的属性可以分为物理属性、化学属性等。流的属性包含属性名称和属性值，流的属性不同则流不同。概念设计阶段流的属性仅取定性值。

Flow is the basic object to be considered in any design problem. It contains the key physical information in the product model. Flow is usually divided into material flow，energy flow and signal flow，and can be further refined. Materials are best represented by materials，and information is more specifically represented by parameters. Flow has attributes to describe the state of flow. The attributes of flow can be divided into physical attributes，chemical attributes and so on. The attributes of a flow include the attribute name and the attribute value. Different attributes of a flow make different flows. Only qualitative values are taken for the attributes of the flow in conceptual design phase.

假定存在两个名称相同的流，如果流 1 具有 k 个属性，流 2 具有的 n 个属性中有 m 个属性与流 1 相同，则流 2 相对流 1 的一致性程度（Dc）可用下式计算：

Suppose there are two streams with the same name. If stream 1 has k attributes and stream 2 has n attributes, m of which are the same as stream 1, then the consistency degree（Dc）of stream 2 relative to stream 1 can be calculated as follows：

$$Dc = \frac{m}{k} \times 100\%$$

要将多个效应组合成效应链，邻接效应的输入流与输出流必须相容。邻接效应的输入流与输出流必须相容是指邻接效应的输入流与输出流名称相同，且输入流与输出流的一致性程度 $Dc = 100\%$，称为效应相容规则，简记为 $W_1 = W_2$。

To combine multiple effects into an effect chain, the input and output flows of adjacency effects must be compatible. The input flow and output flow of adjacency effect must be compatible, which means that the input flow and output flow of adjacency effect have the same name, and the consistency degree of input flow and output flow $Dc = 100\%$, which is called effect compatibility rule, abbreviated as $W_1 = W_2$.

在不限制转换次数的情况下，在理论上实现两个不同流之间的转换可能有无穷多种，效应链的长度也各不相同。从输入流 W_i 到输出流 W_o（$W_i \neq W_o$）的所用可能转换路径中，最短路径长度 $P_{\min}$ 是 $W_i \rightarrow W_o$ 转换的最小值。

Without limiting the number of transitions, there may be infinitely many transitions between two different streams in theory, and the length of the effect chain is also different. From input stream W_i to output stream W_o（$W_i \neq W_o$）, the shortest path length $P_{\min}$ is the minimum value of $W_i \rightarrow W_o$ conversion.

基于效应相容规则和效应模式将多个效应推理组合成效应链可以有完全匹配法、最短路径法和近似匹配法三种效应链推理方法。

Based on effect compatibility rule and effect pattern, there are three effect chain reasoning methods：perfect matching method, shortest path method and approximate matching method.

7.2.3.1　完全匹配法
7.2.3.1　Perfect matching method

基于效应相容规则，给出了两种推理模型：正向搜索推理模型和反向搜索推理模型。首先，输入预期的输入输出转换 $T = [W_i][W_o]$，并设定最大效应链长度 $N_{\max}$。然后，选择推理模型，依据流相容规则搜索效应。正向推理模型中，依据 $W_i = W_{i1}$ 搜索效应，确定每一个效应的输出流（W_{Po1}）。如果 $W_{Po1} = W_o$，则确定实现预期输入/输出转换的效应链，并标记效应链路径长度 $P(W_i, W_o) = 1$，推理次数 $tr = 1$。如果第一次推理不满足期望的输出流，则将效应的输出流（W_{Po1}）作为新的输入流（$W_{i2} = W_{Po1}$）进行第二次推理，以此类推，直到推理次数与最大效应链长度相等为止。反向推理模型中，依据 $W_{Pi} = W_{Po1}$ 搜索效应，确定每一个效应的输出流（W_{Pi1}）。如果 $W_{Pi1} = W_{Pi}$，则确定实现预期输入/输出转换的效应链，并标记效应链

路径长度 P (W_i, W_o) =1，推理次数 tr =1。如果第一次推理不满足期望的输出流，则将效应的输出流（W_{Pi1}）作为新的输出流（$W_{o2} = W_{Pi1}$）进行第二次推理，以此类推，直到推理次数与最大效应链长度相等为止。最后，对效应链进行评价以获得最优组合解。

Based on the effect compatibility rule, two reasoning models are proposed: forward search reasoning model and reverse search reasoning model. First, input the expected input-output conversion $T=$ [W_i] [W_o], and set the maximum effect chain length N_{max}. Then, the inference model is selected to search the effect according to the flow compatibility rule. In the forward reasoning model, the output stream (W_{Po1}) of each effect is determined according to $W_i = W_{i1}$ search effect. If $W_{Po1} = W_o$, the effect chain to achieve the desired input/output conversion is determined, and the path length P (W_i, W_o) of the effect chain is marked as 1, the number of reasoning tr =1. If the first inference does not meet the expected output stream, the output stream of the effect (W_{Po1}) is used as the new input stream ($W_{i2} = W_{Po1}$) for the second inference, and so on, until the number of inference is equal to the length of the maximum effect chain. In the reverse reasoning model, the output stream (W_{pi1}) of each effect is determined according to the search effect of $W_{Pi} = W_{Po1}$. If $W_{Pi1} = W_{Pi}$, the effect chain to achieve the desired input/output conversion is determined, and the path length P (W_i, W_o) = 1 and the inference times tr =1 are marked. If the first inference does not meet the expected output stream, the output stream of effect (W_{Pi1}) is used as the new output stream ($W_{o2} = W_{pi1}$) for the second inference, and so on, until the number of inference is equal to the length of the maximum effect chain. Finally, the effect chain is evaluated to obtain the optimal combination solution.

7.2.3.2 最短路径法
7.2.3.2 The shortest path method

基于完全匹配法可以确定实现输入流到输出流转换的最短效应链路径长度，将这些最短效应链路径知识收集起来，形成最短效应链路径知识库。借助最短效应链路径知识库，设计者可以迅速地找到最短的搜索路径，实现输入流到输出流的转换。该方法有效地收敛了解空间，提高了求解效率。

Based on the perfect matching method, the shortest effect chain path length to realize the transformation from input stream to output stream can be determined, and the shortest effect chain path knowledge can be collected to form the shortest effect chain path knowledge base. With the help of the shortest effect chain path knowledge base, designers can quickly find the shortest search path and realize the transformation from input stream to output stream. This method effectively converges the solution space and improves the efficiency of solution.

7.2.3.3 近似匹配法
7.2.3.3 Approximate matching method

完全流匹配法和最短路径法要求邻接效应的输入流与输出流之间满足效应相容规则。在效应知识库中规定较小的情况下，要求效应链中的输入流与输出流完全匹配时才会导致无解，而且不利于创新解的产生。为了解决上述问题，可以形成效成链的过程中允许输入流与输出流的近似匹配，即按给定的一致性程度（$Dc_0 \leqslant 100\%$）进行匹配。

The complete flow matching method and the shortest path method require that the input flow and output flow of adjacency effect meet the effect compatibility rule. In the case of a small effect knowledge base, when the input stream and output stream in the effect chain are required to match completely, there will be no solution, and it is not conducive to the generation of innovative solutions. In order to solve the above problems, the approximate matching between the input stream and the output stream can be allowed in the process of forming the effective chain, that is, matching according to the given consistency degree ($Dc_0 \leqslant 100\%$).

近似匹配法包括正向近似匹配推理模型和反向近似匹配推理模型两种推理模型。两种近似匹配推理模型与完全匹配法中的两种推理模型相似，只是依据输入/输出流将多个效应结合成为效应链时不再遵循效应相容规则，而是按 $Dc \geqslant Dc_0$ 进行匹配，近似匹配法利用输入流与输出流之间的近似匹配增加了创新的可能性，但对于产生的效应链中效应间的相容性要进行检验。

The approximate matching method includes two inference models: forward approximate matching inference model and reverse approximate matching inference model. The two approximate matching reasoning models are similar to the two reasoning models in the complete matching method, but when combining multiple effects into an effect chain based on the input/output flow, the effect compatibility rule is no longer followed, but the matching is carried out according to $Dc \geqslant Dc_0$. The approximate matching method increases the possibility of innovation by using the approximate matching between the input flow and the output flow, but the compatibility between the effects in the resulting effect chain needs to be tested.

7.3 基于效应的功能设计过程
7.3 Effect based functional design process

功能设计是产品设计的核心阶段。在该阶段，设计人员根据用户需求确定产品的总功能，并将总功能分解力分功能及功能元，功能与能量、物料、信号三种流组成的网络结构即为待设计产品的功能结构；确定每个功能元的原理解，并将所有功能元的原理解合成得到待设计产品的原理解。

Function design is the technical stage of product design. In this stage, the designer determines the total function of the product according to the user's demand, and divides the total power into function and function element. The network structure composed of function, energy, material and signal is the functional structure of the product to be designed. The principle solution of each function element is determined, and the principle solution of all function elements is synthesized to obtain the principle solution of the product to be designed.

效应与产品之间存在关联性，可用于产品设计中原理解的确定。通过设计目录、功能量矩阵等工具在效应知识库中进行效应的查找和组合，获得满足产品功能的原理解，统称为基于效应的功能设计。

There is correlation between effect and product, which can be used to determine the original understanding in product design. Through the search and combination of effects in the effect knowledge base by means of design catalog, function quantity matrix and other tools, theprinciple solution satisfying the product function is obtained, which is collectively referred to as effect based functional design.

7.3.1　基本概念
7.3.1　Basic concepts

7.3.1.1　功能
7.3.1.1　Function

功能是功能设计中的一个重要概念。功能是对一定设计环境下用以实现设计意图的输入/输出之间关系的抽象描述。由于设计初期各种信息不完备，所以设计者对设计意图的认识和描述是比较抽象和不确定的。功能的实现建立在与环境发生物质、能量和信号交换关系的基础上，功能是一个开发体系。功能通常采用"动词+名词"的形式描述。

Function is an important concept in function design. Function is an abstract description of the relationship between input and output used to achieve design intent in a certain design environment. Due to the incomplete information at the beginning of the design, the designer's understanding and description of the design intention are abstract and uncertain. The realization of function is based on the exchange of material, energy and signal with the environment. Function is a development system. Function is usually described in the form of "Verb + noun".

为了规范产品功能，学者们进行了很多研究。Malmqvist 认为 TRIZ 中的功能比较具体不适于功能结构的建立。基于上述分类和直接进化理论对 TRIZ 中的 30 种功能进行扩展、语义规定和重新分类，建立了标准的功能集，包括操作集和流集，见表 7-1 和表 7-2。

In order to standardize the product function, scholars have done a lot of research. Malmqvist thinks that the function of TRIZ is more specific and not suitable for the establishment of functional structure. Based on the above classification and direct evolution theory, 30 functions in TRIZ are extended, semantically defined and reclassified, and a standard function set is established, including operation set and flow set, as shown in Table 7-1 and Table 7-2.

表 7-1　操作集简表

Table 7-1　Operation set summary

类操作 Class operation	基本操作 Basic operation
产生 Produce	合成，生产 Synthesis, production
变化 Change	增加，减少，转变，相变，成形，控制 Increase, decrease, transform, phase change, forming, control
结合 Combine	混合，嵌入，装配，连接 Mix, embed, assemble, connect
分离 Separate	分开，分解，抽取，净化 Separate, decompose, extract, purify
积聚 Gather	吸收，存储，聚集 Absorption, storage, aggregation
运动 Motion	移动，传输，旋转，振动，提升，引导 Move, transmit, rotate, vibrate, lift, guide
测量 Measure	检测，度量，测量 Test, measure, measure
保持 Keep	预防，维持，稳定 Prevent, maintain, stabilize
消除 Eliminate	破坏，去除 Destroy, remove

表 7-2　流集简表

Table 7-2　Flow set summary

类流 Class flow	子流 Subflow
物料 Materiel	固体，液体，气体，化合物，混合物，几何体，松散物质，多孔物质，结构物质，粒子，分子和亚分子，等离子体 Solid, liquid, gas, compound, mixture, geometry, loose matter, porous matter, structural matter, particle, molecule and sub molecule, plasma
能量 Energy	力，运动，形变，热能，机械波和声波，电场，磁场，电磁感应，电磁波和光，核能与放射性 Force, motion, deformation, thermal energy, mechanical wave and sound wave, electric field, magnetic field, electromagnetic induction, electromagnetic wave and light, nuclear energy and radioactivity

类流 Class flow	子流 Subflow
参数 Parameter	固体参数，表面参数，几何参数，形变参数，流体参数，气体参数，浓度参数，量参数，化学参数，力参数，运动参数，过程参数，热参数，机械波与声波参数，电场参数，磁场参数，电磁感应参数，电磁波和光参数，放射性参数 Solid parameters, surface parameters, geometric parameters, deformation parameters, fluid parameters, gas parameters, concentration parameters, quantity parameters, chemical parameters, force parameters, motion parameters, process parameters, thermal parameters, mechanical and acoustic parameters, electric field parameters, magnetic field parameters, electromagnetic induction parameters, electromagnetic wave and optical parameters, radioactive parameters

通过功能分解建立功能结构，如图 7-8 所示，可以实现系统由抽象到具体的转化，降低功能求解的复杂度。功能结构中总功能、分功能、功能元间以逻辑与、或关系联接形成树型结构，称为功能树；同一层功能之间以串联、并联、环形或控制关系联接形成链型结构，称为功能链；功能树和功能链分别描述功能间的纵向和横向关系。

The functional structure is established by functional decomposition, as shown in Figure 7-8, which can realize the transformation of the system from abstract to concrete and reduce the complexity of functional solution. In the functional structure, the tree structure is formed by the connection of logic and, or relationship among the total function, sub function and functional element, which is called the functional tree; the chain structure is formed by the connection of series, parallel, circular or control relationship among the functions of the same layer, which is called the functional chain; the function tree and the functional chain describe the vertical and horizontal relationship between functions respectively.

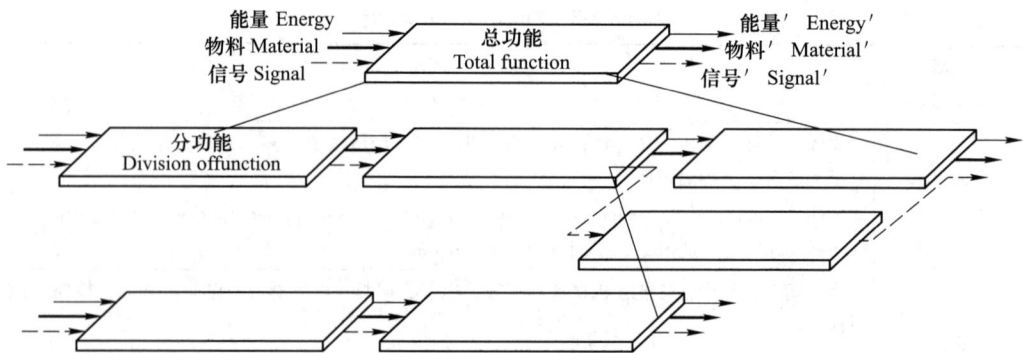

图 7-8　功能结构

Figure 7-8　Function structure

7.3.1.2 行为

7.3.1.2 Behavior

行为（Behavior）是系统输入/输出状态的描述。描述系统输入、输出之间的关系的行为称为外部行为。对于复杂系统，外部行为通常分解为一系列容易实现的子行为，每个子行为由系统结构的全体或其中的一部分来表现。子行为间存在着因果关系和结构关系。因果关系描述了相邻两个子行为的输出、输入之间的连接关系；结构关系描述了内部行为中的子行为之间的组成关系。将子行为按因果次序形成外部行为的因果过程称为内部行为。内部行为既描述了子行为间的因果关系，又体现了外部行为的实现方式。内部行为的发生导致外部行为的实现，一个外部行为可以由多个内部行为分别实现。为保证内部行为的实现，在流转换过程中相邻子行为的输入、输出必须相容，并且要满足相应的约束条件。

Behavior is the description of system input/output state. The behavior that describes the relationship between system input and output is called external behavior. For complex systems, external behaviors are usually decomposed into a series of easily implemented sub behaviors, and each sub behavior is represented by all or part of the system structure. There are causal and structural relationships among the sub behaviors. Causality describes the connection between the output and input of two adjacent sub behaviors, and structural relationship describes the composition of sub behaviors in internal behaviors. The cause and effect process in which sub behaviors form external behaviors in the order of cause and effect is called internal behavior. Internal behavior not only describes the causal relationship between sub behaviors, but also reflects the realization of external behavior. The occurrence of internal behavior leads to the realization of external behavior. An external behavior can be realized by multiple internal behaviors. In order to ensure the realization of internal behavior, the input and output of adjacent sub behaviors must be compatible and meet the corresponding constraints in the process of flow transformation.

7.3.1.3 结构

7.3.1.3 Structure

原理结构（PS，Principle Structure）是对组成产品子结构以及子结构之间配合关系的一种抽象或定性的描述。产品原理结构模型通常由以下几部分组成：子结构（SS，Sub-Structure）和联接结构（CS，Connect Structure），它们各自发挥自身的作用，并通过联接面（CSs，Conncet Surfaces）相互耦合，形成产品总功能或外部行为实现结构。

Principle Structure (PS) is an abstract or qualitative description of the product substructure and the relationship between the substructures. The productprinciple structure model usually consists of the following parts: Sub Structure (SS) and Connect Structure (CS). They play their own roles and couple with each other through the Connect Surfaces

（CSs）to form the overall function or external behavior realization structure of the product.

产品原理结构模型是对产品组成部分以及组成部分之间配合关系的一种抽象或定性的表达，层次化的树状结构描述不同层结构之间的纵向逻辑关系，链状结构描述功能树中同一层结构之间的横向组合关系。因此，产品原理结构模型是一种网状结构，另外，产品原理结构模型虽然是一种产品实际结构在原理上的表达，但它也对应着一定的功能，反映输入流与输出流之间的转换。因此，产品原理结构模型中效应结构之间是有次序的，要描述流在系统中的流动。如果效应结构与其他效应结构建立了关系，则其他效应结构就会对该结构施加组合约束（形状、位置约束、尺寸、运动约束等）。实际上，产品原理结构中，效应结构通常被施加了多个组合约束，因而产品原理结构模型需要综合考虑效应结构的每一组合约束才能得到。

The productprinciple structure model is an abstract or qualitative expression of the product components and the coordination relationship between them. The hierarchical tree structure describes the vertical logical relationship between different layer structures, and the chain structure describes the horizontal combination relationship between the same layer structures in the function tree. Therefore, the product principle structure model is a kind of network structure. In addition, although the product principle structure model is an expression of the actual product structure in principle, it also corresponds to certain functions, reflecting the transformation between input flow and output flow. Therefore, in the product principle structure model, the effect structures are ordered to describe the flow in the system. If the effect structure has a relationship with other effect structures, other effect structures will impose combined constraints (shape, position, size, motion, etc.) on the structure. In fact, in the product principle structure, the effect structure is usually imposed with multiple combination constraints, so the product principle structure model needs to consider each combination constraint of the effect structure.

7.3.2　基于效应的基本映射单元
7.3.2　Basic mapping unit based on effect

基于效应进行功能，行为和结构间的映射有以下几种基本映射单元。

The mapping between function, behavior and structure is based on effect.

7.3.2.1　总功能→外部行为映射
7.3.2.1　Total function → external behavior mapping

在设计初期，设计者对设计问题的描述和认识是比较抽象和不确定的，对待设计系统的输入/输出往往考虑不周全。功能到行为的映射是问题描述具体化的过程。

一个系统通常具有多个功能，其中一个是主功能，系统存在的意义在于实现该功能。其他功能为辅助功能，系统实现辅助功能的目的是更好地实现主功能。系统总功能的实现要以主功能为出发点，然后才能围绕主功能选择必需的辅助功能。系统的主功能由执行机构具体完成。

通过专利分析可以确定功能（功能元）与效应之间的相关性，功能元与效应之间是一种多对多的对应关系。设计人员根据用户需求确定产品的总功能和主功能，依据功能效应对应关系确定实现主功能的效应集，并对效应集中的效应进行筛选。根据选定效应的输入/输出流，由系统完整性和可用资源确定系统输入/输出流，实现总功能到外部行为的映射。图 7-9 所示产品黑箱模型描述了产品总功能与输入/输出之间的关系，使设计问题描述具体化。

In the early stage of design, the designer's description and understanding of the design problem is abstract and uncertain, and the input/output of the design system is often not fully considered. The mapping from function to behavior is the process of problem description concretization.

A system usually has many functions, one of which is the main function. The significance of the system is to realize the function. Other functions are auxiliary functions, and the purpose of the system to realize the auxiliary functions is to better realize the main functions. The realization of the total function of the system should be based on the main function, and then the necessary auxiliary functions can be selected around the main function. The main function of the system is completed by the actuator.

Through patent analysis, we can determine the correlation between function (functional element) and effect, which is a many to many correspondence. The designer determines the total function and main function of the product according to the user's needs, determines the effect set to realize the main function according to the corresponding relationship of function effect, and screens the effects in the effect set. According to the input/output flow of the selected effect, the input/output flow of the system is determined by the system integrity and available resources to realize the mapping from the total function to the external behavior. The black box model of the product shown in Figure 7-9 describes the relationship between the total function of the product and the input/output, which makes the description of the design problem concrete.

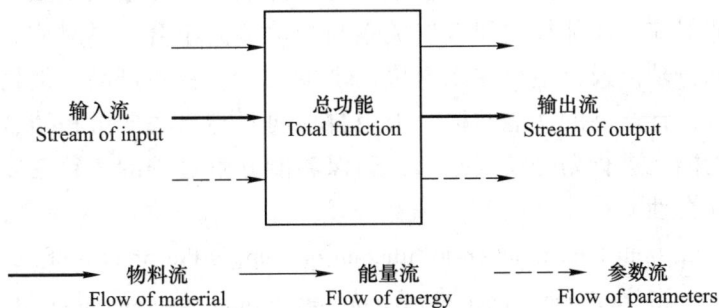

输入流　　　　　总功能　　　　　输出流
Stream of input　Total function　Stream of output

物料流　　　　　能量流　　　　　参数流
Flow of material　Flow of energy　Flow of parameters

图 7-9　产品黑箱模型

Figure 7-9　Product black box model

7.3.2.2　外部行为→子行为

7.3.2.2　External behavior → sub behavior

外部行为到子行为的映射是确定系统输入/输出状态转换因果次序的过程。依据

图 7-9 中的系统输入/输出流和选定实现主功能的效应，利用效应模式和效应链推理方法构建效应链。效应链中每一效应输入/输出状态的转换都与一个子行为对应，而效应链对应的输入/输出状态转换次序则与内部行为对应，内部行为的发生导致外部行为的实现。基于效应的外部行为到子行为映射建立行为模型，描述外部行为、内部行为和子行为间因果关系，可依据流的转换路径及其连通性对待设计系统进行检验。

The mapping from external behavior to sub behavior is a process to determine the causal order of system input/output state transition. According to the system input/output flow in Figure 7-9 and the effect selected to realize the main function, the effect chain is constructed by using the effect mode and effect chain reasoning method. In the effect chain, the transition of each effect input/output state corresponds to a sub behavior, and the transition order of the effect chain corresponds to the internal behavior. The occurrence of the internal behavior leads to the realization of the external behavior. Based on the effect mapping from external behavior to sub behavior, the behavior model is established to describe the causal relationship among external behavior, internal behavior and sub behavior. The flow transformation path and its connectivity can be used to test the design system.

7.3.2.3　总功能→功能元映射

7.3.2.3　Total function → function element mapping

总功能到功能元的映射是通过功能分解建立功能结构的过程。按实际情况构建效应链，再依据功能效应对应关系确定效应链中每一效应的功能（功能元），建立产品功能链，实现总功能到功能元自顶向下的分解。依据系统完整性定律和三流原则对功能链中的功能元进行模块划分，并确定功能模块间接口关系。功能模块与分功能对应，功能模块间接口关系与分功能间组合关系对应，实现功能链中的功能元到分功能及其组合关系自底向上的抽取，构建产品功能树。功能树和功能链构成待设计产品的功能结构。采用自顶向下与自底向上相结合的方法对各个分功能或功能元进行划分及其排列，确保功能分解过程的一致性以及分功能和功能元解的存在性。

The mapping from total function to function element is the process of building function structure through function decomposition. According to the actual situation, the effect chain is constructed, and then the function (function element) of each effect in the effect chain is determined according to the corresponding relationship of function effect, and the product function chain is established to realize the decomposition from the total function to the function element. According to the law of system integrity and thethree flow principle, the functional elements in the functional chain are divided into modules, and the interface relationship between functional modules is determined. The function module corresponds to the sub function, and the interface relationship between the function modules corresponds to the combination relationship between the sub functions. The bottom-up extraction from the function element to the sub function and its combination relationship in the function chain is realized, and the product function tree is constructed. Function tree and function chain constitute the function structure of the product to be designed. The top-down and bottom-up methods are used to divide and arrange each sub function or function element, so as to ensure the consistency of function decomposition process and the existence of sub function and function element solutions.

7.3.2.4 功能元→子结构映射

7.3.2.4 Function element → substructure mapping

功能元到子结构的映射是产生满足功能元的子结构的过程。通过专利分析确定专利中产品的结构信息，进而确定与结构相关的效应，建立效应与结构之间的相关性。效应和结构之间是多对多的关系。对于给定的功能元，依据功能与效应、效应与结构之间的相关性，形成基于效应的功能元与子结构间的映射关系。

The mapping from function element to substructure is the process of generating substructure satisfying function element. Through patent analysis, the structure information ofproducts in patent is determined, and then the structure related effects are determined, and the correlation between effects and structure is established. The relationship between effect and structure is many to many. For a given function element, according to the correlation between function and effect, effect and structure, the mapping relationship between function element and substructure based on effect is formed.

7.3.2.5 子结构→原理结构

7.3.2.5 Substructure →principle structure

子结构到原理结构的映射是确定实现功能元的子结构后，对子结构进行适当的组合、调整形成产品原理结构的过程。子结构间的可组合性由输入输出流、连接结构和联接面几何特征决定。由于效应与子结构间是多对多的映射关系，所以需要依据行为模型对产品原理结构中可能存在的无效或冗余结构进行检验和修正。

The mapping from substructure to principle structure is the process of properly combining and adjusting the substructures to form the product principle structure after the substructure of function element is determined. The composability of substructures is determined by the input-output flow, the connection structure and the geometry of the connection surface. Due to the many to many mapping relationship between effect and substructure, it is necessary to check and correct the invalid or redundant structure in the product principle structure according to the behavior model.

7.3.3　基于效应模功能设计过程
7.3.3　Functional design process based on EMD

效应是产品功能、行为和结构存在的科学依据。将多输入/输出流多极效应模型与 FBS 框架集成，确定效应、功能、行为和结构之间的内在因果关系，建立扩展效应驱动的功能行为结构模型（EE-FBS），揭示效应在功能、行为和结构转换过程中的桥梁作用，如图 7-10 所示。

Effect is the scientific basis for the existence of product function, behavior and structure. Integrate themulti input/output multi pole effect model with the FBS framework to determine the internal causal relationship among effect, function, behavior and structure, establish the extended effect driven functional behavior structure model (EE-FBS), and reveal the bridge role of effect in the process of function, behavior and structure transformation, as shown in Figure 7-10.

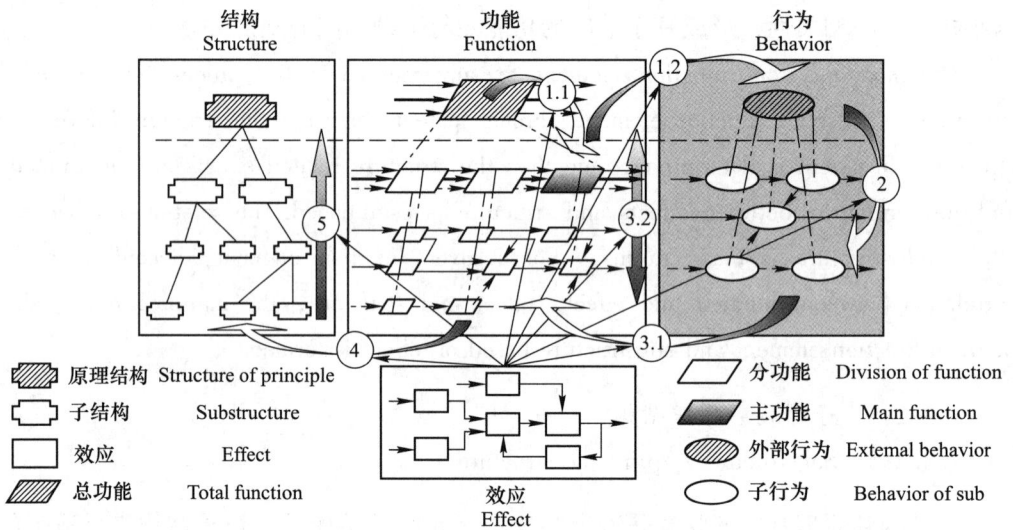

图 7-10　基于效应模功能设计过程模型

Figure 7-10　Functional design process model based on EMD

EE-FBS 模型以效应、功能、行为和结构基本概念为研究基础，以标准的操作集和流集为各映射单元的通用接口，利用形式化方法给出映射单元的恰当表示方式，基于效应模式和推理方法形成支持产品功能分解和功能到结构映射的系统化方法。

功能分析过程如下。

（1）总功能→外部行为映射：确定产品总功能与系统输入/输出之间的关系，使问题描述具体化。

（2）外部行为→子行为：确定系统输入/输出状态转换的次序，建立行为模型，检验流的转换路径及其连通性。

（3）总功能→功能元映射：采用自顶向下与自底向上相结合的方法推理可能的功能分解路线，构建待设计产品的功能结构。

The EE-FBS model is based on the basic concepts of effect, function, behavior and structure. The standard operation set and flow set are used as the common interfaces of each mapping unit. The appropriate representation of mapping unit is given by using formal method. Based on effect pattern and reasoning method, a systematic method supporting product function decomposition and function to structure mapping is formed.

The process of functional analysis is as follows.

（1）Total function → external behavior mapping：determine the relationship between the total function of the product and the system input/output to make the problem description concrete.

（2）External behavior → sub behavior：determine the order of system input/output state transition, establish behavior model, and test flow transition path and its connectivity.

（3）Total function → function element mapping：the top-down and bottom-up methods are used to infer the possible functional decomposition routes and construct the functional structure of the product to be designed.

功能到结构映射过程如下。

（1）功能元→子结构映射：确定功能结构中每一功能元对应的子结构。

（2）子结构→原理结构：将子结构按输入/输出流、连接结构和连接面几何特征组合成实现总功能的产品原理结构。

The mapping process from function to structure is as follows.

（1）Function element → substructure mapping：determine the corresponding substructure of each function element in the function structure.

（2）Substructure →principle structure：the product principle structure is composed of substructures according to input/output flow, connection structure and geometric characteristics of connection surface to realize the overall function.

基于 EE-FBS 模型的功能设计以产品功能为前提，在一定抽象层上通过推理建立模型，并分别表示在效应层和行为层中，通过进一步推理从已有设计知识或设计实例中去发现和组合出设计方案，形成产品原理结构。所发现的设计方案由设计者进行评价、决策和修正以实现需求功能。基于这一思想的功能设计过程如图 7-11 所示。

The function design based on EE-FBS model takes the product function as the premise, establishes the model through reasoning on a certain abstract level, and expresses it in the effect level and the behavior level respectively. Through further reasoning, it finds and combines the design scheme from the existing design knowledge or design cases, and forms the product principle structure. The design scheme is evaluated, decided and modified by the designer to realize the requirement function. The function design process based on this idea is shown in Figure 7-11.

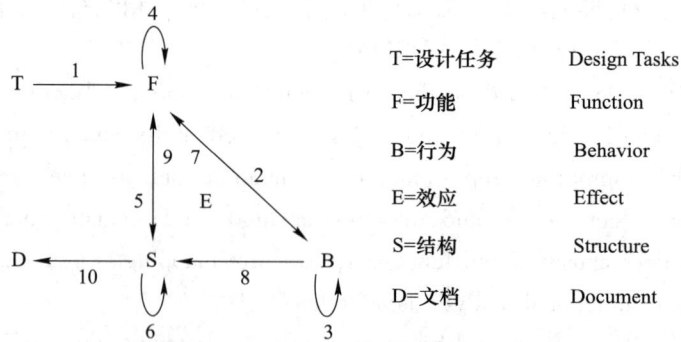

图 7-11　基于 EE-FBS 模型功能设计过程

Figure 7-11　Functional design process based on EE-FBS model

1—抽象，由设计任务抽象出产品总功能；2—映射，确定系统的输入/输出；

3—推理，确定子行为及其之间关系，建立行为模型；4—分解，将总功能分解为分功能和功能元，

建立功能结构；5—映射，确定功能元对应的子结构；6—组合，将子结构组合形成原理结构；7~9—检验，

依据行为模型分别对功能结构以及原理结构的可靠性和冗余进行检验和修正，验证原理结构是否满足产品

总功能，如不满足需求，则回退到 1~6 中某一阶段，重新进行推理和求解；

10—收录，将原理结构转换为设计文档

1—Abstract, the total function of the product is abstracted from the design task;

2—Mapping, determine the input/output of the system; 3—Reasoning, determine sub behaviors and their relationships, and establish behavior model; 4—Decomposition, the total function is divided into sub function and function element, and the function structure is established; 5—Mapping, determine the corresponding substructure of function element; 6—Combination, the combination of substructures to form the principle structure; 7~9—Inspection, according to the behavior model, the reliability and redundancy of the functional structure and the principle structure are inspected and modified to verify whether the principle structure meets the total function of the product; If it does not meet the requirements, it will go back to a certain stage in 1~6, reasoning and solving again; 10—Included, transform principle structure into design document

7.4　本章小结
7.4　Summary of this chapter

　　对于一个给定的问题，运用物理、化学和几何效应可以使解决方案更理想和简单地实现。本章介绍效应的概念、应用效应进行功能设计一般过程，并用工程实例说明了效应的应用。设计人员如能掌握，必将增加其创新能力。

　　For a given problem, the application of physical, chemical and geometric effects can make the solution more ideal and simple. This chapter introduces the concept of effect, the general process of applying effect to function design, and illustrates the application of effect with engineering examples. If designers can master it, they will increase their innovation ability.

8 应用案例分析
Chapter 8 Application Case Analysis

8.1 基于 TRIZ 理论的含油轴承粉料制备工艺及设备开发
8.1 Preparation process and equipment development of oil bearing powder based on TRIZ theory

本节主要从以下五个方面进行分析：

（1）问题背景和描述；

（2）问题分析过程；

（3）问题求解过程；

（4）问题的解；

（5）取得成果与效益。

The Section is mainly analyzed from the following five aspects:

（1）Background and description of the problem;

（2）Problem analysis process;

（3）Problem solving process;

（4）The solution of the problem;

（5）Achievements and benefits.

8.1.1 问题背景和描述
8.1.1 Problem background and description

8.1.1.1 问题的背景
8.1.1.1 Background of the problem

烧结含油轴承，铁基约占 65%，铜基约占 35%。用途极其广泛，运输机械用约占 41%，电气机械用约占 33%，办公机械占 21%，照相机、计量仪表及其他用约占 5%，含油轴承分类见图 8-1。

For sintered oil-bearing, 65% is iron-based and 35% is copper-based. It is widely used, with 41% for transportation machinery, 33% for electrical machinery, 21% for office machinery, and 5% for cameras, measuring instruments and others, the classification of oil bearing is shown in Figure 8-1.

含油轴承小型化，附加值增高。现在烧结含油轴承大体上一年生产 20 多亿个，组装在我们身边的机器中，平均每人每年约使用 2 个烧结金属含油轴承。

图 8-1　含油轴承

Figure 8-1　Oil bearing

The oil bearing is miniaturized and the added value is increased. At present, there are about 2 billion sintered oil-bearing units a year, which are assembled in the machines around us. On average, each person uses about 2 sintered metal oil-bearing units a year.

含油轴承的自润滑原理与运转特性轴承在使用过程中其内表面与轴的外表面之间形成摩擦。为了使轴承正常顺利地工作，必须对其进行润滑。润滑的目的在于减小摩擦与磨损，特别是后者。含油轴承运动如图 8-2 所示。

Self lubrication principle and operation characteristics of oil bearing friction is formed between the inner surface of the bearing and the outer surface of the shaft. In order to make the bearing work normally and smoothly, it must be lubricated. The purpose of lubrication is to reduce friction and wear, especially the latter. oil bearing movement is shown in Figure 8-2.

烧结含油轴承是利用烧结金属具有可控孔隙度的特点，在其材料的联通孔隙中含浸以润滑油，在使用时能够自动提供润滑油的一类特殊的滑动轴承。

The sintered oil-bearing is a kind of special sliding bearing which can provide lubricating oil automatically in use by using the characteristics of sintered metal with controllable porosity and impregnating lubricating oil in the connecting pores of its material.

由于润滑油的提供，在轴承的内径面与轴的轴面之间被一层流体油膜相隔离，使旋转能够轻松圆滑地进行。

Due to the supply of lubricating oil, a layer of fluid oil film is separated between the inner diameter surface of the bearing and the shaft surface of the shaft, so that the rotation can be carried out easily and smoothly.

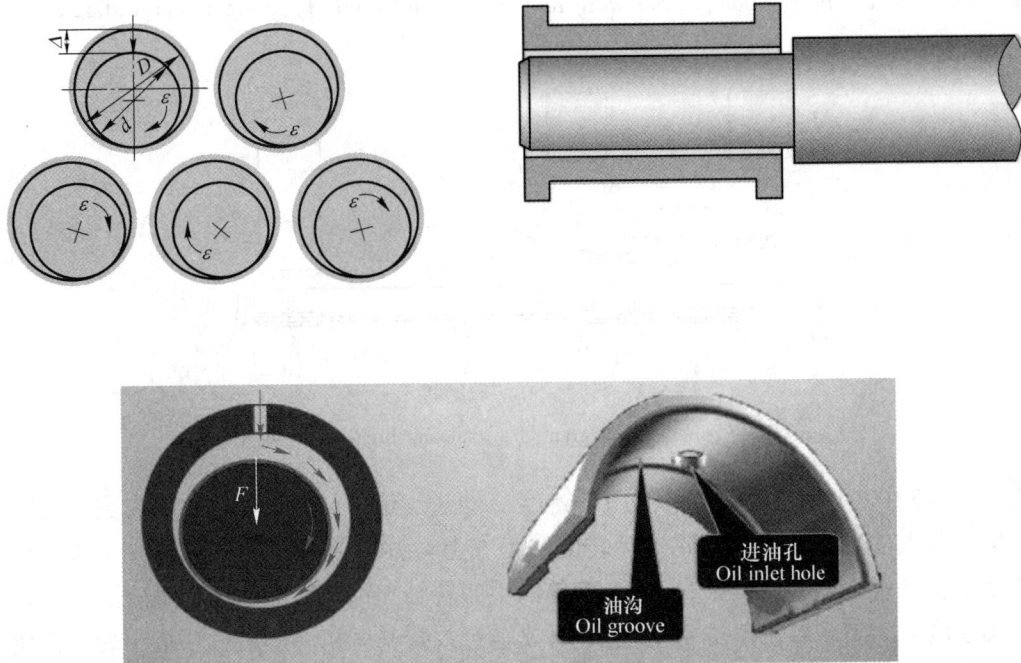

图 8-2　含油轴承运动

Figure 8-2　Oil bearing movement

8.1.1.2　问题的描述

8.1.1.2　Description of the problem

A　定义技术系统实现的功能

A　Define the function of the technology system

问题所在技术系统为 Cu/Fe 粉体机械球磨系统。

该技术系统的功能为研磨破碎 Cu、Fe 粉体。

实现该功能的约束有 Cu、Fe 粉体原始粒度、研磨方法、球料比、填充率、球磨时间以及表面活性剂对产物粒度。

The technical system of the problem is Cu/Fe powder mechanical ball milling system.

The function of the system is to grind and crush Cu and Fe powders.

The constraints to realize this function include original particle size of Cu and Fe powder, grinding method, ball to material ratio, filling rate, ball milling time and the effect of surfactant on product particle size.

B　现有技术系统的工作原理

B　Working principle of prior art system

将铁粉+铜粉+乙醇放置在高能球磨机中，将铁粉和铜粉充分混合，磨碎，示意图如图 8-3 所示。

The iron powder, copper powder and ethanol were placed in the high-energy ball mill, the iron powder and copper powder were fully mixed and ground, the schematic diagram is shown in Figure 8-3.

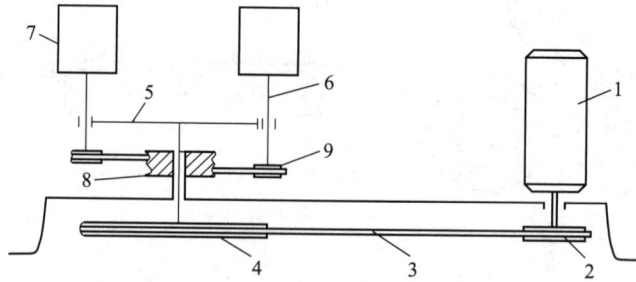

图 8-3　行星式高能球磨机示意图

Figure 8-3　Schematic diagram of a planetary high-energy ball mill

图 8-3 中与调速电机 1 固联的小皮带轮 2 通过皮带 3 与大皮带轮 4 构成皮带传动机构，与大皮带轮 4 固联并同轴运转的转盘 5 上对称布置有若干球磨筒 7 （图中仅有 2 个，且省去了磨筒支架），每个磨筒的中心转轴 6 都与转盘 5 构成回转副，并且转轴 6 的下部固联有行星带轮 9，带轮 9 又通过皮带与同机座固联的中心带轮 8 构成皮带传动。当调速电机启动后，转盘 5 便会转动起来，同时球磨筒 7 便开始做行星运动。这种行星式高能球磨机呈立式，即各旋转体的轴心线都与地面相垂直。

In the Figure 8-3 the small pulley 2 which is fixedly connected with the speed regulating motor 1 forms a belt transmission mechanism with the large pulley 4 through the belt 3. A number of ball milling cylinders 7 are symmetrically arranged on the rotary table 5 which is fixedly connected with the large pulley 4 and runs coaxially. The central rotating shaft 6 of each grinding cylinder and the turntable 5 form a rotary pair, and the lower part of the rotating shaft 6 is fixedly connected with a planetary pulley 9, which in turn forms a belt drive with the central pulley 8 fixedly connected with the same base through a belt. When the speed regulating motor is started, the turntable 5 will rotate, and the ball milling cylinder 7 will start to make planetary motion. The planetary high-energy ball mill is vertical, that is, the axis line of each rotating body is perpendicular to the ground.

C　当前技术系统存在的问题

C　Problems in current technology system

球磨后粉体 Fe、Cu 粉体，呈不规则层片状粒度，且呈现偏正态分布，造成混料不均匀，在压坯和烧结后组织中的油隙分布就不均匀，从而恶化含油轴承的性能且缩短寿命。

After ball milling, Fe and Cu powders show irregular lamellar particle size and partial normal distribution, resulting in uneven mixture and uneven distribution of oil gap in the compact and sintered structure, which worsens the performance and service life of oil bearing.

D 问题出现的条件和时间

D The condition and time of the problem

依据上述当前系统存在的问题，需要说明以下内容：

（1）原料中 Cu 粒度 3~5μm 和 Fe 小于 75μm；

（2）铁铜粉体在研磨后体积平均粒径，2h 为 40.97μm、4h 为 40.28μm、6h 为 29.47μm，实验数据图如图 8-4 所示；

（3）随球磨时间延长体积平均径减小，但仍然呈现偏正态分布；

（4）铁铜粉体研磨后的分布区间太大，会造成混料不均。

According to the above problems existing in the current system, the following contents need to be explained:

（1）The particle size of Cu is 3-5μm and Fe is less than 75μm;

（2）The volume average particle size of Fe Cu powder after grinding, 2h is 40.97μm, 4h is 40.28μm, 6h is 29.47μm, experimental data plot is shown in Figure 8-4;

（3）With the increase of milling time, the volume average diameter decreases, but it still presents a partial normal distribution;

（4）The distribution range of iron copper powder after grinding is too large, which will cause uneven mixing.

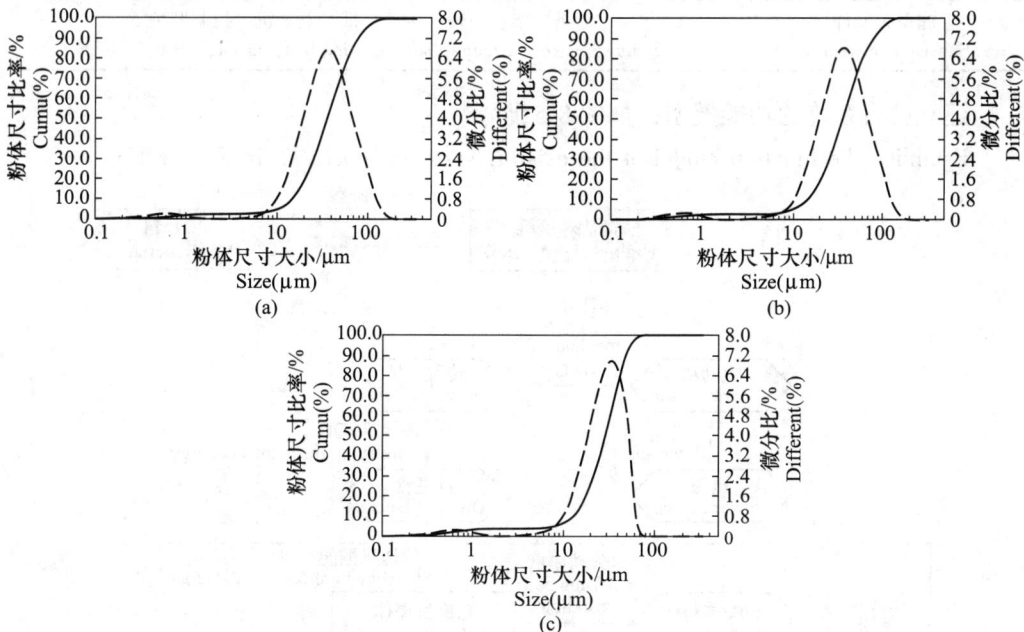

图 8-4 实验数据图

Figure 8-4 Experimental data plot

（a）2h：40.97μm；（b）4h：40.28μm；（c）6h：29.47μm

E 问题或类似问题的现有解决方案及其缺点

E Existing solutions to problems or similar problems and their shortcomings

通过延长球磨时间，调高机械合金化的程度，并提高粉体颗粒的混合均匀性，但生产效率低。

By prolonging the milling time, increasing the degree of mechanical alloying and improving the mixing uniformity of powder particles, the production efficiency is low.

8.1.2　问题分析

8.1.2　Problem analysis

8.1.2.1　功能分析

8.1.2.1　Functional analysis

系统分析见表 8-1。

Systems analysis is shown in Table 8-1.

表 8-1　系统分析

Table 8-1　Systems analysis

制品 Products	Cu、Fe 混合粉体 Mixed powder of Cu and Fe
系统元件 System components	Cu/Fe 粉体、乙醇、磨球、研磨罐 Cu/Fe powder, ethanol, grinding ball, grinding tank
超系统元件 Supersystem element	卡具支架、转轴、转动皮带、电动机、控制开关 Fixture bracket, rotating shaft, rotating belt, motor, control switch

建立已有系统的功能模型，如图 8-5 所示。

Establish the function model of the existing system, as shown in Figure 8-5.

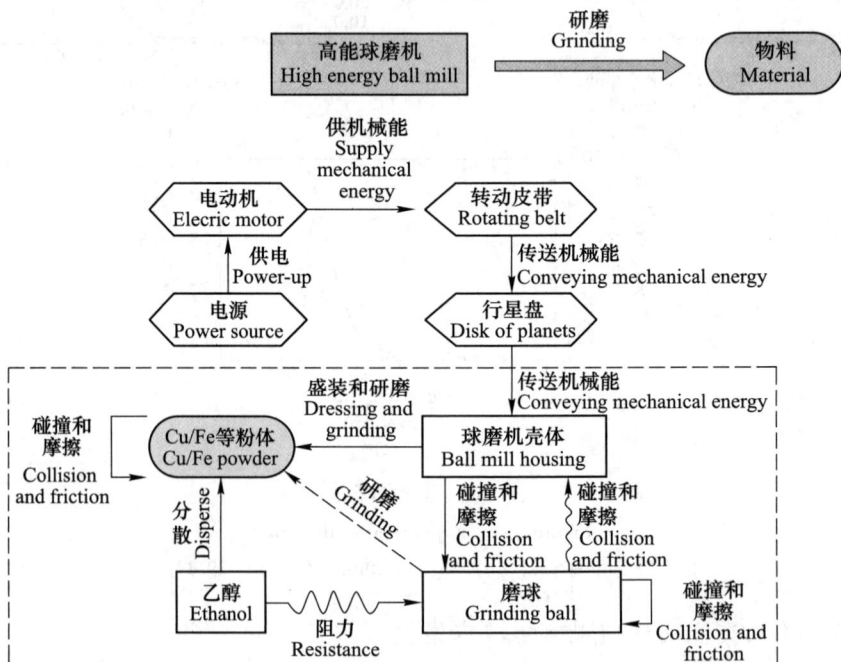

图 8-5　系统功能分析图

Figure 8-5　System function analysis diagram

8. 1. 2. 2 因果分析

8. 1. 2. 2 Causal analysis

应用因果链分析法确定产生问题的原因，如图 8-6 所示。

Using causal chain analysis to determine the cause of the problem，as shown in Figure 8-6.

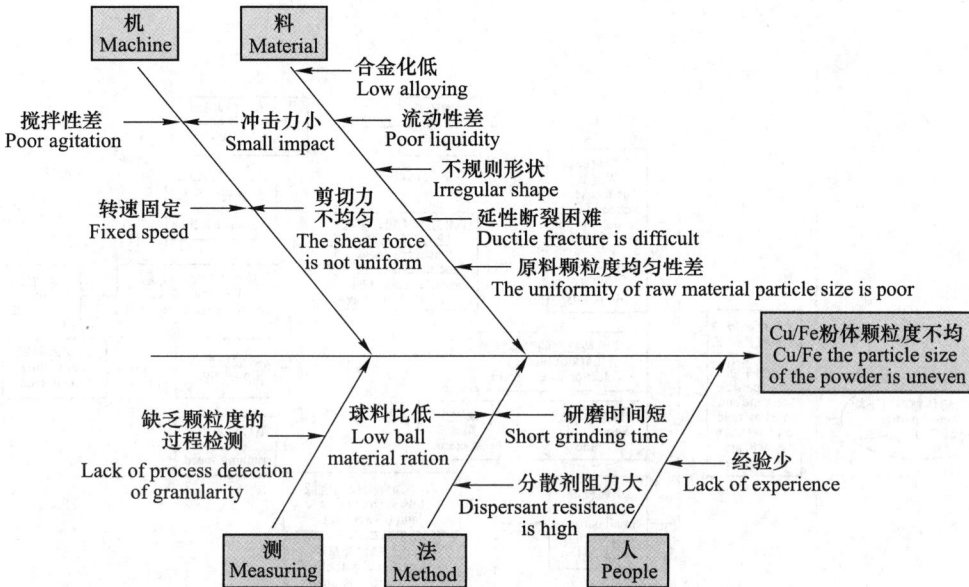

图 8-6 因果分析

Figure 8-6 Causal analysis

应用因果链分析法确定产生问题的原因，具体分析如图 8-7 所示。

Using causal chain analysis to determine the cause of the problem，the specific analysis is shown in Figure 8-7.

8. 1. 2. 3 冲突区域确定（问题关键点确定）

8. 1. 2. 3 Determination of conflict area（determination of key points）

（1）问题关键点 1：作用力与 Cu、Fe 颗粒破碎程度不匹配。

（2）问题关键点 2：研磨时间不足粒破碎和冷焊长大程度未达到平衡。

（3）问题关键点 3：作用力使粉体成球性困难。

（1）The key point of the problem 1：the force does not match the crushing degree of Cu and Fe particles.

（2）The key point of the problem 2：grinding time is not enough，particle breakage and cold welding growth is not balanced.

（3）The key point of the problem 3：the force makes the powder spheroidizing difficult.

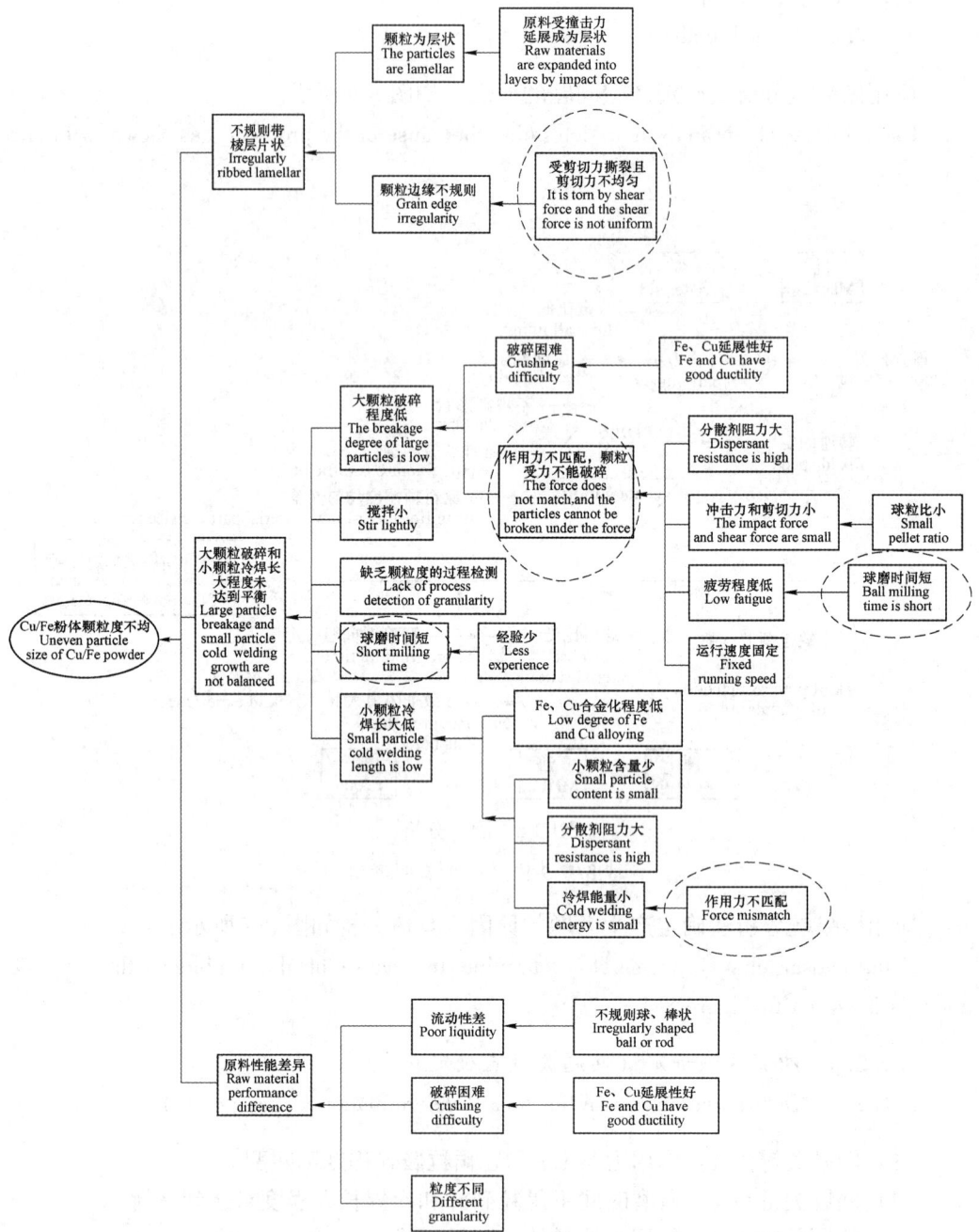

图 8-7　因果分析

Figure 8-7　Causal analysis

8.1.2.4　理想解分析

8.1.2.4　Analysis of ideal solution

理想解分为最终理想解和次理想解。最终理想解是指 Fe、Cu 球的颗粒是圆形、大小一致；次理想解是指球磨 4h，粒径为 20μm。

理想解分析主要对以下问题进行回答。

（1）设计的最终目的是什么？Fe、Cu 球的颗粒是圆形、大小一致。

（2）理想解是什么？改善球料比和分散剂，适当延长球磨时间，并对研磨后的粉体料分级，对颗粒进行修复。

（3）达到理想解的障碍是什么？研磨时粉体不能分级，不能对粉体表面修复。

（4）出现这种障碍的结果是什么？粉体颗粒度不均，冲击受力形成多棱形貌。

（5）不出现这种障碍的条件是什么？创造这些条件存在的可用资源是什么？采用气动流化，使得颗粒之间相互碰撞，形成无棱形貌，并对粉体分级；可用资源流化床、惰性气体和筛子。

The ideal solutions are divided into final ideal solution and sub-ideal solution. The final ideal solution is that the particles of Fe and Cu spheres are round and of the same size. Sub-ideal solution refers to ball milling for 4h and particle size of 20μm.

The ideal solution analysis mainly answers the following questions.

（1）What is the ultimate goal of design? The particles of Fe and Cu spheres are round and of the same size.

（2）What is the ideal solution? Improve the ball to material ratio and dispersant, extend the ball milling time appropriately, and grade the milled powder to repair the particles.

（3）What are the obstacles to the ideal solution? During grinding, the powder can not be graded and the surface of the powder can not be repaired.

（4）What is the result of this obstacle? The particle size of the powder is not uniform, and the impact force forms a polygonal morphology.

（5）What are the conditions for the absence of such obstacles? What are the resources available to create these conditions? Pneumatic fluidization is used to make the particles collide with each other to form a non edge morphology, the powder is graded; resource fluidized bed, inert gas and sieve can be used.

依据理想解分析得到方案为：采用气动流化，使得颗粒之间相互碰撞，形成无棱形貌，并对粉体分级。

According to the ideal solution analysis, the scheme is as follows: aerodynamic fluidization is used to make the particles collide with each other to form a non edge morphology; and the powder is graded.

8.1.2.5　可用资源分析

8.1.2.5　Analysis of available resources

可用资源分析见表 8-2。

Analysis of available resources are shown in Table 8-2.

表 8-2　可用资源分析

Table 8-2　Analysis of available resources

项目 Project	类别 Category	资源名称 Resource name	可用性分析 Usability analysis
内部资源 Internal resources	物质资源 Material resources	Fe、Cu 的颗粒 Particles of Fe and Cu	Fe、Cu 颗粒之间相互碰撞消除棱角 Collision between Fe and Cu particles to eliminate edges and corners
		磨球 Grinding ball	通过调整磨球搭配和球料比增加对 Fe、Cu 颗粒的作用力，提高破碎率 Increase the force on Fe and Cu particles by adjusting the grinding ball collocation and ball material ratio to improve the crushing rate
		球磨机壳体 Ball mill shell	盛装并与磨球碰撞研磨 Fe、Cu 颗粒 Pack and grind Fe and Cu particles with grinding ball
	场资源 Field resources	乙醇 Ethanol	分散细颗粒，防止发生团聚 Disperse fine particles to prevent agglomeration
		冲击势能 Impact potential energy	调整电机转速。增加磨球对 Fe、Cu 颗粒的冲击力，提高破碎率和破碎程度 Adjust the motor speed. The impact force of grinding ball on Fe and Cu particles is increased to improve the crushing rate and degree
外部资源 External resources	物质资源 Material resources	电动机 Motor	调整电动机的转速，改变冲击力 Adjust the speed of the motor to change the impact force
超系统资源 Supersystem resources	物质资源 Material resources	激光粒度仪 Laser particle sizer	测量 Fe、Cu 颗粒的颗粒度 Measure the particle size of Fe and Cu particles
		烘箱 Oven	对 Fe、Cu 粉体烘干 Drying of Fe and Cu powders
		筛子 Sieve	Fe、Cu 粉体颗粒分级 Classification of Fe and Cu powders

8.1.3 问题求解

8.1.3 Problem solving

8.1.3.1 问题关键点 1 作用力与 Cu、Fe 颗粒破碎程度不匹配

8.1.3.1 The key point of problem 1 The force does not match the crushing degree of Cu and Fe particles

A 工具 1：冲突解决理论（技术）

A Tool 1：conflict resolution theory（technology）

技术冲突解决过程如下。

（1）冲突描述。为了提高球磨系统的"颗粒的破碎率"，需要增加作用力，但这样做会导致系统的功率增加。

（2）转换成 TRIZ 标准冲突。改善的参数为 7 运动物体的体积；恶化的参数为 24 功率。

（3）查找冲突矩阵，得到如下发明原理，见表 8-3。

The technology conflict resolution process is as follows.

（1）Conflict description. In order to improve the "particle breakage rate" of the ball milling system, we need to increase the force, but doing so will lead to an increase in the power of the system.

（2）Conversion to TRIZ standard conflict. Improved parameters is 7volume of moving object；deteriorated parameter is 24power.

（3）By searching the conflict matrix, the following principles of the invention are obtained, as shown in Table 8-3.

表 8-3 技术冲突分析

Table 8-3 Technical conflict analysis

改善的参数 Improved parameters	恶化的参数 Deteriorating parameters	对应的发明原理 Corresponding principles of invention
运动物体的体积 Volume of moving object	功率 Power	35、6、13、18

➢方案 1：依据发明原理 35——参数变化

得到解如下：改变物体浓度或黏度。

方案描述：将球料比由 10∶1 调整为 15∶1，乙醇的添加量保持不变，这样相当于稀释了磨料的浓度，增强了磨球对磨料的冲击和剪切力，从而提高了粉体的破碎效率。

➢Scheme 1：according to the principle of invention 35——parameter change

The solution is as follows：change the concentration or viscosity of the object.

Scheme description：the ratio of ball to material is adjusted from 10∶1 to 15∶1；the addition of ethanol remains unchanged, which is equivalent to diluting the concentration of abrasive, enhancing the impact and shear force of grinding ball on abrasive, thus improving the crushing efficiency of powder.

➤**方案 2：依据 13 反向的发明原理**

得到解如下：将一个问题说明中所规定的操作改为相反的操作。

方案描述：采用可反向旋转的电动机，当球料罐正向旋转 0.5h 后，反向旋转 0.5h，以改变粉体的受力方向，增强粉体受力的均匀性，加速疲劳，从而提高了粉体的破碎效率。

➤**Scheme 2：according to the invention principle of 13 reverse**

The solution is as follows：change the operation specified in a problem description to the opposite operation.

Scheme description：the motor with reverse rotation is adopted. When the spherical material tank rotates for 0.5 hours in the forward direction, it rotates for 0.5 hours in the reverse direction, so as to change the stress direction of powder, enhance the uniformity of powder stress, accelerate fatigue, and improve the crushing efficiency of powder.

➤**方案 3：依据 18 振动的发明原理**

得到解如下：使物体处于振动状态。

方案描述：在球料罐上下加入弹簧装置，使得球料罐在转动的过程中产生上下的振动，增强粉体受力的方向，加速破碎，从而提高了粉体的破碎效率。

➤**Scheme 3：according to the Dnvention Principle of 18 vibration**

The solution is as follows：put an object in a state of vibration.

Scheme description：the spring device is added to the top and bottom of the spherical tank, which makes the spherical tank vibrate up and down in the process of rotation, enhances the direction of the powder force, and accelerates the crushing, so as to improve the crushing efficiency of the powder.

➤**方案 4：依据 6 多用性的发明原理**

得到解如下：是一个物体能完成多项功能，可以减少原设计中完成这些功能的多个物体的数量。

方案描述：将变频器由固定频率，改变为动态调频，即在研磨过程中，根据粉体的状态，动态地调整球罐的速度，提高粉体的破碎率。

➤**Scheme 4：according to the invention principle of 6 versatility**

The solution is as follows：one object can complete multiple functions, which can reduce the number of multiple objects to complete these functions in the original design.

Scheme description：the frequency converter is changed from fixed frequency to dynamic frequency modulation, that is, in the grinding process, according to the state of powder, the speed of spherical tank is dynamically adjusted to improve the crushing rate of powder.

B　工具 2：冲突解决理论（物理）

B　Tool 2：conflict resolution theory（physics）

物理冲突解决过程如下。

（1）冲突描述。为了"提高破碎率"，需要参数"作用力"为"正"，但又为了"减少功率"，需要参数"作用力"为"负"，即某个参数既要"正"又要"负"。

（2）选用4条分离原理当中的"时间分离原理10"原理，得到解决方案。

The physical conflict resolution process is as follows.

（1）Conflict description. In order to "improve the crushing rate", the parameter "force" needs to be "positive", but in order to "reduce power", the parameter "force" needs to be "negative", that is, a parameter should be "positive" and "negative".

（2）Choose the principle of "time separationprinciple 10" among the four separation principles to get the solution.

➤**方案：依据10预操作发明原理**

得到解如下：在操作前，使物体局部或全部产生所需要的变化。

方案描述：在机械球磨前先对 Cu、Fe 颗粒加热，然后快淬，使 Cu、Fe 颗粒的脆性增强，改善研磨过程的脆断能力，如图 8-8 所示。

➤**Scheme：according to the principle of 10 preoperation invention**

The solution is as follows：before operation，make the required changes to the whole or part of the object.

Scheme description：in order to improve the brittleness of Cu and Fe particles，the Cu and Fe particles were heated and then quenched before ball milling，as shown in Figure 8-8.

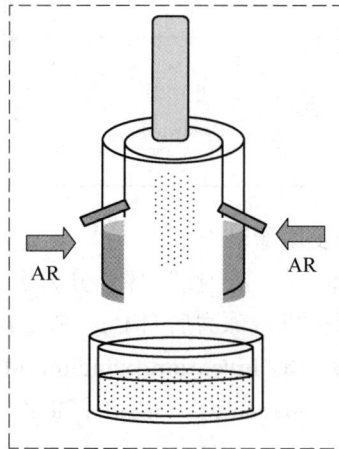

图 8-8 模型图

Figure 8-8 Illustration of model

8.1.3.2 问题关键点2 颗粒破碎和冷焊长大程度未达到平衡

8.1.3.2 The key point of the promble Particle breakage and cold welding growth are not balanced

➤**工具：冲突解决理论**

技术冲突解决过程如下。

（1）冲突描述。为了提高球磨系统的"颗粒破碎和冷焊长大程度的一致性"，需要增加研磨时间，但这样做了会导致系统的效率降低。

（2）转换成 TRIZ 标准冲突。改善的参数为运动物体的体积；恶化的参数为生产率。

（3）查找冲突矩阵，得到如下发明原理，见表8-4。

➤Tool：conflict resolution theory

The technology conflict resolution process is as follows.

（1）Conflict description. In order to improve the "consistency of particle breakage andcold welding growth degree" of ball milling system, we need to increase the grinding time, but this will reduce the efficiency of the system.

（2）Conversion to TRIZ standard conflict. Improved parameter is volume of moving object；deteriorating parameter is productivity.

（3）By searching the conflict matrix, the following principles of the invention are obtained, as shown in Table 8-4.

表 8-4 技术冲突分析

Table 8-4 Technical conflict analysis

改善的参数 Improved parameters	恶化的参数 Deteriorating parameters	对应的发明原理 Corresponding principles of invention
运动物体的体积 Volume of moving object	生产率 Productivity	10、6、2、34

➤**方案1：依据2分离的发明原理**

得到解如下：将一个物体中的"干扰"部分分离出去。

方案描述：在 Cu、Fe 颗粒机械球磨后对 Cu、Fe 颗粒分级。

➤**Scheme 1：according to the invention principle of 2 separation**

The solution is as follows：separate the "interference" part of an object.

Scheme description：Cu and Fe particles were graded after mechanical ball milling.

➤**方案2：依据34抛弃与修复的发明原理**

得到解如下：立即修复一个物体中所损耗的部分。

方案描述：在机械球磨过程中及时对磨球表面进行清洁处理，保证磨球的球磨效果。

➤**Scheme 2：according to the invention principle of 34 discard and repair**

The solution is as follows：repair the damaged part of an object immediately.

Scheme Description：In the process of mechanical ball milling, the surface of the ball should be cleaned in time to ensure the ball milling effect.

8.1.3.3 问题关键点 3 作用力不均匀使粉体成球状困难

8.1.3.3 The key point of the problem 3 It is difficult for the powder to be spherical due to the uneven force

A 工具 1 模型构建

A Tool 1: model building

（1）建立问题的物质-场模型。

（2）根据所建问题的物质-场模型，应用标准解解决流程，得到标准解为：第二类改进物质-场。

（3）依据选定的标准解，得到问题的解决方案。

（1）The matter field model of the problem is established.

（2）According to the matter field model of the problem, the standard solution process is applied, and the standard solution is: the second kind of improved matter field.

（3）According to the selected standard solution, the solution of the problem is obtained.

➤**方案：依据 No.15 并联物质-场模型标准解**

得到问题的解如下：可控性差的系统需要改进，但是无法改变已有系统的要素。使用第二个场作用于 S_2。

采用惰性气体吹动 Cu、Fe 粉体，形成流化态，通过高速气流的带动，使颗粒之间碰撞，摩擦，逐渐形成球状。

➤**Scheme: according to the standard solution of No.15 parallel matter field model**

The solution of the problem is as follows: the system with poor controllability needs to be improved, but the elements of the existing system cannot be changed. The second field is applied to S_2.

Inert gas is used to blow Cu and Fe powders to form fluidization state. Driven by high-speed air flow, the particles collide and rub with each other to form a ball gradually.

B 工具 2：物质-场分析及 76 个标准解

B Tool 2: matter field analysis and 76 standard solutions

（1）根据所建问题的物质-场模型，应用标准解解决流程，得到标准解为：第二类改进物质-场。

（2）No.14 串联物质-场模型。

（3）S_2 通过 F_1 作用于 S_3，S_3 再通过 F_1 作用于 S_1，把单一的模型变换成一串联模型。两个模型的串联顺序独立可控。

（4）依据选定的标准解，得到问题的解决方案。

（1）According to the matter field model of the problem, the standard solution process is applied, and the standard solution is: the second kind of improved matter field.

（2）No.14 series matter field model.

（3）S_2 acts on S_3 through F_1, S_3 acts on S_1 through F_1, and transforms a single model into a series model. The series sequence of two models can be controlled independently.

（4）According to the selected standard solution, the solution of the problem is obtained.

➢**方案：依据 No. 14 串联物质-场模型标准解**

得到问题的解如下：在球磨机中添加硬的细颗粒，增加细颗粒与颗粒之间的冲击力和碰撞概率，提高频率，如图 8-9 所示。

➢**Scheme：according to the standard solution of No. 14 series matter field model**

The solution of the problem is as follows：add hard fine particles in the ball mill, increase the impact force and collision probability between fine particles, and increase the frequency, as shown in Figure 8-9.

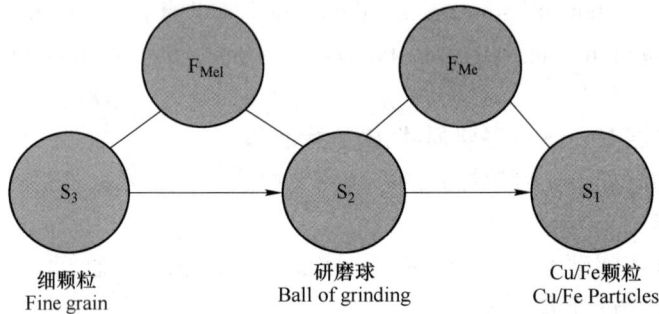

图 8-9　物质-场模型图

Figure 8-9　Model diagram of matter field

C　工具 3：效应

C　Tool 3：effect

（1）确定问题要实现的功能为"破碎+固态"。

（2）查找效应知识库，得到可用的效应为"fluidisation（流态化）"（可以有多个效应），依据该效应得到问题的解决方案。

（1）The function to be realized is "crushing + solid state".

（2）The available effect is "fluidization"（there can be multiple effects），and the solution of the problem is obtained according to the effect.

➢**方案 1：依据"fluidisation"效应**

得到如下解：采用惰性气体是颗粒在研磨过程中，形成流态化。

➢**Scheme 1：according to the "fluidization" effect**

The following solution is obtained：inert gas is used to form fluidization of particles in the grinding process.

（1）确定问题要实现的功能为"固态+破碎"。

（2）查找效应知识库，得到可用的效应为" Friction（摩擦）"，依据该效应得到问题的解决方案。

（1）The function of the problem is "solid state + crushing".

（2）The available effect is "friction" by searching the effect knowledge base，and the solution of the problem is obtained according to the effect.

➤**方案 2：依据 "Friction" 效应**

得到如下解：采用表面有粗糙度的研磨球，增加摩擦力。

➤**Scheme 2：according to the "friction" effect**

The following solution is obtained：grinding ball with surface roughness is used to increase friction.

8.1.4 问题的解
8.1.4 Problem solving

8.1.4.1 根据 TRIZ 理论对以上方案进行可用性评价

8.1.4.1 According to TRIZ theory，evaluate the usability of the above schemes

可用性评价见表8-5。

Availability evaluation is shown in Table 8-5.

表 8-5 可用性评价
Table 8-5 Usability evaluation

序号 Serial number	方案要点 Key points of the scheme	所用创新原理 Innovation principles used	可用性评估 Usability evaluation
1	将球料比由 10：1 调整为 15：1 Adjust the ball to material ratio from 10：1 to 15：1	发明原理 35 Principles of invention 35	1.244
2	采用可反向旋转的电动机，0.5h 反向旋转 The motor can rotate in reverse direction for half an hour	发明原理 13 Principle of invention 13	1.342
3	在球料罐上下加入弹簧装置 The spring device is added above and below the spherical material tank	发明原理 18 Principles of invention 18	1.473
4	将变频器由固定频率，改变为动态调频 Change the frequency converter from fixed frequency to dynamic frequency modulation	发明原理 6 Principle of invention 6	1.463
5	球磨前先对 Cu、Fe 颗粒加热，然后快淬 Before ball milling, Cu and Fe particles were heated and then rapidly quenched	条件分离 Conditional separation	1.505
6	球磨过程中对磨球表面进行清洁处理 Clean the surface of grinding ball during ball milling	发明原理 2 Principle of invention 2	1.228
7	在球磨机中添加硬的细颗粒 Adding hard fine particles to the ball mill	14 串联物质-场模型 14 series matter field model	1.342
8	采用惰性气体使颗粒在研磨过程中，形成流态化研磨 Inert gas is used to make particles form fluidization grinding in the grinding process	效应 Effect fluidization	1.445

序号 Serial number	方案要点 Key points of the scheme	所用创新原理 Innovation principles used	可用性评估 Usability evaluation
9	采用表面有粗糙度的研磨球，增加摩擦力 Grinding ball with surface roughness is used to increase friction	效应 Effect friction	1. 236

8. 1. 4. 2 可用性评估

8. 1. 4. 2 Usability evaluation

评价指标体系主要有以下几个方面：
(1) 颗粒分布 ($A = 0.3$)；
(2) 粒度 ($B = 0.3$)；
(3) 形状 ($C = 0.3$)；
(4) 效率 ($D = 0.1$)。

其中，A 代表改进后粒度分布系数/原来粒度分布粒度系数；B 代表改进后粒度系数/原来粒度系数；C 代表改进后粒度形状系数/原来粒度形状系数；D 代表原来球磨时间/改进后球磨时间。

The evaluation index system mainly includes the following aspects：
(1) Particle distribution ($A = 0.3$)；
(2) Particle size ($B = 0.3$)；
(3) Shape ($C = 0.3$)；
(4) Efficiency ($d = 0.1$) .

Among them, A represents improved particle size distribution coefficient/original particle size distribution coefficient；B represents improved particle size coefficient/original particle size coefficient；C represents improved particle size shape coefficient/original particle size shape coefficient；D represents original ball milling time/improved ball milling time.

可用性评估见表 8-6。

Usability evaluation is shown in Table 8-6.

表 8-6 可用性评估
Table 8-6 Availability assessment

指标体系	颗粒分布 A	粒度 B	形状 C	效率 D
权重	0. 3	0. 3	0. 3	0. 1
系数	a	b	g	t
可用性 $h = \sum AbBgCtD$				

8. 1. 4. 3 最终理想解

8. 1. 4. 3 The final ideal solution

最终理想解如图 8-10 所示。

The final ideal solution is shown in Figure 8-10.

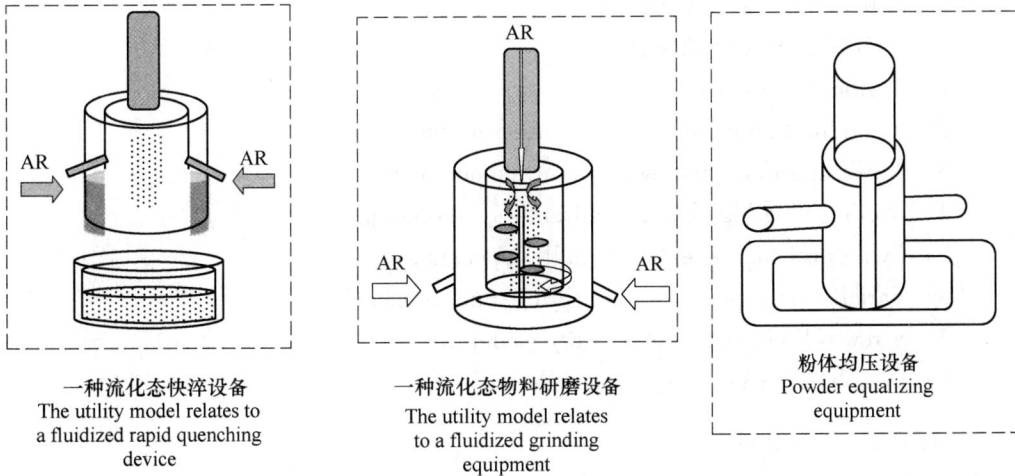

一种流化态快淬设备
The utility model relates to
a fluidized rapid quenching
device

一种流化态物料研磨设备
The utility model relates
to a fluidized grinding
equipment

粉体均压设备
Powder equalizing
equipment

图 8-10 最终理想解
Figure 8-10 The final ideal solution

8.1.5 取得成果与效益
8.1.5 Achievements and benefits

8.1.5.1 发明专利受理证明
8.1.5.1 Acceptance certificate of invention patent

（1）颗粒物流化研磨设备，发明专利，申请号或专利号：201711014858.3。

（2）流化快淬设备，发明专利，申请号或专利号：201711014889.9。

（3）粉体均压制样设备，发明专利，申请号或专利号：2017110143431.1。

（1）Particle flow grinding equipment, invention patent, application number or patent number：201711014858.3.

（2）Fluidized rapid quenching equipment, invention patent, application number or patent number：201711014889.9.

（3）Sample pressing equipment for powder, patent for invention, application number or patent number：2017110143431.1.

8.1.5.2 依据发明原理正在准备申请的专利
8.1.5.2 Patents under application according to the principle of invention

（1）一种振动式磨料罐（发明专利）。

（2）一种流化态磨料罐（发明专利）。

（3）一种自清洁磨球（发明专利）。

（4）一种循环高能球磨设备（发明专利）。

（5）圆筒形高能球磨机（外观设计）。

（6）变频振动性弹簧（实用新型）。

（7）螺旋自清洁球（实用新型）。

（8）可拆卸压头（外观设计）。

（1）A vibrating abrasive tank（invention patent）.

（2）A fluidized abrasive tank（invention patent）.

（3）A self cleaning grinding ball（invention patent）.

（4）A circulating high energy ball mill（invention patent）.

（5）Cylindrical high energy ball mill（appearance design）.

（6）Variable frequency vibrating spring（utility model）.

（7）Screw self cleaning ball（utility model）.

（8）Detachable RAM（appearance design）.

8.1.5.3 效益分析

8.1.5.3 Benefit analysis

采用原理优化后 CuFe 轴承材料的性能指标及效益：每年生产约 10000t，可节约成本 670 万~860 万元，具体效益分析见表 8-7。

The performance index and benefit of CUFE bearing material optimized by the principle：the annual production is about 10000 tons，and the cost can be saved by 6.7~8.6 million yuan，specific benefit analysis is shown in Table 8-7.

表 8-7 效益分析

Table 8-7 Benefit analysis

Fe_xCu_{100-x}	压溃强度/MPa	含油率/%	硬度 HB	时间/h
$x = 25$	283	22.13	32.12	4.5
$x = 20$	302	22.25	33.10	4.5
GB/T 6804	214	16	23	

8.2 电磁式铁屑清扫机性能优化设计

8.2 Performance optimization design of electromagnetic scrap iron sweeper

本节主要从以下五个方面进行分析：

（1）问题背景和描述；

（2）问题分析过程；

（3）问题求解过程；

（4）问题的解；

（5）取得成果与效益。

The section is mainly analyzed from the following five aspects:

(1) Background and description of the problem;

(2) Problem analysis process;

(3) Problem solving process;

(4) The solution of the problem;

(5) Achievements and benefits.

8.2.1 问题背景和描述

8.2.1 Problem background and description

8.2.1.1 问题的背景

8.2.1.1 Background of the problem

为工厂提供一种电磁式铁屑清扫机,如图 8-11 所示。这种清扫机可以将铁屑自动收集和输入至收集器中,清扫快捷、方便、省时、省力,从而可以大大提高清扫工作的效率,并减轻工人的劳动强度。但是电磁铁的磁吸力和耗电量无法控制,需要根据铁屑的大小、质量调整电磁铁的吸力和布置方式,最大程度地节省蓄电池的电量和清扫效果。

This kind of sweeper can automatically collect and input the iron scraps into the collector, illustration of model is shown in Figure 8-11. Which is fast, convenient, time-saving and labor-saving, so as to greatly improve the efficiency of cleaning work and reduce the labor intensity of workers. However, the magnetic attraction and power consumption of the electromagnet can not be controlled. It is necessary to adjust the attraction and layout of the electromagnet according to the size and quality of the iron chips, so as to save the battery power and cleaning effect to the greatest extent.

图 8-11 模型图

Figure 8-11 Illustration of model

8.2.1.2　问题的描述

8.2.1.2　Description of the problem

A　定义技术系统实现的功能

A　Define the function of the technology system

问题所在技术系统为电磁式铁屑清扫机。

该技术系统的功能为铁屑吸附、转移、收集。

实现该功能的约束有蓄电池电量、电磁铁性能。

The technical system of the problem is electromagnetic scrap cleaner.

The function of the technology system is iron filings adsorption, transfer, collection.

The constraints to achieve this function are battery power, electromagnet performance.

B　现有技术系统的工作原理

B　Working principle of prior art system

电磁式铁屑清扫机，它包括壳体、前轮、万向轮、手推杆、收集箱、蓄电池、电动机、滚轮、电磁铁、电刷滑环、隔离板，壳体为长方形；多块电磁铁均布固定在滚轮上，电磁铁正负极导线通过电刷滑环与电源开关的正负接线柱相连接，正负接线柱与蓄电池相连接。隔离板为圆筒体，套装在滚轮的电磁铁外周，隔离板的圆周后侧位于收集箱的前端上方。

The utility model relates to an electromagnetic iron chip cleaning machine, which comprises a shell, a front wheel, a universal wheel, a hand push rod, a collection box, a storage battery, a motor, a roller, an electromagnet, an electric brush slip ring, and an isolating plate; A plurality of electromagnets are uniformly distributed and fixed on the roller, the positive and negative pole wires of electromagnets are connected with the positive and negative terminals of the power switch through the brush slip ring, and the positive and negative terminals are connected with the storage battery. The isolation plate is a cylinder body, which is sheathed on the periphery of the electromagnet of the roller, and the back of the circumference of the isolation plate is located above the front end of the collection box.

利用滚轮上的电磁铁将铁屑吸附在隔离板上，电动机带动滚轮和电磁铁转动，铁屑在隔离板上随电磁铁的转动而移动，最后从隔离板末端落入下方的收集箱内。

The electromagnet on the roller is used to adsorb the iron filings on the isolation plate. The motor drives the roller and electromagnet to rotate. The iron filings on the isolation plate move with the rotation of the electromagnet, and finally fall into the collection box below from the end of the isolation plate.

本发明利用电动机来驱动电磁铁转动，通过调速器实现电机转速的调节，以适应复杂情况下的作业，并通过蓄电池为设备整体提供动力和自动化操作，达到自动化清扫铁屑和铁粉的目的。

The invention uses the motor to drive the electromagnet to rotate, realizes the speed adjustment of the motor through the speed governor, so as to adapt to the complex situation, and provides power and automatic operation for the whole equipment through the storage battery, so as to achieve the purpose of automatic cleaning of iron filings and iron powder.

C　当前技术系统存在的问题

C　Problems in current technology system

技术问题 1：电磁铁较多，耗电量较大，需要提高电能的利用率。

解决方案：电磁铁布置较多，而转到靠近地面位置的电磁铁才起到吸附作用，需要控制该位置的电磁铁通电，而其他部分的电磁铁断电，从而起到高效省电的目的。

Technical problem 1: there are many electromagnets and the power consumption is large, so it is necessary to improve the utilization rate of electric energy.

Solution: there are many electromagnets arranged, and the electromagnet which is close to the ground can play the role of adsorption. It is necessary to control the electromagnet in this position to be powered on, while the electromagnets in other parts are powered off, so as to achieve the purpose of high efficiency and power saving.

技术问题 2：根据铁屑大小调节电磁力。

解决方案：铁屑大小物理量转变为电量信号，输入给控制器，控制器再控制电磁铁的电流大小。

Technical problem 2: adjust the electromagnetic force according to the size of scrap iron.

Solution: the physical quantity of iron chips is transformed into electricity signal, which is input to the controller, and then the controller controls the current of the electromagnet.

技术问题 3：整机尺寸较大，不宜在狭窄空间使用。

解决方案：滚筒式改为圆盘式。

Technical problem 3: the overall size is large and should not be used in narrow spaces.

Solution: change the drum type to disc type.

D　问题出现的条件和时间

D　The condition and time of the problem

依据上述当前系统存在的问题，需要说明以下内容。

（1）问题是否是在某一个特殊的条件下才发生？是，该电磁清扫机在机加工车间或铁粉较多的场地。

（2）问题是否是在某一时间内发生？是，机加工后产生的铁屑或铁粉。

According to the above problems existing in the current system, the following contents need to be explained.

（1）Does the problem arise under a particular condition? Yes, the electromagnetic sweeper is used in machining workshops or places with more iron powder.

（2）Does the problem occur at a certain time? Yes, scrap iron or iron powder produced after machining.

E　问题或类似问题的现有解决方案及其缺点

E　Existing solutions to problems or similar problems and their shortcomings

（1）采用更换电磁铁为永久磁铁，带来的问题是：磁力不可调。

（2）增加电磁铁电流控制器，控制电流，达到节电的目的。缺点：系统更加复杂。

（3）改变电磁铁在滚筒上的布置，改善吸附效果，效果待验证。

（1）If the electromagnet is replaced as permanent magnet, the problem is that the magnetic force is not adjustable.

（2）The electromagnet current controller is added to control the current to achieve the purpose of power saving. Shortcomings：the system is more complex.

（3）The effect of changing the arrangement of electromagnet on the drum to improve the adsorption effect needs to be verified.

F　新系统的要求

F　Requirements of the new system

电磁铁改为永久磁铁，改变滚筒的电磁铁布置方式，滚筒也改为圆盘式。增加刮板，以提高铁屑收集效果。铁屑收集箱下增加永久磁铁，用来吸附圆盘上铁屑。

The electromagnet is changed to permanent magnet, the arrangement of electromagnet of drum is changed, and the drum is also changed to disc type. Add scraper to improve the collection effect of scrap iron. A permanent magnet is added under the iron chip collecting box to absorb the iron chips on the disc.

8.2.1.3　问题求解流程

8.2.1.3　Problem solving process

求解过程如图 8-12 所示。

Problem solving process is shown in Figure 8-12.

8.2.2　问题分析

8.2.2　**Problem analysis**

8.2.2.1　功能分析

8.2.2.1　Functional analysis

系统分析见表 8-8。

Systems analysis is shown in Table 8-8.

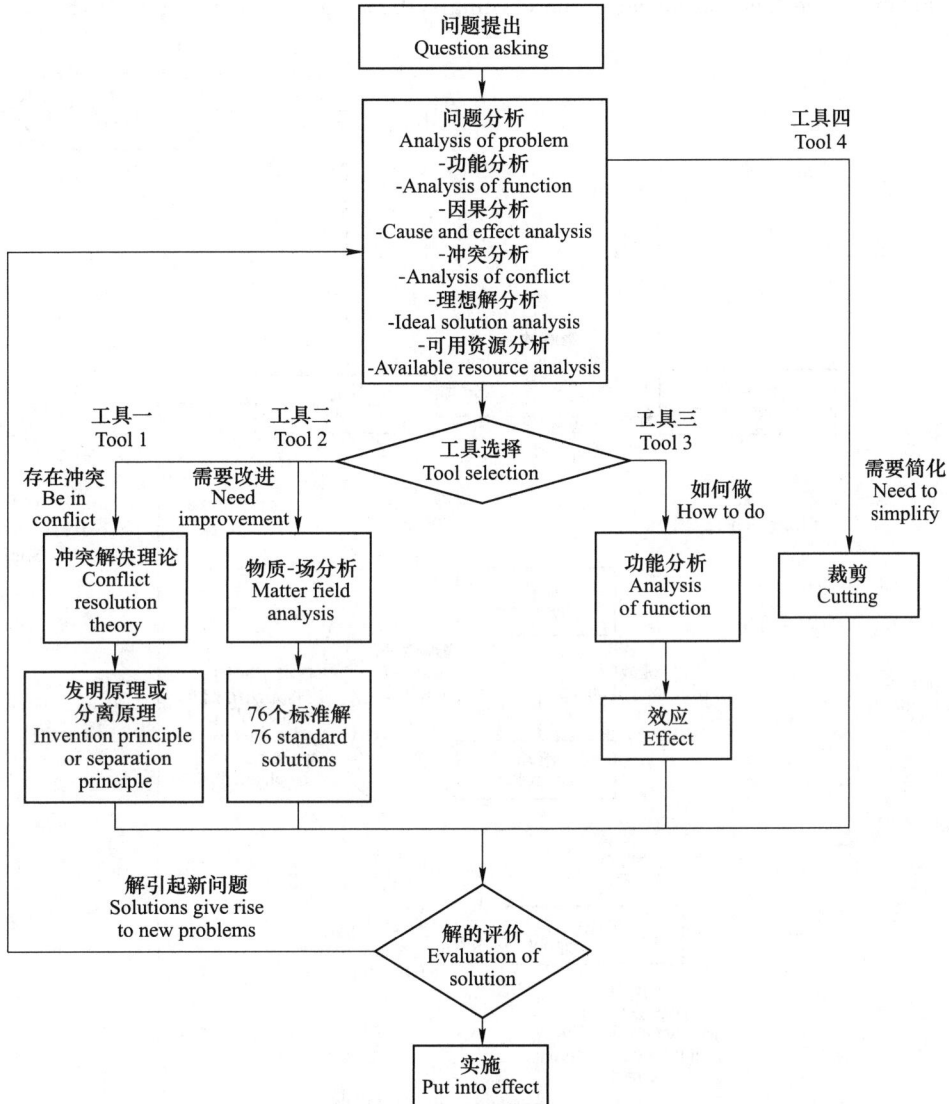

图 8-12 求解流程

Figure 8-12 Solve the process

表 8-8 系统分析

Table 8-8 Systems analysis

制品 Products	铁屑、铁粉 Iron filings, iron powder
系统元件 System components	电磁铁、电机、蓄电池、滚轮、外壳 Electromagnet, motor, battery, roller and shell
超系统元件 Supersystem element	地面 Ground

建立已有系统的功能模型，如图 8-13 所示。

Establish the function model of the existing system, as shown in Figure 8-13.

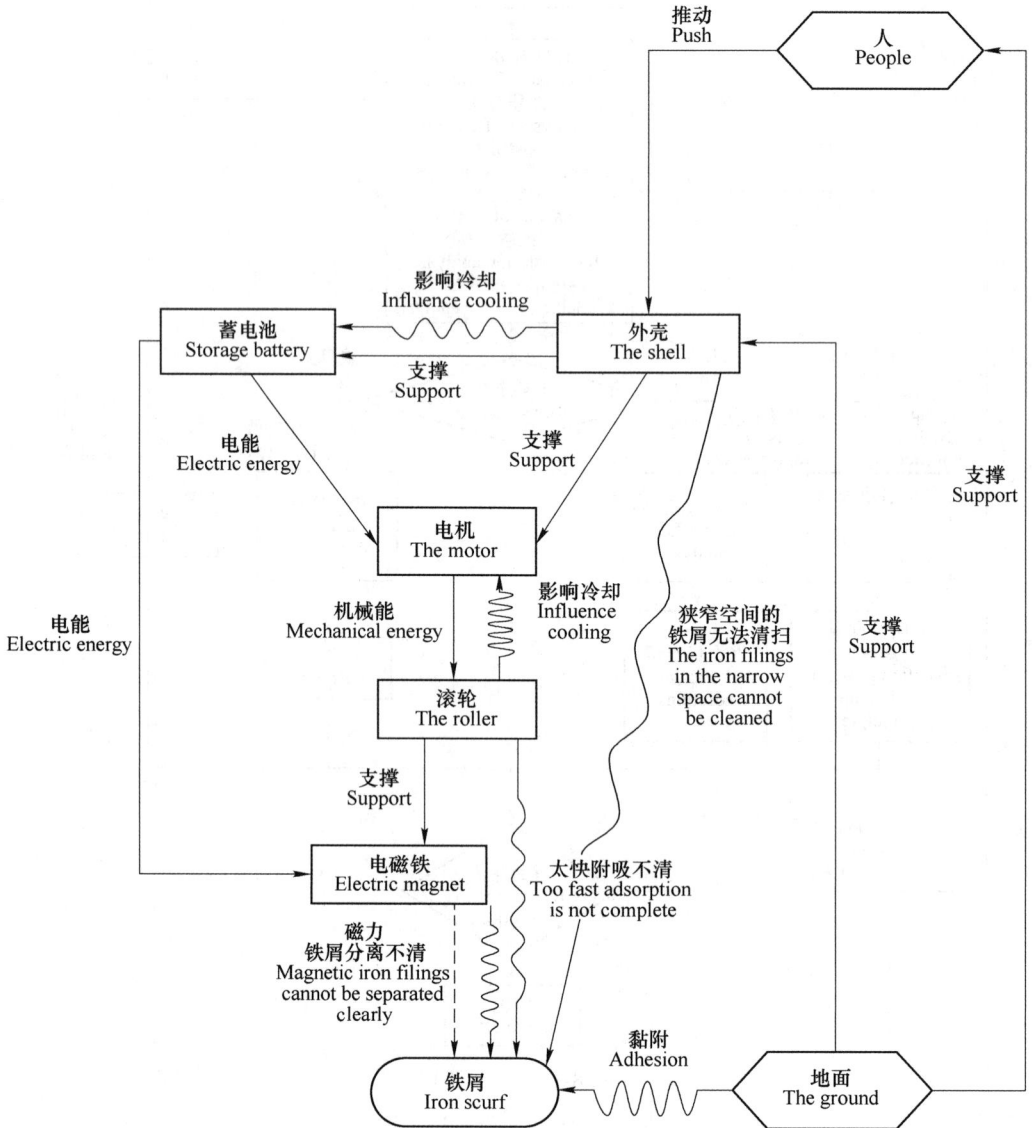

图 8-13　功能模型

Figure 8-13　Functional model

8.2.2.2　因果分析

8.2.2.2　Causal analysis

应用因果链分析法确定产生问题的原因，如图 8-14 所示。

Using causal chain analysis to determine the cause of the problem, as shown in Figure 8-14.

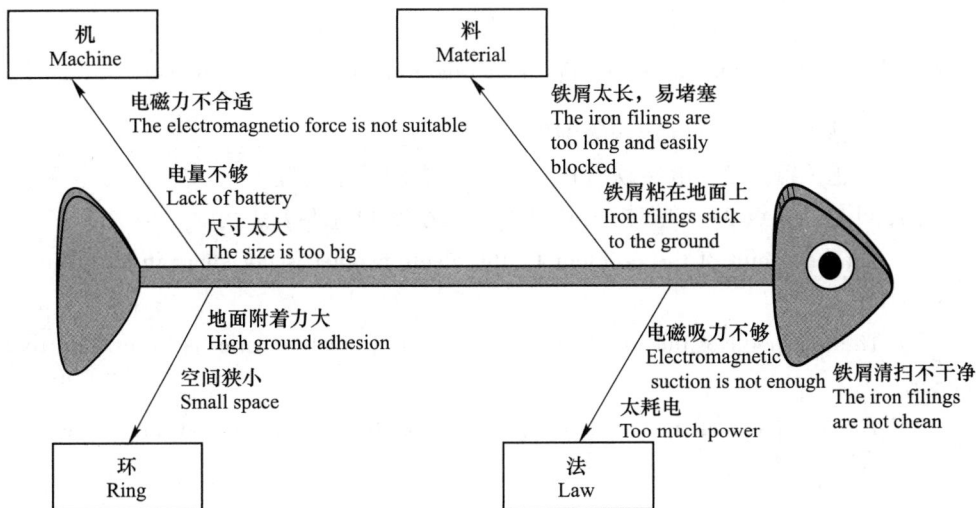

(a)

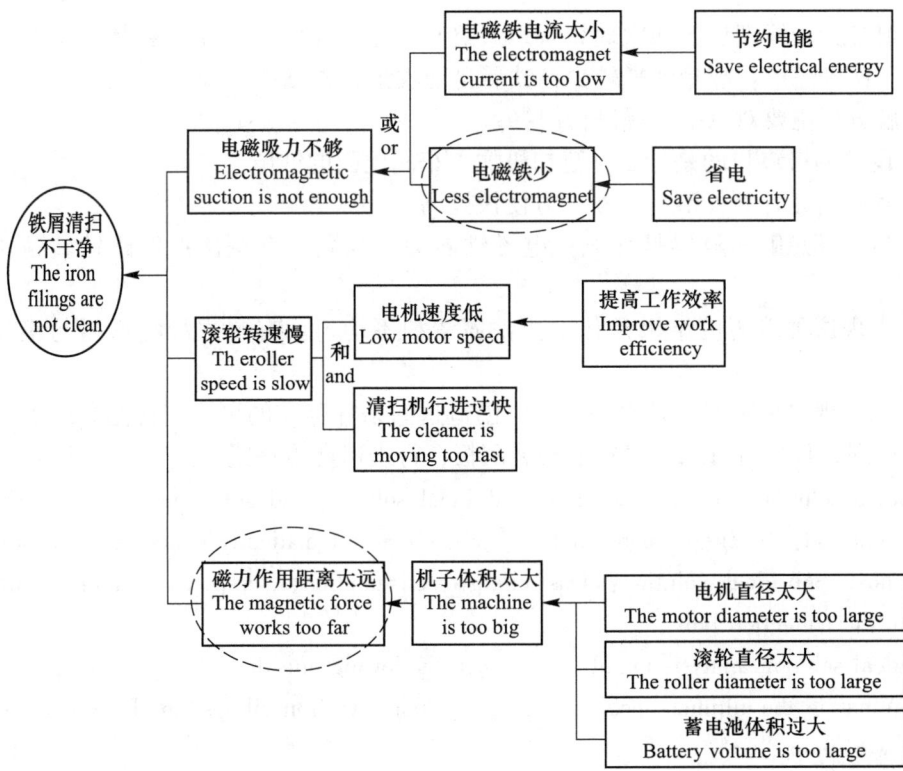

(b)

图 8-14   模型分析图

Figure 8-14   Model analysis diagram

（a）鱼骨展示图；（b）功能模型图

（a）Fish bone display；（b）Functional model diagram

8.2.2.3 冲突区域确定（问题关键点确定）
8.2.2.3 Determination of conflict area（determination of key points）

（1）问题关键点 1：电磁铁吸附铁屑不干净。

（2）问题关键点 2：电磁铁转速低于清扫机的行进速度。

（3）问题关键点 3：清扫机尺寸过大，狭小空间进不去。

（1）The key point of the problem 1: the electromagnet is not clean in absorbing iron filings.

（2）The key point of the problem 2: the speed of electromagnet is lower than that of sweeper.

（3）The key point of the problem 3: the size of the sweeper is too large to enter the narrow space.

8.2.2.4 理想解分析
8.2.2.4 Analysis of ideal solution

理想解分为最终理想解和次理想解。最终理想解：不消耗能量，铁屑自动集中到收集箱。次理想解：能量消耗较少，铁屑自动收集到收集箱。

理想解分析主要对以下问题进行回答。

（1）设计的最终目的是什么？清扫机加工车间地面的铁屑。

（2）理想解是什么？清扫干净，方便快捷高效。

（3）达到理想解的障碍是什么？电磁铁磁力不均匀，有剩磁；电磁铁转速不合适。

（4）出现这种障碍的结果是什么？铁屑清扫不均匀；有剩磁影响铁屑与滚轮分离。

（5）不出现这种障碍的条件是什么？创造这些条件存在的可用资源是什么？电磁铁斜向排列，且电流可调；滚轮上安装刮板；行进速度传感器。

The ideal solutions are divided into final ideal solution and sub-ideal solution. The final ideal solution: no energy consumption, iron chips automatically concentrated to the collection box. Sub-ideal solution: less energy consumption, scrap iron automatically collected to the collection box.

The ideal solution analysis mainly answers the following questions.

（1）What is the ultimate goal of design? Clean the iron filings on the ground of machining workshop.

（2）What is the ideal solution? Clean, convenient and efficient.

（3）What are the obstacles to the ideal solution? The magnetic force of the electromagnet is uneven and has remanence; improper speed of electromagnet.

（4）What is the result of this obstacle? The cleaning of iron scraps is uneven; there is remanence effect on the separation of scrap iron and roller.

（5）What are the conditions for the absence of such obstacles? What are the resources available to create these conditions? The electromagnets are arranged obliquely and the current is adjustable; the scraper is installed on the roller; the travel speed sensor.

依据理想解分析得到方案为：

（1）电磁铁斜向排列，并根据铁屑大小调节电流大小；

（2）滚轮上的剩余铁屑用刮板去掉；

（3）电机转速根据行进速度调节。

According to the ideal solution analysis, the scheme is as follows:

（1）The electromagnets are arranged obliquely, and the current is adjusted according to the size of iron chips;

（2）The remaining iron chips on the roller are removed by scraper;

（3）The motor speed is adjusted according to the traveling speed.

8.2.2.5 可用资源分析
8.2.2.5 Analysis of available resources

可用资源分析见表8-9。

Analysis of available resources are shown in Table 8-9.

表 8-9 可用资源分析
Table 8-9 Analysis of available resources

项目 Project	类别 Category	资源名称 Resource name	可用性分析（初步方案） Usability analysis（preliminary scheme）
内部资源 Internal resources	物质资源 Material resources	滚轮 Roller	滚轮改为圆盘 Change roller to disc
		电磁铁 Electromagnet	磁力可控 The magnetic force is controllable
		蓄电池 Battery	大容量电池 Large capacity battery
	场资源 Field resources	磁场 Magnetic field	电磁力吸附铁屑 Adsorption of iron filings by electromagnetic force
		机械能 Mechanical energy	电机驱动滚轮或圆盘 The motor drives the roller or disc
		电场 Electric field	电池提供电能给电磁铁和电机 The battery supplies electricity to the electromagnet and motor
	其他资源 Other resources		

项目 Project	类别 Category	资源名称 Resource name	可用性分析（初步方案） Usability analysis (preliminary scheme)
外部资源 External resource	物质资源 Material resources	永久磁铁 Permanent magnet	用强永磁体替代电磁铁，提供强磁力， 结构简化，可控性降低 Using strong permanent magnet instead of electromagnet can provide strong magnetic force, simplify structure and reduce controllability
		蓄电池 Battery	提高电池容量 Increase battery capacity
	场资源 Field resources	磁场 Magnetic field	电磁场、磁场 Electromagnetic field, magnetic field
	其他资源 Other resources		
超系统资源 Supersystem resources	物质资源 Material resources	人 People	使用操作培训 Operation training
	场资源 Field resources	地面 （重力场） Ground (gravity field)	地面的支撑作用，提供地面的摩擦力，保证机器前进 The supporting function of the ground provides the friction force of the ground and ensures the progress of the machine
	其他资源 Other resources		

8.2.3　问题求解

问题关键点　以"提高清扫性能"为入手点解决问题。

8.2.3　Problem solving

The key point of the problem　To solve the problem by "improving the cleaning performance".

8.2.3.1　工具1：冲突解决理论（技术）

8.2.3.1　Tool 1：conflict resolution theory (technology)

技术冲突解决过程 1 如下。

（1）冲突描述。为了提高系统的"清扫性能（电磁铁的磁吸力）"，需要改善电磁铁的安装排列，但这样做了会导致系统的更加复杂，成本提高，技术难度加大。

（2）转换成 TRIZ 标准冲突。改善的参数为 No. 3 运动物体的长度；恶化的参数为 No. 36 装置的复杂性。

The technology conflict resolution process 1 is as follows.

（1）Conflict description. In order to improve the "cleaning performance（magnetic attraction of electromagnet）" of the system, we need to improve the installation arrangement of electromagnets, but this will lead to more complex system, higher cost and more technical difficulty.

（2）Conversion to TRIZ standard conflict. Improved parameter is No. 3 length of moving object; deteriorating parameters is complexity of No. 36 device.

技术冲突解决过程 2 如下。

（1）冲突描述。为了提高系统的"清扫性能（电磁铁的磁吸力）"，需要增大电流，但这样做了会导致系统的能耗过大。

（2）转换成 TRIZ 标准冲突。改善的参数为 No. 10 力；恶化的参数为 No. 22 能耗过大。

（3）查找冲突矩阵，得到如下发明原理，见表 8-10。

The technology conflict resolution process 2 is as follows.

（1）Conflict description. In order to improve the "cleaning performance（magnetic attraction of electromagnet）" of the system, we need to increase the current, but doing so will lead to excessive energy consumption of the system.

（2）Conversion to TRIZ standard conflict. Improved parameter is No. 10 force; deteriorated parameter is No. 22 excessive energy consumption.

（3）By searching the conflict matrix, the following principles of the invention are obtained, as shown in Table 8-10.

表 8-10 技术冲突分析

Table 8-10 Technical conflict analysis

改善的参数 Improved parameters	恶化的参数 Deteriorating parameters	对应的发明原理 Corresponding principles of invention	改善的参数 Improved parameters
电磁吸力 Magnetic adhesion	能量损耗 Energy loss	14 曲面化和 15 动态化 14 curved and 15 dynamic	电磁吸力 Magnetic adhesion
运动物体的长度 The length of a moving object	装置的复杂性 Complexity of devices	1 分割、19 周期性、 26 复制、24 中介物 1 division, 19 periodicity, 26 replication, 24 mediator	运动物体的长度 The length of a moving object
运动物体的面积 Area of moving object	装置的复杂性 Complexity of devices	14 曲面化、1 分割、13 反向 14 curved, 1 split, 13 reverse	运动物体的面积 Area of moving object
速度 Speed	能量损失 Energy loss	14 曲面化、20 有效作用的连续性、 19 周期性作用、35 参数变化 14 curved surface, 20 continuity of effective action, 19 periodic action, 35 parameter change	速度 Speed

➤ 方案 1：依据 No. 26 复制 发明原理的第 1 条

得到解如下：把电磁铁换为永久磁铁，如图 8-15 所示。

➤ **Scheme 1：according to Article 1 of No. 26 reproduction invention principle**

The solution is as follows：change electromagnet into permanent magnet，as shown in Figure 8-15.

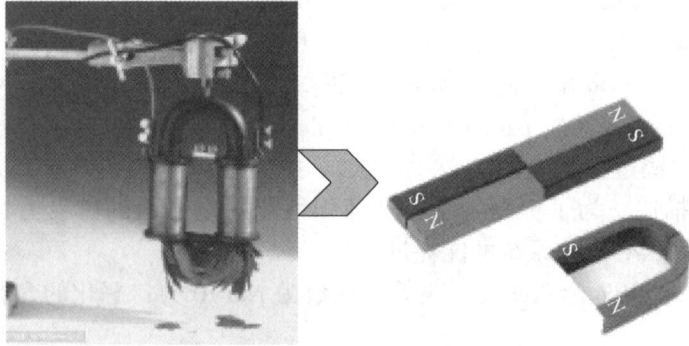

图 8-15　模型图

Figure 8-15　Illustration of model

➤ **方案 2：依据 No. 24 中介物 发明原理的第 2 条 "将一容易移动的物体与另一物体暂时接合"**

得到解如下：磁铁安装在圆盘上，使铁屑容易转移，如图 8-16 所示。

➤ **Scheme 2：according to Article 2 of No. 24 intermediary invention principle "temporarily connect one easily movable object with another"**

The solution is asfollows：the magnet is installed on the disc，which makes the iron filings easy to transfer，as shown in Figure 8-16.

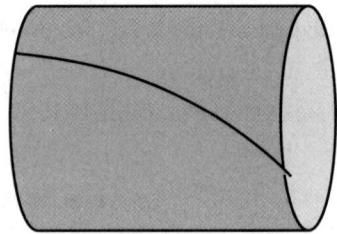

图 8-16　方案的原理图或示意图

Figure 8-16　Schematic or schematic diagram of the scheme

➤ **方案 3：依据 No. 15 动态化 发明原理的第 1 条 "自动调整，达到最优"**

得到解如下：电磁铁增加电流控制器，已控制通过电磁铁电流的大小。

➤ **Scheme 3：according to Article 1 of No. 15 dynamic invention principle "automatic adjustment to achieve optimal"**

The solution is as follows：the electromagnet adds a current controller to control the current through the electromagnet.

8.2.3.2　**工具 2：冲突解决理论（物理）**

8.2.3.2　Tool 2：conflict resolution theory（physics）

物理冲突解决过程如下。

The physical conflict resolution process is as follows.

（1）冲突描述：为了改善 "清扫性能"，需要参数 "电流" 为 "大"，但又为

了 "节能"，需要参数 "电流" 为 "小"，即，某个参数既要 "大" 又要 "小"。

（2）选用 4 条分离原理（空间分离、时间分离、基于条件的分离、整体与部分分离）当中的 "基于条件的分离" 原理，得到解决方案。

（1）Conflict description：in order to improve the cleaning performance, the parameter "current" needs to be "large", but in order to "save energy", the parameter "current" needs to be "small", that is, a parameter needs to be "large" and "small".

（2）Choose the "condition based separation" principle among the four separation principles（space separation, time separation, condition based separation, whole and part separation）to get the solution.

➤ **方案 1**

当铁屑附着在地面较强时，加大电流；当附着力较小时，减小电流。

➤ **Scheme 1**

When the iron filings adhere to the ground strongly, increase the current; when the adhesion is small, the current is reduced.

➤ **方案 2**

用永久磁铁替换电磁铁。

➤ **Scheme 2**

Replace the electromagnet with a permanent magnet.

8.2.3.3　工具 3：物质-场分析及 76 个标准解

8.2.3.3　Tool 3：matter field analysis and 76 standard solutions

（1）建立问题的物质-场模型。

（2）根据所建问题的物质-场模型，应用标准解解决流程，得到标准解为：No. 32（2.4.8）利用动态、可变、或可调整的磁场。

（3）依据选定的标准解，得到问题的解决方案。No. 32（2.4.8）标准解为：利用动态、可变、或可调整的磁场。

（1）Establish the matter field model of the problem.

（2）According to the matter field model of the problem, the standard solution process is applied：No. 32（2.4.8）utilizes dynamic, variable, or adjustable magnetic fields.

（3）According to the selected standard solution, the solution of the problem is obtained. The standard solution of No. 32（2.4.8）is to use dynamic, variable or adjustable magnetic field.

➤ **方案 1：依据 No. 32（2.4.8）标准解**

得到问题的解如下：用电流控制器，控制电流的大小。铁屑大时，电流大；铁屑小，时电流小。改进之后的物质-场模型如图 8-17 所示。

➤ **Scheme 1：according to No. 32（2.4.8）standard solution**

The solution of the problem is as follows：use current controller to control the current. When the iron chip is large, the current is large; when the iron chip is small, the current is small. The improved matter field model is shown in Figure 8-17.

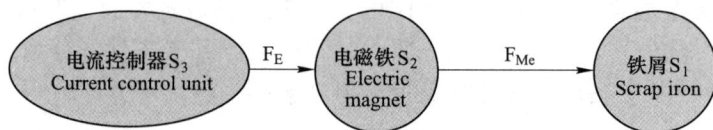

图 8-17　功能结构图

Figure 8-17　Functional structure diagram

➤ **方案 2：依据 No. 32（2. 4. 8）标准解**

得到问题的解如下：用电流控制器，控制不同电磁铁电流的通电时间。吸铁屑时，通电；不吸铁屑时，断电。改进之后的物质-场模型如图 8-17 所示。

➤ **Scheme 2：according to No. 32（2. 4. 8）standard solution**

The solution of the problem is as follows： the current controller is used to control the power on time of different electromagnet currents. When the iron chips are absorbed, the electromagnet is powered on； when the iron chips are not absorbed, the electromagnet is powered off. The improved matter field model is shown in Figure 8-17.

➤ **方案 3：依据 No. 32（2. 4. 8）标准解**

得到问题的解如下：变化滚轮的转速，控制吸附效果。铁屑多时，高速；铁屑少时，低速。改进之后的物质-场模型如图 8-18 所示。

➤ **Scheme 3：according to No. 32（2. 4. 8）standard solution**

The solution of the problem is as follows： change the rotation speed of the roller to control the adsorption effect. High speed when there are more iron chips； low speed when there areless iron chips. The improved matter field model is shown in Figure 8-18.

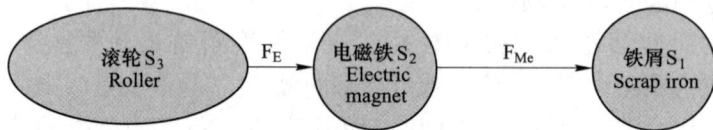

图 8-18　功能结构图

Figure 8-18　Functional structure diagram

➤ **方案 4：依据 No. 32（2. 4. 8）标准解**

得到问题的解如下：变化电磁铁在滚轮的安装形态，控制吸附效果。改进之后的物质-场模型如图 8-19 所示。

➤ **Scheme 4：according to No. 32（2. 4. 8）standard solution**

The problem solution is as follows： change the installation form of the electromagnet in the roller to control the adsorption effect. The improved matter field model is shown in Figure 8-19.

8. 2. 3. 4　工具 4：裁剪

8. 2. 3. 4　Tool 4：cutting

（1）裁剪电磁铁。将电磁铁裁剪，用永久磁铁替换，主要是为了减少电能的消

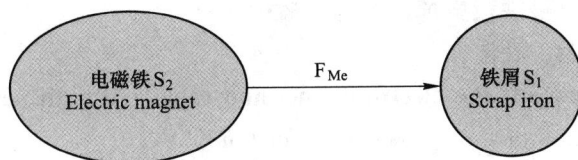

图 8-19　功能结构图

Figure 8-19　Functional structure diagram

耗，并减小系统的复杂程度。

（2）裁剪电机。裁剪电机，用机械系统替换，减小能耗。

（1）Cutting electromagnet. The main purpose of cutting electromagnet and replacing it with permanent magnet is to reduce the power consumption and the complexity of the system.

（2）Cutting motor. Cutting motor is replaced by mechanical system to reduce energy consumption.

➤ **方案 1：将电机裁剪掉**

理由：成本高，耗电，占用空间。裁剪后功能模型分析图如图 8-20 所示。

➤ **Scheme 1：cut off the motor**

Reason：high cost, power consumption and space occupation. Tailored functional model analysis diagram is shown on Figure 8-20.

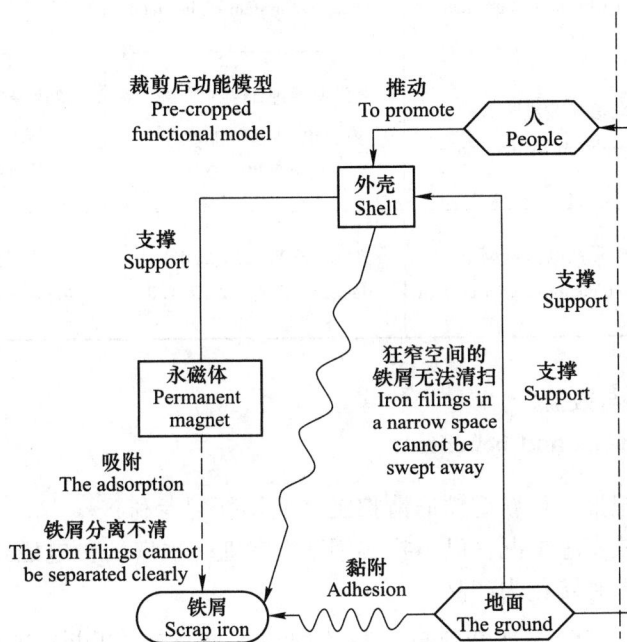

图 8-20　裁剪后功能模型分析图

Figure 8-20　Tailored functional model analysis diagram

➤ **方案 2：将电磁铁裁剪掉，换为永磁体**

理由：结构复杂，耗电。

➤ **Scheme 2：cut off the electromagnet and replace it with permanent magnet**

Reason：complex structure，power consumption.

8.2.4　问题的解

8.2.4　Solution of the problem

上述方案汇总见表 8-11。

Summary of the above schemes are shown in Table 8-11.

表 8-11　可用性评估

Table 8-11　Availability assessment

序号 Serial number	方案 Programme	所用创新原理 Innovation principles used	可用性评估 Usability evaluation
1	将电机裁剪掉，齿轮传动代替 Cut out the motor and replace it with gear drive	发明原理 28：机械系统替代 Principle of invention 28：mechanical system replacement	系统简化 System simplification
2	将电磁铁裁剪掉，换为永磁体 Cut off the electromagnet and replace it with permanent magnet	发明原理 28：机械系统替代 Principle of invention 28：mechanical system replacement	提高节能效果 Improve energy saving effect
3	将滚轮改成圆盘 Change the roller into a disc	发明原理 24：中介物 Principle of invention 24：intermediary	高度降低，便于清理工作 The height is reduced to facilitate cleaning
4	电磁铁电流可调 Adjustable electromagnet current	物质-场 No. 32 (2.4.8) Matter field No. 32 (2.4.8)	提高节能效果 Improve energy saving effect

8.2.5　取得成果与效益

8.2.5　Achievements and benefits

专利名称：拟报一种新型铁屑清扫机（实用新型专利）。

已取得效益或实施情况：已申报实用新型专业一项（一种电磁式铁屑清扫机）。

预期效益：专利转化为产品。

Patent name：a new type of scrap iron cleaning machine（utility model patent）.

Achieved benefits or implementation：one utility model specialty has been declared（an electromagnetic iron chip cleaning machine）.

Expected benefits：transforming patents into products.

8.3 提升自动感应门灵敏度
8.3 Improve the sensitivity of automatic induction door

本书主要从以下五个方面进行分析：
(1) 问题背景和描述；
(2) 问题分析过程；
(3) 问题求解过程；
(4) 问题的解；
(5) 取得成果与效益。

This section is mainly analyzed from the following five aspects：
(1) Background and description of the problem；
(2) Problem analysis process；
(3) Problem solving process；
(4) The solution of the problem；
(5) Achievements and benefits.

8.3.1 问题背景和描述
8.3.1 Problem background and description

8.3.1.1 问题的背景
8.3.1.1 Background of the problem

自动感应门广泛应用于办公楼、厂房、超市、机场等场所。利用人体红外传感器实现的红外感应自动门受限于传感器、透镜和环境等影响，使自动感应门存在一定的探测盲区，且探测距离有限，给系统的使用带来了不便，模型图如图 8-21 所示。如何提高系统灵敏度，提高使用者体感是自动门领域的一个技术难点。

Automatic induction door is widely used in office buildings, factories, supermarkets, airports and other places. Due to the influence of sensor, lens and environment, the infrared induction automatic door based on human infrared sensor has a certain detection blind area, and the detection distance is limited, which brings inconvenience to the use of the system, the illustration of model is shown in Figure 8-21. How to improve the sensitivity of the system and the user's body feeling is a technical difficulty in the field of automatic door.

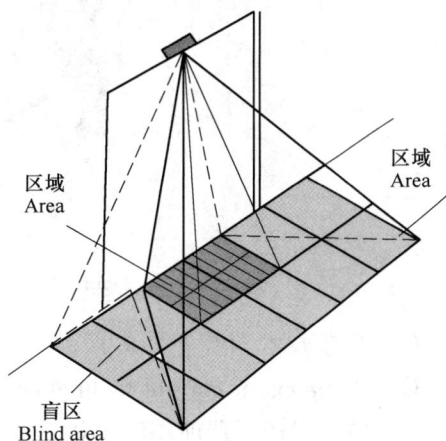

图 8-21 模型图

Figure 8-21 Illustration of model

8.3.1.2　问题的描述

8.3.1.2　Description of the problem

A　定义技术系统实现的功能

A　Define the function of the technology system

问题所在技术系统为自动感应门系统。

该技术系统的功能为识人开门。

实现该功能的约束有：在固定范围内（3m内）消除识人盲区，实现人到门前无等待。

The problem lies in the technical system: automatic induction door system.

The function of the technology system is to recognize people and open the door.

The constraints to realize this function include: eliminating blind area within a fixed range (within 3m) and realizing no waiting in front of the door.

B　现有技术系统的工作原理

B　Working principle of prior art system

系统通过人体红外传感器识别靠近自动门的人体发出的特定波长红外线，从而产生控制自动门电机的控制信号，实现自动开门。系统框图如图 8-22 所示。

The system can recognize the specific wavelength infrared emitted by the human body close to the automatic door through the human body infrared sensor, so as to generate the control signal to control the automatic door motor and realize the automatic door opening. The system block diagram is shown in Figure 8-22.

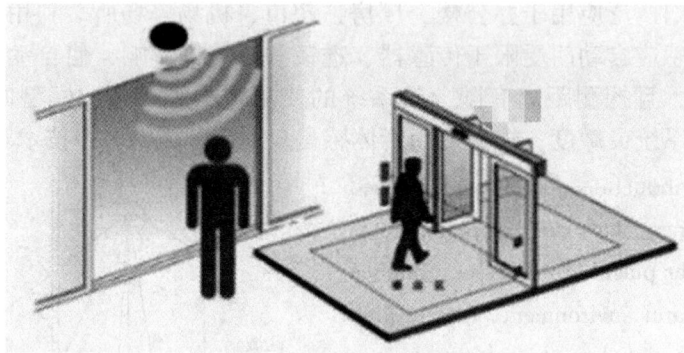

图 8-22　示意图

Figure 8-22　Diagrammatic sketch

C　当前技术系统存在的问题

C　Problems in current technology system

问题 1：受传感器前端滤镜接受光线角度的不同，使从不同的角度接近传感器的人的识别距离产生差异，甚至产生盲区。

Problem 1: the different angle of light received by the front-end filter of the sensor makes the recognition distance of people approaching the sensor from different angles different, and even produces blind area.

问题 2：受传感器感应距离（灵敏度）限制，自动门控系统在人体快速移动时，不能及时将门打开。

Problem 2: limited by the sensing distance (sensitivity) of the sensor, the automatic door control system can not open the door in time when the human body moves rapidly.

利用人体红外传感器实现的红外感应自动门受限于传感器、透镜和环境等因素的影响，使其存在一定的探测盲区，且探测距离有限，给系统的使用带来了不便。如何提高系统灵敏度，提高使用者体感是自动门领域的一个技术难点。

受传感器前端滤镜接受光线角度的不同，使从不同的角度接近传感器的人的识别距离产生差异，甚至产生盲区。

Due to the influence of sensor, lens, environment and other factors, the infrared induction automatic door based on human infrared sensor has a certain detection blind area, and the detection distance is limited, which brings inconvenience to the use of the system. How to improve the sensitivity of the system and the user's body feeling is a technical difficulty in the field of automatic door.

Due to the different angle of light received by the front filter of the sensor, the recognition distance of people approaching the sensor from different angles is different, and even the blind area is generated.

D 问题出现的条件和时间

D The condition and time of the problem

针对问题 1：当人体从传感器（自动门）侧面接近时，自动门反应迟钝甚至无反应。

针对问题 2：当人体快速（大于 2m/s）接近自动门时，自动门打开不及时。

Aiming at problem 1: when the human body approaches from the side of the sensor (automatic door), the automatic door is slow to respond or even has no response.

Aiming at problem 2: when the human body approaches the automatic door quickly (more than 2m/s), the automatic door is not opened in time.

E 问题或类似问题的现有解决方案及其缺点

E Existing solutions to problems or similar problems and their shortcomings

针对问题 1：可以采用微波传感器替代人体红外传感器，缺点是传感器不能检测处于静止状态的人或者物。当人在门口静止时，容易夹到人体，甚至引起误伤。

针对问题 2：提高门控电机转速，加大自动门打开速度，从而减少开门时间。缺点是门速度过大容易引起误伤，危险性增大；并且增大了机械部件的磨损。

Aiming at problem 1: we can use microwave sensor instead of human infrared sensor, the disadvantage is that the sensor can not detect people or objects in a static state. When people are still at the door, it is easy to clip the human body, and even cause accidental injury.

Aiming at the second problem: increase the speed of the door control motor, increase the opening speed of the automatic door, so as to reduce the opening time. The disadvantage is that the door speed is too high, which is easy to cause accidental injury, increase the risk, and increase the wear of mechanical parts.

F　新系统的要求

F　Requirements of the new system

提升系统灵敏性，使人体在任何方位接近自动门时都能实现自动开门。提高自动门反应灵敏性，减少识别误差。减少误动作，防止误伤人体。

Enhance the sensitivity of the system, so that the human body can automatically open the door when approaching the automatic door in any direction. The sensitivity of automatic door is improved and the recognition error is reduced. Reduce misoperation and prevent injury to human body.

8.3.2　问题分析

8.3.2　Problem analysis

8.3.2.1　功能分析

8.3.2.1　Functional analysis

系统分析见表 8-12.

Systems analysis is shown in Table 8-12.

表 8-12　系统分析

Table 8-12　Systems analysis

制　品 System product	门 Door
系统元件 System components	人、人体红外传感器（含透镜）、控制系统、门控驱动器、电机、传感器支撑 People, human body infrared sensor (including lens), control system, gate driver, motor, sensor support
超系统元件 Supersystem element	电源、其他物、光、墙 Power, other things, light, wall

系统的功能模型如图 8-23 所示。

The function model of the system is shown in Figure 8-23.

控制器软件功能模型如图 8-24 所示。

Function model of controller software is shown in Figure 8-24.

8.3.2.2　因果分析

8.3.2.2　Causal analysis

应用因果链分析法确定产生问题的原因，如图 8-25 所示。

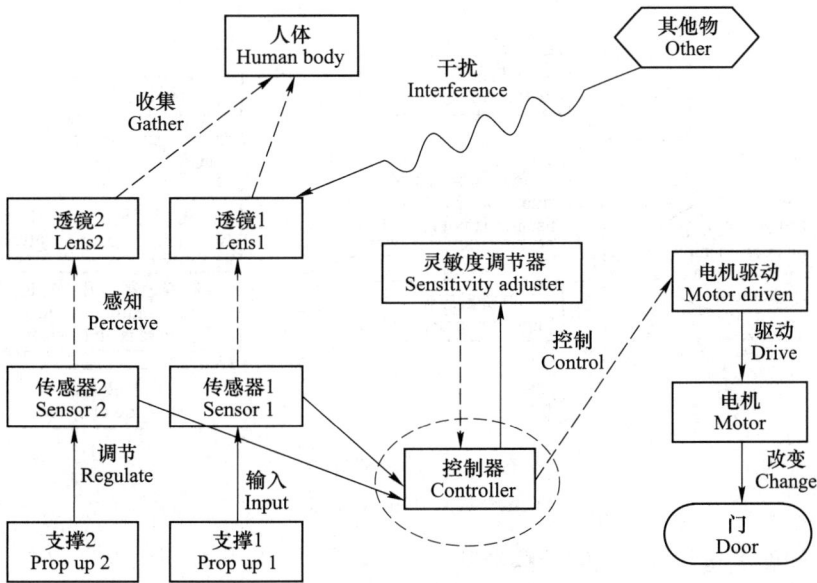

图 8-23 模型分析图

Figure 8-23 Model analysis diagram

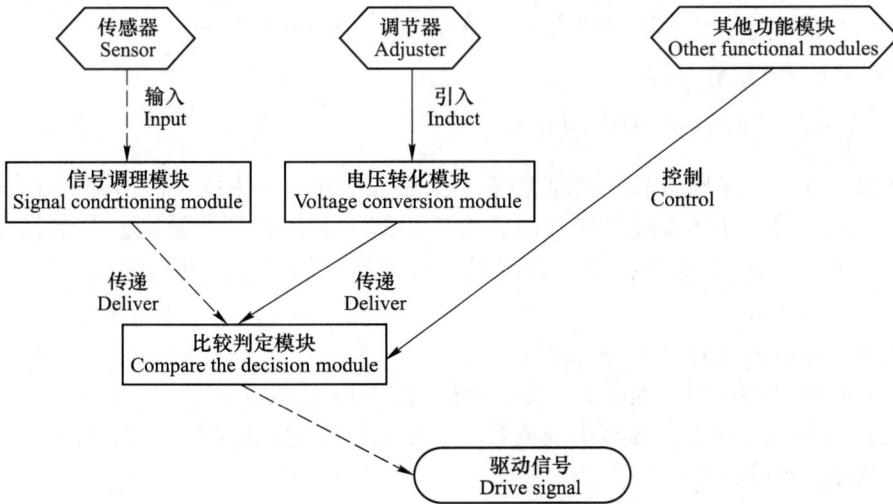

图 8-24 模型分析图

Figure 8-24 Model analysis diagram

Using causal chain analysis to determine the cause of the problem, as shown in Figure 8-25.

8.3.2.3 冲突区域确定 (问题关键点确定)

8.3.2.3 Determination of conflict area (determination of key points)

(1) 问题关键点 1: 传感器探测角度有限, 使探测区域灵敏度有差异。

(2) 问题关键点 2: 电机转速慢。

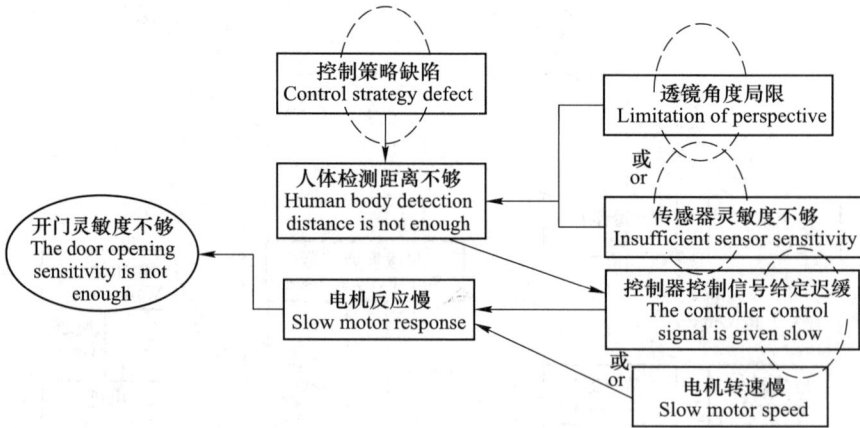

图 8-25　因果链分析

Figure 8-25　Causal analysis

（3）问题关键点 3：控制策略缺陷。

（1）The key point of the problem 1：the sensor detection angle is limited, so that the sensitivity of detection area is different.

（2）The key point of the problem 2：slow motor speed.

（3）The key point of the problem 3：defects of control strategy.

8.3.2.4　理想解分析

8.3.2.4　Analysis of ideal solution

理想解分为最终理想解和次理想解。最终理想解：人体从任何角度，以任何速度接近自动门时，都能实现准确开门。次理想解：提高识别灵敏度，在半径 3m 范围内，人体以 2m/s 的速度接近自动门时，自动门能够打开；并且实现减少识别误差，减少误动作。

理想解分析主要对以下问题进行回答。

（1）设计的最终目的是什么？提高灵敏度，消除误动作。

（2）理想解是什么？提高识别灵敏度，使人体接近自动门时已经开门；识别人体接近意图，消除误动作。

（3）达到理想解的障碍是什么？探测手段不足，识别判定方法不足。

（4）出现这种障碍的结果是什么？有盲区，误动作。

The ideal solutions are divided into final ideal solution and sub-ideal solution. The final ideal solution：when the human body approaches the automatic door from any angle and at any speed, it can open the door accurately. Sub ideal solution：to improve the recognition sensitivity, when the human body approaches the automatic door at the speed of 2m/s within the radius of 3m, the automatic door can be opened, and the recognition error and misoperation can be reduced.

The ideal solution analysis mainly answers the following questions.

（1）What is the ultimate goal of design? Improve sensitivity and eliminate misoperation.

（2）What is the ideal solution? Improve the recognition sensitivity, make the human body close to the automatic door has opened; identify the human body close to the intention, eliminate misoperation.

（3）What are the obstacles to the ideal solution? The detection means and identification methods are insufficient.

（4）What is the result of this obstacle? There are blind areas and misoperations.

依据理想解分析得到方案为：改进传感器探测模式，优化软件判定开门时间算法。

According to the ideal solution analysis, the scheme is: improve the sensor detection mode, optimize the software to determine the opening time algorithm.

可行性分析见表8-13。

Feasibility analysis is shown in Table 8-13.

表 8-13　可行性分析

Table 8-13　Feasibility analysis

类别 Category	资源名称 Resource name	可用性分析（初步方案） Usability analysis（preliminary scheme）
物质资源 Material resources	透镜 Lens	可改 It can be changed
	传感器 Sensor	不变 Unchanged
	控制系统 Control system	可优化 Optimizable
	电机 Electric machinery	可改动 Modifiable
	门 Door	可调节 Adjustable
	支撑 Brace	
场资源 Field resources	光 Light	
	电 Electric	

8.3.2.5　可用资源分析

8.3.2.5　Analysis of available resources

可用资源分析见表8-14。

Analysis of available resources are shown in Table 8-14.

表 8-14　可用资源分析

Table 8-14　Analysis of available resources

类别 Category		资源名称 Resource name	可用性分析（初步方案） Usability analysis（preliminary scheme）
外部资源 External resources	物质资源 Material resources	支撑物 A support	
	场资源 Field resources	电磁 Electromagnetism	
		机械 Mechanics	
		光 Light	
	其他资源 Other resources		
超系统资源 Supersystem resources	物质资源 Material resources	场所、人 Place，people	
		地面 Ground	
		空间 Space	
	场资源 Field resources	光 Light	

8.3.3　问题求解

问题关键点　以"提升探测区域"为入手点解决问题。

8.3.3　Problem solving

The key point of the problem To solve the problem with "enhance the detection area" as the starting point.

8.3.3.1　工具 1：冲突解决理论

8.3.3.1　Tool 1：conflict resolution theory

技术冲突解决过程如下。

（1）冲突描述：为了减少红外门系统的"盲区范围"，需要提升传感器灵敏度，但这样做了会导致系统误动作提升。

（2）转换成 TRIZ 标准冲突。改善的参数为 28 测量精度；恶化的参数为 27 可靠性。

（3）查找冲突矩阵，得到如下发明原理，见表 8-15。

The technology conflict resolution process is as follows.

(1) Conflict description: in order to reduce the "blind area" of the infrared gate system, we need to improve the sensitivity of the sensor, but doing so will lead to the improvement of the system misoperation.

(2) Conversion to TRIZ standard conflict. Improved parameter is 28 measurement accuracy; deteriorating parameter is 27 reliability.

(3) By searching the conflict matrix, the following principles of the invention are obtained, as shown in Table 8-15.

表 8-15 技术冲突分析

Table 8-15 Technical conflict analysis

改善的参数 Improved parameter	恶化的参数 Deteriorating parameter	对应的发明原理 Corresponding principles of invention
28	27	5、11、1、23

➤ 方案 1: 依据 No.1 分割, 第 (1) 条

将单侧传感器 (含透镜) 分割成两个, 减小单传感器探测区域, 从而实现减少盲区, 提高感应灵敏度。

➤ Scheme 1: according to No.1 division, Article (1)

The single side sensor (including lens) is divided into two parts to reduce the detection area of single sensor, so as to reduce the blind area and improve the sensitivity.

➤ 方案 2: 依据 No.1 分割, 第 (3) 条

将单侧传感器 (含透镜) 分割成传感器和透镜, 将单传感器的透镜增加为两个, 成左右分布, 将感应到的红外线折射给传感器感光元件, 增大感光区域, 从而减少感应盲区, 模型图如图 8-26 所示。

➤ Scheme 2: according to No.1 division, Article (3)

The single side sensor (including lens) is divided into sensor and lens, and the lens of single sensor is increased to 2, which is distributed left and right. The infrared ray is refracted to the sensor sensitive element to increase the sensitive area, so as to reduce the sensing blind area, the illustration of model is shown in Figure 8-26.

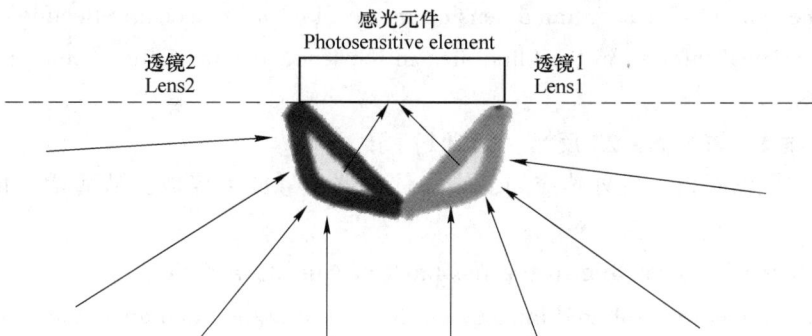

图 8-26 模型图

Figure 8-26 Illustration of model

> **方案 3：依据 No. 5 合并，第（1）条**

将系统两侧两个传感器合并成一个传感器，增加两侧透镜，将探测区域内红外线折射到传感器，模型图如图 8-27 所示。

> **Scheme 3：according to No. 5 merger，Article（1）**

The two sensors on both sides of the system are combined into one sensor, and the lenses on both sides are added to refract the infrared ray in the detection area to the sensor, the illustration of model is shown in Figure 8-27.

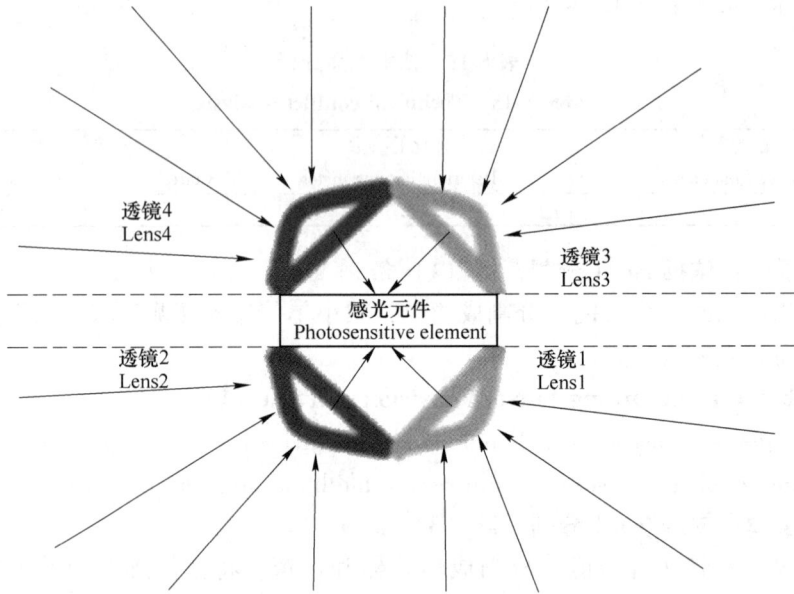

图 8-27　模型图

Figure 8-27　Illustration of model

> **方案 4：依据 No. 11 预补偿，第（1）条**

针对传感器对盲区红外感应弱，增加反射面，将原来盲区红外线反射到透镜，示意图如图 8-28 所示。

> **Scheme 4：according to No. 11 pre compensation，Article（1）**

For the sensor's weak infrared sensing in the blind area, add a reflecting surface to reflect the original infrared in the blind area to the lens, diagrammatic sketch is shown in Figure 8-28.

> **方案 5：依据 No. 23 反馈，第（1）条**

针对传感器对盲区红外感应弱，增加传感器信号放大倍数，从而增大传感器探测区域。

> **Scheme 5：according to the feedback of No. 23，Article（1）**

In view of the weak infrared induction of the sensor to the blind area, the amplification factor of the sensor signal is increased, so as to increase the detection area of the sensor.

物理冲突解决过程如下。

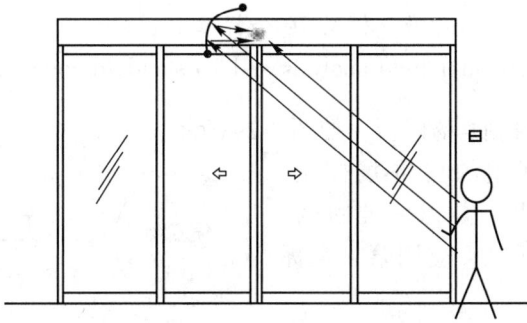

图 8-28　示意图

Figure 8-28　Diagrammatic sketch

（1）冲突描述：为了"提高系统响应速度"，需要参数"传感器灵敏度调节器阈值电压"为"小"，但又为了系统抗干扰性能，需要参数"阈值电压"为"大"，即，阈值电压既要"大"又要"小"。

（2）选用4条分离原理（空间分离、时间分离、基于条件的分离、整体与部分分离）当中的"时间分离"原理，得到解决方案。

（3）查找与该分离原理对应的发明原理有"1、7、9、10、11、15、16、18、19、20、21 等"。根据选定的发明原理，得到解决方案。

The physical conflict resolution process is as follows.

（1）Conflict description: in order to "improve the response speed of the system", the parameter "threshold voltage of sensor sensitivity regulator" needs to be "small", but for the anti-interference performance of the system, the parameter "threshold voltage" needs to be "large", that is, the threshold voltage should be "large" and "small".

（2）Choose the "time separation" principle among the four separation principles (space separation, time separation, condition based separation, whole and part separation) to get the solution.

（3）The invention principles corresponding to the separation principle are "1, 7, 9, 10, 11, 15, 16, 18, 19, 20, 21, etc.". According to the selected invention principle, the solution is obtained.

➤ 方案 6：依据 No. 1 发明原理

得到解如下：在探测人体时，降低传感器判定阈值电压，提前检测到人体经过；在判定电机是否驱动时，提高阈值电压，保障系统稳定性。通过传感器信号变化强度，判定信号输出。

➤ Scheme 6: according to the principle of No. 1 invention

The solution is as follows: when detecting the human body, the threshold voltage of the sensor is reduced to detect the passing of the human body in advance; when determining whether the motor is driven, the threshold voltage is increased to ensure the stability of the system. The signal output is determined by the change intensity of the sensor signal.

8.3.3.2   工具 2：物质-场分析及 76 个标准解

8.3.3.2   Tool 2：matter field analysis and 76 standard solutions

（1）建立问题的物质-场模型，如图 8-29 所示。

（2）根据所建问题的物质-场模型，应用标准解解决流程，得到标准解为：该问题是检测/测量问题，应用第 4 类标准解得到。

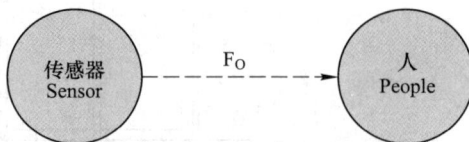

图 8-29　功能结构图

Figure 8-29   Functional structure diagram

（3）依据选定的标准解，得到问题的解决方案。No.44 标准解为：假如 No.43 不可能，测量一复制品或肖像。

（1）The matter field model of the problem is established, as shown in Figure 8-29.

（2）According to the matter field model of the built problem, apply the standard solution solution process, and the standard solution is obtained as follows：this problem is a detection/measurement problem, using the type 4 standard solution.

（3）According to the selected standard solution, the solution of the problem is obtained. The standard solution of No.44 is：if No.43 is impossible, measure a copy or portrait.

➤ **方案 1：依据 No.44 标准解**

得到问题的解如下：通过摄像机获取检测区域图像，通过图像处理分析人在图像中位置，从而实现识别人体的目的。改进之后的物质-场模型如图 8-30 所示。

➤ **Scheme 1：according to No.44 standard solution**

The solution of the problem is as follows：the image of detection area is obtained by camera, and the position of human in the image is analyzed by image processing, so as to realize the purpose of human body recognition. The improved matter field model is shown in Figure 8-30.

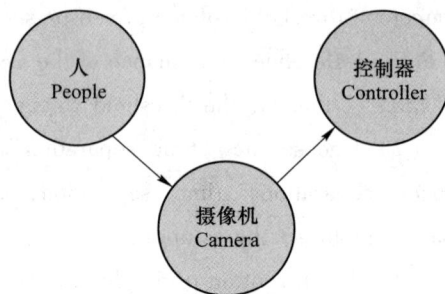

图 8-30　功能结构图

Figure 8-30   Functional structure diagram

依据选定的标准解，得到问题的解决方案。No.48 标准解为：在环境中增加附加物使其对系统产生场，检测或测量场对系统的影响。

According to the selected standard solution, the solution of the problem is obtained. The standard solution of No.48 is to add an additive to the environment to produce a field for the system, and to detect or measure the influence of the field on the system.

➤ **方案 2：依据 No.48 标准解**

得到问题的解如下：在环境中增加接近开关感受人体重力，从而产生电信号，控制器通过接受电信号识别人体接近。

改进之后的物质-场模型如图 8-31 所示。

➤ **Scheme 2: according to No. 48 standard solution**

The solution of the problem is as follows: in the environment, a proximity switch is added to sense the gravity of human body, so as to generate electric signal. The controller recognizes the human body approaching by receiving the electric signal.

The improved matter field model is shown in Figure 8-31.

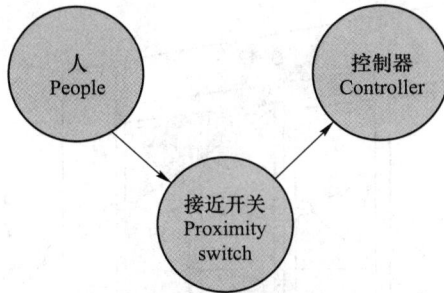

图 8-31　功能结构图

Figure 8-31　Functional structure diagram

8.3.3.3　工具 3：效应

8.3.3.3　Tool 3：effect

（1）确定问题要实现的功能为"检测位置"（measure position）。

（2）查找效应知识库，从 51 个建议注重得到可用的效应为"LIDAR、Photogrammetry、Radar"，依据该效应得到问题的解决方案。

1）LIDAR 效应：测量被测量物体反射回的光或者其他形式电磁波的时间差达到测距的目的。

2）Photogrammetry 效应：用图像识别技术测量物体形状。

3）Radar 效应：利用电磁波检测物体的形状、高度、速度等的方法。

4）网络效应库。

（1）The function to determine the problem is "measure position".

（2）Search the effect knowledge base, from 51 suggestions, the available effects are "LIDAR, Photogrammetry, Radar", according to the effect to get the solution of the problem.

1）LIDAR effect: measure the time difference of light or other forms of electromagnetic wave reflected by the measured object to achieve the purpose of ranging.

2）Photogrammetry effect: measuring object shape with image recognition technology.

3）Radar effect: a method to detect the shape, height and speed of an object by using electromagnetic wave.

4）Network effect library.

➤ **方案 1：依据 LIDAR 效应**

得到如下解：主动向需探测区域发射不可见光（红外线），监测红外线反射的变动情况；当有人体进入探测区域时，人体会将红外线反射回探测装置，来确定人体位置和移动，示意图如图 8-32 所示。

➢ **Scheme 1：according to LIDAR effect**

The following solution is obtained：when a human body enters the detection area，the human body will reflect the infrared back to the detection device to determine the position and movement of the human body，the diagrammatic sketch is shown in Figure 8-32.

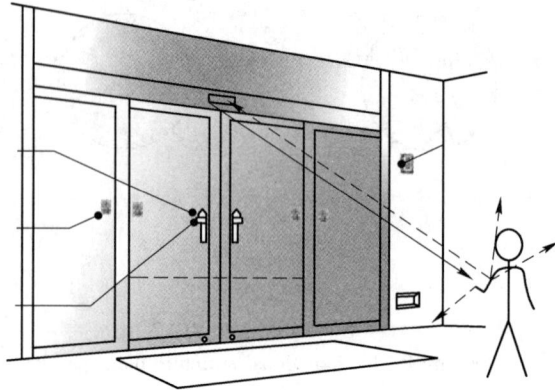

图 8-32　示意图

Figure 8-32　Diagrammatic sketch

➢ **方案 2：依据 Photogrammetry 效应**

得到如下解：利用基于图像处理的算法探测人体。通过分析广角摄像机图像，根据人体识别算法确定人体位置和姿态，来确定人体通过门与否的意图，实现自动门打开或者关闭，结构示意图如图 8-33 所示。

➢ **Scheme 2：according to the Photogrammetry effect**

The following solution is obtained：the algorithm based on image processing is used to detect human body. Through the analysis of wide-angle camera images，according to the human body recognition algorithm to determine the position and posture of the human body，to determine whether the intention of the human body through the door or not，to achieve automatic door opening or closing，structural representation is shown in Figure 8-33.

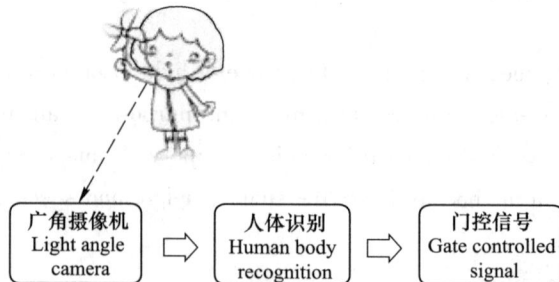

图 8-33　结构示意图

Figure 8-33　Structural representation

➤ **方案 3：依据 Radar 效应**

得到如下解：探测装置主动发射超声波，接收被人体反射回的超声波来确定人体位置和距离。

➤ **Scheme 3：according to the Radar effect**

The following solution is obtained：the detection device actively emits ultrasonic waves and receives the ultrasonic waves reflected by the human body to determine the position and distance of the human body.

8.3.4 问题的解

8.3.4 Solution of the problem

方案汇总见表 8-16。

Scheme summary is shown in Table 8-16.

表 8-16 可用性评估

Table 8-16 Availability assessment

序号 Serial number	方案 Programme	所用创新原理 Innovation principles used	可用性评估 Usability evaluation
1	将单侧传感器分割为 2 个 One side sensor is divided into two parts	技术冲突 No. 1.1 Technical conflict No. 1.1	可用☆ ☆ ☆ Usable
2	将单侧透镜分割为 2 个 The unilateral lens is divided into two parts	技术冲突 No. 1.3 Technical conflict No. 1.3	可用☆ Usable
3	合并两侧传感器为 1 个 Combine the two sensors into one	技术冲突 No. 5.1 Technical conflict No. 5.1	可用☆ Usable
4	增加反射面 Add reflector	技术冲突 No. 11.1 Technical conflict No. 11.1	可用，增加超系统 Usable，adding up to the supersystems
5	增加传感器信号放大倍数 Increase the amplification factor of sensor signal	技术冲突 No. 23.1 Technical conflict No. 23.1	不可用 Unusable
6	分离判断用的阈值电压 Threshold voltage for separation judgment	物理冲突 No. 1 Physical conflict No. 1	可用☆ ☆ ☆ ☆ Usable
7	在环境中（地面）增加电开关 Add electric switch in environment（ground）	物质-场模型 No. 48 Matter-filed model No. 48	不可用 Unusable
8	使用主动红外线检测人体 Using active infrared to detect human body	LIDAR 效应 LIDAR effect	可用☆ ☆ ☆ Usable
9	使用图像处理技术检测人体 Using image processing technology to detect human body	Photogrammetry 效应 Photogrammetry effect	可用☆ ☆ ☆ Usable
10	使用超声波检测人体 Using ultrasound to detecthuman body	Radar 效应 Radar effect	可用☆ ☆ ☆ Usable

最终解为：在探测人体时，降低传感器判定阈值电压①，提前检测到人体经过；在判定电机是否驱动时，提高阈值电压②，保障系统稳定性，如图 8-34 所示。通过传感器信号变化强度，判定信号输出。

The final solution is as follows：when detecting the human body，reduce the threshold voltage of the sensor to detect the passing of the human body in advance；when determining whether the motor is driven，increase the threshold voltage to ensure the stability of the system， as shown in Figure 8-34. The signal output is determined by the change intensity of the sensor signal.

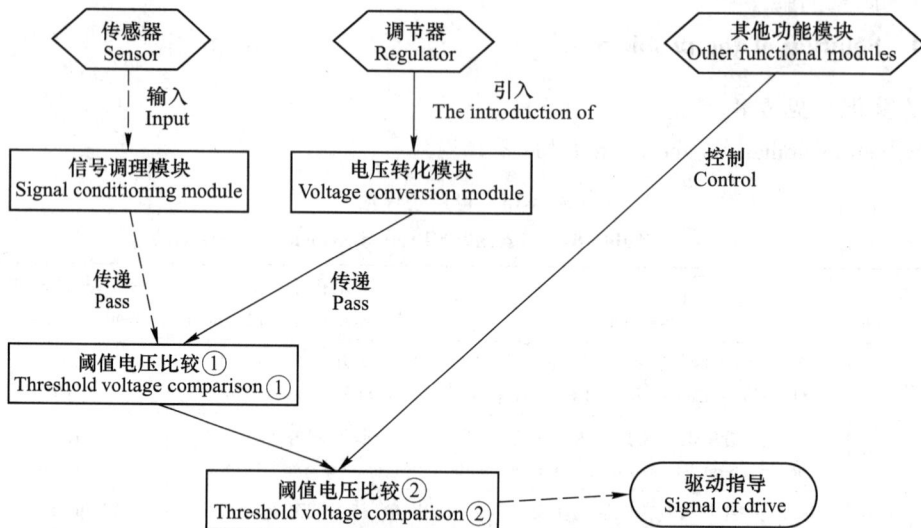

图 8-34　功能结构图

Figure 8-34　Functional structure diagram

8.3.5　取得成果与效益

8.3.5　Achievements and benefits

预期专利名称：
（1）一种多传感器自动感应门控装置，实用新型，正在申请；
（2）一种能识别人体出入意图的智能门控系统，实用新型，正在申请。

Expected patent name：
（1）The utility model relates to a multi-sensor automatic induction door control device；
（2）The utility model relates to an intelligent door control system which can recognize the intention of human body entering and leaving.

8.4　如何解决盒尺划伤手问题

8.4　How to solve the hand scratch problem of box ruler

本节主要从以下四个方面进行分析：

（1）问题背景和描述；

（2）问题分析过程；

（3）问题求解过程；

（4）问题的解。

The section is mainly analyzed from the following four aspects：

（1）Background and description of the problem；

（2）Problem analysis process；

（3）Problem solving process；

（4）The solution of the problem.

8.4.1 问题背景和描述
8.4.1 Problem background and description

8.4.1.1 问题的背景
8.4.1.1 Background of the problem

建筑施工领域用的盒尺（见图 8-35），在实际使用中很容易划到手，主要原因有以下几点：

（1）测量范围较长，尺带容易回折，方向难以预测；

（2）尺带的材质以金属为主；

（3）为了保证回卷的力量，发条弹簧的张力很大；

（4）金属材质质量大，边沿锋利。

The box ruler（see Figure 8-35）used in the field of construction is easy to get in the actual use. The main reasons are as follows：

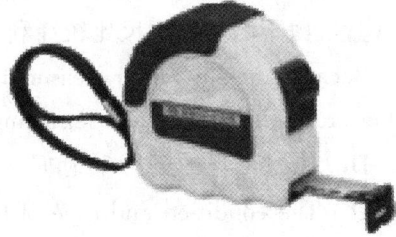

图 8-35 模型图
Figure 8-35 Illustration of model

（1）The measurement range is long, the tape is easy to fold back, and the direction is difficult to predict；

（2）The material of the tape is mainly metal；

（3）In order to ensure the rewinding force, the spring tension is very large；

（4）Metal material quality, sharp edge.

8.4.1.2 问题的描述
8.4.1.2 Description of the problem

A 定义技术系统实现的功能

A Define the function of the technology system

问题所在技术系统为盒尺。

该技术系统的功能为测量长度。

实现该功能的约束有测量长度。

The technical system of the problem is box ruler.

The function of the technology system is measuring length.

The constraints to realize this function are measuring length.

B　现有技术系统的工作原理

B　Working principle of prior art system

盒尺由外壳、尺条、制动开关、尺钩、提带、尺簧等构件构成。盒尺里面装有发条弹簧，在拉出测量长度时，实际是拉长标尺及弹簧的长度，一旦测量完毕，卷尺里面的弹簧会自动收缩，标尺在弹簧力的作用下也跟着收缩，所以卷尺就会卷起来。

The box ruler is composed of a shell, a ruler bar, a brake switch, a ruler hook, a lifting belt, a ruler spring and other components. There is a spring inside the tape. When the tape is pulled out to measure the length, it actually lengthens the length of the scale and the spring. Once the measurement is finished, the spring inside the tape will shrink automatically, and the scale will also shrink under the action of the spring force, so the tape will roll up.

C　当前技术系统存在的问题

C　Problems in current technology system

盒尺由于测量的钢尺比较锋利，在拉开和回缩的过程容易划伤手。

Because the steel ruler measured by the box ruler is sharp, it is easy to scratch hands in the process of pulling and retracting.

D　问题出现的条件和时间

D　The condition and time of the problem

依据上述当前系统存在的问题，需要说明以下内容。

（1）问题是否是在某一个特殊的条件下才发生？

（2）在测量过程中，在拉开或者回尺的时候容易划伤手。

According to the above problems existing in the current system, the following contents need to be explained.

（1）Does the problem arise under a particular condition?

（2）In the process of measurement, it is easy to scratch hands when pulling or returning the ruler.

E　问题或类似问题的现有解决方案及其缺点

E　Existing solutions to problems or similar problems and their shortcomings

在下面描述针对当前系统存在的问题，是否已经尝试了一些方法来解决问题，这些方法有什么缺点。

In the following description, in view of the problems existing in the current system, whether some methods have been tried to solve the problems, and what are the shortcomings of these methods.

F 新系统的要求

F Requirements of the new system

测量用尺不锋利, 拉开或者回收速度可控性强。

The measuring ruler is not sharp, and the pulling or recycling speed is controllable.

8.4.1.3 问题求解流程

8.4.1.3 Problem solving process

功能结构图如图 8-12 所示。

The functional structure diagram is shown in Figure 8-12.

8.4.2 问题分析

8.4.2 Problem analysis

8.4.2.1 功能分析

8.4.2.1 Functional analysis

系统分析见表 8-17。

Systems analysis is shown in Table 8-17.

表 8-17 系统分析
Table 8-17 Systems analysis

制 品 Product	被测量物 Measurements
系统元件 System component	钢尺带、回尺簧、空心轴、外壳、制动开关 Steel ruler tape, ruler spring, hollow shaft, housing, brake switch
超系统元件 Supersystem components	人 People

建立已有系统的功能模型, 如图 8-36 所示。

Establish the function model of the existing system is shown in Figure 8-36.

8.4.2.2 因果分析

8.4.2.2 Causal analysis

应用因果链分析法确定产生问题的原因, 如图 8-37 所示。

Using causal chain analysis to determine the cause of the problem, as shown in Figure 8-37.

8.4.2.3 冲突区域确定 (问题关键点确定)

8.4.2.3 Determination of conflict area (determination of key points)

(1) 问题关键点 1: 钢尺较薄。

(2) 问题关键点 2: 拉伸和回尺速度快。

固定 Fixed
外壳 The shell
固定 Fixed
人 People
储存 Storag
划伤 Scratch
拉动 Pull
控制 Control
空心轴 Hollow core shaft
支撑 Prop up
尺带 Feet with
控制 Control
固定 Fixed
收拉 Close to pull
测量 Measuremen
制动开关 Brake off switch
回尺簧 Rule return spring
被测量对象 Object being measured

人员 Personnel
机械 Mechanical
材料 Material
钢尺较硬 The steel ruler is stiff
保护措施不当 Improper protection measures
钢尺回收速度快 Steel ruler recovery speed is fast
钢尺较薄 The steel ruler is thin
盒尺划伤手
Box ruler cuts hand
操作不当 Improper operation
测量距离长 The measurement distance is too long
方法 Methods
环境 The environment

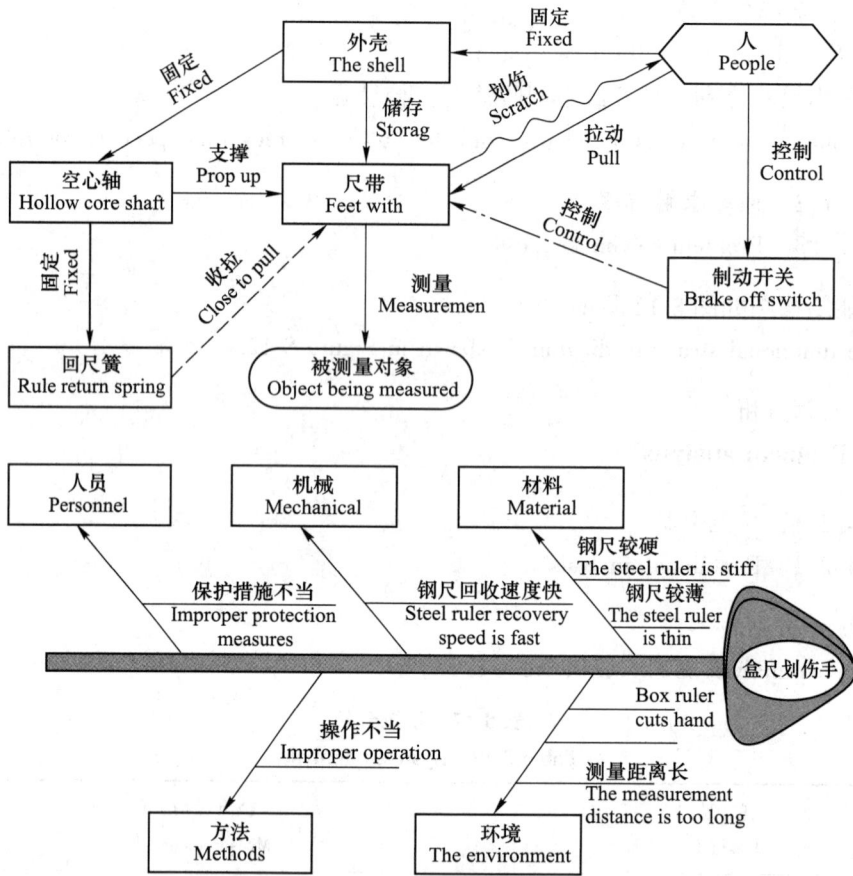

图 8-36 功能结构图

Figure 8-36 Functional structure diagram

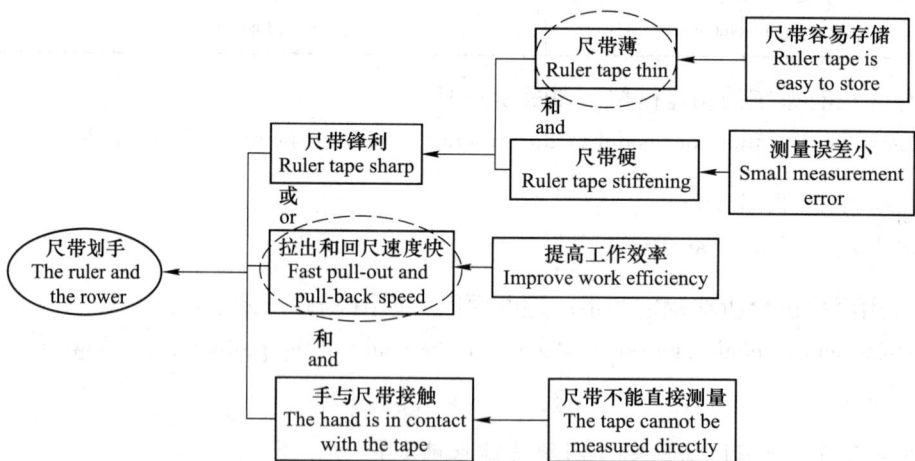

尺带薄 Ruler tape thin
尺带容易存储 Ruler tape is easy to store
和 and
尺带锋利 Ruler tape sharp
尺带硬 Ruler tape stiffening
测量误差小 Small measurement error
或 or
尺带划手 The ruler and the rower
拉出和回尺速度快 Fast pull-out and pull-back speed
提高工作效率 Improve work efficiency
和 and
手与尺带接触 The hand is in contact with the tape
尺带不能直接测量 The tape cannot be measured directly

图 8-37 功能结构图

Figure 8-37 Functional structure diagram

（1）The key point of the problem 1: the steel ruler is thin.

（2）The key point of the problem 2：the speed of drawing and back is fast.

8.4.2.4　理想解分析

8.4.2.4　Analysis of ideal solution

理想解分析主要对以下问题进行回答。
（1）设计的最终目的是什么？不划伤手的盒尺。
（2）理想解是什么？钢尺自动测量。
（3）达到理想解的障碍是什么？钢尺必须与手接触。
（4）出现这种障碍的结果是什么？划伤手。

The ideal solution analysis mainly answers the follwing questions.

（1）What is the ultimate goal of design？ Box ruler without scratching hands.

（2）What is the ideal solution？ Automatic measurement with steel ruler.

（3）What are the obstacles to the ideal solution？ The steel ruler must be in contact with the hand.

（4）What is the result of this obstacle？ Scratch hands.

8.4.2.5　可用资源分析

8.4.2.5　Analysis of available resources

可用资源分析见表8-18。

Analysis of available resources are shown in Table 8-18.

表 8-18　可用资源分析
Table 8-18　Analysis of available resources

类别 Category		资源名称 Resource name	可用性分析（初步方案） Usability analysis（preliminary scheme）
内部 资源 Inside resources	物质资源 Material resources	回尺簧 Return ruler spring	
		尺带 Ulnar band	
		外壳 Shell	
	场资源 Field resources	机械场 Mechanical field	
	其他资源 Other resources		
外部资源 External resources	物质资源 Material resources	柔性材料 Flexible material	
	场资源 Field resources	机械场 Mechanical field	
	其他资源 Other resources		

类别 Category		资源名称 Resource name	可用性分析（初步方案） Usability analysis（preliminary scheme）
超系统资源 Supersystem resources	物质资源 Material resources		
	场资源 Field resources		
	其他资源 Other resources	人 People	

8.4.3　问题求解
8.4.3　Problem solving

8.4.3.1　问题关键点 1　以"钢尺较薄"为入手点解决问题

8.4.3.1　The key point of the problem 1　To solve the problem with "thin steel ruler" as the starting point

A　工具 1：冲突解决理论

A　Tool 1：conflict resolution theory

技术冲突解决过程如下。

（1）冲突描述：为了减小盒尺中尺带系统的"锋利性"，需要增加尺带厚度，但这样做了会导致系统尺带弯折不便，导致体积增大，成本增加。

（2）转换成 TRIZ 标准冲突。改善的参数为 31 物体产生的有害因素；恶化的参数为 08 静止物体体积、23 物质损失、33 可操作性。

（3）查找冲突矩阵，得到如下发明原理，见表 8-19。

The technology conflict resolution process is as follows.

（1）Conflict description：in order to reduce the "sharpness" of the tape system in the box ruler，we need to increase the thickness of the tape，but doing so will lead to inconvenient bending of the tape system，increase the volume and cost.

（2）Conversion to TRIZ standard conflict. Improved parameters is 31 harmful factors caused by objects；deteriorating parameters is 08 volume of stationary object，23 mass loss，33 operability.

（3）By searching the conflict matrix，the following principles of the invention are obtained，as shown in Table 8-19.

➤ **方案 1：依据 No. 10 预操作发明原理**

（1）在操作开始前，使物体局部或全部产生所需的变化。

（2）预先对物体进行特殊安排，使其在时间上有准备，或已处于易操作的位置。

表 8-19　技术冲突分析
Table 8-19　Technical conflict analysis

改善的参数 Improved parameters	恶化的参数 Deteriorating parameters	对应的发明原理 Corresponding principles of invention
物体产生的有害因素 Harmful factors caused by objects	物质损失 Material loss	1. 分割 1. Segmentation
物体产生的有害因素 Harmful factors caused by objects	静止物体体积 Volume of stationary object	4. 不对称 4. Asymmetry
物体产生的有害因素 Harmful factors caused by objects	物质损失 Material loss	10. 预操作 10. Pre operation
物体产生的有害因素 Harmful factors caused by objects	静止物体体积 Volume of stationary object	18. 振动 18. Vibration
物体产生的有害因素 Harmful factors caused by objects	静止物体体积 Volume of stationary object	30. 柔性壳体或薄膜 30. Flexible shell or membrane
物体产生的有害因素 Harmful factors caused by objects	物质损失 Material loss	34. 抛弃与修复 34. Abandonment and restoration
物体产生的有害因素 Harmful factors caused by objects	静止物体体积 Volume of stationary object	35. 参数变化 35. Parameter change

得到解如下：制作专用手套用来保护手指，在测量前先戴上。

➤ **Scheme 1：according to the principle of No. 10 pre operation invention**

（1）Before the start of operation, make the required changes to the whole or part of the object.

（2）Make special arrangements in advance for the object to be ready in time or in a good condition easy to operate location.

The solution is as follows：make special gloves to protect fingers and wear them before measurement.

➤ **方案 2：依据 No. 30 柔性壳体或薄膜**

发明原理：用柔性壳体或薄膜代替传统材料。

得到解如下：将钢尺材料改为 PET 聚酯材料，此材料耐疲劳性，耐摩擦性、尺寸稳定性都很好，可代替原钢尺带。

➤ **Scheme 2：according to No. 30 flexible shell or membrane**

Principle of invention：flexible shell or film is used to replace traditional materials.

The solution is as follows：the steel ruler material is changed into PET polyester material, which has good fatigue resistance, friction resistance and dimensional stability, and can replace the original steel ruler belt.

将钢尺边缘包裹一层薄的柔性材料，如图 8-38 所示。

Wrap the edge of the steel ruler with a thin layer of flexible material, as shown in Figure 8-38.

图 8-38　模型图

Figure 8-38　Illustration of model

（1）冲突描述：为了"避免划伤手"，需要参数"卷尺厚度"为"厚"，但又为了"携带方便"，需要参数"卷尺的厚度"为"薄"，即，卷尺的厚度某个参数既要"厚"又要"薄"。

（2）选用 4 条分离原理（空间分离、时间分离、基于条件的分离、整体与部分分离）当中的"基于条件的分离"原理，得到解决方案。

(1) Conflict description：in order to "avoid scratching hands", the parameter "tape thickness" needs to be "thick", but for "convenience of carrying", the parameter "tape thickness" needs to be "thin", that is, a parameter of tape thickness needs to be "thick" and "thin".

(2) Choose the "condition based separation" principle among the four separation principles (space separation, time separation, condition based separation, whole and part separation) to get the solution.

➤ **方案 3：空间分离**

元件的某一部分有特性 P，另一部分有特性-P，在空间上分离该两部分。

解决方案：将尺带设计成边缘厚，中间薄，外壳也根据钢尺进行设计。

➤ **Scheme 3：spatial separation**

One part of the element has characteristic P, and the other part has characteristic-P, which separates the two parts in space.

Solution：the tape is designed with thick edge and thin middle, and the shell is also designed according to the steel ruler.

➤ **方案 4：基于条件的分离**

在某一条件，元件具有特性 P，在另外一条件，该元件具有特性-P，按条件分离 P 与-P。

解决方案：改造外壳，在刚尺拉出头的位置加一段悬挑出来的头，如图 8-39 所示。

➤ **Scheme 4：conditional separation**

In one condition，the element has the characteristic P，in another condition，the element has the characteristic-P，and P and-P are separated according to the condition.

Solution：transform the shell，add a section of overhanging head at the position where the rigid ruler pulls out the head, as shown in Figure 8-39.

B 工具 2：物质-场分析及 76 个标准解

B Tool 2: matter field analysis and 76 standard solutions

（1）建立问题的物质-场模型，如图 8-40 所示。

（1）The matter field model of the problem is established, as shown in Figure 8-40.

图 8-39 模型图

Figure 8-39 Illustration of model

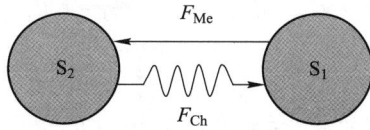

图 8-40 模型分析图

Figure 8-40 Model analysis diagram

S_2—尺带；S_1—手指；

S_2—Ruler hand；S_1—Finger

期望作用 F_{Me}—拉力；有害作用 F_{Ch}—（划伤手）力

Effect of expectation—pull；Harmful effect—(cut one's hand)force

（2）根据所建问题的物质-场模型，应用标准解解决流程，得到标准解为：No. 1. 2. 1，No. 1. 2. 2，No. 1. 2. 3，No. 1. 2. 4。

（2）According to the matter field model of the problem, the standard solution process is applied：No. 1. 2. 1，No. 1. 2. 2，No. 1. 2. 3，No. 1. 2. 4.

（3）依据选定的标准解，得到问题的解决方案。No. 1. 2. 1 标准解为：当前设计中同时存在有用和有害作用，S_1 和 S_2 不必直接接触，引入 S_3 消除有害作用。

（3）According to the selected standard solution, the solution of the problem is obtained. The standard solution of No. 1. 2. 1 is：there are both useful and harmful effects in the current design, S_1 and S_2 do not need to be directly contacted, and S_3 is introduced to eliminate the harmful effects.

➤ 方案：依据 No. 9 标准解

得到问题的解如下：给钢尺带保护套（减小锐度）、拉出时会同时带出一截保护套，回收最后时此段保护套同时缩回。

改进之后的物质-场模型如图 8-41 所示。

➤ Scheme：according to No. 9 standard solution

The solution of the problem is as follows：the steel ruler is provided with a protective cover (to reduce the sharpness). When it is pulled out, a section of the protective cover will be taken out at the same time. When it is finally recovered, the protective cover will be retracted at the same time.

The improved matter field model is shown in Figure 8-41.

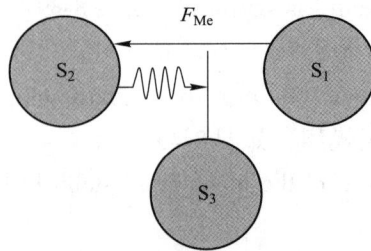

图 8-41　模型分析图

Figure 8-41　Model analysis diagram

S_1—手指；S_2—尺带；S_3—保护套

S_1—Finger；S_2—Ruler hand；S_3—Protective sleeve

8.4.3.2　问题关键点 2　以"钢尺拉收速度快"为入手点解决问题

8.4.3.2　The key point of the problem 2　To solve the problem from the point of "steel ruler pulling and retracting fast"

➢ 工具：冲突解决理论

物理冲突解决过程如下。

➢ Tool：conflict resolution theory

The physical conflict resolution process is as follows.

（1）冲突描述：为了"避免划伤手"，需要参数"速度"为"慢"，但又为了"提高工作效率"，需要参数"速度"为"快"，即，卷尺的厚度某个参数既要"快"又要"慢"。

（2）选用 4 条分离原理（空间分离、时间分离、基于条件的分离、整体与部分分离）当中的"基于条件的分离"原理，得到解决方案。

（1）Conflict description：in order to "avoid scratching hands", the parameter "speed" needs to be "slow", but in order to "improve work efficiency", the parameter "speed" needs to be "fast", that is, a certain parameter of tape thickness should be "fast" and "slow".

（2）Choose the "condition based separation" principle among the four separation principles (space separation, time separation, condition based separation, whole and part separation) to get the solution.

➢ 方案：基于条件的分离

在某一条件下，元件具有特性 P，在另一条件，该元件具有特性-P，按条件分离 P 与-P。

解决方案：在钢尺的出口处加一个装置，使其在拉出时摩擦力小，速度快；在回尺时摩擦力大，速度慢。

➢ Scheme：conditional separation

Under one condition, the element has characteristic P, and under another condition, the element has characteristic-P. P and-P are separated according to the condition.

Solution: add a device at the exit of the steel ruler to make it pull out with small friction and fast speed; when the ruler is returned, the friction force is large and the speed is slow.

8.4.4 问题的解
8.4.4 Solution of the problem

上述方案汇总见表 8-20。

Summary of the above schemes are shown in Table 8-20.

表 8-20 可用性评估

Table 8-20 Availability assessment

序号 Serial number	方案 Programme	所用创新原理 Innovation principles used	可用性评估 Usability evaluation
1	制作专用手套用来保护手指，在测量前先戴上 Make special gloves to protect fingers and wear them before measurement	预操作发明原理 Principle of pre operation invention	
2	将钢尺材料改为 PET 聚酯材料，此材料耐疲劳性，耐摩擦性、尺寸稳定性都很好，可代替原钢尺带 The steel ruler material is changed into PET polyester material, which has good fatigue resistance, friction resistance and dimensional stability, and can replace the original steel ruler belt	柔性壳体或薄膜发明原理 Principle of flexible shell or membrane	
3	将钢尺边缘包裹一层薄的柔性材料 Wrap the edge of the steel ruler with a thin layer of flexible material	柔性壳体或薄膜发明原理 Principle of flexible shell or membrane	
4	将尺带设计成边缘厚，中间薄，外壳也根据钢尺进行设计 The tape is designed to be thick at the edge and thin in the middle, and the shell is also designed according to the steel ruler	空间分离 Spatial separation	
5	改造外壳：在钢尺拉出头的位置加一段悬挑出来的头 Transform the shell: add a section of overhanging head at the position where the steel ruler pulls out the head	基于条件的分离 Condition based separation	

序号 Serial number	方案 Programme	所用创新原理 Innovation principles used	可用性评估 Usability evaluation
6	给钢尺带保护套（减小锐度）、拉出时会同时带出一截保护套，回收最后时此段保护套同时缩回 The steel ruler is provided with a protective cover（to reduce the sharpness）. When it is pulled out, a section of the protective cover will be taken out at the same time. When it is finally recovered, the protective cover will be retracted at the same time	当前设计中同时存在有用和有害作用，S_1 和 S_2 不必直接接触，引入 S_3 消除有害作用 In the current design, there are both useful and harmful effects, S_1 and S_2 do not need to contact directly, and S_3 is introduced to eliminate the harmful effects	
7	在钢尺的出口处加一个装置，使其在拉出时摩擦力小，速度快；在回尺时摩擦力大，速度慢 A device is added at the exit of the steel ruler, so that the friction force is small and the speed is fast when the steel ruler is pulled out; when the ruler is returned, the friction force is large and the speed is slow	基于条件的分离 Condition based separation	

最终解为：在钢尺的出口处加一个装置，使其在拉出时摩擦力小，速度快；在回尺时摩擦力大，速度慢。

The final solution is as follows：a device is added at the exit of the steel ruler, so that the friction force is small and the speed is fast when the steel ruler is pulled out；when the ruler is returned, the friction force is large and the speed is slow.

8.5　儿童书写姿势矫正装置
8.5　Children's writing posture correction device

本节主要从以下五个方面进行分析：

（1）问题背景和描述；

（2）问题分析过程；

（3）问题求解过程；

（4）问题的解；

（5）取得成果与效益。

This section is mainly analyzed from the following five aspects：

（1）Background and description of the problem；

（2）Problem analysis process；

(3) Problem solving process;

(4) The solution of the problem;

(5) Achievements and benefits.

8.5.1 问题背景和描述
8.5.1 Problem background and description

8.5.1.1 问题的背景
8.5.1.1 Background of the problem

儿童如果书写姿势不正确则直接影响书写的质量与速度，必然制约儿童今后写字水平的提高。4~8岁的儿童正处在学习写字初期，如果写字姿势不正确，容易造成脊髓弯曲，右手发育不良甚至畸形等后果；坐姿歪斜、弯腰曲背，会造成眼睛离书和作业本距离太近，眼睛斜视或视角不正，眼球长期调整过度，形成近视，这些不良习惯影响学生的身体发育，不及时矫治，还可能引发一系列负面影响。

If children's writing posture is not correct, it will directly affect the quality and speed of writing, which will inevitably restrict the improvement of children's writing level in the future. Children aged 4-8 are in the early stage of learning to write. If the writing posture is not correct, it is easy to cause spinal cord bending, right hand dysplasia and even deformity; sitting askew, bending back, will cause eyes too close to the book and homework, eye strabismus or angle of view is not correct, eye long-term excessive adjustment, the formation of myopia, these bad habits affect the physical development of students, not timely correction, may also cause a series of negative effects.

8.5.1.2 问题的描述
8.5.1.2 Description of the problem

A 定义技术系统实现的功能

A Define the function of the technology system

问题所在技术系统为儿童书写姿势矫正装置。

该技术系统的功能为预防、矫正。

实现该功能的约束有儿童的身高（90-120cm）、书桌高（60-90cm）。

The problem lies in the technical system: children's writing posture correction device.

The function of the technology system is: prevention, correction.

The constraints to achieve this function are: children's height (90-120cm), desk height (60-90cm).

B 现有技术系统的工作原理

B Working principle of prior art system

现有的书写姿势矫正器，不用托下巴，让孩子自然抬头，底部采用高精密防滑垫，不采用螺纹固定，桌子厚度，桌子有抽屉都不受影响，都可直接放上使用，用写字板上的夹子固定纸，写字板没有固定在桌上，容易移动；采用握笔器可以矫正握笔姿势将握笔器套筒拿在手上，另一只手用旋转的方法将笔插入笔筒，将笔插入笔筒后，调整到合适位置。技术系统的工作原理如图 8-42 所示。

The existing writing posture correction device does not need to hold the chin, so that children can naturally look up. The bottom adopts high-precision anti-skid pad, and does not use thread fixation. The thickness of the table and the drawer of the table are not affected, and can be directly put into use. The paper is fixed with the clip on the writing board, and the writing board is not fixed on the table, so it is easy to move; the pen holder can correct the posture of holding the pen, hold the sleeve of the pen holder in the hand, and insert the pen into the pen holder with the other hand by rotating. After inserting the pen into the pen holder, adjust it to the appropriate position. Working principle of ant system is shown in Figure 8-42.

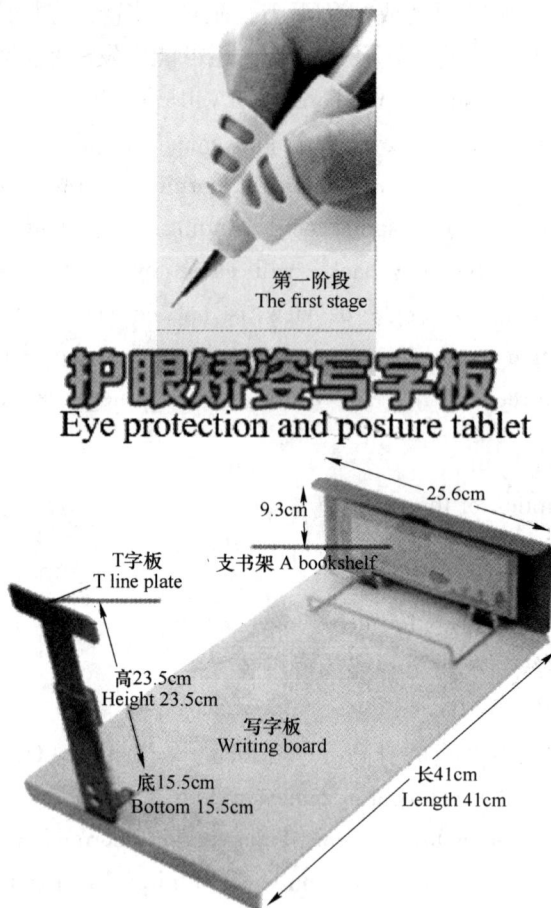

图 8-42　工作原理示意图

Figure 8-42　Working principle diagram

C　当前技术系统存在的问题

C　Problems in current technology system

技术问题 1：现有的握笔姿势矫正器只矫正手指与笔尖的距离，很多儿童写字时会把整个手腕扭转，笔朝向自己。

解决方案：设计一种阻止手腕扭转的装置，在不知不觉中起到矫正书写姿势的目的。

Technical problem 1: the existing pen holding posture corrector only corrects the distance between the finger and the tip of the pen, and many children will twist the whole wrist when writing, with the pen facing themselves.

Solution: design a device to prevent wrists from twisting, which can correct writing posture unconsciously.

技术问题 2：现有的坐姿矫正器只矫正前胸、手臂、眼睛的与书本的相对位置，有些孩子习惯写字时跷二郎腿，目前没有矫正腿部的装置。

解决方案：设计一种书写时矫正腿部位置的装置。

Technical problem 2: the existing sitting posture orthosis only corrects the relative position of the front chest, arms, eyes and books. Some children are used to crossing their legs when writing, and there is no leg correction device at present.

Solution: design a device to correct the leg position when writing.

技术问题 3：目前，大部分只是矫正握笔姿势的器具，针对纸张摆放位置的矫正装置极少，很多儿童写字时纸张总是倾斜向一边。

解决方案：设计一种矫正纸张摆放位置的装置。

Technical problem 3: at present, most of them are just devices for correcting the posture of holding pen. There are few devices for correcting the position of paper. When many children write, the paper is always tilted to one side.

Solution: design a device to correct the position of paper.

D 问题出现的条件和时间

D The condition and time of the problem

在教室里上课、在书桌上写作业的时候；在儿童读书、写字的时候。

In the classroom, when doing homework on the desk; when children read and write.

E 问题或类似问题的现有解决方案及其缺点

E Existing solutions to problems or similar problems and their shortcomings

将书写板的背面粘贴双面胶，固定在书桌上，使用一段时间后，双面胶黏度下降，无法固定在书桌上。

Stick double-sided tape on the back of the writing board and fix it on the desk. After using for a period of time, the viscosity of the double-sided tape decreases and cannot be fixed on the desk.

F 新系统的要求

F Requirements of the new system

手腕矫正装置根据儿童的手臂、手掌尺寸可调。纸张矫正装置根据书桌的尺寸可调，腿部矫正装置根据腿的长短可调。

The wrist correction device can be adjusted according to the size of children's arms and palms. The paper straightening device can be adjusted according to the size of the desk, and the leg straightening device can be adjusted according to the length of the leg.

8.5.1.3　问题求解流程
8.5.1.3　Problem solving process

功能结构图如图 8-37 所示。

Functional structure diagram is shown in Figure 8-37.

8.5.2　问题分析
8.5.2　Problem analysis

8.5.2.1　功能分析
8.5.2.1　Functional analysis

系统分析见表 8-21。

Systems analysis is shown in Table 8-21.

表 8-21　系统分析
Table 8-21　Systems analysis

制品 Products	书桌、纸、书、笔 Desk, paper, book, pen
系统元件 System components	握笔器、夹子、T字板、支书架、平板 Pen holder, clip, T-board, book holder, flat board
超系统元件 Supersystem element	人、地面 People, ground

建立已有系统的功能模型，如图 8-43 所示。

Establish the function model of the existing system is shown in Figure 8-43.

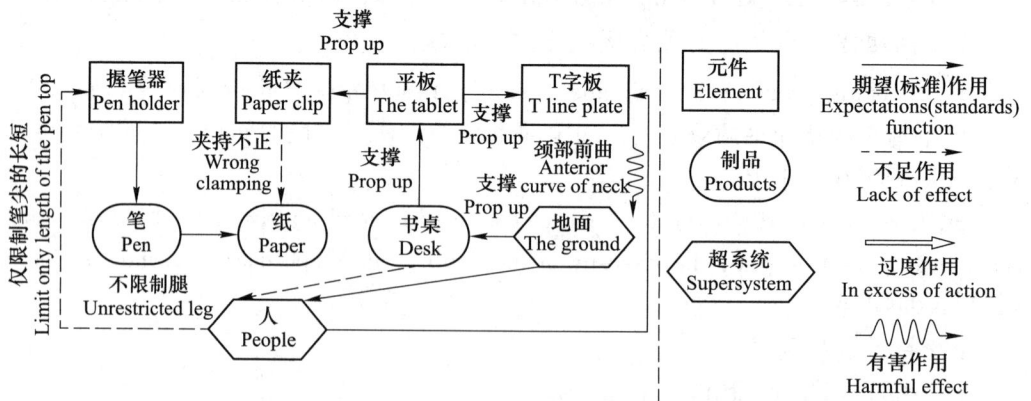

图 8-43　功能结构图

Figure 8-43　Functional structure diagram

8.5.2.2 因果分析

8.5.2.2 Causal analysis

具体分析如图 8-44 所示。

The specific analysis is shown in Figure 8-44.

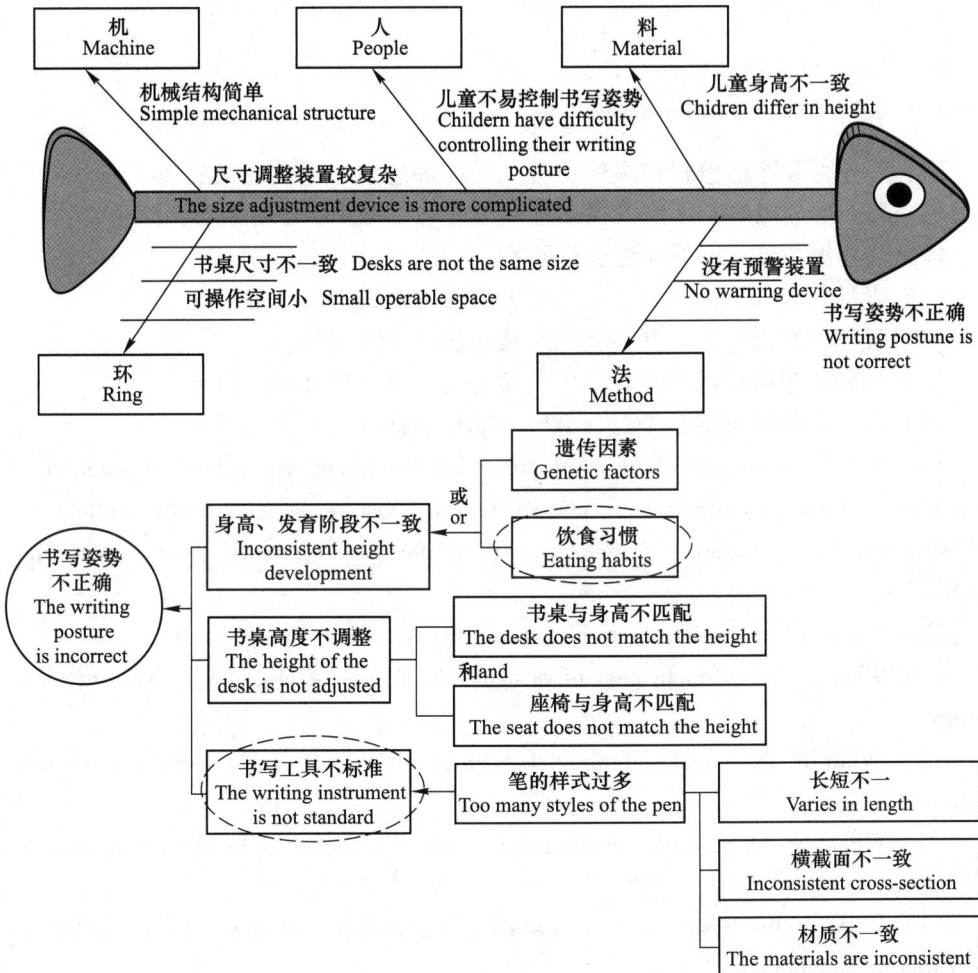

图 8-44 因果链分析

Figure 8-44 Causal analysis

8.5.2.3 冲突区域确定（问题关键点确定）

8.5.2.3 Determination of conflict area (determination of key points)

（1）问题关键点 1：握笔器只能矫正笔尖距离手指的距离，手腕扭转时，无法调节。

（2）问题关键点 2：纸夹只能夹持纸张，无法调节纸张相对于书桌的平行度和垂直度。

（3）问题关键点 3：腿部位置无法调节。

（1）The key point of the problem 1：the pen holder can only correct the distance between the pen tip and the finger, when the wrist is twisted, it cannot be adjusted.

（2）The key point of the problem 2：the paper clip can only hold the paper, and can't adjust the parallelism and perpendicularity of the paper relative to the desk.

（3）The key point of the problem 3：leg position cannot be adjusted.

8.5.2.4　理想解分析

8.5.2.4　Analysis of ideal solution

理想解分为最终理想解和次理想解。最终理想解：不使用矫正器，学生自发矫正书写姿势。次理想解：按照人机工程学设计书写姿势矫正器。

理想解分析主要对以下问题进行回答。

（1）设计的最终目的是什么？矫正儿童不正确的书写姿势。

（2）理想解是什么？让儿童自发形成正确的书写姿势。

（3）达到理想解的障碍是什么？儿童身高、书桌尺寸不一致。

（4）出现这种障碍的结果是什么？不能按照标准矫正书写姿势。

The ideal solutions are divided into final ideal solution and sub-ideal solution. The final ideal solution：students can correct writing posture spontaneously without using orthosis. Sub ideal solution：design of writing posture correction device according to ergonomics.

The ideal solution analysis mainly answers the following questions.

（1）What is the ultimate goal of design? Correction of children's incorrect writing posture.

（2）What is the ideal solution? Let children spontaneously form correct writing posture.

（3）What are the obstacles to the ideal solution? Children's height and desk size are inconsistent.

（4）What is the result of this obstacle? The writing posture cannot be corrected according to the standard.

按照儿童身高划分系列；按照书桌大小划分系列；依据理想解分析得到方案为：把矫正器设计成尺寸可调节的装置。

Divide the series according to the height of children; divide the series according to the size of the desk; according to the analysis of ideal solution, the scheme is to design the orthodontic device as a device with adjustable size.

8.5.2.5　可用资源分析

8.5.2.5　Analysis of available resources

可用资源分析见表 8-22。

Analysis of available resources are shown in Table 8-22.

表 **8-22** 可用资源分析

Table 8-22　Analysis of available resources

类别 Category		资源名称 Resource name	可用性分析（初步方案） Usability analysis（preliminary scheme）
内部 资源 Inside resources	物质资源 Material resources	纸夹 Paper clip	将纸夹与平移机构设计成一体式结构 The paper clip and translation mechanism are designed as an integrated structure
	场资源 Field resources	机械能 Mechanical energy	机构运动 Mechanism movement
	其他资源 Other resources		
外部资源 External resources	物质资源 Material resources	书桌 Desk	书桌的高低适宜 The height of the desk is suitable
		书本、纸张 Books，paper	与安装的夹子的大小匹配 Match the size of the clip installed
	场资源 Field resources	重力场 Field of gravity	
	其他资源 Other resources		
超系统资源 Supersystem resources	物质资源 Material resources	人 People	使用矫正器 Use of orthotics
	场资源 Field resources	地面（重力场） Ground（gravity field）	地面支撑书桌 Floor supported desk
	其他资源 Other resources		

8.5.3　问题求解

8.5.3　Problem solving

问题关键点　以"矫正写字姿势"为入手点解决问题。

The key points of the problem　To solve the problem with "correcting writing posture" as the starting point.

8.5.3.1　工具1：冲突解决理论

8.5.3.1　Tool 1：conflict resolution theory

技术冲突解决过程如下。

（1）冲突描述：为了达到系统的"手腕矫正功能"，需要增加弯曲机构，但这样做了会导致系统的约束过多。

（2）转换成 TRIZ 标准冲突。改善的参数为 No. 12 形状；恶化的参数为 No. 25 时间损失。

Technology conflict resolution process is as follows.

（1）Conflict description: in order to achieve the "wrist correction function" of the system, we need to add a bending mechanism, but doing so will lead to excessive constraints of the system.

（2）Conversion to TRIZ standard conflict. Improved parameter is No. 12 shape; deteriorating parameter is No. 25 time loss.

（1）冲突描述：为了达到系统的"纸张矫正功能"，需要 3 连杆矫正机构，但这样做了会导致系统更加复杂，成本提高。

（2）转换成 TRIZ 标准冲突。改善的参数为 No. 3 运动物体的长度；恶化的参数为 No. 36 装置的复杂性。

（1）Conflict description: in order to achieve the "paper correction function" of the system, we need a 3-link correction mechanism, but doing so will lead to more complex system and higher cost.

（2）Conversion to TRIZ standard conflict. Improved parameter is No. 3 length of moving object; deteriorating parameters is complexity of No. 36 device.

（1）冲突描述：为了达到系统的"腿部矫正功能"，需要变更机构垂直方向的高度，但这样做了会导致系统的更加复杂，成本提高。

（2）转换成 TRIZ 标准冲突。改善的参数为 No. 10 力；恶化的参数为 No. 22 能量损失。

（3）查找冲突矩阵，得到如下发明原理，见表 8-23。

（1）Conflict description: in order to achieve the "leg correction function" of the system, we need to change the vertical height of the mechanism, but this will lead to more complex system and higher cost.

（2）Conversion to TRIZ standard conflict. Improved parameter is No. 10 force; deteriorating parameter is No. 22 energy loss.

（3）By searching the conflict matrix, the following principles of the invention are obtained, as shown in Table 8-23.

表 8-23　技术冲突分析

Table 8-23　Technical conflict analysis

改善的参数 Improved parameters	恶化的参数 Deteriorating parameters	对应的发明原理 Corresponding principles of invention
形状 Shape	时间损失 Time lost	14 曲面化、10 预操作、34 抛弃与修复、35 维数变化 14 curved surface, 10 pre operation, 34 discard and repair, 35 dimension change
运动物体的长度 The length of a moving object	装置的复杂性 Complexity of devices	1 分割、19 周期性、26 复制、24 中介物 1 division, 19 periodicity, 26 replication, 24 mediator
力 Power	能量损失 Energy loss	14 曲面化、15 动态化 14 curved and 15 dynamic

➤ **方案 1：依据 No. 14 曲面化发明原理的第 1 条**

得到解如下：把将约束部分换为球形。

➤ **Scheme 1：according to Article 1 of No. 14 curved surface invention principle**

The solution is as follows：replace the constrained part with a sphere.

方案模型图如图 8-45 所示。

Illustration of model is shown in Figure 8-45.

➤ **方案 2：依据 No. 24 中介物 发明原理的第 1 条 "使用中介物传递某一物体或某一种中间过程"**

得到解如下：采用 3 连杆机构传递运动。

➤ **Scheme 2：according to Article 1 of No. 24 intermediary invention principle "use intermediary to transfer an object or an intermediate process"**

The solution is as follows：3-bar linkage is used to transfer motion.

方案的原理图或示意图，如图 8-46 所示。

Schematic diagram or schematic diagram of the scheme，as shown in Figure 8-46.

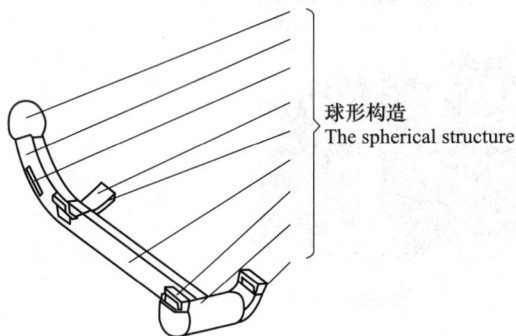

图 8-45　模型图

Figure 8-55　Illustration of model

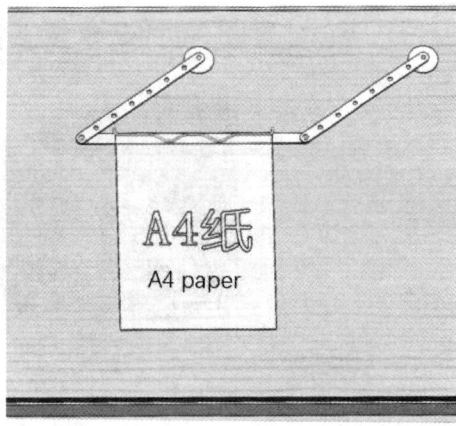

图 8-46　模型分析图

Figure 8-46　Model analysis diagram

➤ **方案 3：依据 No. 15 动态化发明原理的第 3 条 "如果一个物体是静止的，使之变为可变的"**

得到解如下：增加螺旋机构，使之可以调节尺寸。

➤ **Scheme 3：according to Article 3 of No. 15 dynamic invention principle "if an object is static，make it variable"**

The solution is as follows：screw mechanism is added to adjust the size.

方案的原理图或示意图，如图 8-47 所示。

Schematic diagram or schematic diagram of the scheme，as shown in Figure 8-47.

➤ **方案 4：依据 No. 14 曲面化发明原理**

得到解如下：将腿部约束机构变为圆盘形，如图 8-48 所示。

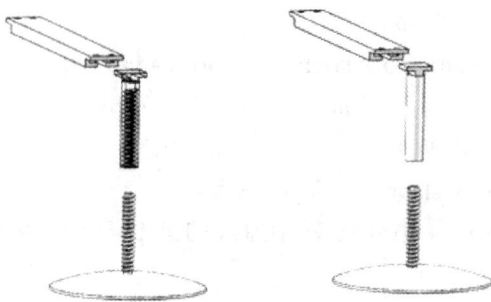

图 8-47 结构图

Figure 8-47 Assumption diagram

➢ **Scheme 4: according to the invention principle of No. 14**

The solution is as follows: change the leg restraint mechanism into a disc shape, as shown in Figure 8-48.

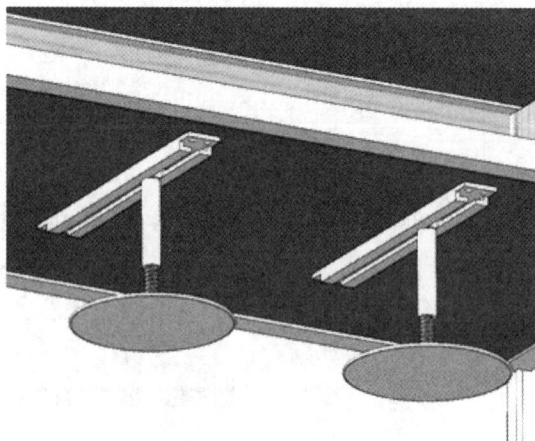

图 8-48 方案的原理图或示意图

Figure 8-48 Schematic or schematic diagram of the scheme

（1）冲突描述：为了"有效矫正写字姿势"，需要参数"形状"为"复杂"，但又为了"容易操作"，需要参数"形状"为"简单"，即，某个参数既要"复杂"又要"简单"。

（2）选用4条分离原理（空间分离、时间分离、基于条件的分离、整体与部分分离）当中的"基于条件的分离"原理，得到解决方案。

（1）Conflict description: in order to "effectively correct writing posture", the parameter "shape" needs to be "complex", but in order to "easy to operate", the parameter "shape" needs to be "simple", that is, a parameter needs to be "complex" and "simple".

（2）Choose the "condition based separation" principle among the four separation principles (space separation, time separation, condition based separation, whole and part separation) to get the solution.

➢方案 5：当需要矫正手腕姿势时，安装手腕矫正器。

➢方案 6：当需要矫正纸张位置时，安装纸张矫正器。

➢方案 7：当需要矫正腿部姿势时，安装腿部矫正器。

➢ **Scheme 5**: when the wrist posture needs to be corrected, install a wrist orthosis.

➢ **Scheme 6**: when the paper position needs to be corrected, install the paper corrector.

➢ **Scheme 7**: when the leg posture needs to be corrected, install leg orthosis.

8.5.3.2　工具 2：物质-场分析及 76 个标准解

8.5.3.2　Tool 2: matter field analysis and 76 standards

（1）建立问题的物质-场模型，如图 8-49 所示。

（2）根据所建问题的物质-场模型，应用标准解解决流程，得到标准解为：No. 3（1.1.3）系统不能改变，但允许使用一个永久或暂时的外部附加成分 S_3 改变 S_1 或 S_2。

（3）依据选定的标准解，得到问题的解决方案。

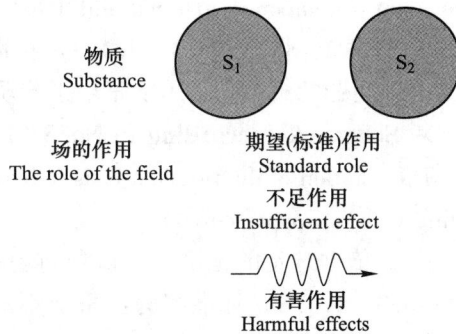

图 8-49　功能结构图
Figure 8-49　Functional structure diagram

（1）The matter field model of the problem is established, as shown in Figure 8-49.

（2）According to the matter field model of the problem, the standard solution process is applied: No. 3 (1.1.3) system cannot be changed, but it is allowed to use a permanent or temporary external additional component S_3 to change S_1 or S_2.

（3）According to the selected standard solution, the solution of the problem is obtained.

No. 3（1.1.3）标准解为：系统不能改变，但允许使用一个永久或暂时的外部附加成分 S_3 改变 S_1 或 S_2。

The standard solution of No. 3 (1.1.3) is: the system cannot be changed, but a permanent or temporary external additional component S_3 is allowed to change S_1 or S_2.

➢ **方案 1：依据 No. 3（1.1.3）标准解**

得到问题的解如下：用手腕矫正器矫正书写时手腕的位置。

改进之后的物质-场模型如图 8-50 所示。

➢ **Scheme 1: according to the standard solution of No. 3 (1.1.3)**

The solution of the problem is as follows: correct the position of the wrist when writing with a wrist orthosis.

The improved matter field model is shown in Figure 8-50.

图 8-50　功能结构图

Figure 8-50　Functional structure diagram

（4）依据选定的标准解，得到问题的解决方案。

No. 3（1. 1. 3）标准解为：系统不能改变，但允许使用一个永久或暂时的外部附加成分 S_3 改变 S_1 或 S_2。

（4）According to the selected standard solution, the solution of the problem is obtained.

The standard solution of No. 3（1. 1. 3）is: the system cannot be changed, but a permanent or temporary external additional component S_3 is allowed to change S_1 or S_2.

➤ **方案 2：依据 No. 3（1. 1. 3）标准解**

得到问题的解如下：用纸张矫正器矫正书写时纸张的正确位置。

➤ **Scheme 2：according to No. 3（1. 1. 3）standard solution**

The solution of the problem is as follows: correct the correct position of the paper when writing with the paper corrector.

（5）依据选定的标准解，得到问题的解决方案。

No. 3（1. 1. 3）标准解为：系统不能改变，但允许使用一个永久或暂时的外部附加成分 S_3 改变 S_1 或 S_2。

（5）According to the selected standard solution, the solution of the problem is obtained.

The standard solution of No. 3（1. 1. 3）is: the system cannot be changed, but a permanent or temporary external additional component S_3 is allowed to change S_1 or S_2.

➤ **方案 3：依据 No. 3（1. 1. 3）标准解**

得到问题的解如下：用腿部矫正器矫正书写时腿的正确的位置。

➤ **Scheme 3：according to the standard solution of No. 3（1. 1. 3）**

The solution of the problem is as follows: use leg orthosis to correct the correct position of the leg when writing.

改进之后的物质-场模型如图 8-51 所示。

The improved matter field model is shown in Figure 8-51.

图 8-51　功能结构图

Figure 8-51　Functional structure diagram

8.5.3.3 工具3：裁剪

8.5.3.3 Tool 3：cutting

（1）裁剪丁字板。将丁字板剪裁，减小系统的复杂程度。

（2）裁剪丁字板。将丁字板剪裁，减小系统的复杂程度。理由：长时间书写，容易疲劳，结构复杂，结构不合理。

（1）Cutting T-board. The T-board is cut to reduce the complexity of the system.

（2）Cutting T-board. The T-board is cut to reduce the complexity of the system. Reason：writing for a long time，easy to fatigue，complex structure，unreasonable structure.

8.5.4 问题的解

8.5.4 Solution of the problem

上述方案汇总见表8-24。

Summary of the above schemes are shown in Table 8-24.

表 8-24 可用性评估

Table 8-24 Availability assessment

方案 Programme	所用创新原理 Innovation principles used	可用性评估 Usability evaluation
将丁字板裁剪掉 Cut off the T-board	发明原理28：机械系统替代 Principle of invention 28：mechanical system	

最终解为：去掉丁字板，完善手腕、纸张、腿部矫正装置。

The final solution is：remove the T-board, improve the wrist, paper, leg correction device.

8.5.5 取得成果与效益

8.5.5 Achievements and benefits

专利名称：拟报两种实用新型专利（一种儿童书写纸张矫正器、一种儿童书写腿部矫正器）。

其他成果：无。

已取得效益或实施情况：已申报实用新型专业一项（一种儿童书写手腕矫正器）。

预期效益：专利转化为产品。

Patent name：two utility model patents（one for children's writing paper appliance and one for children's writing leg appliance）are proposed.

Other achievements：none.

Achieved benefits or implementation：a practical new specialty has been declared（a kind of writing wrist orthosis for children）.

Expected benefits: transforming patents into products.

8.5.6 创新课题与创新成果

8.5.6 Innovative topics and achievements

已完成创新课题汇总见表 8-25。

Summary of innovation projects completed are shown in Table 8-25.

表 8-25 效益分析
Table 8-25 Benefit analysis

课题名称 Subject name	技术创新方法 (采用了什么 创新方法) Technological innovation methods (what innovative methods is used)	课题简介 (做什么，解决什么问题, 形成什么创新方案) Brief introduction of the project (what to do, what to solve, what kind of innovative plan will be formed)	取得成果 (该课题取得的专利、论文、 经济或社会效益等，如无 成果该列可删除) Results achieved (patents, papers, economic or social benefits, etc., if there are no results, the column can be deleted)
儿童书写姿势 矫正装置 Children's writing posture correction device	TRIZ 理论：物理冲突、 技术冲突、裁剪 TRIZ theory: physical conflict, technical conflict and tailoring	结构完善，性能优化 Perfect structure and optimized performance	实用新型专利 1 项 One utility model patent

8.6 提高乙酰水杨酸的产量

8.6 Increase the yield of acetylsalicylic acid

本节主要从以下四个方面进行分析：

(1) 问题背景和描述；

(2) 问题分析过程；

(3) 问题求解过程；

(4) 问题的解。

This section is mainly analyzed from the follwing four aspects:

(1) Background and description of the problem;

(2) Problem analysis process;

(3) Problem solving process;

(4) The solution of the problem.

8.6.1 问题背景和描述
8.6.1 Problem background and description

8.6.1.1 问题的背景
8.6.1.1 Background of the problem

乙酰水杨酸即阿司匹林，为一种解热止痛药物，有报道表明，人们正在发现它的某些新功能。

阿司匹林是由水杨酸（邻羟基苯甲酸）与乙酸酐进行酯化反应而得的，模型分子式如图 8-52 所示。水杨酸分子中的羧基与酚羟基之间形成分子内氢键，阻碍了酚羟基的酰化。为了使酰化反应顺利进行，常加入浓硫酸或磷酸将氢键破坏。

Acetylsalicylic acid（aspirin）is a kind of antipyretic and analgesic drug. It has been reported that some new functions of aspirin are being found.

Aspirin is prepared by esterification of salicylic acid（o-hydroxybenzoic acid）with acetic anhydride，the molecular formula of the model is shown in Figure 8-52. The formation of intramolecular hydrogen bond between carboxyl group and phenolic hydroxyl group in salicylic acid hindered the acylation of phenolic hydroxyl group. In order to carry out acylation smoothly，concentrated sulfuric acid or phosphoric acid is often added to destroy the hydrogen bond.

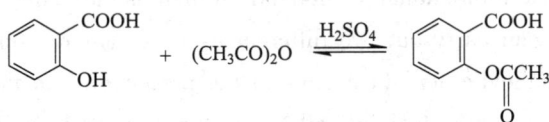

图 8-52　模型分子式

Figure 8-52　Model molecular formula

8.6.1.2 问题的描述
8.6.1.2 Description of the problem

A　定义技术系统实现的功能

A　Define the function of the technology system

问题所在技术系统为乙酰水杨酸制备实验。

该技术系统的功能为制备乙酰水杨酸。

实现该功能的约束有催化剂、水浴加热、药品的量取。

The technical system of the problem is：acetylsalicylic acid preparation experiment.

The function of the system is to prepare acetylsalicylic acid.

The constraints to achieve this function include：catalyst，water bath heating，and drug dosage.

B　现有技术系统的工作原理

B　Working principle of prior art system

实验制备过程如图 8-53 所示。

Experimental preparation process is shown in Figure 8-53.

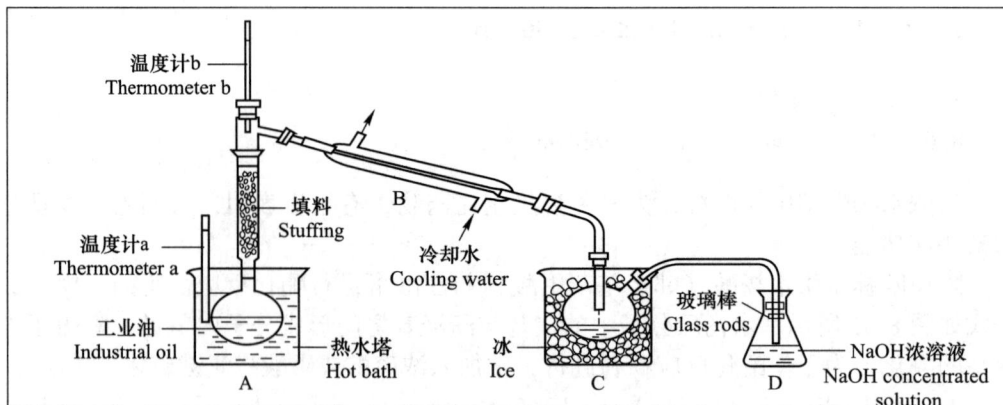

图 8-53　实验制备过程

Figure 8-53　Experimental preparation process

水杨酸是一个双官能团化合物，它既是酚又是羧酸，因此它能进行两种不同的酯化反应，它既可与醇反应，乙酸酐存在下，形成乙酰水杨酸（阿司匹林），而在过量甲醇存在下，产品则是水杨酸甲酯（冬青油）。用水杨酸与乙酸酐反应制备乙酰水杨酸，原理如图 8-54 所示。

Salicylic acid is a bifunctional compound, which is not only a phenol but also a carboxylic acid, so it can carry out two different esterification reactions. It can react with alcohol to form acetylsalicylic acid (aspirin) in the presence of acetic anhydride, and the product is methyl salicylate (Holly oil) in the presence of excessive methanol. Acetylsalicylic acid was prepared by the reaction of salicylic acid with acetic anhydride is shown in Figure 8-54.

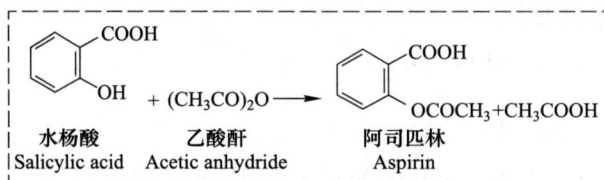

图 8-54　制备原理

Figure 8-54　Preparation principle

C　当前技术系统存在的问题

C　Problems in current technology system

（1）药品的量取存在实验浪费和误差问题。

（2）浓硫酸作为催化剂，存在健康危害、环境危害及燃爆危险。

（3）水浴加热，温度不易掌握，易造成产率低。

（1）There are problems of waste and error in the measurement of drugs.

（2）Concentrated sulfuric acid, as a catalyst, is hazardous to health, environment and explosion.

(3) When heated in water bath, the temperature is not easy to master and the yield is low.

D 问题出现的条件和时间

D The condition and time of the problem

(1) 称取水杨酸 1.98g 于锥形瓶（150mL），在通风条件下用吸量管取乙酸酐 5mL，加入锥形瓶进行反应。

(2) 滴入 5 滴浓硫酸，摇动使固体全部溶解，盖上带玻璃管的胶塞，在事先预热的水浴中加热 10~15min。

(3) 水浴装置：将反应液体转移至 250mL 烧杯并冷却至室温（可能会没有晶析出）。

(1) Weigh 1.98g salicylic acid in a conical flask（150mL），under the condition of ventilation, 5mL of acetic anhydride was taken by pipette and added into conical flask for reaction.

(2) Add 5 drops of concentrated acid, shake to dissolve all the solids, cover the rubber plug with glass tube, and heat in the preheated water bath for 10~15min.

(3) Water bath device：transfer the reaction liquid to a 250mL beaker and cool it to room temperature（no crystal may precipitate）.

E 问题或类似问题的现有解决方案及其缺点

E Existing solutions to problems or similar problems and their shortcomings

若用 3mL 可减少副反应发生，易于晶体析出，提高产率。

n（水杨酸）：n（乙酸酐）= 1：（2~3）较为合适。

浓硫酸用量要控制（$V < 0.2$mL），浓硫酸作用在于破坏水杨酸分子内氢键，降低反应温度（150~160℃）到 85~90℃发生，避免高温副反应发生，提高产品纯度、产率。

冷却时搅拌要激烈，否则会析出块状物，影响后续实验。

If 3mL is used, the side reaction can be reduced, the crystal is easy to precipitate and the yield can be increased.

n（salicylic acid）：n（acetic anhydride）= 1：（2-3）is more suitable.

The dosage of concentrated sulfuric acid should be controlled（$V < 0.2$mL）. The function of concentrated sulfuric acid is to break the intramolecular hydrogen bond of salicylic acid, reduce the reaction temperature（150-160℃）to 85-90℃, avoid high temperature side reaction, and improve the purity and yield of the product.

When cooling, the stirring should be intense, otherwise the lumps will precipitate, which will affect the subsequent experiments.

F 新系统的要求

F Requirements of the new system

控制好反应温度（85~90℃），否则温度过高将增加副产物的生成。

The reaction temperature (85-90℃) should be well controlled, otherwise the formation of by-products will be increased if the temperature is too high.

8.6.2 问题分析
8.6.2 Problem analysis

8.6.2.1 功能分析
8.6.2.1 Functional analysis

系统分析见表8-26。

Systems analysis is shown in Table 8-26.

表 8-26 系统分析
Table 8-26 Systems analysis

制品 Products	乙酰水杨酸 Acetylsalicylic acid
系统元件 System components	水杨酸、乙酸酐、浓硫酸、圆底烧瓶、结晶物、冰水、抽滤瓶、移液管、天平 Salicylic acid, acetic anhydride, concentrated sulfuric acid, round bottom flask, crystal, ice water, filter bottle, pipette, balance
超系统元件 Supersystem element	烧杯、温度计、酒精灯、烘箱、玻璃棒 Beaker, thermometer, alcohol lamp, oven, glass rod

建立已有系统的功能模型，如图8-55所示。

Establish the function model of the existing system is shown in Figure 8-55.

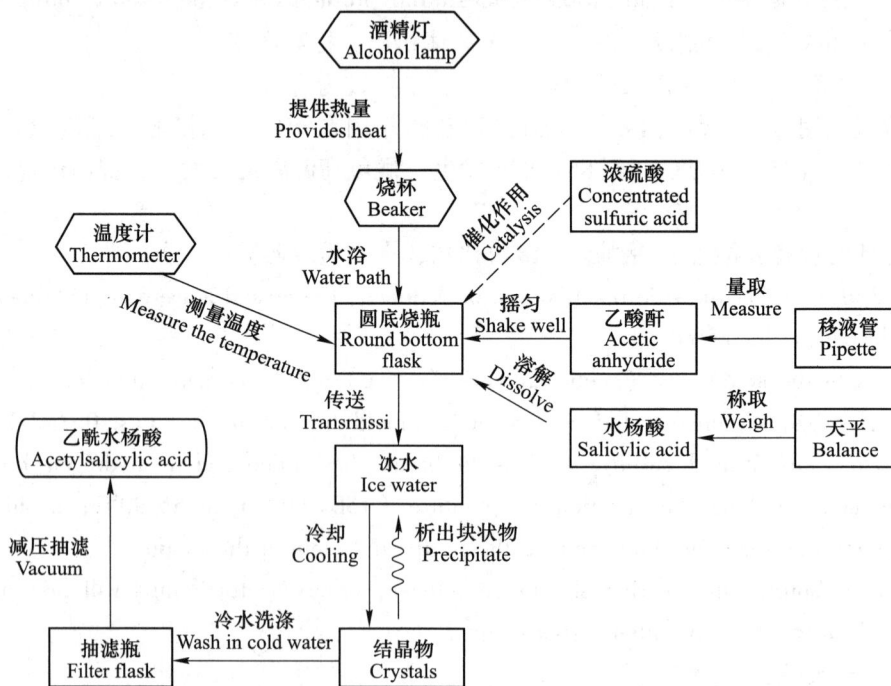

图 8-55 功能结构图

Figure 8-55 Functional structure diagram

8.6.2.2 因果分析

8.6.2.2 Causal analysis

因果链分析如图 8-56 所示。

The causal analysis is shown in Figure 8-56.

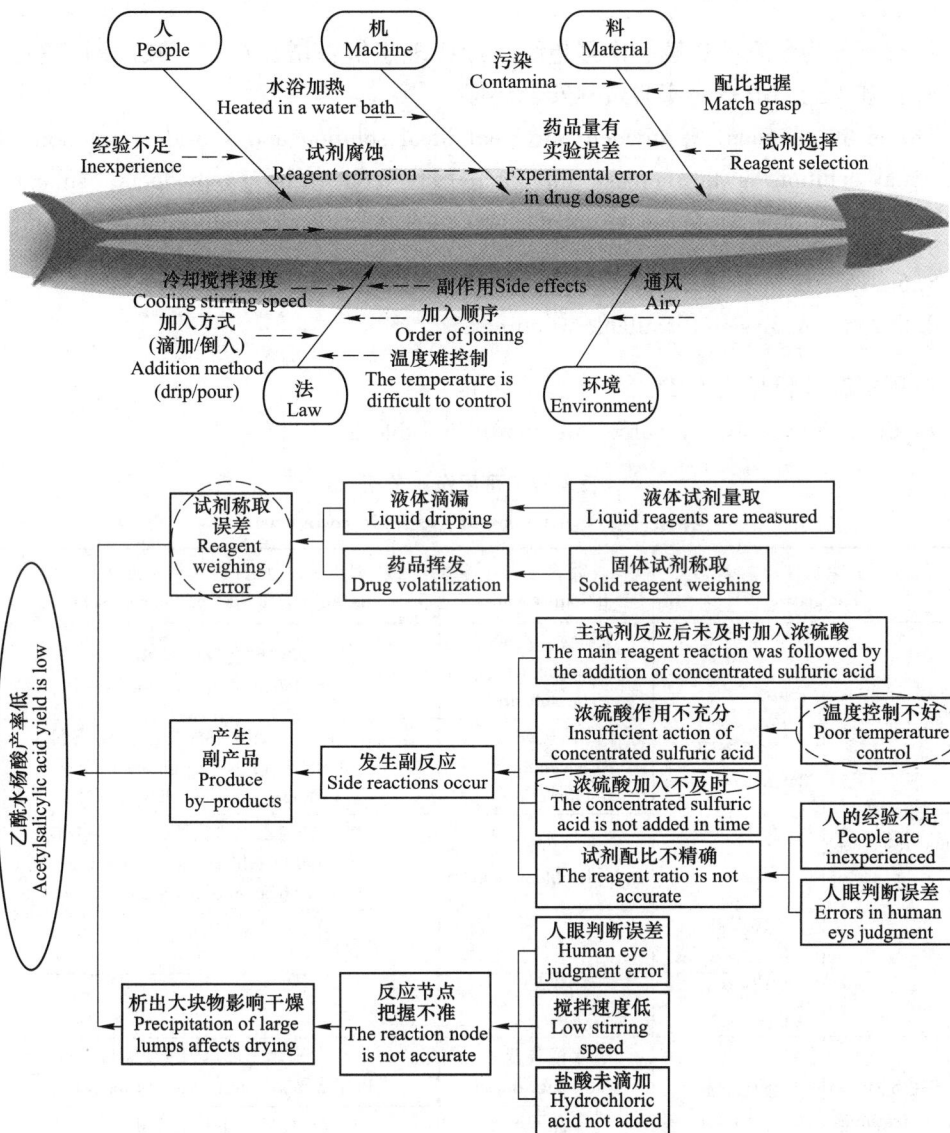

图 8-56 因果链分析

Figure 8-56 Causal analysis

8.6.2.3 冲突区域确定（问题关键点确定）

8.6.2.3 Determination of conflict area (determination of key points)

（1）问题关键点 1：实验试剂用量的准确性。

（2）问题关键点 2：反应温度的控制。

（1）The key point of the problem 1：accuracy of reagent dosage.

（2）The key point of the problem 2：control of reaction temperature.

8.6.2.4　理想解分析
8.6.2.4　Analysis of ideal solution

理想解分为最终理想解和次理想解。最终理想解：增加产率、减产副产物；次理想解：减少药品浪费、实验过程安全环保。

The ideal solutions are divided into final ideal solution and sub-ideal solution. The final ideal solution is to increase the yield and reduce the by-products; suboptimal solution：reduce drug waste, experimental process safety and environmental protection.

8.6.2.5　可用资源分析
8.6.2.5　Analysis of available resources

可用资源分析见表 8-27。

Analysis of available resources are shown in Table 8-27.

表 8-27　可用资源分析

Table 8-27　Analysis of available resources

类别 Category		资源名称 Resource name	可用性分析（初步方案） Usability analysis（preliminary scheme）
内部资源 Internal resources	物质资源 Material resources	水杨酸、乙酸酐 Salicylic acid, acetic anhydride	发生酰化反应，形成酯 Acylation occurs to form esters
		浓硫酸 Concentrated sulfuric acid	催化剂（破坏水杨酸分子内氢键） Catalyst（breaking intramolecular hydrogen bond of salicylic acid）
		盐酸 Hydrochloric acid	中和提纯乙酰水杨酸时的碳酸氢钠 Sodium bicarbonate for neutralization and purification of acetylsalicylic acid
	场资源 Field resources		
	其他资源 Other resources		
外部资源 External resources	物质资源 Material resources	水浴装置 Water bath device	预热、加热到反应温度 Preheat and heat to reaction temperature
		冰水 Ice water	使粗品晶体完全析出 The coarse crystal is completely separated out
超系统资源 Supersystem resources	物质资源 Material resources	抽滤装置 Suction filter	提纯粗品 Purified crude product
		干燥装置 Drying device	干燥产品 Dry products
		乙醇 Ethanol	增加水杨酸、乙酰水杨酸溶解度 Increase the solubility of salicylic acid and acetylsalicylic acid

8.6.3 问题求解
8.6.3 Problem solving

8.6.3.1 问题关键点 1 以"实验试剂用量的准确性"为入手点解决问题

8.6.3.1 The key point of the problem 1 To solve the problem with "the accuracy of experimental reagent dosage" as the starting point

➢ 工具：冲突解决理论

➢ Tool：conflict resolution theory

技术冲突解决过程如下。

（1）冲突描述：为了提高乙酰水杨酸制备系统的"产率"，需要精确实验试剂用量，但这样做了会导致系统的常规称量方式难以应用。

（2）转换成 TRIZ 标准冲突。改善的参数为物质损耗、称取精准；恶化的参数为易用性、可靠性。

（3）查找冲突矩阵，得到如下发明原理，见表 8-28.

Technology conflict resolution process is as follows.

（1）Conflict description：in order to improve the "yield" of the acetylsalicylic acid preparation system, we need to accurately test the reagent dosage, but doing so will make it difficult to apply the conventional weighing method of the system.

（2）Conversion to TRIZ standard conflict. Improved parameters is material loss and accurate weighing；deteriorating parameters is ease of use, reliability.

（3）By searching the conflict matrix, the following principles of the invention are obtained, as shown in Table 8-28.

表 8-28 技术冲突分析
Table 8-28 Technical conflict analysis

改善的参数 Improved parameters	恶化的参数 Deteriorating parameters	对应的发明原理 Corresponding principles of invention
物质损耗 Material loss	易用性 Ease of use	15、35、5
称取精准 Accurate weighing	可靠性 Reliability	5、11、1、23、29

➢ 方案 1：依据 No. 15 动态化发明原理

如果一个物体是刚性的，使之变成可活动的或可改变的，得到解如下：利用真空气体将盛放挥发性液体水杨酸的容器调整为可压式压出，既可以预防挥发，又能防止与空气反应发生变质。

➢ Scheme 1：according to the No. 15 dynamic invention principle

If an object is rigid, making it movable or changeable, the solution is as follows：using vacuum gas to adjust the container containing volatile liquid salicylic acid to press out, it can not only prevent volatilization, but also prevent deterioration caused by reaction with air.

➢ **方案 2：依据 No. 35 参数改变发明原理**

改变压力，得到解如下：利用真空气体将盛放挥发性液体水杨酸的容器调整为可压式压出，既可以预防挥发，又能防止与空气反应发生变质。

➢ **Scheme 2：according to the No. 35 parameter change invention principle**

Change the pressure, the solution is as follows: using vacuum gas to adjust the container containing volatile liquid salicylic acid to press out, it can not only prevent volatilization, but also prevent deterioration caused by reaction with air.

➢ **方案 3：依据 No. 5 合并发明原理**

在时间上合并相似或相连的操作，得到解如下：将试剂瓶与量筒的功能进行结合，使其既可以存放试剂又可以直接量取体积。

➢ **Scheme 3：according to the No. 5 combined invention principle**

Combining similar or connected operations in time, the solution is as follows: combining the functions of reagent bottle and measuring cylinder, it can store reagent and measure volume directly.

8. 6. 3. 2　问题关键点 2　以"反应温度的控制"为入手点解决问题

8. 6. 3. 2　The key point of the problem 2 To solve the problem with "control of reaction temperature" as the starting point

➢ 工具：冲突解决理论

➢ Tool：conflict resolution theory

技术冲突解决过程如下。

（1）冲突描述：为了提高乙酰水杨酸制备系统的"产率"，需要控制好实验反应过程中的温度，但这样做了会导致系统的副产物产生，降低产率。

（2）转换成 TRIZ 标准冲突。改善的参数为控制复杂性；恶化的参数为设计复杂性。

（3）查找冲突矩阵，得到如下发明原理，见表 8-29.

Technology conflict resolution process is as follows.

（1）Conflict description：in order to improve the "yield" of acetylsalicylic acid preparation system, we need to control the temperature in the experimental reaction process, but doing so will lead to the production of by-products in the system and reduce the yield.

（2）Conversion to TRIZ standard conflict. Improved parameters is control complexity；deteriorating parameters is design complexity.

（3）By searching the conflict matrix, the following principles of the invention are obtained, as shown in Table 8-29.

表 8-29　技术冲突分析

Table 8-29　Technical conflict analysis

改善的参数 Improved parameters	恶化的参数 Deteriorating parameters	对应的发明原理 Corresponding principles of invention
控制复杂性 Control complexity	设计复杂性 Design complexity	15、10、37、24

➤ **方案 1：依据 No. 15 动态化发明原理**

使一个物体或环境在操作的每一个阶段自动调整，以达到优化的性能，得到解如下：利用水浴加热，水的沸点是 100℃，反应温度要求 80~90℃，可将水浴加热中的水换为水与异丙醇的二元共沸物。

➤ **Scheme 1：according to the No. 15 dynamic invention principle**

Make an object or environment automatically adjust at each stage of operation to achieve optimal performance, the solution is as follows：using water bath heating, the boiling point of water is 100℃, and the reaction temperature is 80-90℃. The water in water bath heating can be replaced by the binary azeotrope of water and isopropanol.

➤ **方案 2：依据 No. 10 预操作发明原理**

在操作开始前，使物体局部或全部产生所需的变化，得到解如下：将从共沸物中取出的含内容物的锥形瓶慢慢加入 3~5mL 冰水，此时反应放热，甚至沸腾，待反应平稳后再加入一定量水，用冰水浴冷却，并不断搅拌，待结晶析出后抽滤。

➤ **Scheme 2：according to the No. 10 pre operation invention principle**

Before the operation, the required changes of the object are made locally or completely, the solution is as follows：slowly add 3-5mL ice water into the conical flask containing contents from the azeotrope. At this time, the reaction is exothermic or even boiling. After the reaction is stable, add a certain amount of water, cool it with ice water bath, and continuously stir it. After crystallization, pump and filter it.

➤ **方案 3：依据 No. 37 热膨胀发明原理**

利用材料的热膨胀或热收缩性质，得到解如下：当水杨酸与乙酸酐混合后，及时加入浓硫酸并加热，预防副反应的发生。

➤ **Scheme 3：according to the No. 37 thermal expansion invention principle**

Using the thermal expansion or thermal shrinkage properties of materials, the solution is as follows：when salicylic acid and acetic anhydride are mixed, concentrated sulfuric acid is added and heated in time to prevent the occurrence of side reactions.

➤ **方案 4：依据 No. 24 中介物发明原理**

使用中介物传递某一物体或某一中间过程，得到解如下：利用杂多酸代替浓硫酸进行催化。

➤ **Scheme 4：according to the No. 24 intermediary invention principle**

Using intermediary to transfer an object or an intermediate process, the solution is as follows：heteropoly acid was used instead of concentrated sulfuric acid.

物理冲突解决过程如下。

Physical conflict resolution process is as follows.

（1）冲突描述：为了"提高产率，需要控制好反应温度"，需要参数"温度区间"为"高（80~90℃）"，但又为了"避免浓硫酸高温危险性"，需要参数"温度"为"低（25℃）"，即，某个参数既要"高"又要"低"。

（1）Conflict description：in order to "improve the yield, it is necessary to control the reaction temperature", the parameter "temperature range" should be "high (80-90℃)", but in order to "avoid the high temperature risk of concentrated sulfuric acid", the parameter "temperature" should be "low (25℃)", that is, a parameter should be "high" and "low".

（2）选用 4 条分离原理（空间分离、时间分离、基于条件的分离、整体与部分分离）当中的"时间分离"原理，得到解决方案。

（2）Choose the "time separation" principle among the four separation principles (space separation, time separation, condition based separation, whole and part separation) to get the solution.

➤ **方案 5：依据 16 未达到或超过的作用发明原理**

得到解如下：如果 100% 达到所希望的效果是困难的，稍微未达到或稍微超过预期的效果将大大简化问题。利用杂多酸的绿色催化剂性能，代替浓硫酸，稳定性高，无污染，减小对仪器的腐蚀性。

➤ **Scheme 5：according to the principle of the invention**

The solution is as follows: if it is difficult to achieve 100% of the desired effect, it will greatly simplify the problem if the expected effect is slightly not achieved or slightly exceeded. Using the green catalyst performance of heteropoly acid instead of concentrated sulfuric acid, it has high stability, no pollution and reduces the corrosion to the instrument.

8.7　改善竖炉向气化炉输送矿石受阻问题
8.7　Improvement of ore transportation from shaft furnace to gasifier

本节主要从以下四个方面进行分析：
（1）问题背景和描述；
（2）问题分析过程；
（3）问题求解过程；
（4）问题的解。

This section is mainly analyzed from the following four aspects:
（1）Background and description of the problem;
（2）Problem analysis process;
（3）Problem solving process;
（4）The solution of the problem.

8.7.1　问题背景和描述
8.7.1　Problem background and description

8.7.1.1　问题的背景
8.7.1.1　Background of the problem

COREX 竖炉内含铁炉料的黏结一直是 COREX 工艺的一个重大难题。印度 VJSL 公司 1 号和 2 号预还原竖炉因炉料黏结而进行清空处理，到 2004 年，年均因炉料黏结产生的清炉次数达到 3 次。南非 COREX-2000 预还原竖炉的运行情况比印度稍好，但每年需要清空作业的次数仍大于 2 次。2014 年以来，宝钢 C-3000 投产过程中，因竖炉内炉料黏结，已进行了 8 次清空作业，竖炉清空不仅需要长时间的休风，而且还要消耗大量的物料和人力，严重影响着 COREX 工艺铁水的竞争力。COREX 流程工作示意图如图 8-57 所示。

　　预还原竖炉内炉料粉化，容易黏结成块，累计到一定的程度后，使得竖炉下部的螺旋排料器排料困难，而被迫进行清炉作业，严重影响预还原竖炉的顺行，降低了设备使用效率，增高了炼铁成本。

The bonding of iron bearing burden in COREX shaft furnace has always been a major problem in COREX process. The No. 1 and No. 2 pre reduction shaft furnaces of VJSL company in India were emptied due to burden bonding. By 2004, the average annual number of furnace cleaning due to burden bonding reached three times. The operation of COREX-2000 pre reduction shaft furnace in South Africa is slightly better than that in India, but the number of emptying operations per year is still more than two times. Since 2014, during the production of Baosteel C-3000, eight times of emptying operations have been carried out due to the sticking of burden in the shaft furnace. The emptying of shaft furnace not only needs a long time of air rest, but also consumes a lot of materials and manpower, which seriously affects the competitiveness of COREX process hot metal. The COREX process diagram is shown in Figure 8-57.

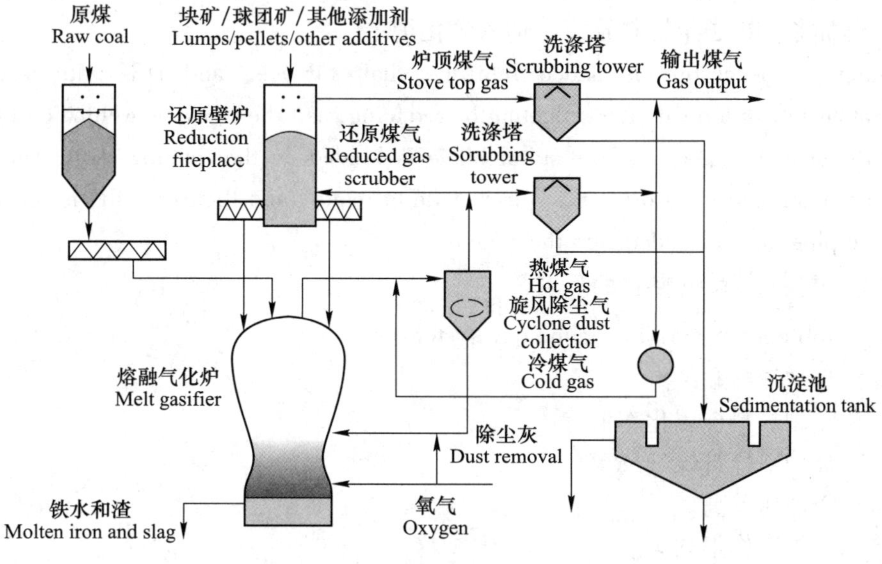

图 8-57　COREX 流程工作示意图

Figure 8-57　COREX process diagram

The burden in the pre reduction shaft furnace is powdered and easy to be caked. After accumulating to a certain extent, it makes it difficult for the spiral discharger at the bottom of the shaft furnace to discharge, and it is forced to clean the furnace, which seriously affects the smooth operation of the pre reduction shaft furnace, reduces the efficiency of the equipment, and increases the cost of ironmaking.

8.7.1.2　问题的描述

8.7.1.2　Description of the problem

A　定义技术系统实现的功能

A　Define the function of the technology system

问题所在技术系统为 COREX 预还原竖炉。

该技术系统的功能为气化炉输送矿石。

实现该功能的约束有：进入竖炉的还原气温度低于 850℃，矿石金属化率不低于 60%~70%，作业率不低于 8400h/a，黏结指数低于 25%。

The technical system of the problem is COREX pre reduction shaft furnace.

The function of the system is to transport ore for gasifier.

The constraints to realize this function are: the temperature of reducing gas entering shaft furnace is lower than 850℃, the metallization rate of ore is not lower than 60%-70%, the operation rate is not lower than 8400h/a, and the caking index is lower than 25%.

B　现有技术系统的工作原理

B　Working principle of prior art system

块矿/球团矿/熔剂加入竖炉，经还原煤气还原后形成一定金属化率的 DRI，套筒焊接在竖炉侧壁，旋转轴上焊接有螺旋叶片，电机带动旋转轴从而带动螺旋叶片转动，进而将 DRI 送至输料管道，加入气化炉中。

Lump ore/pellet/flux is added into the shaft furnace, and DRI with a certain metallization rate is formed after reduction by reducing gas. The sleeve is welded on the side wall of the shaft furnace, and the spiral blade is welded on the rotating shaft. The motor drives the rotating shaft to drive the spiral blade to rotate, and then the DRI is sent to the conveying pipeline and added into the gasifier.

C　当前技术系统存在的问题

C　Problems in current technology system

（1）竖炉炉料黏结。

（2）竖炉炉料金属化率低。

（3）竖炉下降管煤气反窜。

（4）竖炉压差高。

（5）竖炉工作不均匀。

（6）布料过程的粉尘偏析。

（1）Shaft furnace charge bonding.

（2）Low metallization rate of shaft furnace charge.

（3）Reverse channeling of gas in downcomer of shaft furnace.

（4）High differential pressure of shaft furnace.

（5）Uneven operation of shaft furnace.

（6）Dust segregation in distribution process.

D　问题出现的条件和时间

D　The condition and time of the problem

当进入竖炉中煤气温度过高时，造成炉料黏结，超过螺旋排料螺距，排料困难，影响顺行。

当气化炉内约1050℃高温的未经过除尘的高粉尘煤气通过矿石下降管直接反窜进入竖炉，煤气反窜严重则引起竖炉内矿石黏结，尺寸变大，导致螺旋不能正常排料。

当入炉矿粉化严重时，易造成固相黏结，导致炉料尺寸增加，以致螺旋发生堵塞，不能正常向气化炉输料。

When the gas temperature in the shaft furnace is too high, it will cause the burden to bond, exceed the screw discharge pitch, and the discharge is difficult, which will affect the smooth operation.

When the high dust gas with a high temperature of about 1050℃ in the gasifier without dust removal enters the shaft furnace directly through the ore downcomer, the serious reverse channeling of the gas will cause the ore in the shaft furnace to bond, the size will become larger, and the screw can not discharge normally.

When the ore into the gasifier is seriously pulverized, it is easy to cause solid-phase bonding, resulting in the increase of charge size, resulting in the screw blockage, which can not normally feed into the gasifier.

E　问题或类似问题的现有解决方案及其缺点

E　Existing solutions to problems or similar problems and their shortcomings

（1）对入炉矿添加涂层，会降低生产率。

（2）改进螺旋叶片尺寸及螺距分布，竖炉悬料时，此改进不起作用，螺旋叶片直径及螺距见表8-30。

（3）螺旋排料器上方某位置添加破碎装置，不适于大规模工业生产。

表 8-30　螺旋叶片直径及螺距

Table 8-30　Diameter and pitch of spiral blade　　　　　　　　（mm）

项　目 Project	第一段 First part	第二段 Second part	第三段 Third part
改造前叶片直径 Leaf diameter before the modification	900	1000	1100
改造后叶片直径 Leaf diameter after the modification	750	850	1100
螺　距 Pitch	394	460	315. 5

（1）Adding coating to the ore will reduce the productivity.

（2）To improve the size and pitch distribution of the spiral blade, this improvement does not work when the shaft furnace is suspended, diameter and pitch of spiral blade is shown in Table 8-30.

(3) A crushing device is added at a certain position above the screw discharger, which is not suitable for large-scale industrial production.

F　新系统的要求

F　Requirements for the new system

企业竖炉清空周期为 130 天左右，通过对新技术系统的改造，使清空周期延长至 180 天或不再需要休风清炉。

It is known that the clearance cycle of the vertical furnace is about 130 days. Through the transformation of the new technology system, the clearance cycle is extended to 180 days or no longer need to clean the furnace.

8.7.2　问题分析
8.7.2　Problem analysis

8.7.2.1　功能分析
8.7.2.1　Functional analysis

系统分析见表 8-31。

Systems analysis is shown in Table 8-31.

表 8-31　系统分析

Table 8-31　Systems analysis

制　品 Products	矿石 Mineral
系统元件 System components	竖炉、气化炉、螺旋叶片、套筒、电机、输料管道、粉尘、旋转轴、高温煤气、还原煤气、冷却水、块矿/球团矿/熔剂 Shaft furnace, gasifier, spiral blade, sleeve, motor, conveying pipe, dust, rotary shaft, high temperature gas, reducing gas, cooling water, lump/pellet/flux
超系统元件 Supersystem element	电能 Electric energy

建立已有系统的功能模型，如图 8-58 所示。

Establish a functional model of an existing system, as shown in Figure 8-58.

8.7.2.2　因果分析
8.7.2.2　Causal analysis

应用因果链分析法确定产生问题的原因，如图 8-59 所示。

Using causal chain analysis to determine the cause of the problem, as shown in Figure 8-59.

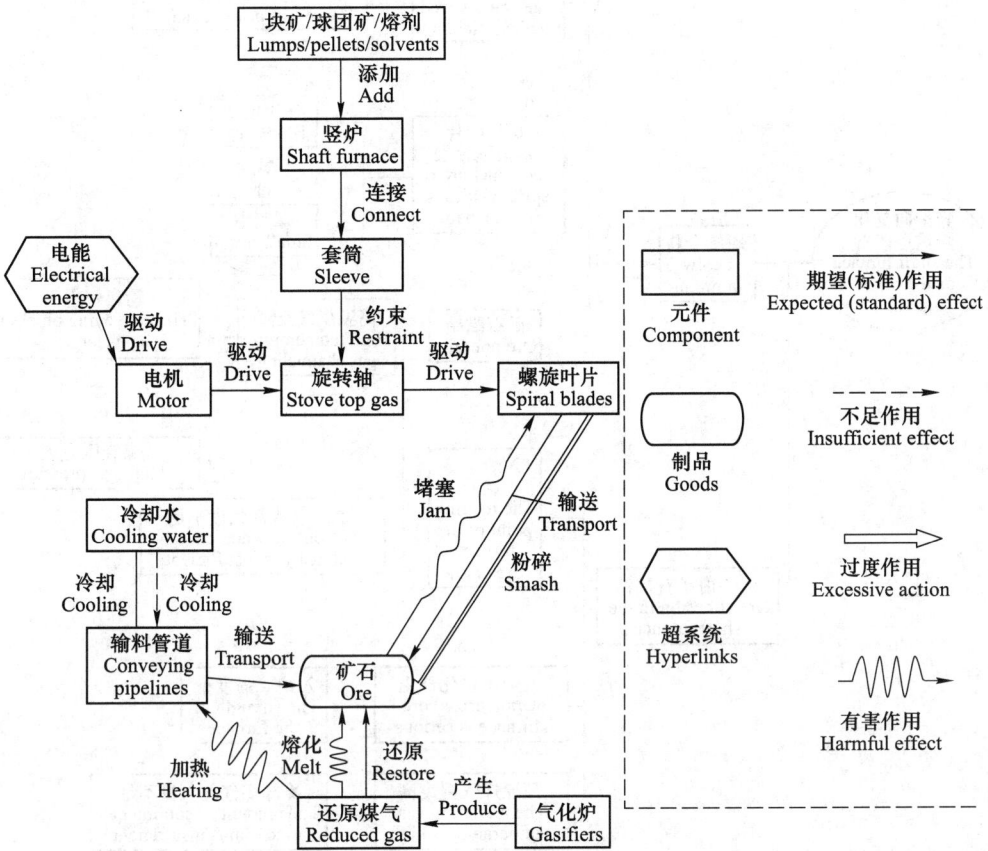

图 8-58 功能结构图

Figure 8-58 Functional structure diagram

8.7.2.3 冲突区域确定（问题关键点确定）

8.7.2.3 Determination of conflict area（determination of key points）

（1）问题关键点 1：叶片尺寸。

（2）问题关键点 2：螺距分布。

（3）问题关键点 3：煤气反窜，如图 8-60 所示。

（1）The key point of the problem 1：blade Size.

（2）The key point of the problem 2：pitch distribution.

（3）The key point of the problem 3：gas channeling，as shown in Figure 8-60.

8.7.2.4 理想解分析

8.7.2.4 Analysis of ideal solution

理想解分为最终理想解和次理想解。最终理想解：螺旋排料器不再发生堵塞；次理想解：螺旋排料器清空周期延长至 180 天左右。

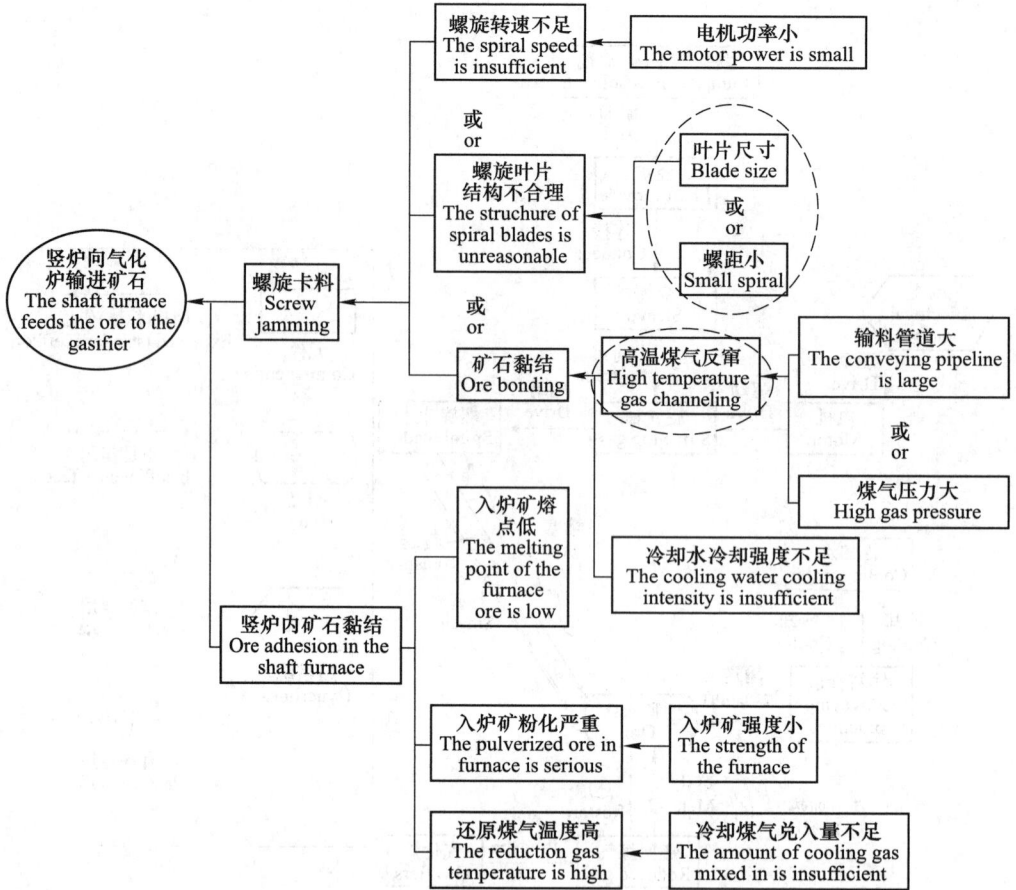

图 8-59 因果链分析

Figure 8-59 Causal analysis

图 8-60 反窜煤气

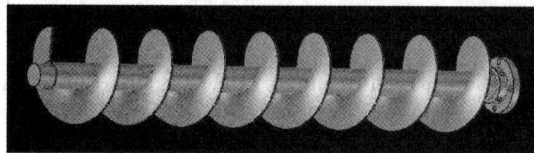

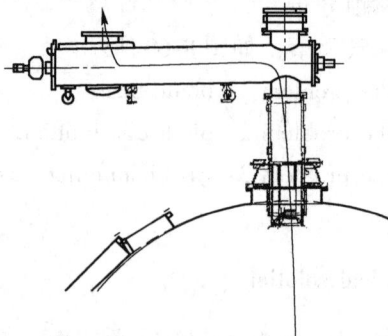

Figure 8-60 Anti-channeling gas

理想解分析主要对以下问题进行回答。

（1）设计的最终目的是什么？延长螺旋排料器清空周期。

（2）理想解是什么？竖炉向气化炉输送矿石过程不再发生堵塞。

（3）达到理想解的障碍是什么？气化炉中会有高温煤气反窜至输料通道、竖炉中矿石黏结。

（4）出现这种障碍的结果是什么？螺旋排料失效，矿石不能加入气化炉。

（5）不出现这种障碍的条件是什么？创造这些条件存在的可用资源是什么？不出现高温煤气反窜或冷却反窜的高温煤气，输料管道处冷却水或高温煤气兑入冷煤气。

The ideal solutions are divided into final solution and sub-ideal solution. The final ideal solution is that the screw discharger is no longer blocked; suboptimal solution: the emptying period of screw discharger is extended to about 180 days.

The ideal solution analysis mainly answers the following questions.

（1）What is the ultimate goal of design? Extending the emptying cycle of screw discharger.

（2）What is the ideal solution? No clogging in the process of ore transportation from shaft furnace to gasifier.

（3）What are the obstacles to the ideal solution? There will be high temperature gas in the gasifier back channeling to the conveying channel and ore in the shaft furnace.

（4）What is the result of this obstacle? Spiral discharge failure, ore can not be added to the gasifier.

（5）What are the conditions for the absence of such obstacles? What are the resources available to create these conditions?

There is no reverse channeling of high-temperature gas or cooling reverse channeling of high-temperature gas, and the cooling water or high-temperature gas at the conveying pipe is mixed with cold gas.

依据理想解分析得到方案为：在输料通道处通入冷却气体或引入冷却水用于冷却从气化炉反窜来的高温煤气。

According to the ideal solution analysis, the scheme is as follows: cooling gas or cooling water is introduced into the feed channel to cool the high temperature gas from the gasifier.

8.7.2.5 可用资源分析

8.7.2.5 Analysis of available resources

可用资源分析见表 8-32。

Analysis of available resources are shown in Table 8-32.

表 8-32 可用资源分析

Table 8-32 Analysis of available resources

类别 Category		资源名称 Resource name	可用性分析（初步方案） Usability analysis（preliminary scheme）
内部资源 Internal resources	物质资源 Material resources	矿石 Mineral	改变矿石的黏结特性 Change the bond property of ore
		螺旋 Screw	改变螺距、叶片尺寸 Changing pitch and blade size
	场资源 Field resources	电场 Electric field	改变螺旋转速 Changing the screw speed
	其他资源 Other resources		
外部资源 External resources	物质资源 Material resources	高温煤气 High temperature gas	冷却 Cooling
	场资源 Field resources	热能 Heat energy	
	其他资源 Other resources		
超系统资源 Supersystem resources	物质资源 Material resources	冷却气体 Cooling gas	
		冷却水 Cooling water	
	场资源 Field resources	热能 Heat energy	
	其他资源 Other resources		

8.7.3 问题求解

8.7.3 Problem solving

8.7.3.1 问题关键点 1 以"改变螺旋叶片尺寸"为入手点解决问题

8.7.3.1 The key point of the problem 1 To solve the problem by "changing the size of the spiral blade"

➤ 工具：冲突解决理论

➤ Tool：conflict resolution theory

技术冲突解决过程如下。

（1）冲突描述：为改善系统的"输送矿石受阻问题"，我们需要改变螺旋叶片尺寸，但这样做了会导致系统的螺旋叶片寿命变化。

（2）转换成 TRIZ 标准冲突。改善的参数为运动物体的面积；恶化的参数为强度（叶片与螺旋轴的连接）。

（3）查找冲突矩阵，得到如下发明原理，见表 8-33。

Technology conflict resolution process is as follows.

（1） Conflict description：in order to improve the problem of "conveying ore blocked", we need to change the size of spiral blade, but this will lead to the change of spiral blade life.

（2） Conversion to TRIZ standard conflict. Improved parameter is area of moving object；deteriorating parameter is strength （connection between blade and spiral shaft）.

（3） By searching the conflict matrix, the following principles of the invention are obtained, as shown in Table 8-33.

表 8-33　技术冲突分析
Table 8-33　Technical conflict analysis

改善的参数 Improved parameters	恶化的参数 Deteriorating parameters	对应的发明原理 Corresponding principles of invention
运动物体的面积（5） Area of moving object（5）	强度（14） Strength（14）	3、15、40、14

发明原理 3：局部质量-1 将物体或环境的均匀结构变成不均匀结构，对螺旋叶片表面进行热处理增加其使用强度、添加涂层或使其具自清洁处理功能。

Invention principle 3：local mass-1 changes the uniform structure of object or environment into non-uniform structure. Heat treatment is carried out on the surface of spiral blade to increase its service strength, add coating or make it have self-cleaning treatment function.

发明原理 15：动态化-3 如果一个物体是静止的，使之变为运动的或可改变的参照电磁振动给料器，使螺旋排料器具振动功能，改善不能向气化炉输料问题。

Principle of invention 15：dynamic-3 if an object is static, it can be changed into a moving or changeable reference electromagnetic vibration feeder, so that the vibration function of the screw discharge device can be improved, and the problem of unable to feed to the gasifier can be solved.

➢ **方案 1：依据 No. 3 发明原理**

得到解如下：对螺旋叶片表面进行热处理增加其使用强度、添加涂层或使其具自清洁处理功能。

➢ **Scheme 1：according to the invention principle of No. 3**

The solution is as follows：the surface of spiral blade is heat treated to increase its strength, add coating or make it self-cleaning.

➢ **方案 2：依据 No. 15 发明原理**

得到解如下：参照电磁振动给料器，使螺旋排料器具振动功能，改善不能向气化炉输料问题。

➢ **Scheme 2: according to the invention principle of No. 15**

The solution is as follows: referring to the electromagnetic vibration feeder, the vibration function of the spiral discharge device is improved, and the problem that the material cannot be transported to the gasifier is improved.

物理冲突解决过程（1）如下。

Physical conflict resolution process (1) is as follows.

（1）冲突描述：为了"改善竖炉向气化炉输送矿石受阻问题"，需要参数"螺旋叶片尺寸"为"正"，但又为了"改善螺旋排料叶片寿命"，需要参数"螺旋叶片尺寸"为"负"，即某个参数既要"正"又要"负"。

（2）选用4条分离原理（空间分离、时间分离、基于条件的分离、整体与部分分离）当中的"空间分离"原理，得到解决方案。

（1）Conflict description: in order to "improve the problem of ore transportation from shaft furnace to gasifier", the parameter "spiral blade size" needs to be "positive", but in order to "improve the service life of spiral discharge blade", the parameter "spiral blade size" needs to be "negative", that is, a parameter needs to be "positive" and "negative".

（2）The "space separation" principle among the four separation principles (space separation, time separation, condition based separation, whole and part separation) is selected to get the solution.

8.7.3.2　问题关键点2　以"改变螺距分布"为入手点解决问题

8.7.3.2　The key point of the problem 2　To solve the problem by "changing the pitch distribution"

（1）冲突描述：为了改善系统的"输送矿石受阻问题"，需要改变螺距分布，但这样做了会导致系统的螺旋可制造性难度增加。

（2）转换成 TRIZ 标准冲突。改善的参数为形状；恶化的参数为可制造性。

（3）查找冲突矩阵，得到如下发明原理，见表 8-34。

（1）Conflict description: in order to improve the problem of "ore blocking", we need to change the pitch distribution, but this will increase the difficulty of screw manufacturability.

（2）Conversion to TRIZ standard conflict. Improved parameter is shape; deteriorating parameter is manufacturability.

（3）By searching the conflict matrix, the following principles of the invention are obtained, as shown in Table 8-34.

表 8-34　技术冲突分析

Table 8-34　Technical conflict analysis

改善的参数 Improved parameters	恶化的参数 Deteriorating parameters	对应的发明原理 Corresponding principles of invention
形状（12） Shape（12）	可制造性（32） Manufacturability（32）	17、32、1、28

➢ **方案 1：依据 No. 1 发明原理**

得到解如下：将螺旋叶片分成容易组装及拆卸的部分（连接性）。

➢ **Scheme 1：according to the invention principle of No. 1**

The solution is as follows：divide the spiral blade into parts easy to assemble and disassemble（connectivity）.

➢ 工具：效应

（1）确定问题要实现的功能为："move solid"（动词+名词）；

（2）查找效应知识库，得到可用的效应为 "vibration"（可以有多个效应，依据该效应得到问题的解决方案。

➢ Tool：effect

（1）Determine that the function of the problem is "move solid"（verb + noun）；

（2）By searching the effect knowledge base, the available effect is "vibration"（there can be multiple effects）, and the solution of the problem is obtained according to the effect.

8.7.3.3 问题关键点 3 以"煤气反窜"为入手点解决问题

8.7.3.3 The key point of the problem 3 Solve the problem with "gas anti channeling" as the starting point

A 工具 1：冲突解决理论

A Tool 1：conflict resolution theory

技术冲突解决过程如下。

（1）冲突描述：为改善系统的"输送矿石受阻问题"，我们需要改变输料管道，但这样做了会导致系统的生产率变化。

（2）转换成 TRIZ 标准冲突。改善的参数为静止物体的面积；恶化的参数为生产率。

（3）查找冲突矩阵，得到如下发明原理，见表 8-35.

Technology conflict resolution process is as follows.

（1）Conflict description：in order to improve the "ore blocking problem" of the system, we need to change the conveying pipeline, but doing so will lead to the productivity change of the system.

（2）Conversion to TRIZ standard conflict. Improved parameter is area of stationary object；deteriorating parameter is productivity.

（3）By searching the conflict matrix, the following principles of the invention are obtained, as shown in Table 8-35.

表 8-35 技术冲突分析

Table 8-35 Technical conflict analysis

改善的参数 Improved parameters	恶化的参数 Deteriorating parameters	对应的发明原理 Corresponding principles of invention
静止物体的面积（6） Area of stationary object（6）	生产率（39） Productivity（39）	10、15、17、7

➢ **方案 1：依据 No. 15 发明原理**

得到解如下：使输料管道在输料过程中能够根据进入其内的煤气量自动调整尺寸，以最大程度抑制煤气反窜。

➢ **Scheme 1：according to the invention principle of No. 15**

The solution is as follows：the size of the conveying pipeline can be automatically adjusted according to the amount of gas entering the pipeline during the conveying process, so as to restrain the gas channeling to the greatest extent.

➢ **方案 2：依据 No. 7 发明原理**

得到解如下：将输料管道采取套装的形式，与气化炉连接处采用小口径管道（抑制煤气反窜量），与螺旋排料器连接处采用大口径管道（使矿石易于进入管道，提高生产率）。

➢ **Scheme 2：according to the invention principle of No. 7**

The solution is as follows：the feeding pipe is in the form of a suit, the small diameter pipe is used at the connection with the gasifier (to inhibit the gas reverse channeling), and the large diameter pipe is used at the connection with the screw discharger (to make the ore easy to enter the pipe and improve the productivity).

B　工具 2：物质-场分析及 76 个标准解

B　Tool 2：matter field analysis and 76 standard solutions

（1）建立问题的物质-场模型，如图 8-61 所示。

（1）Establish the matter field model of the problem, as shown in Figure 8-61.

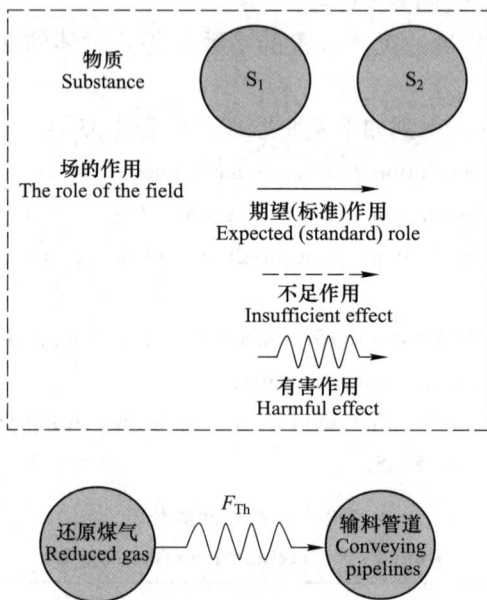

图 8-61　物质-场模型

Figure 8-61　The matter field model

（2）依据选定的标准解，得到问题的解决方案。

No. 11 标准解为：有害作用是由一个场引起的，引入要素 S_3 吸收有害效应。

（2）According to the selected standard solution, the solution of the problem is obtained.

The standard solution of No. 11 is that the harmful effect is caused by a field, and the element S_3 is introduced to absorb the harmful effect.

➢ **方案：依据 No. 11 标准解**

得到问题的解如下：在输料管道处安装抽气装置，吸收反窜入输料管道的还原煤气。

➢ **Scheme：according to the standard solution of No. 11**

The solution of the problem is as follows：a gas extraction device is installed at the conveying pipeline to absorb the reducing gas flowing into the conveying pipeline.

C 工具 3：效应

C Tool 3：effect

➢ **方案：依据"vacuum"效应**

得到如下解：在输料管道处安装一真空泵装置，抽除反窜至输料管道的还原煤气。

➢ **Scheme：according to the "vacuum" effect**

The following solution is obtained：a vacuum pump device is installed at the conveying pipeline to remove the reducing gas from the reverse channeling to the conveying pipeline.

8.7.4 问题的解

8.7.4 Solution of problem

上述方案汇总见表 8-36。

Summary of the above schemes are shown in Table 8-36.

表 8-36 可用性评估

Table 8-36 Availability assessment

序号 Serial number	方案 Programme	所用创新原理 Innovation principles used	可用性评估 Usability evaluation
1	对螺旋叶片表面进行热处理增加其使用强度 Heat treatment is carried out on the surface of spiral blade to increase its service strength	发明原理 3 Principle of invention 3	
2	螺旋叶片添加涂层 Spiral blade coating	发明原理 3 Principle of invention 3	
3	螺旋排料器具自清洁处理功能 Self cleaning function of screw discharge device	发明原理 3 Principle of invention 3	
4	参照电磁振动给料器，使螺旋排料器具振动功能 According to the electromagnetic vibration feeder, the vibration function of the spiral discharge device is improved	发明原理 15 Principle of invention 15	

序号 Serial number	方案 Programme	所用创新原理 Innovation principles used	可用性评估 Usability evaluation
5	将螺旋叶片分成容易组装及拆卸的部分 （连接性） Divide the spiral blade into parts easy to assemble and disassemble (connectivity)	发明原理 1 Principle of invention 1	
6	使输料管道在输料过程中能够根据进入其内的 煤气量自动调整尺寸，以最大程度抑制煤气反窜 The size of the conveying pipeline can be automatically adjusted according to the amount of gas entering the pipeline during the conveying process, so as to restrain the gas channeling to the greatest extent	发明原理 15 Principle of invention 15	
7	将输料管道采取套装的形式，与气化炉连接 处采用小口径管道（抑制煤气反窜量）， 与螺旋排料器连接处采用大口径管道 （使矿石易于进入管道，提高生产率） The feeding pipe is in the form of a suit, the small diameter pipe is used at the connection with the gasifier (to inhibit the gas reverse channeling), and the large diameter pipe is used at the connection with the screw discharger (to make the ore easy to enter the pipe and improve the productivity)	发明原理 7 Principle of invention 7	
8	在输料管道处安装真空泵，吸收反窜 入输料管道的还原煤气 A vacuum pump is installed at the conveying pipeline to absorb the reducing gas flowing into the conveying pipeline	No. 11 有害作用是由一 个场引起的，引入要素 S_3 吸收有害效应 The harmful effect of No. 11 is caused by a field, and S_3 is introduced to absorb the harmful effect	

依据上面得到的若干创新解，通过评价，确定最优解。

最终解为：

（1）对螺旋叶片进行热处理增加其强度，同时添加一涂层（该涂层不与矿石润湿），并使螺旋叶片可拆分，以适应不同状态下的排料；

（2）输料管道采用"漏斗型"管道；

（3）在输料管道处安装一真空装置，用于抽除反窜至输料管道的还原煤气。

Based on the above innovative solutions, the optimal solution is determined by evaluation.

The final solution is as follows:

(1) Heat treatment is carried out on the spiral blade to increase its strength, and a coating is added at the same time (the coating is not wetted with the ore), so that the spiral blade can be separated to adapt to the discharge in different states;

(2) The "funnel type" pipeline is used for material conveying;

(3) A vacuum device is installed at the feed pipe to remove the reducing gas from the feed pipe.

8.8 本章小结
8.8 Summary of this chapter

本章通过对7个应用案例的分析，从背景、问题分析、问题求解和实际应用价值等方面详细介绍了如何运用 TRIZ 工具解决实际问题。本章介绍效应的概念、应用效应进行功能设计一般过程，并用工程实例说明了效应的应用。设计人员如能掌握，将增加其创新能力。

This chapter introduces how to use TRIZ tools to solve practical problems in terms of background, problem analysis, problem solving and practical application value. This chapter introduces the concept and application effect of effect for the general process of functional design, and illustrates the application of effect with engineering examples. If the designers can master it, they will certainly increase their innovation ability.

参考文献

References

［1］孙永伟，谢尔盖·伊克万科. TRIZ：打开创新之门的金钥匙（Ⅰ+Ⅱ）［M］. 北京：科学出版社，2015.

［2］赵敏，张武城，王冠殊. TRIZ 进阶及实战大道至简的发明方法［M］. 北京：机械工业出版社，2015.

［3］莱昂纳德·契储金. TRIZ 研究与实践：连接创造力、工程与创新［M］. 北京：科学出版社，2020.

［4］姚威，韩旭，储昭卫. 创新之道：TRIZ 理论与实战精要［M］. 北京：清华大学出版社，2019.

［5］檀润华. C-TRIZ 及应用—发明过程解决理论［M］. 北京：高等教育出版社，2018.

［6］檀润华. TRIZ 及应用：技术创新过程与方法［M］. 北京：高等教育出版社，2010.

［7］谢尔盖·伊克万科. TRIZ 创新指引：技术系统进化趋势［M］. 北京：电子工业出版社，2018.

［8］维克多·费，尤金·里温. 需求导向创新：基于 TRIZ 的新产品开发［M］. 北京：科学出版社，2010.

［9］成思源，周金平，郭钟宁. 技术创新方法实战：TRIZ 训练与应用［M］. 北京：化学工业出版社，2014.

［10］赵敏. TRIZ 入门及实践［M］. 北京：科学出版社，2009.